The Millennials

AMERICANS
BORN 1977 to 1994

The Millennials

AMERICANS
BORN 1977 to 1994

3rd EDITION

BY THE NEW STRATEGIST EDITORS

New Strategist Publications, Inc.
Ithaca, New York

New Strategist Publications, Inc.
P.O. Box 242, Ithaca, New York 14851
800/848-0842; 607/273-0913
www.newstrategist.com

ISBN 1-885070-88-8

Printed in the United States of America

Table of Contents

Chapter 5. Labor Force

Chapter 6. Living Arrangements

Chapter 7. Population

Chapter 8. Spending

Chapter 9. Time Use

Chapter 10. Wealth

Tables

Chapter 1. Education

Chapter 2. Health

Chapter 3. Housing

Chapter 4. Income

Chapter 7. Population

Chapter 8. Spending

Chapter 9. Time Use

Chapter 10. Wealth

Illustrations

Chapter 5. Labor Force

Chapter 6. Living Arrangements

Chapter 7. Population

Chapter 8. Spending

Chapter 9. Time Use

Introduction

Literally the new kids in town, the Millennial generation—America's children, teens, and youngest adults—is the most mysterious. The characteristics of Millennials are only now beginning to emerge as the oldest graduate from college and enter the workforce. The third edition of *The Millennials: Americans Born 1977 to 1994* provides a demographic and socioeconomic profile of the generation. Because Millennials are the children of Baby Boomers, the generation has attracted the media spotlight. Because of the generation's size, business and government are paying attention to Millennial wants and needs.

The Millennial generation, aged 11 to 28 in 2005, numbers 75 million and accounts for 25 percent of the total population—close to the Baby Boom's 26 percent share. For convenience, children under age 11 are also included in the Millennial profile in this book. The post-Millennial group adds another 44 million people, for a total of 119 million people under age 29 in the United States in 2005—a substantial 40 percent of the population.

The Millennial generation's beginning marked the end of the small Generation X, also known as the baby-bust generation. The oldest Millennials were born in 1977, when the long anticipated echo boom of births began. In that year, the number of births ticked up to 3.3 million. This increase followed a 12-year lull in births called Generation X. By 1980, annual births were up to 3.6 million. By 1990, they topped 4 million. Altogether, 68 million babies were born between 1977 and 1994. The number of Millennials has grown beyond the 68 million because of immigration.

Like every other generation of Americans, Millennials are defined by their numbers. And like the large Baby Boom before them, the Millennial generation's entrance is making waves. Public schools are straining with enrollment not seen since Boomers filled classrooms. Colleges and universities that had been competing for scarce Gen Xers now pick and choose from among the best as applications soar. Millennials are also making their mark in the housing market, the homeownership rate among young adults rising faster than that of older age groups. In time, Millennials will also make their mark on the labor market and will shape the nation's families with their own lifestyles and values.

Every generation of Americans is unique, shaped not only by its numbers but also by the historical moment. Millennials are no exception. Already, three distinct characteristics are emerging, characteristics that will reshape American society as Millennials mature. One, Millennials are racially and ethnically diverse—so diverse, in fact, that in many parts of the country the term "minority" no longer has meaning for their peer group. Two, they are fiercely independent thanks to divorce, day care, single parents, latch key lifestyles, and the technological revolution that has put the joy stick squarely in their hands. Three, Millennials feel powerful. Raised by indulgent parents, they have a sense of security not shared by Gen Xers. Optimistic about the future, Millennials see opportunity where others see problems.

The Millennials: Americans Born 1977 to 1994 examines the youth generation from two perspectives—as independent individuals establishing themselves in the household and labor market, and as workers, householders, parents, and consumers. Because about half the Millennial generation is not yet independent, the second perspective is on the lifestyles of children—examining, for example, the labor force participation of mothers, day care arrangements, and the spending of married couples with children. Together, the two perspectives provide a comprehensive picture of children, teens, and the youngest adults.

How to use this book

The Millennials: Americans Born 1977 to 1994 is designed for easy use. It is divided into ten chapters, organized alphabetically: Education, Health, Housing, Income, Labor Force, Living Arrangements, Population, Spending, Time Use, and Wealth.

The third edition of *The Millennials* includes statistics on the education, living arrangements, labor force participation, health, incomes, spending, and time use of the youngest generation and its parents. The socioeconomic estimates presented here are the all-important mid-decade demographics, offering enough of a trend line into the 21st century to guide researchers in their business plans or government policies. *The Millennials* presents labor force data for 2005, including the government's new labor force projections. It contains new data on the health of the population, including updated estimates of the sexual activity and drug use of teens and young adults. The Census Bureau's latest population projections are also included in the book, showing the growth of young adults over the next decade. *The Millennials* also presents the latest estimates of household wealth from the recently released Federal Reserve Board's 2004 Survey of Consumer Finances. New to this edition is the Time Use chapter, with many tables based on the Bureau of Labor Statistics' new American Time Use Survey. The results show Millennials getting more sleep than older age groups, and despite their wired reputation they spend more time watching television than playing on computers.

Most of the tables in *The Millennials* are based on data collected by the federal government, in particular the Census Bureau, the Bureau of Labor Statistics, the National Center for Education Statistics, the National Center for Health Statistics, the Centers for Disease Control and Prevention, and the Federal Reserve Board. The federal government is the best source of up-to-date, reliable information on the changing characteristics of Americans. Also included in *The Millennials* are the latest data on alcohol, cigarette, and drug use among teenagers from the University of Michigan's Institute for Social Research, and the book includes results from the

2005 American Freshman Survey fielded by UCLA's Higher Education Research Institute.

The Millennials includes the demographic and lifestyle data most important to researchers. Most of the tables are based on data collected by the federal government, but they are not simply reprints of government spreadsheets—as is the case in many reference books. Instead, each table is individually compiled and created by New Strategist's editors, with calculations designed to reveal the trends. The task of extracting and processing raw data from the government's web sites at times requires hours of effort to create a single table. The effort is worthwhile, however, because each table tells a story about Millennials and their families, a story explained by the accompanying text and chart, which analyze the data and highlight future trends. If you need more information than the tables and text provide, you can plumb the original source listed at the bottom of each table.

The book contains a comprehensive table list to help you locate the information you need. For a more detailed search, see the index at the back of the book. Also at the back of the book are the bibliography and the glossary, which defines the terms and describes the many surveys referenced in the tables and text.

Each new generation of Americans is unique and surprising in its own way. With *The Millennials: Americans Born 1977 to 1994* on your bookshelf, you won't be surprised by the unique characteristics of this exciting generation of Americans.

1

Education

■ The oldest members of the Millennial generation have graduated from college and are embarking on a career. The youngest are still in elementary school. Consequently, the educational attainment of Millennials is rising rapidly.

■ Among Millennials, Asian women have the highest level of education and Hispanic men the lowest. Twenty-four percent of the Asian women and only 4 percent of the Hispanic men have a college degree.

■ Among households with children under age 14, fully 77 percent are satisfied with the elementary school in their area. Only 7 percent are not satisfied.

■ SAT scores are rising. The average verbal SAT score rose 9 points between 1990–91 and 2003–04. The average math SAT score rose 18 points during those years.

■ The proportion of dependents aged 18 to 24 enrolled in college rises from a low of 24 percent for those with a family income of less than $20,000 to a high of 68 percent for those with a family income of $150,000 or more.

■ Among the nation's 17 million college students in 2004, more than 13 million were under age 30 and most belonged to the Millennial generation (the oldest Millennials turned 27 in that year).

Most Millennials Are in High School and College

Most of those in their twenties have college experience.

The oldest members of the Millennial generation have graduated from college and are embarking on a career. The youngest are still in elementary school. The educational attainment of Millennials, who spanned the broad age group from 10 to 27 in 2004, is rising rapidly. Among 18-to-19-year-olds, 28 percent have college experience. The figure rises to 55 percent in the 20-to-24 age group. Women are further along than men. Sixty percent of 20-to-24-year-old women have college experience compared with only 50 percent of their male counterparts.

Among women aged 20 to 24, 14 percent are college graduates. The figure is a smaller 9 percent among men in the age group. Since it takes, on average, six years to get a bachelor's degree today, it is little wonder so few in their early twenties have earned a college degree. Among 25-to-29-year-olds, fully 31 percent of women and 26 percent of men have a college degree.

■ Millennial women appear to be more serious about education than their male counterparts. This could narrow the income gap between men and women in the years ahead.

Among people in their twenties, women are more likely to be college graduates

(percent of people aged 20 to 29 with a college degree, by sex, 2004)

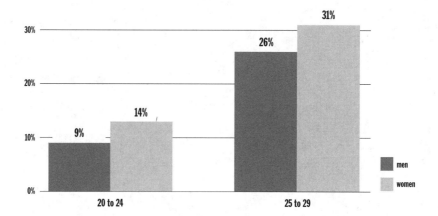

Table 1.1 Educational Attainment of Millennials, 2004

(number and percent distribution of people aged 15 or older, aged 15 to 27, and aged 15 to 29 in selected age groups, by highest level of education, 2004; numbers in thousands)

	total 15 or older	15 to 27	selected age groups 15 to 17	18 to 19	20 to 24	25 to 29
Total people	**227,529**	**52,076**	**12,829**	**7,485**	**20,339**	**19,008**
Not a high school graduate	46,521	20,364	12,614	3,289	2,871	2,554
High school graduate	68,302	11,927	137	2,116	6,239	5,557
Some college, no degree	41,617	12,258	67	2,044	7,698	3,891
Associate's degree	16,992	2,159	3	32	1,191	1,549
Bachelor's degree	35,994	4,760	6	4	2,217	4,358
Master's degree	12,713	460	–	–	104	785
Professional degree	2,966	107	–	–	13	218
Doctoral degree	2,426	41	–	–	5	96
High school graduate or more	181,010	31,712	213	4,196	17,467	16,454
Some college or more	112,708	19,785	76	2,080	11,228	10,897
Bachelor's degree or more	54,099	5,368	6	4	2,339	5,457
Total people	**100.0%**	**100.0%**	**100.0%**	**100.0%**	**100.0%**	**100.0%**
Not a high school graduate	20.4	39.1	98.3	43.9	14.1	13.4
High school graduate	30.0	22.9	1.1	28.3	30.7	29.2
Some college, no degree	18.3	23.5	0.5	27.3	37.8	20.5
Associate's degree	7.5	4.1	0.0	0.4	5.9	8.1
Bachelor's degree	15.8	9.1	0.0	0.1	10.9	22.9
Master's degree	5.6	0.9	–	–	0.5	4.1
Professional degree	1.3	0.2	–	–	0.1	1.1
Doctoral degree	1.1	0.1	–	–	0.0	0.5
High school graduate or more	79.6	60.9	1.7	56.1	85.9	86.6
Some college or more	49.5	38.0	0.6	27.8	55.2	57.3
Bachelor's degree or more	23.8	10.3	0.0	0.1	11.5	28.7

Note: "–" means number is less than 500, percentage is less than 0.05, or sample is too small to make a reliable estimate.
Source: Bureau of the Census, Educational Attainment in the United States: 2004, detailed tables; Internet site http://www
.census.gov/population/www/socdemo/education/cps2004.html; calculations by New Strategist

Table 1.2 Educational Attainment of Millennial Men, 2004

(number and percent distribution of men aged 15 or older, aged 15 to 27, and aged 15 to 29 in selected age groups, by highest level of education, 2004; numbers in thousands)

	total 15 or older	15 to 27	selected age groups 15 to 17	18 to 19	20 to 24	25 to 29
Total men	**110,158**	**26,362**	**6,411**	**3,928**	**10,262**	**9,543**
Not a high school graduate	23,418	10,725	6,306	1,907	1,639	1,413
High school graduate	32,507	6,485	67	1,097	3,454	3,032
Some college, no degree	19,666	5,888	32	913	3,709	1,919
Associate's degree	7,309	967	2	10	546	692
Bachelor's degree	17,502	2,031	4	1	866	2,015
Master's degree	6,192	189	–	–	34	318
Professional degree	1,937	53	–	–	12	113
Doctoral degree	1,626	22	–	–	5	41
High school graduate or more	86,739	15,635	105	2,021	8,626	8,130
Some college or more	54,232	9,150	38	924	5,172	5,098
Bachelor's degree or more	27,257	2,295	4	1	917	2,487
Total men	**100.0%**	**100.0%**	**100.0%**	**100.0%**	**100.0%**	**100.0%**
Not a high school graduate	21.3	40.7	98.4	48.5	16.0	14.8
High school graduate	29.5	24.6	1.0	27.9	33.7	31.8
Some college, no degree	17.9	22.3	0.5	23.2	36.1	20.1
Associate's degree	6.6	3.7	0.0	0.3	5.3	7.3
Bachelor's degree	15.9	7.7	0.1	0.0	8.4	21.1
Master's degree	5.6	0.7	–	–	0.3	3.3
Professional degree	1.8	0.2	–	–	0.1	1.2
Doctoral degree	1.5	0.1	–	–	0.0	0.4
High school graduate or more	78.7	59.3	1.6	51.5	84.1	85.2
Some college or more	49.2	34.7	0.6	23.5	50.4	53.4
Bachelor's degree or more	24.7	8.7	0.1	0.0	8.9	26.1

Note: "–" means number is less than 500, percentage is less than 0.05, or sample is too small to make a reliable estimate.
Source: Bureau of the Census, Educational Attainment in the United States: 2004, detailed tables; Internet site http://www
.census.gov/population/www/socdemo/education/cps2004.html; calculations by New Strategist

Table 1.3 Educational Attainment of Millennial Women, 2004

(number and percent distribution of women aged 15 or older, aged 15 to 27, and aged 15 to 29 in selected age groups, by highest level of education, 2004; numbers in thousands)

			selected age groups			
	total 15 or older	15 to 27	15 to 17	18 to 19	20 to 24	25 to 29
Total women	**117,371**	**25,715**	**6,418**	**3,557**	**10,077**	**9,465**
Not a high school graduate	23,099	9,639	6,310	1,382	1,231	1,140
High school graduate	35,795	5,444	69	1,019	2,786	2,525
Some college, no degree	21,951	6,368	35	1,131	3,989	1,972
Associate's degree	9,682	1,191	1	22	645	856
Bachelor's degree	18,491	2,730	3	3	1,352	2,343
Master's degree	6,521	271	–	–	70	468
Professional degree	1,029	53	–	–	2	106
Doctoral degree	801	18	–	–	–	55
High school graduate or more	94,270	16,075	108	2,175	8,844	8,325
Some college or more	58,475	10,631	39	1,156	6,058	5,800
Bachelor's degree or more	26,842	3,072	3	3	1,424	2,972
Total women	**100.0%**	**100.0%**	**100.0%**	**100.0%**	**100.0%**	**100.0%**
Not a high school graduate	19.7	37.5	98.3	38.9	12.2	12.0
High school graduate	30.5	21.2	1.1	28.6	27.6	26.7
Some college, no degree	18.7	24.8	0.5	31.8	39.6	20.8
Associate's degree	8.2	4.6	0.0	0.6	6.4	9.0
Bachelor's degree	15.8	10.6	0.0	0.1	13.4	24.8
Master's degree	5.6	1.1	–	–	0.7	4.9
Professional degree	0.9	0.2	–	–	0.0	1.1
Doctoral degree	0.7	0.1	–	–	–	0.6
High school graduate or more	80.3	62.5	1.7	61.1	87.8	88.0
Some college or more	49.8	41.3	0.6	32.5	60.1	61.3
Bachelor's degree or more	22.9	11.9	0.0	0.1	14.1	31.4

Note: "–" means number is less than 500, percentage is less than 0.05, or sample is too small to make a reliable estimate.
Source: Bureau of the Census, Educational Attainment in the United States: 2004, detailed tables; Internet site http://www
.census.gov/population/www/socdemo/education/cps2004.html; calculations by New Strategist

Asian Women Are the Best-Educated Millennials

Hispanic men are the least educated.

Among people aged 15 to 27, Asian women have the highest level of education. Already, 24 percent have a bachelor's degree. Asian men rank second in educational attainment, with 21 percent having a college degree.

Hispanics are the least educated among Millennials. Only 48 percent of Hispanic men and 51 percent of Hispanic women aged 15 to 27 are high school graduates. Just 4 percent have a college degree. Many Hispanics are immigrants from countries with little formal schooling.

■ Although the educational attainment of Millennials will rise as more of them complete high school and go to college, the gaps by race and Hispanic origin will persist.

Asians are far better educated than others

(percent of people aged 15 to 27 with college experience, by race and Hispanic origin, 2004)

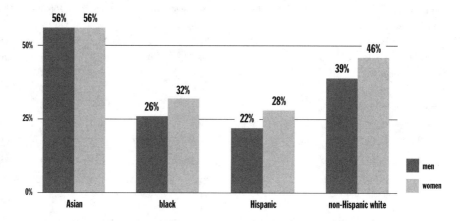

Table 1.4 Educational Attainment of Millennials by Race and Hispanic Origin, 2004

(number and percent distribution of people aged 15 to 27 by educational attainment, race, and Hispanic origin, 2004; numbers in thousands)

	total	Asian	black	Hispanic	non-Hispanic white
Total people aged 15 to 27	**52,076**	**2,416**	**7,760**	**9,288**	**32,189**
Not a high school graduate	20,364	735	3,409	4,728	11,343
High school graduate	11,927	323	2,064	2,245	7,200
Some college, no degree	12,258	698	1,630	1,633	8,187
Associate's degree	2,159	110	223	305	1,500
Bachelor's degree	4,760	432	376	341	3,565
Master's degree	460	80	45	22	308
Professional degree	107	34	12	9	52
Doctoral degree	41	5	–	4	32
High school graduate or more	31,712	1,682	4,350	4,559	20,844
Some college or more	19,785	1,359	2,286	2,314	13,644
Bachelor's degree or more	5,368	551	433	376	3,957
Total people aged 15 to 27	**100.0%**	**100.0%**	**100.0%**	**100.0%**	**100.0%**
Not a high school graduate	39.1	30.4	43.9	50.9	35.2
High school graduate	22.9	13.4	26.6	24.2	22.4
Some college, no degree	23.5	28.9	21.0	17.6	25.4
Associate's degree	4.1	4.6	2.9	3.3	4.7
Bachelor's degree	9.1	17.9	4.8	3.7	11.1
Master's degree	0.9	3.3	0.6	0.2	1.0
Professional degree	0.2	1.4	0.2	0.1	0.2
Doctoral degree	0.1	0.2	–	0.0	0.1
High school graduate or more	60.9	69.6	56.1	49.1	64.8
Some college or more	38.0	56.3	29.5	24.9	42.4
Bachelor's degree or more	10.3	22.8	5.6	4.0	12.3

Note: Asians and blacks are those identifying themselves as being of the race alone and those identifying themselves as being of the race in combination with other races; non-Hispanic whites are those identifying themselves as being white alone and not Hispanic. Numbers will not add to total because not all races are shown and Hispanics may be of any race; "–" means number is less than 500, percentage is less than 0.05, or sample is too small to make a reliable estimate.
Source: Bureau of the Census, Educational Attainment in the United States: 2004, detailed tables; Internet site http://www .census.gov/population/www/socdemo/education/cps2004.html; calculations by New Strategist

Table 1.5 Educational Attainment of Millennial Men by Race and Hispanic Origin, 2004

(number and percent distribution of men aged 15 to 27 by educational attainment, race, and Hispanic origin, 2004; numbers in thousands)

	total	Asian	black	Hispanic	non-Hispanic white
Total men aged 15 to 27	**26,362**	**1,225**	**3,708**	**4,938**	**16,296**
Not a high school graduate	10,725	383	1,706	2,585	5,999
High school graduate	6,485	156	1,031	1,263	3,969
Some college, no degree	5,888	368	750	774	3,946
Associate's degree	967	58	76	127	700
Bachelor's degree	2,031	206	123	165	1,515
Master's degree	189	41	22	15	109
Professional degree	53	10	5	4	35
Doctoral degree	22	1	–	2	19
High school graduate or more	15,635	840	2,007	2,350	10,293
Some college or more	9,150	684	976	1,087	6,324
Bachelor's degree or more	2,295	258	150	186	1,678
Total men aged 15 to 27	**100.0%**	**100.0%**	**100.0%**	**100.0%**	**100.0%**
Not a high school graduate	40.7	31.3	46.0	52.3	36.8
High school graduate	24.6	12.7	27.8	25.6	24.4
Some college, no degree	22.3	30.0	20.2	15.7	24.2
Associate's degree	3.7	4.7	2.0	2.6	4.3
Bachelor's degree	7.7	16.8	3.3	3.3	9.3
Master's degree	0.7	3.3	0.6	0.3	0.7
Professional degree	0.2	0.8	0.1	0.1	0.2
Doctoral degree	0.1	0.1	–	0.0	0.1
High school graduate or more	59.3	68.6	54.1	47.6	63.2
Some college or more	34.7	55.8	26.3	22.0	38.8
Bachelor's degree or more	8.7	21.1	4.0	3.8	10.3

Note: Asians and blacks are those identifying themselves as being of the race alone and those identifying themselves as being of the race in combination with other races; non-Hispanic whites are those identifying themselves as being white alone and not Hispanic. Numbers will not add to total because not all races are shown and Hispanics may be of any race; "–" means number is less than 500, percentage is less than 0.05, or sample is too small to make a reliable estimate.
Source: Bureau of the Census, Educational Attainment in the United States: 2004, detailed tables; Internet site http://www .census.gov/population/www/socdemo/education/cps2004.html; calculations by New Strategist

Table 1.6 Educational Attainment of Millennial Women by Race and Hispanic Origin, 2004

(number and percent distribution of women aged 15 to 27 by educational attainment, race, and Hispanic origin, 2004; numbers in thousands)

	total	Asian	black	Hispanic	non-Hispanic white
Total women aged 15 to 27	**25,715**	**1,192**	**4,053**	**4,351**	**15,891**
Not a high school graduate	9,639	353	1,705	2,137	5,338
High school graduate	5,444	170	1,031	981	3,230
Some college, no degree	6,368	329	882	859	4,242
Associate's degree	1,191	54	153	181	802
Bachelor's degree or more	2,730	225	252	176	2,050
Master's degree	271	38	23	7	198
Professional degree	53	22	6	5	17
Doctoral degree	18	4	–	2	13
High school graduate or more	16,075	842	2,347	2,211	10,552
Some college or more	10,631	672	1,316	1,230	7,322
Bachelor's degree or more	3,072	289	281	190	2,278
Total women aged 15 to 27	**100.0%**	**100.0%**	**100.0%**	**100.0%**	**100.0%**
Not a high school graduate	37.5	29.6	42.1	49.1	33.6
High school graduate	21.2	14.3	25.4	22.5	20.3
Some college, no degree	24.8	27.6	21.8	19.7	26.7
Associate's degree	4.6	4.5	3.8	4.2	5.0
Bachelor's degree	10.6	18.9	6.2	4.0	12.9
Master's degree	1.1	3.2	0.6	0.2	1.2
Professional degree	0.2	1.8	0.1	0.1	0.1
Doctoral degree	0.1	0.3	–	0.0	0.1
High school graduate or more	62.5	70.6	57.9	50.8	66.4
Some college or more	41.3	56.4	32.5	28.3	46.1
Bachelor's degree or more	11.9	24.2	6.9	4.4	14.3

Note: Asians and blacks are those identifying themselves as being of the race alone and those identifying themselves as being of the race in combination with other races; non-Hispanic whites are those identifying themselves as being white alone and not Hispanic. Numbers will not add to total because not all races are shown and Hispanics may be of any race; "–" means number is less than 500, percentage is less than 0.05, or sample is too small to make a reliable estimate.
Source: Bureau of the Census, Educational Attainment in the United States: 2004, detailed tables; Internet site http://www .census.gov/population/www/socdemo/education/cps2004.html; calculations by New Strategist

Most Young Children Attend School

The percentage of 3- and 4-year-olds enrolled in school rises with mother's education.

Many of today's young children have parents belonging to the Millennial generation (aged 10 to 27 in 2004). During their early childhood, a large proportion of Millennials found themselves in preschool as their Boomer mothers went to work. Now Millennials are taking advantage of preschool opportunities for their children. The percentage of 3-to-4-year-olds enrolled in nursery school or kindergarten has grown substantially over the years. In 2004, most 3-to-4-year-olds were in school.

Mother's labor force status has a surprisingly small effect on nursery school or kindergarten enrollment. Among 3-to-4-year-olds whose mother works full-time, 58 percent are enrolled in school. Among those whose mother is not in the labor force, 48 percent are in school. A mother's educational attainment is a more important factor in the school enrollment of young children. Among 3-to-4-year-olds, nearly 68 percent of those whose mother has a bachelor's degree are in nursery school or kindergarten compared with a much smaller 39 percent of children whose mother did not graduate from high school.

■ Enrolling children in preschool has become the norm, especially for working women and college graduates.

The school enrollment of young children has grown substantially

(percent of 3-to-4-year-olds enrolled in nursery school or kindergarten, 1980 and 2004)

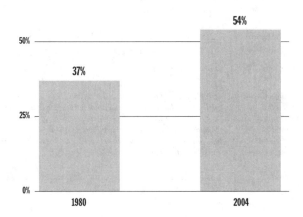

Table 1.7 Three- and Four-Year-Olds Enrolled in School, 1980 to 2004

(percentage of three and four-year-olds enrolled in nursery school or kindergarten, 1980 to 2004)

Year	Percentage
2004	54.0%
2003	55.1
2002	54.5
2001	52.2
2000	52.1
1999	54.2
1998	52.1
1997	52.6
1996	48.3
1995	48.7
1994	47.3
1993	40.1
1992	39.7
1991	40.5
1990	44.4
1989	39.1
1988	38.2
1987	38.3
1986	39.0
1985	38.9
1984	36.3
1983	37.6
1982	36.4
1981	36.0
1980	36.7

Source: Bureau of the Census, School Enrollment, Historical Tables, Internet site http://www.census.gov/population/www/socdemo/school.html

Table 1.8 School Enrollment Status of Children Aged 3 to 6 by Labor Force Status of Mother, 2004

(number and percent distribution of children aged 3 to 6 by labor force status of mother and school enrollment status, by age of child, 2004; numbers in thousands)

	total	not enrolled	nursery school	kindergarten	elementary school
Aged 3 to 4	**7,788**	**3,535**	**3,934**	**319**	**0**
Mother employed full-time	3,090	1,298	1,660	132	0
Mother employed part-time	1,360	510	813	36	0
Mother unemployed	336	151	161	25	0
Mother not in the labor force	3,002	1,575	1,300	127	0
Aged 5	**3,646**	**247**	**431**	**2,733**	**236**
Mother employed full-time	1,489	71	171	1,162	85
Mother employed part-time	639	40	62	502	35
Mother unemployed	166	14	27	116	8
Mother not in the labor force	1,352	121	170	953	108
Aged 6	**3,711**	**86**	**65**	**579**	**2,980**
Mother employed full-time	1,574	27	24	216	1,307
Mother employed part-time	687	8	8	134	537
Mother unemployed	152	1	5	23	121
Mother not in the labor force	1,298	50	28	206	1,014

PERCENT DISTRIBUTION BY SCHOOL ENROLLMENT STATUS

	total	not enrolled	nursery school	kindergarten	elementary school
Aged 3 to 4	**100.0%**	**45.4%**	**50.5%**	**4.1%**	**0.0%**
Mother employed full-time	100.0	42.0	53.7	4.3	0.0
Mother employed part-time	100.0	37.5	59.8	2.6	0.0
Mother unemployed	100.0	44.9	47.9	7.4	0.0
Mother not in the labor force	100.0	52.5	43.3	4.2	0.0
Aged 5	**100.0**	**6.8**	**11.8**	**75.0**	**6.5**
Mother employed full-time	100.0	4.8	11.5	78.0	5.7
Mother employed part-time	100.0	6.3	9.7	78.6	5.5
Mother unemployed	100.0	8.4	16.3	69.9	4.8
Mother not in the labor force	100.0	8.9	12.6	70.5	8.0
Aged 6	**100.0**	**2.3**	**1.8**	**15.6**	**80.3**
Mother employed full-time	100.0	1.7	1.5	13.7	83.0
Mother employed part-time	100.0	1.2	1.2	19.5	78.2
Mother unemployed	100.0	0.7	3.3	15.1	79.6
Mother not in the labor force	100.0	3.9	2.2	15.9	78.1

Source: Bureau of the Census, School Enrollment—Social and Economic Characteristics of Students: October 2004, detailed tables; Internet site http://www.census.gov/population/www/socdemo/school/cps2004.html; calculations by New Strategist

Table 1.9 School Enrollment Status of Children Aged 3 to 6 by Education of Mother, 2004

(number and percent distribution of children aged 3 to 6 by educational attainment of mother and school enrollment status, by age of child, 2004; numbers in thousands)

	total	not enrolled	nursery school	kindergarten	elementary school
Aged 3 to 4	**7,788**	**3,535**	**3,934**	**319**	**0**
Not a high school graduate	1163	709	386	69	0
High school graduate	2,182	1,115	985	81	0
Some college or associate's degree	2,274	1,014	1,169	91	0
Bachelor's degree or more	2,169	697	1,394	79	0
Aged 5	**3,646**	**247**	**431**	**2,733**	**236**
Not a high school graduate	516	64	57	349	47
High school graduate	950	65	82	743	60
Some college or associate's degree	1,085	70	142	816	57
Bachelor's degree or more	1,096	48	150	826	72
Aged 6	**3,711**	**86**	**65**	**579**	**2,980**
Not a high school graduate	533	26	13	99	396
High school graduate	1,047	34	28	152	834
Some college or associate's degree	1,127	16	15	175	920
Bachelor's degree or more	1,003	9	9	154	830

PERCENT DISTRIBUTION BY SCHOOL ENROLLMENT STATUS

	total	not enrolled	nursery school	kindergarten	elementary school
Aged 3 to 4	**100.0%**	**45.4%**	**50.5%**	**4.1%**	**0.0%**
Not a high school graduate	100.0	61.0	33.2	5.9	0.0
High school graduate	100.0	51.1	45.1	3.7	0.0
Some college or associate's degree	100.0	44.6	51.4	4.0	0.0
Bachelor's degree or more	100.0	32.1	64.3	3.6	0.0
Aged 5	**100.0**	**6.8**	**11.8**	**75.0**	**6.5**
Not a high school graduate	100.0	12.4	11.0	67.6	9.1
High school graduate	100.0	6.8	8.6	78.2	6.3
Some college or associate's degree	100.0	6.5	13.1	75.2	5.3
Bachelor's degree or more	100.0	4.4	13.7	75.4	6.6
Aged 6	**100.0**	**2.3**	**1.8**	**15.6**	**80.3**
Not a high school graduate	100.0	4.9	2.4	18.6	74.3
High school graduate	100.0	3.2	2.7	14.5	79.7
Some college or associate's degree	100.0	1.4	1.3	15.5	81.6
Bachelor's degree or more	100.0	0.9	0.9	15.4	82.8

Source: Bureau of the Census, School Enrollment—Social and Economic Characteristics of Students: October 2004, detailed tables; Internet site http://www.census.gov/population/www/socdemo/school/cps2004.html; calculations by New Strategist

Most Millennials Are Students

Two-thirds of people under age 30 are in school.

Among the nation's 75 million students, fully 71 million are under age 30. More than 90 percent of children aged 5 to 17 are in school. The figure falls with age, but remains above 50 percent through age 20.

The number of students enrolled in kindergarten through 12th grade stood at 53 million in 2004 (37 million in grades K through 8, and nearly 17 million in grades 9 through 12). These lofty numbers have not been seen since the Baby-Boom generation filled classrooms decades ago.

Only 13 percent of students enrolled in school below the college level are in privately owned institutions. The percentage in private school falls with age, from 48 percent among nursery schoolers to just 8 percent of high school students.

■ School enrollment will remain at record-high levels thanks to immigration and the beginning of childbearing by the large Millennial generation.

School enrollment drops sharply among people in their early twenties

(percent of people aged 18 to 24 enrolled in school, by age, 2004)

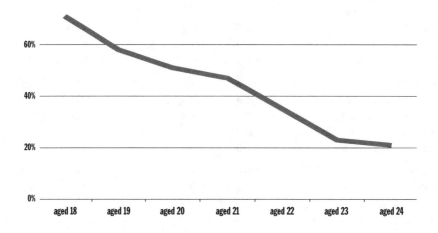

Table 1.10 School Enrollment by Age, 2004

(number of people aged 3 or older, and number and percent enrolled in school, by age, 2004; numbers in thousands)

	total	enrolled	
		number	percent
Total people	**277,467**	**75,461**	**27.2%**
Under age 30	108,904	71,099	65.3
Aged 3	4,089	1,583	38.7
Aged 4	4,339	2,969	68.4
Aged 5	3,934	3,662	93.1
Aged 6	3,994	3,899	97.6
Aged 7	3,802	3,725	98.0
Aged 8	4,004	3,931	98.2
Aged 9	3,922	3,855	98.3
Aged 10	4,044	3,995	98.8
Aged 11	4,067	3,999	98.3
Aged 12	4,337	4,275	98.6
Aged 13	4,290	4,227	98.5
Aged 14	4,242	4,192	98.8
Aged 15	4,211	4,135	98.2
Aged 16	4,472	4,275	95.6
Aged 17	4,084	3,811	93.3
Aged 18	3,784	2,685	71.0
Aged 19	3,917	2,276	58.1
Aged 20	3,981	2,030	51.0
Aged 21	3,995	1,874	46.9
Aged 22	3,891	1,381	35.5
Aged 23	4,107	953	23.2
Aged 24	4,273	888	20.8
Aged 25 to 29	19,125	2,479	13.0
Aged 30 or older	168,563	4,364	2.6

Source: Bureau of the Census, School Enrollment—Social and Economic Characteristics of Students: October 2004, detailed tables; Internet site http://www.census.gov/population/www/socdemo/school/cps2004.html; calculations by New Strategist

Table 1.11 Enrollment in Nursery School through College, 2004

(number and percent distribution of people attending nursery school through college, fall 2004; numbers in thousands)

	number	percent distribution
TOTAL STUDENTS	75,461	100.0%
Total, kindergarten through 12th	53,338	70.7
Nursery school	4,739	6.3
Kindergarten	3,992	5.3
Elementary and middle, total	32,555	43.1
1st grade	4,254	5.6
2nd grade	3,708	4.9
3rd grade	3,972	5.3
4th grade	3,882	5.1
5th grade	3,890	5.2
6th grade	4,313	5.7
7th grade	4,199	5.6
8th grade	4,337	5.7
High school, total	16,791	22.3
9th grade	4,339	5.8
10th grade	4,477	5.9
11th grade	3,990	5.3
12th grade	3,985	5.3
College, total	17,383	23.0
1st year	4,150	5.5
2nd year	3,807	5.0
3rd year	3,291	4.4
4th year	2,757	3.7
5th year	1,324	1.8
6th year	2,054	2.7

Source: Bureau of the Census, School Enrollment—Social and Economic Characteristics of Students: October 2004, detailed tables; Internet site http://www.census.gov/population/www/socdemo/school/cps2004.html; calculations by New Strategist

Table 1.12 Enrollment in Private School, 2004

(number and percent distribution of people attending nursery school through high school by control of school, 2004; numbers in thousands)

		private	
	total	number	percent
Total students	**57,810**	**7,489**	**13.0%**
Nursery school	4,739	2,252	47.5
Kindergarten	3,992	575	14.4
Elementary and middle	32,521	3,389	10.4
High school	16,557	1,272	7.7

Source: Bureau of the Census, School Enrollment—Social and Economic Characteristics of Students: October 2004, detailed tables; Internet site http://www.census.gov/population/www/socdemo/school/cps2004.html; calculations by New Strategist

Most Parents Are Satisfied with the Local Elementary School

But some are so bothered by their school they want to move.

Complaints about public schools have become commonplace, but in fact few households with elementary-school-aged children are not satisfied with the local public elementary school. Among households with children under age 14, fully 77 percent are satisfied with the public elementary school in their area. Only 7 percent are not satisfied. Three percent of households are so bothered by the local school that they want to move.

Just as most parents are satisfied with the local school, most also participate in school activities. Among elementary and secondary school children, 70 percent of parents report attending a class event during the past year, and 88 percent attended a general school meeting. Participation is greatest among the most-educated parents.

■ While the great majority of parents are satisfied with the local elementary school, the more than 2 million dissatisfied parents are one of the pressure points for educational reform.

Educated parents are most likely to attend their children's events

(percent of children whose parents attended a class event, by education of parent, 2003)

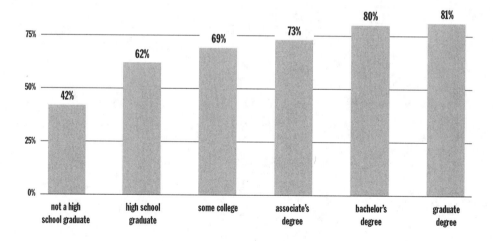

Table 1.13 Satisfaction with Local Elementary School, 2003

(number and percent distribution of households with children aged 5 to 15 by school attendance status of children; and number and percent distribution of households with children under age 14 by attitude toward and location of local elementary school, 2003; numbers in thousands)

	number	percent distribution
Households with children aged 5 to 15	**27,158**	**100.0%**
Children attend public school, K–12	22,834	84.1
Children attend private school, K–12	2,922	10.8
Children attend ungraded school, preschool	343	1.3
Children are home schooled	395	1.5
Children are not in school	808	3.0
Households with children under age 14	**31,081**	**100.0**
Satisfactory public elementary school	24,010	77.2
Unsatisfactory public elementary school	2,169	7.0
So bothered by school they want to move	992	3.2
Public elementary school less than 1 mile from home	17,544	56.4
Public elementary school 1 mile or more from home	12,234	39.4

Note: Numbers will not add to total because more than one category may apply and not reported is not shown.
Source: Bureau of the Census, American Housing Survey for the United States in 2003, Internet site http://www.census.gov/hhes/ www/housing/ahs/ahs03/tab28.htm; calculations by New Strategist

Table 14. Parental Involvement in School Activities, 2003

(percent of elementary and secondary school children whose parents reported participating in school activities, and number of times per week parent helps child with homework, by selected characteristics of child and parent, 2003)

	attended a general school meeting	attended a parent-teacher conference	attended a class event	volunteered at school	number of times per week parent helped with homework			
					less than one	one or two	three or four	five or more
Total children	**87.7%**	**77.1%**	**69.9%**	**41.8%**	**25.9%**	**35.6%**	**26.5%**	**12.0%**
Race and Hispanic origin of child								
Black, non-Hispanic	88.7	78.7	63.3	32.0	17.0	34.9	30.7	17.5
Hispanic	82.6	78.1	60.9	27.7	16.9	38.1	29.2	15.8
White, non-Hispanic	88.7	76.4	74.1	48.4	30.7	35.7	24.2	9.4
Other, non-Hispanic	87.5	77.6	68.5	37.2	23.5	30.1	32.3	14.1
Educational attainment of parent								
Not a high school graduate	69.8	67.8	42.4	15.6	18.6	44.8	23.2	13.4
High school graduate	83.8	75.4	62.1	30.3	23.1	35.8	28.4	12.7
Some college	88.5	78.0	69.1	38.8	24.6	35.6	27.6	12.3
Associate's degree	88.6	76.6	73.0	39.7	26.8	35.7	26.2	11.3
Bachelor's degree	92.0	79.8	80.1	53.9	28.7	34.2	26.1	10.9
Graduate degree	94.6	79.4	80.8	61.8	30.7	33.4	24.2	11.8
Child attending public school, total	**86.7**	**75.9**	**68.0**	**38.5**	**26.0**	**35.9**	**26.4**	**11.7**
Elementary and middle (kindergarten to 8th grade)	90.9	85.1	71.7	42.8	16.8	35.3	32.9	15.0
Secondary school (grades 9 to 12)	76.9	54.8	59.4	28.5	50.6	37.6	9.0	2.7
Child attending private school, total	**95.7**	**86.6**	**85.6**	**68.7**	**24.7**	**33.1**	**27.7**	**14.5**
Elementary and middle (kindergarten to 8th grade)	96.6	91.6	88.4	73.4	17.8	30.4	33.6	18.3
Secondary school (grades 9 to 12)	93.0	72.2	77.6	55.2	46.9	41.8	8.9	2.4

Source: National Center for Education Statistics, Digest of Education Statistics 2004; http://nces.ed.gov/programs/digest/d04/list_tables2.asp#c2_6; calculations by New Strategist

Few High School Students Have Jobs

Employment is not the norm among high school students.

Among the nation's 14 million high school students, fewer than 3 million have jobs. The 21 percent who are employed is lower than the 27 percent of 2000.

The percentage of high school students with jobs rises with age. Only 7 percent of students aged 15 are employed. The figure rises to 26 percent among 16-to-17-year-olds. Among 18-to-19-year-old high school students, 34 percent are employed. Even among older high school students—those aged 20 or older—only 36 percent are employed.

■ The many extracurricular activities in which today's teens are involved make it difficult for them to work.

The percentage of high school students with jobs has declined

(percent of students enrolled in high school who are employed, 2000 and 2004)

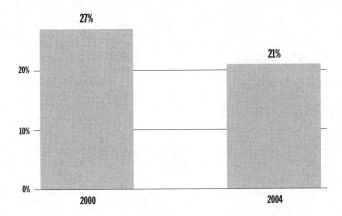

Table 1.15 High School Students by Age and Employment Status, 2004

(number and percent distribution of high school students by age and employment status, 2004)

	total	employed	
		number	percent
Students enrolled in high school	**13,522**	**2,865**	**21.2%**
Aged 15	3,962	266	6.7
Aged 16 to 17	7,862	2,010	25.6
Aged 18 to 19	1,266	432	34.1
Aged 20 or older	432	157	36.3

Source: Bureau of the Census, School Enrollment—Social and Economic Characteristics of Students: October 2004, detailed tables; Internet site http://www.census.gov/population/www/socdemo/school/cps2004.html; calculations by New Strategist

SAT Scores Rise

Most demographic segments have made gains.

The number of high school students who take the Scholastic Assessment Test expanded enormously over the past few decades. Once limited to the elite, the SAT has been embraced by the masses—as have the nation's college campuses. Despite the greater numbers of students taking the test, SAT scores are rising.

The average verbal SAT score rose 9 points between 1990–91 and 2003–04. The biggest gainers by race and Hispanic origin are Asians—up 22 points. The average math SAT score rose 18 points overall between 1990–91 and 2003–04, including a 29-point rise for Asians. Blacks and Hispanics made the smallest gains on both verbal and math scores.

■ Gains in SAT test scores suggest students are learning more of what they need to know at school—or preparing better for the test.

Verbal and math scores are up

(average verbal and math SAT scores, 1990–91 and 2003–04)

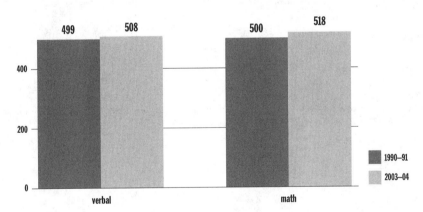

Table 1.16 Scholastic Assessment Test Scores by Sex, Race, and Hispanic Origin, 1990–91 and 2003–04

(average SAT scores and change in scores by sex, race, and Hispanic origin of student, 1990–91 and 2003–04)

	2003–04	1990–91	change
VERBAL SAT			
Total students	**508**	**499**	**9**
Female	504	495	9
Male	512	503	9
American Indian	483	470	13
Asian	507	485	22
Black	430	427	3
Hispanic	461	458	3
White	528	518	10
Other	494	486	8
MATH SAT			
Total students	**518**	**500**	**18**
Female	501	482	19
Male	537	520	17
American Indian	488	468	20
Asian	577	548	29
Black	427	419	8
Hispanic	465	462	3
White	531	513	18
Other	508	492	16

Source: National Center for Education Statistics, Digest of Education Statistics 2004; http://nces.ed.gov/programs/digest/d04/list_tables2.asp#c2_6; calculations by New Strategist

The Majority of High School Grads Go to College

Women are more likely than men to go to college.

Going to college is no longer an elite privilege, but the norm. Most high school graduates continue their education on a college campus. Although male high school graduates were once more likely than their female counterparts to go to college, today the opposite is the case. In 2003, 66.5 percent of girls and a smaller 61.2 percent of boys who had graduated from high school in the previous 12 months had started college by October.

Non-Hispanic white high school graduates are much more likely than black or Hispanic graduates to go to college—66.2 percent of non-Hispanic whites go to college within 12 months of graduating from high school versus 57.5 percent of blacks and 54.6 percent of Hispanics.

■ As the cost of colleges rises, college enrollment rates may fall as families struggle to pay tuition.

Women have a higher college enrollment rate than men

(percent of people aged 16 to 24 who graduated from high school in the previous 12 months and had enrolled in college as of October, by sex, 2003)

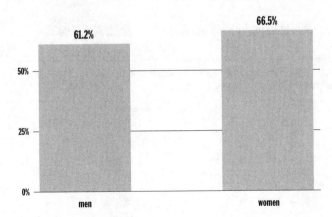

Table 1.17 College Enrollment Rates by Sex, 1990 to 2003

(percent of people aged 16 to 24 graduating from high school in the previous 12 months who were enrolled in college as of October of each year, by sex; percentage point difference in enrollment rates of men and women, 1990–2003)

	men	women	percentage point difference
2003	61.2%	66.5%	−5.3
2002	62.1	68.4	−6.3
2001	60.1	63.5	−3.4
2000	59.9	66.2	−6.3
1999	61.4	64.4	−3.0
1998	62.4	69.1	−6.7
1997	63.6	70.3	−6.7
1996	60.1	69.7	−9.6
1995	62.6	61.3	1.3
1994	60.6	63.2	−2.6
1993	59.9	65.2	−5.3
1992	60.0	63.8	−3.8
1991	57.9	67.1	−9.2
1990	58.0	62.2	−4.2

Source: National Center for Education Statistics, Digest of Education Statistics 2004; http://nces.ed.gov/programs/digest/d04/list_tables3.asp#c3; calculations by New Strategist

Table 1.18 College Enrollment Rates by Race and Hispanic Origin, 1990 to 2003

(percent of people aged 16 to 24 graduating from high school in the previous 12 months who were enrolled in college as of October of each year, by race and Hispanic origin, 1990–2003)

	black	non-Hispanic white	Hispanic
2003	57.5%	66.2%	–
2002	59.4	69.1	54.6%
2001	55.0	64.3	52.7
2000	54.9	65.7	49.0
1999	58.9	66.3	47.5
1998	61.9	68.5	51.8
1997	58.5	68.2	54.6
1996	56.0	67.4	56.7
1995	51.2	64.3	51.2
1994	50.8	64.5	55.0
1993	55.6	62.9	55.4
1992	48.2	64.3	58.1
1991	46.4	65.4	51.6
1990	46.8	63.0	51.7

Note: Hispanic enrollment rates are a three-year moving average. "–" means data are not available.
Source: National Center for Education Statistics, Digest of Education Statistics 2004; http://nces.ed.gov/programs/digest/d04/list_tables3.asp#c3; calculations by New Strategist

Most Children from Affluent Families Go to College

The majority of dependents aged 18 to 24 with family incomes of $50,000 or more are in college.

Family income is one of the best predictors of whether children have the opportunity to go to college. Among the nation's 16 million dependent family members aged 18 to 24, nearly half—46 percent—are in college. The proportion rises with income from a low of 24 percent for those with a family income of less than $20,000 to a high of 68 percent for those with a family income of $150,000 or more.

Among children in college, those from upper-income families are more likely to attend four-year schools. The figure ranges from a low of 63 percent for those with family incomes below $20,000 to a high of 81 percent for those with an income of $100,000 or more. Family income also affects whether children attend college full-time.

■ Many children from less-affluent families attend school part-time because they must work to pay the bills.

College attendance rises with family income

(percent of dependent family members aged 18 to 24 attending college, by household income, 2004)

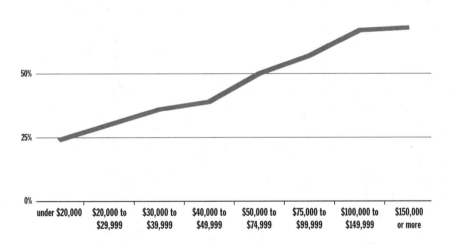

Table 1.19 Children in College by Family Income, 2004

(number and percent of dependent primary family members aged 18 to 24 by household income and college enrollment status, 2004; numbers in thousands)

	total	enrolled in college	
		number	percent
Total dependent primary family members aged 18 to 24	**15,720**	**7,191**	**45.7%**
Under $20,000	1,790	422	23.6
$20,000 to $29,999	1,214	362	29.8
$30,000 to $39,999	1,508	540	35.8
$40,000 to $49,999	1,107	434	39.2
$50,000 to $74,999	2,962	1,483	50.1
$75,000 to $99,999	1,825	1,049	57.5
$100,000 to $149,999	1,632	1,094	67.0
$150,000 or more	980	662	67.6
Income not reported	2,701	1,144	42.4

Source: Bureau of the Census, School Enrollment—Social and Economic Characteristics of Students: October 2004, detailed tables; Internet site http://www.census.gov/population/www/socdemo/school/cps2004.html; calculations by New Strategist

Table 1.20 Children in College by Family Income and Enrollment Status, 2004

(number of dependent primary family members aged 18 to 24 enrolled in college by household income, type of institution, and attendance status, 2004; numbers in thousands)

	total	type of institution		attendance status	
		two-year college	four-year college	full-time student	part-time student
Dependent primary family members aged 18 to 24 enrolled in college	**7,191**	**1,808**	**5,383**	**6,392**	**799**
Under $20,000	422	155	267	371	51
$20,000 to $29,999	362	118	244	286	76
$30,000 to $39,999	540	162	378	476	64
$40,000 to $49,999	434	113	321	359	75
$50,000 to $74,999	1,483	408	1,075	1,329	154
$75,000 to $99,999	1,049	267	782	951	98
$100,000 to $149,999	1,094	207	887	1,000	94
$150,000 or more	662	128	534	624	38
Income not reported	1,144	251	893	994	150
Dependent primary family members aged 18 to 24 enrolled in college	**100.0%**	**25.1%**	**74.9%**	**88.9%**	**11.1%**
Under $20,000	100.0	36.7	63.3	87.9	12.1
$20,000 to $29,999	100.0	32.6	67.4	79.0	21.0
$30,000 to $39,999	100.0	30.0	70.0	88.1	11.9
$40,000 to $49,999	100.0	26.0	74.0	82.7	17.3
$50,000 to $74,999	100.0	27.5	72.5	89.6	10.4
$75,000 to $99,999	100.0	25.5	74.5	90.7	9.3
$100,000 to $149,999	100.0	18.9	81.1	91.4	8.6
$150,000 or more	100.0	19.3	80.7	94.3	5.7
Income not reported	100.0	21.9	78.1	86.9	13.1

Source: Bureau of the Census, School Enrollment—Social and Economic Characteristics of Students: October 2004, detailed tables; Internet site http://www.census.gov/population/www/socdemo/school/cps2004.html; calculations by New Strategist

Millennials Are the Majority of Undergraduates

Most Millennial college students attend four-year schools full-time.

Among the nation's 17 million college students in 2004, more than 13 million were under age 30 and belonged to the Millennial generation (the oldest Millennials turned 27 in that year). Among the 8 million Millennials in four-year undergraduate programs, 87 percent attend school full-time. Among the 3 million in two-year undergraduate programs, 69 percent are full-time students.

More than 3 million students attend the nation's graduate schools, and just over half are under age 30. Among graduate students under age 30, nearly two-thirds attend graduate school full-time.

■ With Millennials heading to college, many middle-aged parents face stiff college tuition bills.

Millennial college students are likely to attend school full-time

(percent distribution of college students under age 30 by type of program and attendance status, 2004)

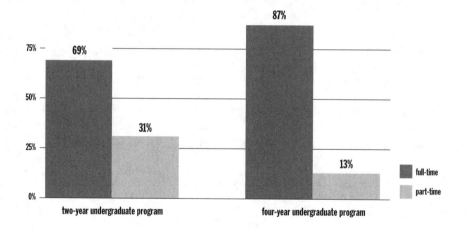

Table 1.21 College Students by Age and Attendance Status, 2004

(number and percent distribution of people aged 15 or older enrolled in institutions of higher education by age and attendance status, 2004; numbers in thousands)

| | | undergraduate | | | | | | graduate school | | |
| | | two-year | | | four-year | | | | | |
	total	total	full-time	part-time	total	full-time	part-time	total	full-time	part-time
Total enrolled	**17,383**	**4,340**	**2,602**	**1,738**	**9,665**	**7,816**	**1,849**	**3,378**	**1,572**	**1,806**
Under age 30	13,214	3,168	2,187	981	8,312	7,239	1,073	1,730	1,115	615
Aged 15 to 17	199	74	59	15	113	112	1	11	11	0
Aged 18 to 19	3,685	1,168	968	200	2,507	2,394	113	9	9	0
Aged 20 to 21	3,778	803	554	249	2,898	2,697	201	76	76	0
Aged 22 to 24	3,149	568	327	241	1,862	1,508	354	717	548	169
Aged 25 to 29	2,403	555	279	276	932	528	404	917	471	446
Aged 30 or older	4,172	1,172	417	755	1,352	576	776	1,648	456	1,192

PERCENT DISTRIBUTION BY ATTENDANCE STATUS

Total enrolled	–	**100.0%**	**60.0%**	**40.0%**	**100.0%**	**80.9%**	**19.1%**	**100.0%**	**46.5%**	**53.5%**
Under age 30	–	100.0	69.0	31.0	100.0	87.1	12.9	100.0	64.5	35.5
Aged 15 to 17	–	100.0	79.7	20.3	100.0	99.1	0.9	100.0	100.0	0.0
Aged 18 to 19	–	100.0	82.9	17.1	100.0	95.5	4.5	100.0	100.0	0.0
Aged 20 to 21	–	100.0	69.0	31.0	100.0	93.1	6.9	100.0	100.0	0.0
Aged 22 to 24	–	100.0	57.6	42.4	100.0	81.0	19.0	100.0	76.4	23.6
Aged 25 to 29	–	100.0	50.3	49.7	100.0	56.7	43.3	100.0	51.4	48.6
Aged 30 or older	–	100.0	35.6	64.4	100.0	42.6	57.4	100.0	27.7	72.3

PERCENT DISTRIBUTION BY AGE

Total enrolled	**100.0%**	**100.0%**	**100.0%**	**100.0%**	**100.0%**	**100.0%**	**100.0%**	**100.0%**	**100.0%**	**100.0%**
Under age 30	76.0	73.0	84.1	56.4	86.0	92.6	58.0	51.2	70.9	34.1
Aged 15 to 17	1.1	1.7	2.3	0.9	1.2	1.4	0.1	0.3	0.7	0.0
Aged 18 to 19	21.2	26.9	37.2	11.5	25.9	30.6	6.1	0.3	0.6	0.0
Aged 20 to 21	21.7	18.5	21.3	14.3	30.0	34.5	10.9	2.2	4.8	0.0
Aged 22 to 24	18.1	13.1	12.6	13.9	19.3	19.3	19.1	21.2	34.9	9.4
Aged 25 to 29	13.8	12.8	10.7	15.9	9.6	6.8	21.8	27.1	30.0	24.7
Aged 30 or older	24.0	27.0	16.0	43.4	14.0	7.4	42.0	48.8	29.0	66.0

Note: "–" means not applicable.
Source: Bureau of the Census, School Enrollment—Social and Economic Characteristics of Students: October 2004, detailed tables; Internet site http://www.census.gov/population/www/socdemo/school/cps2004.html; calculations by New Strategist

Most College Students Are Employed

Even among full-time students, half are employed.

Fifty percent of full-time college students have jobs. Thirty-five percent work part-time, while a busy 15 percent work full-time on top of their studies. The proportion of full-time students with full-time jobs increases with age from just 5 percent of those under age 20 to more than one-third of students aged 30 or older.

Among part-time college students, fully 84 percent have jobs. The 65 percent majority works full-time, while just 19 percent work part-time. The percentage of part-time students who work full-time rises with age from 32 percent of those aged under age 20 to more than 70 percent of those aged 25 or older.

■ With college costs rising rapidly, many students have no choice but to work while in school.

The proportion of full-time college students with jobs does not vary much by age

(percent of full-time college students who are employed, by age, 2004)

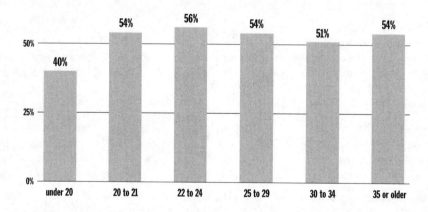

Table 1.22 College Students by Age and Employment Status, 2004

(number and percent distribution of college students by age, attendance status, and employment status, 2004)

	total	employed			total	employed		
		total	full-time	part-time		total	full-time	part-time
Full-time college students	**11,990**	**5,990**	**1,764**	**4,226**	**100.0%**	**50.0%**	**14.7%**	**35.2%**
Under age 20	3,553	1,423	194	1,229	100.0	40.1	5.5	34.6
Aged 20 to 21	3,326	1,781	380	1,401	100.0	53.5	11.4	42.1
Aged 22 to 24	2,384	1,331	393	938	100.0	55.8	16.5	39.3
Aged 25 to 29	1,278	691	348	343	100.0	54.1	27.2	26.8
Aged 30 to 34	548	281	147	134	100.0	51.3	26.8	24.5
Aged 35 or older	901	483	302	181	100.0	53.6	33.5	20.1
Part-time college students	**5,393**	**4,511**	**3,492**	**1,019**	**100.0**	**83.6**	**64.8**	**18.9**
Under age 20	330	247	105	142	100.0	74.8	31.8	43.0
Aged 20 to 21	451	356	209	147	100.0	78.9	46.3	32.6
Aged 22 to 24	765	658	437	221	100.0	86.0	57.1	28.9
Aged 25 to 29	1,125	970	812	158	100.0	86.2	72.2	14.0
Aged 30 to 34	739	631	525	106	100.0	85.4	71.0	14.3
Aged 35 or older	1,983	1,649	1,404	245	100.0	83.2	70.8	12.4

Source: Bureau of the Census, School Enrollment—Social and Economic Characteristics of Students: October 2004, detailed tables; Internet site http://www.census.gov/population/www/socdemo/school/cps2004.html; calculations by New Strategist

Many Young Adults Participate in Adult Education for Job-Related Reasons

Life-long learning is becoming a necessity for job security.

As job security dwindles, many workers are turning to the educational system to try to stay on track. Overall, 33 percent of Americans aged 17 or older participated in work-related adult education during the past 12 months. An even larger 58 percent participated in less formal work-related learning activities, such as seminars offered by employers.

Among 17-to-24-year-olds, 31 percent took part in work-related courses in 2003. The figure rises above 40 percent in the 25-to-29 age group and remains above 40 percent through the 50-to-54 age group. The percentage participating in less-formal work-related learning activities is highest (above 70 percent) among people under age 30.

■ Many Americans who participate in work-related education are training themselves to compete in the increasingly global economy.

More than 40 percent of people aged 25 to 29 took a work-related course in 2003

(percent of people aged 17 or older participating in job- or career-related courses, by age, 2003)

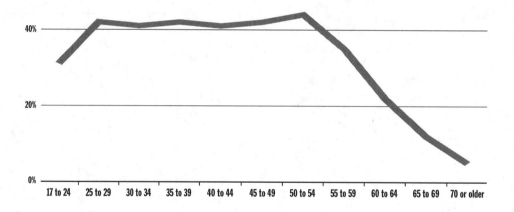

Table 1.23 Participation in Adult Education for Work-Related Reasons, 2003

(percent of people aged 17 or older participating in work-related adult education during the past 12 months, by age and type, 2003; numbers in thousands)

	career- or job-related courses	less formal work-related learning activities
Total people	**33.2%**	**58.3%**
Aged 17 to 24	30.9	73.4
Aged 25 to 29	42.4	75.4
Aged 30 to 34	40.7	68.4
Aged 35 to 39	41.6	67.5
Aged 40 to 44	40.7	70.4
Aged 45 to 49	42.2	65.3
Aged 50 to 54	43.6	65.7
Aged 55 to 59	34.9	56.3
Aged 60 to 64	21.7	39.4
Aged 65 to 69	11.9	27.0
Aged 70 or older	4.7	12.9

Note: Adult education is defined as all education activities except full-time enrollment in higher education credential programs. Examples include part-time college attendance and classes or seminars given by employers.
Source: National Center for Education Statistics, Digest of Education Statistics, 2004, list of tables, Internet site http:// nces.ed.gov/programs/digest/d04/list_tables3.asp#c3b_1; calculations by New Strategist

2

Health

■ The 54 percent majority of children under age 18 are in excellent health, according to their parents. Only 2 percent of parents report their children's health as only fair or poor.

■ Among high school girls, 25 percent are overweight or at risk for becoming overweight. A larger 36 percent think they are overweight, and an even larger 59 percent are trying to lose weight.

■ The 53 percent majority of 11th graders have had sexual intercourse at some point in their lives, and the share tops 60 percent among high school seniors.

■ Twenty-five percent of people aged 12 or older have smoked cigarettes in the past month. The proportion peaks at 43 percent among 22-year-olds.

■ Among 18-to-24-year-olds, 31 percent do not have health insurance—a larger share than in any other age group.

■ Nearly 5 million children (8 percent) have been diagnosed with a learning disability, and more than 4 million (7 percent) have attention deficit disorder.

■ In the 15-to-24 age group, accidents, homicide, and suicide are the leading causes of death.

Most Children Are in Excellent Health

The proportion of people in excellent health falls among young adults, however.

The 54 percent majority of children under age 18 are in excellent health, according to their parents. Not surprisingly, the figure is much higher than that reported by adults, who are prone to stresses and chronic conditions that lead to health problems. Only about 2 percent of parents report that their children's health is only fair or poor.

The situation is different for young adults, who self-reported their health status in a different survey. Only 25 to 27 percent of 18-to-34-year-olds report being in excellent health, although the figure rises to the 61 to 64 percent majority when those reporting "very good" health are included. Seven to 8 percent of young adults report being in fair or poor health.

■ The majority of Americans under age 55 say their health is very good to excellent.

Few children are in poor health

(percent distribution of children under age 18 by parent-reported health status, 2004)

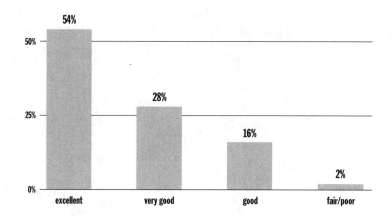

Table 2.1 Health Status of People under Age 35, 2004

(parent- or self-reported health status of people under age 35, by age, 2004)

	excellent	very good	good	fair/poor
Under age 18	54.0%	28.3%	15.9%	1.8%
Under age 5	58.7	26.5	13.5	1.3
Aged 5 to 11	53.9	28.9	15.4	1.8
Aged 12 to 17	50.2	29.0	18.5	2.3
Aged 18 to 24	24.6	36.5	30.3	7.5
Aged 25 to 34	26.5	37.6	27.9	7.2

Source: National Center for Health Statistics, Summary Health Statistics for U.S. Children: National Health Interview Survey, 2004, Series 10, No. 227, 2003, Internet site http://www.cdc.gov/nchs/nhis.htm; and Centers for Disease Control and Prevention, Behavioral Risk Factor Surveillance System Prevalence Data, 2004, Internet site http://apps.nccd.cdc.gov/brfss/

Teens Worry about Being Overweight

Although few are overweight, many are trying to shed pounds.

Among children in both the 6-to-11 and 12-to-19 age groups, only about 16 percent are overweight, according to government studies. Blacks and Hispanics are more likely to be overweight than non-Hispanic whites.

Among high school students, 25 percent of girls are overweight or at risk for becoming overweight. A larger share of girls (36 percent) think they are overweight, and even more are trying to lose weight (59 percent). Thirty-three percent of boys in 9th to 12 grade are overweight or at risk for becoming overweight, but only 24 percent of boys think they are overweight.

Weight problems become more severe among young adults. Fifty-three percent of women aged 20 to 34 are overweight and 28 percent are obese. Among men in the age group, 57 percent are overweight and 22 percent are obese. Thirty percent of 18-to-24-year-olds are trying to lose weight, a figure that rises to 38 percent among 25-to-34-year-olds.

■ Although high school girls are weight conscious, their concern does not seem to prevent the majority of them from becoming overweight in early adulthood.

Many girls think they are overweight

(percent of students in 9th to 12th grade who are overweight or at risk for becoming overweight, percent who think they are overweight, and percent trying to lose weight, by sex, 2003)

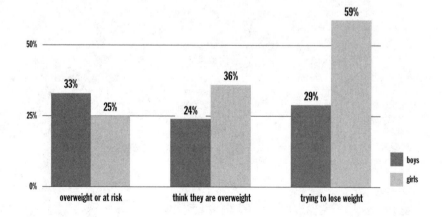

Table 2.2 Overweight Children, 1999–02

(percent of children aged 6 to 19 who are overweight, by sex, race, Hispanic origin, and age, 1999–02)

	6 to 11	12 to 19
Total children	**15.8%**	**16.1%**
Total boys	**16.9**	**16.7**
Black, non-Hispanic	17.0	18.7
Mexican	26.5	24.7
White, non-Hispanic	14.0	14.6
Total girls	**14.7**	**15.4**
Black, non-Hispanic	22.8	23.6
Mexican	17.1	19.9
White, non-Hispanic	13.1	12.7

Note: Being overweight is defined as having a body mass index at or above the sex- and age-specific 95th percentile BMI cutoff points from the 2000 CDC growth charts.
Source: National Center for Health Statistics, Health United States, 2005, Internet site http://www.cdc.gov/nchs/hus.htm

Table 2.3 Weight Problems and Dieting Behavior of 9th to 12th Graders by Sex, 2003

(percent of 9th to 12th graders by weight status and dieting behavior, by sex and grade, 2003)

	total	9th grade	10th grade	11th grade	12th grade
Females					
At risk for becoming overweight*	15.3%	15.6%	15.3%	16.9%	13.2%
Overweight**	9.4	11.2	9.3	8.6	8.0
Described themselves as overweight	36.1	33.1	36.1	36.9	38.7
Were trying to lose weight	59.3	54.1	62.2	60.4	61.7
Ate less food, fewer calories, or foods low in fat to lose weight or to avoid gaining weight in past 30 days	56.2	53.0	58.1	56.4	57.9
Exercised to lose weight or to avoid gaining weight in past 30 days	65.7	65.7	68.9	64.5	63.2
Went without eating for at least 24 hours to lose weight or to avoid gaining weight in past 30 days	18.3	18.8	18.5	19.6	15.7
Took diet pills, powders, or liquids without a doctor's advice to lose weight or avoid gaining weight in past 30 days	11.3	9.2	10.9	12.6	13.0
Vomited or took a laxative to lose weight or to avoid gaining weight in past 30 days	8.4	7.9	9.3	8.8	7.3
Males					
At risk for becoming overweight*	15.5	15.3	14.7	16.6	15.6
Overweight**	17.4	19.0	17.9	17.0	14.7
Described themselves as overweight	23.5	22.6	23.2	24.3	24.1
Were trying to lose weight	29.1	31.2	28.3	28.3	28.0
Ate less food, fewer calories, or foods low in fat to lose weight or to avoid gaining weight in past 30 days	28.9	28.8	27.8	29.4	29.8
Exercised to lose weight or to avoid gaining weight in past 30 days	49.0	50.2	49.8	49.4	46.4
Went without eating for at least 24 hours to lose weight or to avoid gaining weight in past 30 days	8.5	10.7	7.0	8.2	6.9
Took diet pills, powders, or liquids without a doctor's advice to lose weight or avoid gaining weight in past 30 days	7.1	7.0	5.8	7.7	8.5
Vomited or took a laxative to lose weight or to avoid gaining weight in past 30 days	3.7	4.6	3.5	2.6	3.8

* Students at risk of becoming overweight were between the 85th and 95th percentile for body mass index, by age and sex, based on reference data.
** Students classified as overweight were at or above the 95th percentile for body mass index, by age and sex, based on reference data.
Source: Centers for Disease Control and Prevention, "Youth Risk Behavior Surveillance—United States, 2003," Mortality and Morbidity Weekly Report, Vol. 53/SS-2, May 21, 2004, Internet site http://www.cdc.gov/mmwr/indss_2004.html

Table 2.4 Average Measured Weight by Sex and Age, 1960–62 and 1999–02

(average weight in pounds of people aged 20 to 74, by sex and age, 1960–62 and 1999–02; change in pounds 1960–62 to 1999–02)

	1999–02	1960–62	change in pounds
Men aged 20 to 74	**191.0 lbs.**	**166.3 lbs.**	**24.7 lbs.**
Aged 20 to 29	183.4	163.9	19.5
Aged 30 to 39	189.1	169.9	19.2
Aged 40 to 49	196.0	169.1	26.9
Aged 50 to 59	195.4	167.7	27.7
Aged 60 to 74	191.5	158.9	32.6
Women aged 20 to 74	**164.3**	**140.2**	**24.1**
Aged 20 to 29	156.5	127.7	28.8
Aged 30 to 39	163.0	138.8	24.2
Aged 40 to 49	168.2	142.8	25.4
Aged 50 to 59	169.2	146.5	22.7
Aged 60 to 74	164.7	147.3	17.4

Note: Data are based on measured height and weight of a sample of the civilian noninstitutionalized population.
Source: National Center for Health Statistics, Mean Body Weight, Height, and Body Mass Index, United States 1960–2002, Advance Data, No. 347, 2004, Internet site http://www.cdc.gov/nchs/pressroom/04news/americans.htm; calculations by New Strategist

Table 2.5 Weight Status by Sex and Age, 1999–02

(percent of people aged 20 or older who are overweight or obese, by sex and age, 1999–02)

	healthy weight	overweight total	obese
Total people	**32.9%**	**65.2%**	**30.5%**
Total men	**30.4**	**68.6**	**27.5**
Aged 20 to 34	40.3	57.4	21.7
Aged 35 to 44	29.0	70.5	28.5
Aged 45 to 54	24.0	75.7	30.6
Aged 55 to 64	23.8	75.4	35.5
Aged 65 to 74	22.8	76.2	31.9
Aged 75 or older	32.0	67.4	18.0
Total women	**35.4**	**62.0**	**33.4**
Aged 20 to 34	42.6	52.8	28.4
Aged 35 to 44	37.1	60.6	32.1
Aged 45 to 54	33.1	65.1	36.9
Aged 55 to 64	27.6	72.2	42.1
Aged 65 to 74	26.4	70.9	39.3
Aged 75 or older	36.9	59.9	23.6

Note: Data are based on measured height and weight of a sample of the civilian noninstitutionalized population. Being overweight is defined as having a body mass index of 25 or higher. Obesity is defined as a body mass index of 30 or higher. Body mass index is calculated by dividing weight in kilograms by height in meters squared.
Source: National Center for Health Statistics, Health, United States, 2005, Internet site http://www.cdc.gov/nchs/hus.htm

Table 2.6 Weight Loss Behavior by Age, 2000

(percent of people aged 18 or older engaging in selected weight loss behaviors, by age, 2000)

	total	18 to 24	25 to 34	35 to 44	45 to 54	55 to 64	65 or older
Trying to lose weight	38.0%	30.2%	38.0%	40.4%	44.7%	42.6%	30.6%
Trying to maintain weight	58.9	51.9	56.9	59.8	63.1	60.8	58.4
Eating fewer calories to lose/maintain weight*	13.5	11.4	12.1	13.9	15.2	13.2	12.0
Eating less fat to lose/maintain weight*	27.4	25.3	25.8	27.7	28.3	29.1	29.4
Eating fewer calories and less fat to lose/maintain weight*	29.6	25.5	27.0	30.1	32.6	33.0	29.0
Using physical activity or exercise to lose/maintain weight*	60.7	74.7	67.7	64.0	60.5	55.4	43.3
Advised by health professional to lose weight	11.7	4.0	8.4	11.3	16.0	17.7	11.2

* Among those trying to lose or maintain weight.
Source: Centers for Disease Control and Prevention, Behavioral Risk Factor Surveillance System Prevalence Data, 2000, Internet site http://apps.nccd.cdc.gov/brfss/index.asp

Bicycling Is the Most Popular Recreational Activity among Children

But the percentage of children riding bicycles has plunged.

Among selected recreational activities examined by the National Sporting Goods Association, bicycling is most popular among children aged 7 to 11, with more than 9 million (47 percent) taking part at least once in 2004. But a much larger 61 percent of children aged 7 to 11 bicycled ten years earlier. Bicycling is also the most popular recreational activity among 12-to-17-year-olds, but the proportion bicycling at least once in the past year fell from 43 to 31 percent between 1994 and 2004.

The 56 percent majority of high school students are enrolled in physical education classes, but the proportion declines as students progress to just 45 percent of senior boys and 35 percent of senior girls. Fifty-eight percent of high school students played on a sports team in the past year, including 64 percent of boys and 51 percent of girls. Just over half of high school students engage in strengthening exercises during a week's time, with boys more likely to do so than girls.

Among 18-to-24-year-olds, only 42 percent take part in regular leisure-time physical activities. Thirty percent of the age group is physically inactive.

■ The decline in physical activity among children may be one factor in the growing weight problems of young adults.

The percentage of teenagers enrolled in physical education classes declines through high school

(percent of students in 9th to 12th grade enrolled in physical education classes, by sex and grade, 2003)

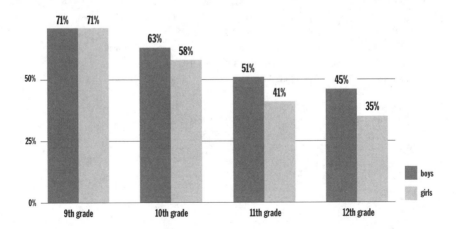

Table 2.7 Sports Participation of Children Aged 7 to 17, 1994 and 2004

(number and percent of people aged 7 to 17 participating in selected sports at least once during past year, by age, 1994 and 2004; percent change in number and percentage point change in participation rate; numbers in thousands)

	2004		1994		percent change in number	percentage point change in rate
	number	percent	number	percent		
AGED 7 TO 11						
Total children	**19,650**	**100.0%**	**18,773**	**100.0%**	**4.7%**	–
Bicycle riding	9,196	46.8	11,403	60.7	−19.4	−13.9
Basketball	5,867	29.9	5,554	29.6	5.6	0.3
Soccer	5,411	27.5	5,494	29.3	−1.5	−1.7
Baseball	4,333	22.1	5,107	27.2	−15.2	−5.2
Fishing	3,583	18.2	4,883	26.0	−26.6	−7.8
Skateboarding	3,439	17.5	1,885	10.0	82.4	7.5
In-line skating	3,313	16.9	6,998	37.3	−52.7	−20.4
Golf	1,027	5.2	670	3.6	53.3	1.7
Snowboarding	971	4.9	210	1.1	362.4	3.8
Skiing (alpine)	659	3.4	646	3.4	2.0	−0.1
Ice hockey	292	1.5	388	2.1	−24.7	−0.6
AGED 12 TO 17						
Total children	**24,988**	**100.0**	**21,579**	**100.0**	**15.8**	–
Bicycle riding	7,770	31.1	9,363	43.4	−17.0	−12.3
Basketball	7,175	28.7	7,951	36.8	−9.8	−8.1
Skateboarding	4,262	17.1	2,012	9.3	111.8	7.7
Fishing	4,103	16.4	4,632	21.5	−11.4	−5.0
Baseball	3,959	15.8	4,148	19.2	−4.6	−3.4
In-line skating	3,913	15.7	5,273	24.4	−25.8	−8.8
Soccer	3,578	14.3	3,536	16.4	1.2	−2.1
Golf	2,487	10.0	1,885	8.7	31.9	1.2
Snowboarding	2,356	9.4	853	4.0	176.2	5.5
Skiing (alpine)	979	3.9	1,966	9.1	−50.2	−5.2
Ice hockey	544	2.2	408	1.9	33.3	0.3

Note: "–" means not applicable.
Source: National Sporting Goods Association, Internet site http://www.nsga.org

Table 2.8   Participation of High School Students in Physical Education Classes, Team Sports, and Strengthening Exercises, 2003

(percent of 9th to 12th graders participating in physical education classes, sports teams, and strengthening exercises, by sex and grade, 2003)

	enrolled in PE class	attended PE class daily (five/week)	played on sports team in past year	strengthening exercises in past week
Total in 9th–12th grade	**55.7%**	**28.4%**	**57.6%**	**51.9%**
Boys	**58.5**	**30.5**	**64.0**	**60.1**
9th grade	70.8	37.7	65.0	63.1
10th grade	63.0	33.5	62.0	60.1
11th grade	50.5	26.0	66.3	62.3
12th grade	44.5	21.4	62.3	54.6
Girls	**52.8**	**26.4**	**51.0**	**43.4**
9th grade	71.2	38.0	55.2	47.9
10th grade	58.3	29.1	53.9	49.2
11th grade	40.8	19.2	47.8	39.8
12th grade	34.6	15.2	45.9	34.4

Note: Strengthening exercises are push-ups, sit-ups, weightlifting, etc., on three days or more during the week preceding the survey.
Source: Centers for Disease Control and Prevention, "Youth Risk Behavior Surveillance—United States, 2003," Mortality and Morbidity Weekly Report, Vol. 53/SS-2, May 21, 2004, Internet site http://www.cdc.gov/mmwr/indss_2004.html

Table 2.9 Leisure-Time Physical Activity Level by Sex and Age, 2003

(percent distribution of people aged 18 or older by leisure-time physical activity level, by sex and age, 2003)

	total	physically inactive	at least some physical activity	regular physical activity
Total people	**100.0%**	**37.6%**	**29.6%**	**32.8%**
Aged 18 to 24	100.0	29.6	28.2	42.3
Aged 25 to 44	100.0	34.0	31.0	34.9
Aged 45 to 54	100.0	36.5	30.8	32.8
Aged 55 to 64	100.0	40.8	30.1	29.2
Aged 65 to 74	100.0	45.8	25.8	28.4
Aged 75 or older	100.0	57.5	24.8	17.7
Total men	**100.0**	**35.4**	**29.2**	**35.4**
Aged 18 to 44	100.0	30.9	29.5	39.6
Aged 45 to 54	100.0	36.4	30.5	33.2
Aged 55 to 64	100.0	39.5	29.7	30.8
Aged 65 to 74	100.0	43.0	24.9	32.1
Aged 75 or older	100.0	48.1	28.9	23.0
Total women	**100.0**	**39.5**	**29.9**	**30.6**
Aged 18 to 44	100.0	34.9	31.1	34.0
Aged 45 to 54	100.0	36.5	31.1	32.4
Aged 55 to 64	100.0	41.9	30.4	27.6
Aged 65 to 74	100.0	48.0	26.6	25.4
Aged 75 or older	100.0	63.7	22.0	14.3

Note: "Physically inactive" are those with no sessions of light/moderate or vigorous leisure-time physical activity of at least 10 minutes duration during past week. "At least some physical activity" includes those who performed at least one light/moderate or vigorous leisure-time physical activity of at least 10 minutes duration during past week, but did not meet the definition for regular leisure-time activity. "Regular physical activity" includes those with three or more sessions per week of vigorous activity lasting at least 20 minutes or five or more sessions per week of light/moderate activity lasting at least 30 minutes.
Source: National Center for Health Statistics, Health, United States, 2005, Internet site http://www.cdc.gov/nchs/hus.htm

The Majority of 11th and 12th Graders Have Had Sex

Many teens have had multiple sexual partners.

The 53 percent majority of 11th graders have had sexual intercourse at some point in their lives, and the share tops 60 percent among high school seniors. The majority of sexually active teens used a condom during or the pill before their last sexual intercourse.

Most teens agree that sexual relations between unmarried 18-year-olds who like each other is OK. But, despite the sexual involvement of many of their peers, 63 to 68 percent of teens disagree that it is OK for unmarried 16-year-olds to have sex. The majority of both boys and girls think cohabitation is acceptable. Interestingly, however, most boys and half of girls do not think divorce is the best solution for couples with marriage problems.

Most teens aged 15 to 17 have not had sexual intercourse with an opposite-sex partner in the past year, but the majority of 18- and 19-year-olds have had sex with an opposite-sex partner in the past year. Among 18-to-19-year-olds who had sex in the past year, a large proportion have had more than one opposite-sex partner—47 percent of men and 43 percent of women.

■ With teenagers sexually active, preventing pregnancy and sexually transmitted diseases is of prime concern to parents and schools.

Girls and boys are almost equally sexually active

(percent of 9th to 12th graders who have had sexual intercourse, by sex, 2003)

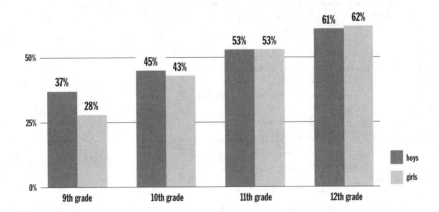

boys
girls

Table 2.10 Sexual Behavior of 9th to 12th Graders by Sex, 2003

(percent of 9th to 12th graders engaging in selected sexual activities, by sex and grade, 2003)

	total	9th grade	10th grade	11th grade	12th grade
Boys					
Ever had sexual intercourse	48.0%	37.3%	45.1%	53.4%	60.7%
First sexual intercourse before age 13	10.4	13.2	11.2	7.5	8.8
Four or more sex partners during lifetime	17.5	14.2	16.4	18.6	22.2
Currently sexually active*	33.8	24.0	30.0	39.2	46.5
Condom use during last sexual intercourse	68.8	71.2	71.8	66.7	67.0
Birth control pill use before last sexual intercourse	13.1	6.6	11.8	14.8	17.5
Girls					
Ever had sexual intercourse	45.3	27.9	43.1	53.1	62.3
First sexual intercourse before age 13	4.2	5.3	5.7	3.2	1.9
Four or more sex partners during lifetime	11.2	6.4	8.8	13.4	17.9
Currently sexually active*	34.6	18.3	31.2	42.9	51.0
Condom use during last sexual intercourse	57.4	66.1	66.4	55.5	48.5
Birth control pill use before last sexual intercourse	20.6	11.6	13.5	24.1	27.2

* Sexual intercourse during the three months preceding the survey.
Source: Centers for Disease Control and Prevention, "Youth Risk Behavior Surveillance—United States, 2003," Mortality and Morbidity Weekly Report, Vol. 53/SS-2, May 21, 2004, Internet site http://www.cdc.gov/mmwr/indss_2004.html

Table 2.11 Attitudes of People Aged 15 to 19 toward Sexual Activity, Childbearing, and Cohabitation, 2002

(percent of people aged 15 to 19 agreeing with statement, by sex, 2002)

	boys	girls
Any sexual act between two consenting adults is all right	73.7%	73.0%
It is all right for unmarried 18-year-olds to have sexual relations if they have strong affection for one another	65.0	60.9
It is all right for unmarried 16-year-olds to have sexual relations if they have strong affection for one another	35.7	30.5
It is OK for an unmarried female to have a child	49.9	64.8
It is better for a person to get married than to go through life being single	69.1	54.5
A young couple should not live together unless they are married	32.3	36.1
Divorce is usually the best solution when a couple can't seem to work out their marriage problems	41.7	48.0

Source: National Center for Health Statistics, Teenagers in the United States: Sexual Activity, Contraceptive Use, and Childbearing, 2002; Vital and Health Statistics Series 23, No. 24, 2004, Internet site http://www.cdc.gov/nchs/nsfg.htm

Table 2.12 Lifetime Sexual Activity of 15-to-44-Year-Olds by Sex, 2002

(number of people aged 15 to 44 and percent distribution by sexual experience with opposite-sex partners during lifetime, by sex and age, 2002; numbers in thousands)

	total		number of opposite-sex partners in lifetime						
	number	percent	none	1	2	3 to 6	7 to 14	15 or more	median
Men aged 15 to 44	**61,147**	**100.0%**	**9.6%**	**12.5%**	**8.0%**	**27.2%**	**19.5%**	**23.2%**	**5.6**
Aged 15 to 19	10,208	100.0	43.5	23.4	9.0	17.0	4.9	2.3	1.6
Aged 20 to 24	9,883	100.0	9.9	15.7	11.6	33.1	13.9	15.8	3.8
Aged 25 to 29	9,226	100.0	5.0	10.0	8.7	29.3	23.1	23.8	5.9
Aged 30 to 34	10,138	100.0	3.0	10.7	6.9	28.4	21.9	29.1	6.4
Aged 35 to 39	10,557	100.0	2.1	8.9	7.0	27.9	25.4	28.7	6.9
Aged 40 to 44	11,135	100.0	1.9	8.8	5.4	25.6	24.2	34.2	8.2
Women aged 15 to 44	**61,561**	**100.0**	**8.6**	**22.5**	**10.8**	**32.6**	**16.3**	**9.2**	**3.3**
Aged 15 to 19	9,834	100.0	37.8	27.2	9.0	19.1	5.0	1.9	1.4
Aged 20 to 24	9,840	100.0	8.9	24.6	13.0	32.2	14.4	6.9	2.8
Aged 25 to 29	9,249	100.0	2.5	22.5	11.7	31.3	20.1	11.9	3.5
Aged 30 to 34	10,272	100.0	1.9	20.5	9.4	38.8	18.0	11.3	3.8
Aged 35 to 39	10,853	100.0	1.1	20.2	11.2	35.8	20.5	11.2	3.9
Aged 40 to 44	11,512	100.0	1.4	20.4	10.5	37.4	19.1	11.2	3.8

Source: National Center for Health Statistics, Sexual Behavior and Selected Health Measures: Men and Women 15–44 Years of Age, United States, 2002, Advance Data, No. 362, 2005, Internet site http://www.cdc.gov/nchs/nsfg.htm

Table 2.13 Past Year Sexual Activity of 15-to-44-Year-Olds by Sex, 2002

(percent distribution of people aged 15 to 44 by sexual experience with opposite-sex partners during the past 12 months, and percent distribution by number of opposite-sex partners in past 12 months, by sex and age, 2002; numbers in thousands)

	total	no opposite-sex partners in past year	one or more opposite-sex partners in past year
Sexual activity in past year			
Total men	**100.0%**	**16.4%**	**83.6%**
Aged 15 to 19	100.0	46.2	53.8
Aged 15 to 17	100.0	58.3	41.6
Aged 18 to 19	100.0	30.5	69.5
Aged 20 to 24	100.0	15.6	84.4
Aged 25 to 29	100.0	11.4	88.6
Aged 30 to 34	100.0	7.4	92.7
Aged 35 to 39	100.0	9.3	90.8
Aged 40 to 44	100.0	9.0	91.1
Total women	**100.0**	**15.3**	**84.7**
Aged 15 to 19	100.0	44.8	55.3
Aged 15 to 17	100.0	58.6	41.4
Aged 18 to 19	100.0	24.8	75.3
Aged 20 to 24	100.0	13.4	86.7
Aged 25 to 29	100.0	6.9	93.0
Aged 30 to 34	100.0	7.9	92.1
Aged 35 to 39	100.0	9.2	90.8
Aged 40 to 44	100.0	10.5	89.5

	total with one or more	one	two	three or more	not reported
Number of sex partners in past year					
Total men	**100.0%**	**75.0%**	**9.6%**	**12.4%**	**3.0%**
Aged 15 to 19	100.0	56.3	21.9	19.9	1.9
Aged 15 to 17	100.0	61.3	20.2	16.8	1.7
Aged 18 to 19	100.0	52.5	23.3	22.2	2.0
Aged 20 to 24	100.0	58.4	15.0	22.9	3.7
Aged 25 to 29	100.0	75.7	7.4	14.1	2.7
Aged 30 to 34	100.0	80.7	7.3	9.4	2.6
Aged 35 to 39	100.0	84.6	5.5	7.5	2.4
Aged 40 to 44	100.0	83.9	6.0	5.8	4.3
Total women	**100.0**	**80.5**	**9.0**	**8.0**	**2.5**
Aged 15 to 19	100.0	58.2	17.5	20.4	3.8
Aged 15 to 17	100.0	59.7	16.9	18.1	5.3
Aged 18 to 19	100.0	57.0	18.1	22.3	2.7
Aged 20 to 24	100.0	70.2	14.5	13.3	2.0
Aged 25 to 29	100.0	81.6	10.1	6.1	2.2
Aged 30 to 34	100.0	86.5	6.1	5.4	2.0
Aged 35 to 39	100.0	86.2	6.7	4.8	2.2
Aged 40 to 44	100.0	88.7	3.8	4.1	3.4

Source: National Center for Health Statistics, Sexual Behavior and Selected Health Measures: Men and Women 15–44 Years of Age, United States, 2002, Advance Data, No. 362, 2005, Internet site http://www.cdc.gov/nchs/nsfg.htm

Table 2.14 Lifetime Same-Sex Sexual Activity of 15-to-44-Year-Olds by Sex, 2002

(percent of people aged 15 to 44 reporting any sexual activity with same-sex partners in their lifetime, by sex, 2002)

	men	women
Total aged 15 to 44	**6.0%**	**11.2%**
Aged 15 to 19	4.5	10.6
Aged 15 to 17	3.9	8.4
Aged 15	2.2	7.2
Aged 16	3.1	13.1
Aged 17	6.6	5.1
Aged 18 to 19	5.1	13.8
Aged 18	4.3	13.7
Aged 19	6.0	13.9
Aged 20 to 24	5.5	14.2
Aged 20 to 21	2.7	13.0
Aged 22 to 24	7.4	15.0
Aged 25 to 44	6.5	10.7
Aged 25 to 29	5.7	14.1
Aged 30 to 44	6.7	9.7

Note: The question about same-sex sexual contact was worded differently for men and women. Women were asked whether they had ever had a sexual experience of any kind with another female. Men were asked whether they had performed any of four specific sexual acts with another male. The question asked of women may have elicited more "yes" answers than the questions asked of men.
Source: National Center for Health Statistics, Sexual Behavior and Selected Health Measures: Men and Women 15–44 Years of Age, United States, 2002, Advance Data, No. 362, 2005, Internet site http://www.cdc.gov/nchs/nsfg.htm; calculations by New Strategist

Birth Rate Has Dropped among Teens and Young Adults

Most 20-to-24-year-old women have not yet had children.

The birth rate for women under age 25 has been falling for decades as a growing number of girls have gone to college and embarked on careers. The birth rate among 15-to-19-year-olds fell 31 percent between 1990 and 2004, while the rate for women aged 20 to 24 fell 13 percent. Just 7 percent of 15-to-19-year-old girls have had children. Among women aged 20 to 24, only 31 percent are mothers. The average woman aged 20 to 24 has had 0.52 children and expects to have an additional 1.92 children, for a total of 2.44 children in her lifetime.

Six percent of women aged 15 to 44 gave birth in the past year, and 2 percent had their first child. Among women aged 15 to 19, only 4 percent gave birth in the past year. The figure rises to 9 percent among 20-to-24-year-olds and peaks at 10 percent among 25-to-29-year-olds.

■ Women in their twenties are experiencing one of the most important transitions in life—becoming a parent for the first time.

Most 25-to-29-year-old women have had children

(percent of women who have had children, by age, 2004)

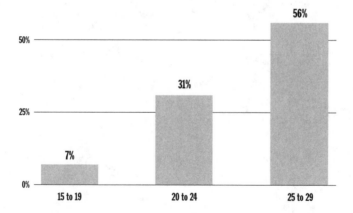

Table 2.15 Birth Rate by Age, 1990 to 2004

(number of live births per 1,000 women in age group, 1990 to 2004; percent change in rate, 1990–2004)

	15 to 19	20 to 24	25 to 29	30 to 34	35 to 39	40 to 44	45 to 49
2004	41.2	101.8	115.5	95.5	45.4	9.0	0.6
2003	41.6	102.6	115.6	95.1	43.8	8.7	0.5
2002	43.0	103.6	113.6	91.5	41.4	8.3	0.5
2001	45.3	106.2	113.4	91.9	40.6	8.1	0.5
2000	47.7	109.7	113.5	91.2	39.7	8.0	0.5
1999	48.8	107.9	111.2	87.1	37.8	7.4	0.4
1998	50.3	108.4	110.2	85.2	36.9	7.4	0.4
1997	51.3	107.3	108.3	83.0	35.7	7.1	0.4
1996	53.5	107.8	108.6	82.1	34.9	6.8	0.3
1995	56.0	107.5	108.8	81.1	34.0	6.6	0.3
1994	58.2	109.2	111.0	80.4	33.4	6.4	0.3
1993	59.0	111.3	113.2	79.9	32.7	6.1	0.3
1992	60.3	113.7	115.7	79.6	32.3	5.9	0.3
1991	61.8	115.3	117.2	79.2	31.9	5.5	0.2
1990	59.9	116.5	120.2	80.8	31.7	5.5	0.2

Percent change

1990 to 2004	–31.2%	–12.6%	–3.9%	18.2%	43.2%	63.6%	200.0%

Source: National Center for Health Statistics, Revised Birth and Fertility Rates for the 1990s and New Rates for the Hispanic Populations 2000 and 2001: United States, National Vital Statistics Report, Vol. 51, No. 12, 2003; and Births: Final Data for 2003, National Vital Statistics Report Vol. 54, No. 2, 2005, Internet site http://www.cdc.gov/nchs/births.htm; and Births: Preliminary Data for 2004, National Vital Statistics Report, Vol. 54, No. 8, 2005, Internet site http://www.cdc.gov/nchs/products/pubs/pubd/nvsr/54/54-pre.htm; calculations by New Strategist

Table 2.16 Number of Children Born to Women Aged 15 to 44, 2004

(total number of women aged 15 to 44, and percent distribution by number of children ever borne, by age, 2004; numbers in thousands)

	total		number of children							
	number	percent	none	one or more	one	two	three	four	five or six	seven+
Aged 15 to 44	**61,588**	**100.0%**	**44.6%**	**55.3%**	**17.2%**	**21.9%**	**10.8%**	**3.6%**	**1.5%**	**0.3%**
Aged 15 to 19	9,964	100.0	93.3	6.6	4.6	1.4	0.6	0.0	0.0	0.0
Aged 20 to 24	10,068	100.0	68.9	31.1	18.3	9.2	2.6	0.8	0.1	0.1
Aged 25 to 29	9,498	100.0	44.2	55.9	23.5	20.7	8.1	2.5	0.9	0.2
Aged 30 to 34	10,082	100.0	27.6	72.4	20.9	28.9	15.8	4.5	2.1	0.2
Aged 35 to 39	10,442	100.0	19.6	80.5	18.8	34.3	18.3	5.8	2.6	0.7
Aged 40 to 44	11,535	100.0	19.3	80.8	17.4	34.5	18.1	7.4	2.9	0.5

Source: Bureau of the Census, Fertility of American Women, Current Population Survey—June 2004, Detailed Tables, Internet site http://www.census.gov/population/www/socdemo/fertility/cps2004.html

Table 2.17 Average Number of Children Borne and Expected, 2002

(average number of children ever borne among women aged 15 to 44, average number of additional births expected, and average number of total births expected, by age, 2002)

	average number of children ever borne	average number of additional births expected	average number of total births expected
Total women aged 15 to 44	**1.28**	**0.99**	**2.27**
Aged 15 to 19	0.09	2.07	2.15
Aged 20 to 24	0.52	1.92	2.44
Aged 25 to 29	1.21	1.15	2.36
Aged 30 to 34	1.58	0.69	2.27
Aged 35 to 39	1.93	0.28	2.21
Aged 40 to 44	2.11	0.08	2.19

Source: National Center for Health Statistics, Fertility, Family Planning, and Reproductive Health of U.S. Women: Data from the 2002 National Survey of Family Growth, Vital and Health Statistics, Series 23, No. 25, December 2005, Internet site http://www.cdc.gov/nchs/nsfg.htm

Table 2.18 Women Giving Birth in the Past Year, 2004

(total number of women aged 15 to 44, number and percent who gave birth in the past year, and number and percent who had a first birth in past year, by age, 2004; numbers in thousands)

	total	gave birth in past year		first birth in past year	
		number	percent	number	percent
Total aged 15 to 44	**61,588**	**3,746**	**6.1%**	**1,474**	**2.4%**
Age					
Aged 15 to 19	9,964	385	3.9	221	2.2
Aged 20 to 24	10,068	882	8.8	433	4.3
Aged 25 to 29	9,498	938	9.9	382	4.0
Aged 30 to 34	10,082	946	9.4	286	2.8
Aged 35 to 39	10,442	443	4.2	120	1.1
Aged 40 to 44	11,535	153	1.3	33	0.3
Race and Hispanic origin					
Asian	3,262	243	7.4	121	3.7
Black	9,065	537	5.9	199	2.2
Hispanic	9,618	817	8.5	269	2.8
Non-Hispanic white	39,120	2,114	5.4	875	2.2
Nativity status					
Native born	52,107	2,953	5.7	1,181	2.3
Foreign born	9,481	794	8.4	293	3.1
Region					
Northeast	11,412	656	5.7	254	2.2
Midwest	13,703	898	6.6	339	2.5
South	22,182	1,338	6.0	530	2.4
West	14,291	854	6.0	352	2.5

Source: Bureau of the Census, Fertility of American Women, Current Population Survey—June 2004, Detailed Tables, Internet site http://www.census.gov/population/www/socdemo/fertility/cps2004.html

The Millennial Generation Accounts for More than One-Third of Births

More than 1.4 million babies were born to women under age 25 in 2004.

Although the birth rate for women under age 25 has been falling, the under-25 age group still accounts for a substantial share of births. (Millennials were aged 10 to 27 in 2004.) Among the 4 million babies born in 2004, 35 percent were born to women under age 25. The great majority of babies born to women under age 20 are first births, but among babies born to women aged 20 to 24 only 47 percent are a first child.

Non-Hispanic whites accounted for fewer than half the babies born to women under age 25 in 2004. Twenty-eight percent of newborns were Hispanic, and 20 percent were black. The younger the mother, the smaller is the non-Hispanic white share. Only 22 percent of babies born to girls under age 15 are non-Hispanic white.

A substantial 35 percent of babies born in 2003 had single mothers. The proportion is a much higher 61 percent among babies born to women under age 25, with the figure ranging from fully 97 percent of those born to girls under age 15 to 53 percent of those born to women aged 20 to 24.

■ In another few years, the majority of the nation's newborns will have mothers belonging to the Millennial generation.

Non-Hispanic whites account for fewer than half the births to women under age 25

(percent distribution of births to women under age 25 by race and Hispanic origin of mother, 2004)

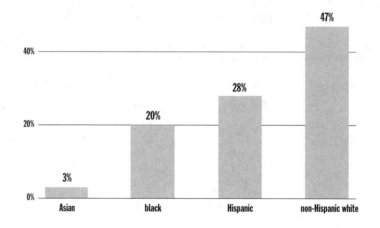

Table 2.19 Births by Age and Birth Order, 2004

(number and percent distribution of births by age and birth order, 2004)

	total	first child	second child	third child	fourth or later child
Total births	**4,115,590**	**1,632,543**	**1,320,853**	**694,584**	**449,049**
Under age 15	6,789	6,642	110	5	0
Aged 15 to 19	415,408	330,238	70,540	11,011	1,508
Aged 20 to 24	1,034,834	483,968	350,739	142,016	53,679
Aged 25 to 29	1,105,297	396,349	370,771	208,216	125,228
Aged 30 to 34	967,008	280,348	342,181	200,365	139,856
Aged 35 to 39	476,123	110,614	155,797	110,077	97,329
Aged 40 or older	110,131	24,385	30,715	22,893	31,449
PERCENT DISTRIBUTION BY BIRTH ORDER					
Total births	**100.0%**	**39.7%**	**32.1%**	**16.9%**	**10.9%**
Under age 15	100.0	97.8	1.6	0.1	0.0
Aged 15 to 19	100.0	79.5	17.0	2.7	0.4
Aged 20 to 24	100.0	46.8	33.9	13.7	5.2
Aged 25 to 29	100.0	35.9	33.5	18.8	11.3
Aged 30 to 34	100.0	29.0	35.4	20.7	14.5
Aged 35 to 39	100.0	23.2	32.7	23.1	20.4
Aged 40 or older	100.0	22.1	27.9	20.8	28.6
PERCENT DISTRIBUTION BY AGE					
Total births	**100.0%**	**100.0%**	**100.0%**	**100.0%**	**100.0%**
Under age 15	0.2	0.4	0.0	0.0	0.0
Aged 15 to 19	10.1	20.2	5.3	1.6	0.3
Aged 20 to 24	25.1	29.6	26.6	20.4	12.0
Aged 25 to 29	26.9	24.3	28.1	30.0	27.9
Aged 30 to 34	23.5	17.2	25.9	28.8	31.1
Aged 35 to 39	11.6	6.8	11.8	15.8	21.7
Aged 40 or older	2.7	1.5	2.3	3.3	7.0

Note: Numbers will not add to total because "not stated" is not shown.
Source: National Center for Health Statistics, Births: Preliminary Data for 2004, National Vital Statistics Report, Vol. 54, No. 8, 2005, Internet site http://www.cdc.gov/nchs/products/pubs/pubd/nvsr/54/54-pre.htm; calculations by New Strategist

Table 2.20 Births by Age, Race, and Hispanic Origin, 2004

(number and percent distribution of births by age, race, and Hispanic origin of mother, 2004)

	total	American Indian	Asian	non-Hispanic black	Hispanic	non-Hispanic white
Total births	**4,115,590**	**43,931**	**229,532**	**576,105**	**944,993**	**2,304,181**
Under age 15	6,789	139	90	2,708	2,364	1,492
Aged 15 to 19	415,408	7,699	7,691	96,718	132,983	169,528
Aged 20 to 24	1,034,834	15,130	30,778	187,797	279,566	518,597
Aged 25 to 29	1,105,297	10,726	65,052	137,445	253,980	633,588
Aged 30 to 34	967,008	6,506	79,726	92,338	177,330	606,165
Aged 35 to 39	476,123	2,984	37,676	46,805	80,765	305,009
Aged 40 or older	110,131	748	8,339	12,295	18,005	69,801

PERCENT DISTRIBUTION BY AGE

Total births	**100.0%**	**100.0%**	**100.0%**	**100.0%**	**100.0%**	**100.0%**
Under age 15	0.2	0.3	0.0	0.5	0.3	0.1
Aged 15 to 19	10.1	17.5	3.4	16.8	14.1	7.4
Aged 20 to 24	25.1	34.4	13.4	32.6	29.6	22.5
Aged 25 to 29	26.9	24.4	28.3	23.9	26.9	27.5
Aged 30 to 34	23.5	14.8	34.7	16.0	18.8	26.3
Aged 35 to 39	11.6	6.8	16.4	8.1	8.5	13.2
Aged 40 or older	2.7	1.7	3.6	2.1	1.9	3.0

PERCENT DISTRIBUTION BY RACE AND HISPANIC ORIGIN

Total births	**100.0%**	**1.1%**	**5.6%**	**14.0%**	**23.0%**	**56.0%**
Under age 15	100.0	2.0	1.3	39.9	34.8	22.0
Aged 15 to 19	100.0	1.9	1.9	23.3	32.0	40.8
Aged 20 to 24	100.0	1.5	3.0	18.1	27.0	50.1
Aged 25 to 29	100.0	1.0	5.9	12.4	23.0	57.3
Aged 30 to 34	100.0	0.7	8.2	9.5	18.3	62.7
Aged 35 to 39	100.0	0.6	7.9	9.8	17.0	64.1
Aged 40 or older	100.0	0.7	7.6	11.2	16.3	63.4

Note: Numbers will not add to total because Hispanics may be of any race.
Source: National Center for Health Statistics, Preliminary Births for 2004, Internet site http://www.cdc.gov/nchs/products/pubs/pubd/hestats/prelim_births/prelim_births04.htm; calculations by New Strategist

Table 2.21 Births to Unmarried Women by Age, Race, and Hispanic Origin, 2003

(total number of births and number and percent to unmarried women, by age, race, and Hispanic origin of mother, 2003)

	total	American Indian	Asian	black	Hispanic	non-Hispanic white
Total births	**4,089,950**	**43,052**	**221,203**	**599,847**	**912,329**	**2,321,904**
Under age 15	6,661	154	104	2,726	2,356	1,399
Aged 15 to 19	414,580	7,690	7,592	100,951	128,524	172,620
Aged 20 to 24	1,032,305	14,645	30,482	196,268	273,311	522,275
Aged 25 to 29	1,086,366	10,524	64,399	139,947	246,361	627,437
Aged 30 to 34	975,546	6,423	75,692	97,529	169,054	626,315
Aged 35 to 39	467,642	2,906	35,074	49,889	75,801	303,354
Aged 40 or older	106,850	710	7,860	12,537	16,922	68,504
BIRTHS TO UNMARRIED WOMEN						
Total births to unmarried women	**1,415,995**	**26,401**	**33,249**	**409,333**	**410,620**	**546,991**
Under age 15	6,469	152	103	2,715	2,224	1,353
Aged 15 to 19	337,201	6,778	5,544	97,000	97,925	132,482
Aged 20 to 24	549,353	10,002	11,115	160,312	146,729	224,941
Aged 25 to 29	287,205	5,293	7,886	83,421	91,644	101,454
Aged 30 to 34	147,555	2,668	5,238	41,692	46,995	52,167
Aged 35 to 39	69,071	1,193	2,580	19,260	20,158	26,352
Aged 40 or older	19,141	315	783	4,933	4,945	8,242
PERCENT OF BIRTHS TO UNMARRIED WOMEN						
Total births	**34.6%**	**61.3%**	**15.0%**	**68.2%**	**45.0%**	**23.6%**
Under age 15	97.1	98.7	99.0	99.6	94.4	96.7
Aged 15 to 19	81.3	88.1	73.0	96.1	76.2	76.7
Aged 20 to 24	53.2	68.3	36.5	81.7	53.7	43.1
Aged 25 to 29	26.4	50.3	12.2	59.6	37.2	16.2
Aged 30 to 34	15.1	41.5	6.9	42.7	27.8	8.3
Aged 35 to 39	14.8	41.1	7.4	38.6	26.6	8.7
Aged 40 or older	17.9	44.4	10.0	39.3	29.2	12.0

Note: Births by race and Hispanic origin will not add to total because Hispanics may be of any race and "not stated" is not shown.
Source: National Center for Health Statistics, Births: Final Data for 2003, National Vital Statistics Reports, Vol. 54, No. 2, 2005, Internet site http://www.cdc.gov/nchs/products/pubs/pubd/nvsr/54/54-pre.htm; calculations by New Strategist

Table 2.22 Births by Age and Method of Delivery, 2003

(number and percent distribution of births by age and method of delivery, 2003)

		vaginal		Caesarean		
	total births	total	after previous Caesarean	total	primary	repeat
Total births	**4,089,950**	**2,949,853**	**51,602**	**1,119,388**	**684,484**	**434,699**
Under age 20	421,241	339,393	1,171	80,182	70,150	10,030
Aged 20 to 24	1,032,305	795,078	9,003	232,579	154,407	78,157
Aged 25 to 29	1,086,366	795,736	14,123	285,231	172,845	112,353
Aged 30 to 34	975,546	665,025	16,004	305,102	170,728	134,296
Aged 35 to 39	467,642	293,643	9,194	171,142	90,685	80,403
Aged 40 or older	106,850	60,978	2,107	45,152	25,669	19,460
PERCENT DISTRIBUTION BY METHOD OF DELIVERY						
Total births	**100.0%**	**72.1%**	**1.3%**	**27.4%**	**16.7%**	**10.6%**
Under age 20	100.0	80.6	0.3	19.0	16.7	2.4
Aged 20 to 24	100.0	77.0	0.9	22.5	15.0	7.6
Aged 25 to 29	100.0	73.2	1.3	26.3	15.9	10.3
Aged 30 to 34	100.0	68.2	1.6	31.3	17.5	13.8
Aged 35 to 39	100.0	62.8	2.0	36.6	19.4	17.2
Aged 40 or older	100.0	57.1	2.0	42.3	24.0	18.2
PERCENT DISTRIBUTION BY AGE						
Total births	**100.0%**	**100.0%**	**100.0%**	**100.0%**	**100.0%**	**100.0%**
Under age 20	10.3	11.5	2.3	7.2	10.2	2.3
Aged 20 to 24	25.2	27.0	17.4	20.8	22.6	18.0
Aged 25 to 29	26.6	27.0	27.4	25.5	25.3	25.8
Aged 30 to 34	23.9	22.5	31.0	27.3	24.9	30.9
Aged 35 to 39	11.4	10.0	17.8	15.3	13.2	18.5
Aged 40 or older	2.6	2.1	4.1	4.0	3.8	4.5

Note: Numbers will not add to total because "not stated" is not shown.
Source: National Center for Health Statistics, Births: Final Data for 2003, National Vital Statistics Reports, Vol. 54, No. 2, 2005,
Internet site http://www.cdc.gov/nchs/products/pubs/pubd/nvsr/54/54-pre.htm; calculations by New Strategist

Cigarette Smoking Is above Average among Millennials

Forty percent of 20-to-25-year-olds have smoked cigarettes in the past month.

Cigarette smoking has been declining in the population as a whole, but among young adults it remains stubbornly high. Either antismoking campaigns are backfiring, or Hollywood's cigarette-smoking role models are overpowering the warnings about the dangers of cigarettes.

Overall, 25 percent of people aged 12 or older smoked cigarettes in the past month, according to a 2004 survey. The proportion surpasses the national average among 17-year-olds and peaks at 43 percent among 22-year-olds.

Cigarette smoking remains popular among teens and young adults although their peers are increasingly likely to disapprove of smoking. Surveys of 8th, 10th, and 12th graders show 80 to 85 percent disapproving of cigarettes in 2005, up from 70 to 82 in 2000. The percentage believing cigarette smoking presents a "great" physical risk has also risen, ranging from 62 percent among 8th graders to 77 percent among 12th graders.

■ Although most teens disapprove of cigarette smoking, most try cigarettes and many take up the haabit.

Many teens and young adults smoke cigarettes

(percent of people who have smoked cigarettes in the past month, by age, 2004)

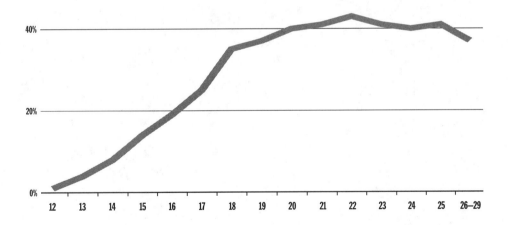

Table 2.23 Cigarette Smoking among People Aged 12 to 29, 2004

(percent of people aged 12 or older and aged 12 to 29 reporting any, past year, and past month use of cigarettes, 2004)

	ever smoked	smoked in past year	smoked in past month
Total people	**67.3%**	**29.1%**	**24.9%**
Aged 12	7.0	3.3	1.1
Aged 13	14.9	8.2	4.3
Aged 14	25.1	15.0	8.4
Aged 15	34.2	21.3	13.5
Aged 16	43.5	29.0	19.1
Aged 17	51.1	34.2	25.4
Aged 18	59.2	43.1	34.8
Aged 19	64.9	47.1	37.2
Aged 20	67.8	49.0	40.3
Aged 21	71.4	49.5	41.2
Aged 22	72.7	50.2	42.9
Aged 23	69.6	47.7	40.6
Aged 24	72.7	47.0	39.7
Aged 25	73.0	46.7	40.5
Aged 26 to 29	72.0	42.9	36.8

Source: SAMHSA, Office of Applied Studies, National Survey on Drug Use and Health, 2004, Internet site http://oas.samhsa .gov/nsduh/2k4nsduh/2k4Results/apph.htm

Table 2.24 Cigarette Use by 9th to 12th Graders, 2003

(percent of 9th to 12th graders who have ever tried cigarette smoking or who have smoked cigarettes in the past 30 days, by sex, 2003)

	lifetime cigarette use	past month cigarette use
Total in 9th–12th grade	**58.4%**	**21.9%**
9th grade	52.0	17.4
10th grade	58.3	21.8
11th grade	60.0	23.6
12th grade	65.4	26.2
Boys	**58.7**	**21.8**
9th grade	53.0	16.0
10th grade	59.0	21.7
11th grade	60.1	23.2
12th grade	64.7	29.0
Girls	**58.1**	**21.9**
9th grade	50.9	18.9
10th grade	57.7	21.9
11th grade	59.8	24.0
12th grade	65.9	23.3

Source: Centers for Disease Control and Prevention, "Youth Risk Behavior Surveillance—United States, 2003," Mortality and Morbidity Weekly Report, Vol. 53/SS-2, May 21, 2004, Internet site http://www.cdc.gov/mmwr/indss_2004.html

Table 2.25 Attitudes toward Cigarette Smoking by 8th, 10th, and 12th Graders, 2000 and 2005

(percent of 8th, 10th, and 12th graders who think smoking one or more packs of cigarettes per day presents a "great" physical risk and percent "disapproving," 2000 and 2005; percentage point change, 2000–05)

	2005	2000	percentage point change
Great risk			
8th graders	61.5%	58.8%	2.7
10th graders	68.1	65.9	2.2
12th graders	76.5	73.1	3.4
Disapprove			
8th graders	85.3	81.9	3.4
10th graders	84.3	76.7	7.6
12th graders	79.8	70.1	9.7

Source: Institute for Social Research, University of Michigan, Monitoring the Future Survey, 2005, Internet site http:// monitoringthefuture.org/data/05data.html#2005data-drugs; calculations by New Strategist

Most Teens Do Not Wait for Legal Drinking Age

The majority of 19- and 20-year-olds have had an alcoholic beverage in the past month.

More than half of Americans aged 12 or older have had an alcoholic beverage in the past month. The figure climbs above 50 percent among 19-year-olds, although the legal drinking age is 21.

Many teens and young adults take part in binge drinking, meaning they have had five or more drinks on one occasion in the past month. Among people aged 18 to 20, more than one in ten participated in heavy drinking during the past month—meaning they binged at least five times during the past month.

Only 24 percent of the nation's high school seniors think having one or two alcoholic drinks nearly every day presents a "great" physical risk. But 71 percent disapprove of doing so. The percentages of teenagers who think drinking every day is risky and who disapprove of it rose slightly between 2000 and 2005.

■ Heavy drinking is a bigger problem among young adults than drug use.

Many teens drink alcohol

(percent of people aged 16 to 20 who have consumed alcoholic beverages in the past month, by age, 2004)

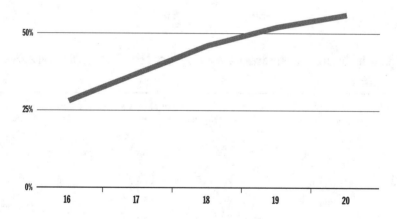

Table 2.26 Alcohol Use by People Aged 12 to 29, 2004

(percent of people aged 12 or older and aged 12 to 29 who drank alcoholic beverages during the past month, by level of alcohol use, 2004)

	drank at any time during past month	binge drinking during past month	heavy drinking during past month
Total people	**50.3%**	**22.8%**	**6.9%**
Aged 12	2.3	1.1	0.1
Aged 13	6.1	2.9	0.4
Aged 14	12.3	5.6	1.0
Aged 15	20.4	12.7	2.2
Aged 16	27.7	18.3	4.5
Aged 17	37.3	26.6	8.1
Aged 18	46.3	33.1	11.0
Aged 19	51.5	37.4	13.9
Aged 20	56.3	40.3	16.3
Aged 21	69.8	48.2	19.2
Aged 22	69.1	46.8	17.8
Aged 23	63.8	43.1	14.3
Aged 24	63.7	40.3	13.7
Aged 25	65.7	41.5	14.8
Aged 26 to 29	63.2	36.8	10.7

Note: Binge drinking is defined as having had five or more drinks on the same occasion on at least one day in the 30 days prior to the survey. Heavy drinking is having had five or more drinks on the same occasion on each of five or more days in 30 days prior to the survey.
Source: SAMHSA, Office of Applied Studies, National Survey on Drug Use and Health, 2004, Internet site http://oas.samhsa .gov/nsduh/2k4nsduh/2k4Results/apph.htm

Table 2.27 Alcohol Use by 9th to 12th Graders, 2003

(percent of 9th to 12th graders who have ever drunk alcohol or who have drunk alcohol in the past 30 days, by sex, 2003)

	lifetime alcohol use	past month alcohol use
Total in 9th–12th grade	**74.9%**	**44.9%**
9th grade	65.0	36.2
10th grade	75.7	43.5
11th grade	78.6	47.0
12th grade	83.0	55.9
Boys	**73.7**	**43.8**
9th grade	64.0	33.9
10th grade	74.9	42.2
11th grade	76.4	47.3
12th grade	82.6	56.0
Girls	**76.1**	**45.8**
9th grade	66.2	38.5
10th grade	76.5	44.9
11th grade	80.9	46.8
12th grade	83.3	55.5

Source: Centers for Disease Control and Prevention, "Youth Risk Behavior Surveillance—United States, 2003," Mortality and Morbidity Weekly Report, Vol. 53/SS-2, May 21, 2004, Internet site http://www.cdc.gov/mmwr/indss_2004.html

Table 2.28 Attitudes toward Drinking Alcohol by 8th, 10th, and 12th Graders, 2000 and 2005

(percent of 8th, 10th, and 12th graders who think having one or two alcoholic drinks nearly every day presents a "great" physical risk and percent "disapproving," 2000 and 2005; percentage point change, 2000–05)

	2005	2000	percentage point change
Great risk			
8th graders	31.4%	30.4%	1.0
10th graders	32.6	32.3	0.3
12th graders	23.7	21.7	2.0
Disapprove			
8th graders	78.7	77.8	0.9
10th graders	76.9	73.8	3.1
12th graders	70.8	70.0	0.8

Source: Institute for Social Research, University of Michigan, Monitoring the Future Survey, 2005, Internet site http://monitoringthefuture.org/data/05data.html#2005data-drugs; calculations by New Strategist

Drug Use Is Prevalent among Teens and Young Adults

More than one in five 18-to-22-year-olds has used an illicit drug in the past month.

Among Americans aged 12 or older, only 8 percent used an illicit drug in the past month. Young adults are much more likely to be current drug users than the average person. The percentage of 15-to-24-year-olds who have used an illicit drug in the past month ranges from 13 to 23 percent.

A 2005 survey of teenagers shows significant but declining drug use. Nine percent of 8th graders used an illicit drug in the past month, down from 12 percent in 2000. The figure rises to 17 percent in 10th grade (down from 23 percent) and to 23 percent in 12th grade (down from 25 percent). The most commonly used drug is marijuana. Forty-five percent of 12th graders have used marijuana at some time in their lives, as have 34 percent of 10th graders and 17 percent of 8th graders.

The recent decline in teen drug use may be due to changing attitudes. A growing share of 12th graders believe smoking marijuana presents a "great" physical risk and most disapprove of regular marijuana use.

■ Protective Boomer parents may be convincing their teens to say no to drugs they once eagerly embraced.

Many teens and young adults use illicit drugs

(percent of people who used illicit drugs in the past month, by age, 2004)

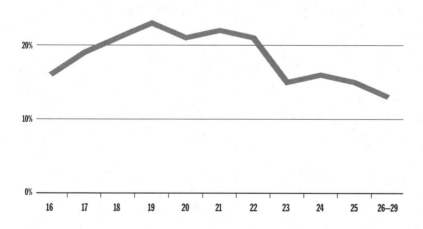

Table 2.29 Illicit Drug Use among People Aged 12 to 29, 2004

(percent of people aged 12 or older and aged 12 to 29 who ever used any illicit drug, who used an illicit drug in the past year, and who used an illicit drug in the past month, by age, 2004)

	ever used illicit drug	used illicit drug in past year	used illicit drug in past month
Total people	**45.8%**	**14.5%**	**7.9%**
Aged 12	11.2	6.7	2.8
Aged 13	18.4	11.6	4.6
Aged 14	25.2	17.8	9.0
Aged 15	34.7	24.6	12.7
Aged 16	42.5	31.0	15.5
Aged 17	48.4	34.9	19.1
Aged 18	53.4	38.8	21.2
Aged 19	56.6	38.6	22.8
Aged 20	59.0	38.1	21.3
Aged 21	62.3	36.6	21.7
Aged 22	62.9	35.1	20.5
Aged 23	59.5	28.3	15.4
Aged 24	59.8	27.6	16.2
Aged 25	60.5	26.7	15.2
Aged 26 to 29	60.0	23.5	13.2

Note: Illicit drugs include marijuana/hashish, cocaine (including crack), heroin, hallucinogens, inhalants, or any prescription-type psychotherapeutic used nonmedically.
Source: SAMHSA, Office of Applied Studies, National Survey on Drug Use and Health, 2004, Internet site http://oas.samhsa
.gov/nsduh/2k4nsduh/2k4Results/apph.htm

Table 2.30   Marijuana Use by 9th to 12th Graders, 2003

(percent of 9th to 12th graders who have ever used marijuana or who have used marijuana in the past 30 days, by sex, 2003)

	lifetime marijuana use	past month marijuana use
Total in 9th–12th grade	**40.2%**	**22.4%**
9th grade	30.7	18.5
10th grade	40.4	22.0
11th grade	44.5	24.1
12th grade	48.5	25.8
Boys	**42.7**	**25.1**
9th grade	33.1	19.6
10th grade	44.2	25.7
11th grade	45.4	27.3
12th grade	51.7	30.0
Girls	**37.6**	**19.3**
9th grade	28.1	17.2
10th grade	36.4	18.2
11th grade	43.5	20.9
12th grade	44.9	21.3

Source: Centers for Disease Control and Prevention, "Youth Risk Behavior Surveillance—United States, 2003," Mortality and Morbidity Weekly Report, Vol. 53/SS-2, May 21, 2004, Internet site http://www.cdc.gov/mmwr/indss_2004.html

Table 2.31 Lifetime Drug Use by 8th, 10th, and 12th Graders, 2000 and 2005

(percent of 8th, 10th, and 12th graders who have ever used illicit drugs by type of drug, 2000 and 2005; percentage point change, 2000–05)

	2005	2000	percentage point change
8th graders			
Any illicit drug	**21.4%**	**26.8%**	**−5.4**
Marijuana	16.5	20.3	−3.8
Inhalants	17.1	17.9	−0.8
Hallucinogens	3.8	4.6	−0.8
Cocaine	3.7	4.5	−0.8
Amphetamines	7.4	9.9	−2.5
Tranquilizers	4.1	4.4	−0.3
Steroids	1.7	3.0	−1.3
10th graders			
Any illicit drug	**38.2**	**45.6**	**−7.4**
Marijuana	34.1	40.3	−6.2
Inhalants	13.1	16.6	−3.5
Hallucinogens	5.8	8.9	−3.1
Cocaine	5.2	6.9	−1.7
Amphetamines	11.1	15.7	−4.6
Tranquilizers	7.1	8.0	−0.9
Steroids	2.0	3.5	−1.5
12th graders			
Any illicit drug	**50.4**	**54.0**	**−3.6**
Marijuana	44.8	48.8	−4.0
Inhalants	11.4	14.2	−2.8
Hallucinogens	8.8	13.0	−4.2
Cocaine	8.0	8.6	−0.6
Amphetamines	13.1	15.6	−2.5
Tranquilizers	9.9	8.9	1.0
Steroids	2.6	2.5	0.1

Source: Institute for Social Research, University of Michigan, Monitoring the Future Survey, 2005, Internet site http:// monitoringthefuture.org/data/05data.html#2005data-drugs; calculations by New Strategist

Table 2.32 Past Month Drug Use by 8th, 10th, and 12th Graders, 2000 and 2005

(percent of 8th, 10th, and 12th graders who have used illicit drugs in the past 30 days, by type of drug, 2000 and 2005; percentage point change, 2000–05)

	2005	2000	percentage point change
8th graders			
Any illicit drug	**8.5%**	**11.9%**	**–3.4**
Marijuana	6.6	9.1	–2.5
Inhalants	4.2	4.5	–0.3
Hallucinogens	1.1	1.2	–0.1
Cocaine	1.0	1.2	–0.2
Amphetamines	2.3	3.4	–1.1
Tranquilizers	1.3	1.4	–0.1
Steroids	0.5	0.8	–0.3
10th graders			
Any illicit drug	**17.3**	**22.5**	**–5.2**
Marijuana	15.2	19.7	–4.5
Inhalants	2.2	2.6	–0.4
Hallucinogens	1.5	2.3	–0.8
Cocaine	1.5	1.8	–0.3
Amphetamines	3.7	5.4	–1.7
Tranquilizers	2.3	2.5	–0.2
Steroids	0.6	1.0	–0.4
12th graders			
Any illicit drug	**23.1**	**24.9**	**–1.8**
Marijuana	19.8	21.6	–1.8
Inhalants	2.0	2.2	–0.2
Hallucinogens	1.9	2.6	–0.7
Cocaine	2.3	2.1	0.2
Amphetamines	3.9	5.0	–1.1
Tranquilizers	2.9	2.6	0.3
Steroids	0.9	0.8	0.1

Source: Institute for Social Research, University of Michigan, Monitoring the Future Survey, 2005, Internet site http://monitoringthefuture.org/data/05data.html#2005data-drugs; calculations by New Strategist

Table 2.33 Attitudes toward Drug Use among 12th Graders, 2000 and 2005

(percentage of high school seniors who think the use of illicit drugs is a "great" physical risk and percent "disapproving" of drug use by people aged 18 or older, by type of use, 2000 and 2005; percentage point change, 2000–05)

	2005	2000	percentage point change
Great risk			
Try marijuana once or twice	16.1%	13.7%	2.4
Smoke marijuana occasionally	25.8	23.4	2.4
Smoke marijuana regularly	58.0	58.3	−0.3
Try cocaine once or twice	50.5	51.1	−0.6
Take cocaine occasionally	66.7	69.5	−2.8
Take cocaine regularly	82.8	86.2	−3.4
Try amphetamines once or twice	37.7	32.6	5.1
Take amphetamines regularly	67.1	66.3	0.8
Try one or two drinks of an alcoholic beverage	8.5	6.4	2.1
Take one or two drinks nearly every day	23.7	21.7	2.0
Smoke one or more packs of cigarettes per day	76.5	73.1	3.4
Take steroids	56.8	57.9	-1.1
Disapprove			
Try marijuana once or twice	55.0	52.5	2.5
Smoke marijuana occasionally	67.8	65.8	2.0
Smoke marijuana regularly	82.0	79.7	2.3
Try cocaine once or twice	88.9	88.2	0.7
Take cocaine regularly	96.0	95.5	0.5
Try amphetamines once or twice	86.1	82.1	4.0
Take amphetamines regularly	94.8	94.1	0.7
Try one or two drinks of an alcoholic beverage	26.4	25.2	1.2
Take one or two drinks nearly every day	70.8	70.0	0.8
Smoke one or more packs of cigarettes per day	79.8	70.1	9.7
Take steroids	88.8	88.8	0.0

Source: Institute for Social Research, University of Michigan, Monitoring the Future Survey, 2005, Internet site http:// monitoringthefuture.org/data/05data.html#2005data-drugs; calculations by New Strategist

Children Account for Nearly One in Five Uninsured Americans

More than 8 million children do not have health insurance.

Among all Americans, 46 million lacked health insurance in 2004—or 16 percent of the population. The figure is 11 percent among children under age 18. Among 18-to-24-year-olds, fully 31 percent do not have health insurance—a larger share than in any other age group. Among 25-to-29-year-olds, a substantial 26 percent are uninsured.

Hispanic children are most likely to be without health insurance. The 21 percent of Hispanic children who are not insured account for 36 percent of all uninsured children—almost equal to the 39 percent share accounted for by non-Hispanic white children. One-third of foreign-born children do not have health insurance versus 10 percent of the native-born.

For 60 percent of the population, an employer provides health insurance. Among 18-to-24-year-olds, however, only 46 percent have employment-based health insurance and just 18 percent have employment-based health insurance through their own employer.

■ Twenty-three percent of medical expenses incurred by children under age 18 in 2003 were covered by Medicaid, the health insurance program for the poor.

Many young adults are without health insurance

(percent of people without health insurance, by age, 2004)

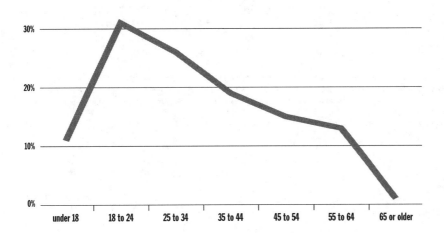

Table 2.34 Health Insurance Coverage of Children, 2004

(number and percent distribution of children under age 18 by age, race, Hispanic origin, and health insurance coverage status, 2004; numbers in thousands)

| | | covered by private or government health insurance | | | | | | | | |
| | | | private insurance | | | government | | | | |
	total	total	total	group health	direct purchase	total	Medicaid	Medicare	military	not covered
NUMBER										
Total children under age 18	**73,821**	**65,553**	**48,462**	**44,892**	**4,166**	**21,922**	**19,847**	**500**	**2,045**	**8,269**
Under age 3	12,164	10,919	7,236	6,794	665	4,504	4,130	103	376	1,245
Aged 3 to 5	11,965	10,776	7,583	7,074	704	4,018	3,704	74	305	1,189
Aged 6 to 11	23,832	21,220	15,861	14,853	1,400	6,987	6,335	183	619	2,613
Aged 12 to 17	25,861	22,638	17,782	16,171	1,397	6,412	5,677	139	745	3,222
Race and Hispanic origin										
Asian	3,712	3,360	2,774	2,517	298	844	695	17	149	352
Black	12,329	10,727	5,941	5,600	411	5,903	5,476	152	414	1,601
Hispanic	14,330	11,312	6,151	5,713	507	6,024	5,747	153	195	3,018
White, non-Hispanic	43,243	39,976	33,446	30,920	2,930	9,102	7,877	172	1,292	3,266
PERCENT DISTRIBUTION										
Total children under age 18	**100.0%**	**88.8%**	**65.6%**	**60.8%**	**5.6%**	**29.7%**	**26.9%**	**0.7%**	**2.8%**	**11.2%**
Under age 3	100.0	89.8	59.5	55.9	5.5	37.0	34.0	0.8	3.1	10.2
Aged 3 to 5	100.0	90.1	63.4	59.1	5.9	33.6	31.0	0.6	2.5	9.9
Aged 6 to 11	100.0	89.0	66.6	62.3	5.9	29.3	26.6	0.8	2.6	11.0
Aged 12 to 17	100.0	87.5	68.8	62.5	5.4	24.8	22.0	0.5	2.9	12.5
Race and Hispanic origin										
Asian	100.0	90.5	74.7	67.8	8.0	22.7	18.7	0.5	4.0	9.5
Black	100.0	87.0	48.2	45.4	3.3	47.9	44.4	1.2	3.4	13.0
Hispanic	100.0	78.9	42.9	39.9	3.5	42.0	40.1	1.1	1.4	21.1
White, non-Hispanic	100.0	92.4	77.3	71.5	6.8	21.0	18.2	0.4	3.0	7.6

Note: Numbers will not add to total because Asians and blacks include those identifying themselves as being of the race alone and those identifying themselves as being of the race in combination with one or more other races, because Hispanics may be of any race, and because not all races are shown. Non-Hispanic whites include only those identifying themselves as being white alone and not Hispanic.
Source: Bureau of the Census, Health Insurance Coverage: 2004, Internet site http://pubdb3.census.gov/macro/032005/health/ toc.htm; calculations by New Strategist

Table 2.35 Children under Age 18 without Health Insurance, 2004

(number and percent distribution of children under age 18 without health insurance by selected characteristics, 2004; numbers in thousands)

	children without health insurance		
	number	percent	percent distribution
Total children under age 18	**8,269**	**11.2%**	**100.0%**
Age			
Under age 3	1,245	10.2	15.1
Aged 3 to 5	1,189	9.9	14.4
Aged 6 to 11	2,613	11.0	31.6
Aged 12 to 17	3,222	12.5	39.0
Race and Hispanic origin			
Asian	352	9.5	4.3
Black	1,601	13.0	19.4
Hispanic	3,018	21.1	36.5
White, non-Hispanic	3,266	7.6	39.5
Region			
Northeast	1,192	9.2	14.4
Midwest	1,311	8.0	15.9
South	3,604	13.5	43.6
West	2,161	12.2	26.1
Family income			
Under $25,000	2,956	18.1	35.7
$25,000 to $49,999	2,532	14.1	30.6
$50,000 to $74,999	1,230	8.5	14.9
$75,000 or more	1,159	4.9	14.0
Family type			
Married couple	4,749	9.3	57.4
Female householder, no spouse present	2,358	13.8	28.5
Male householder, no spouse present	769	19.1	9.3
Nativity			
Native	7,191	10.2	87.0
Foreign born	1,078	33.3	13.0

Note: Numbers will not add to total because Asians and blacks include those identifying themselves as being of the race alone and those identifying themselves as being of the race in combination with one or more other races, because Hispanics may be of any race, and because not all races are shown. Non-Hispanic whites include only those identifying themselves as white alone and not Hispanic.
Source: Bureau of the Census, Health Insurance Coverage: 2004, Internet site http://pubdb3.census.gov/macro/032005/health/ toc.htm; calculations by New Strategist

Table 2.36 Health Insurance Coverage by Age, 2004

(number and percent distribution of people by age and health insurance coverage status, 2004; numbers in thousands)

	total	with health insurance coverage during year			not covered at any time during the year
		total	private	government	
Total people	**291,155**	**245,335**	**198,262**	**79,086**	**45,820**
Under age 18	73,821	65,553	48,462	21,922	8,269
Aged 18 to 24	27,972	19,200	16,229	4,022	8,772
Aged 25 to 34	39,307	29,130	25,765	4,578	10,177
Aged 35 to 44	43,350	35,240	31,883	4,680	8,110
Aged 45 to 54	41,960	35,700	32,414	4,847	6,260
Aged 55 to 64	29,532	25,596	22,174	5,442	3,936
Aged 65 or older	35,213	34,916	21,336	33,595	297
PERCENT DISTRIBUTION BY COVERAGE STATUS					
Total people	**100.0%**	**84.3%**	**68.1%**	**27.2%**	**15.7%**
Under age 18	100.0	88.8	65.6	29.7	11.2
Aged 18 to 24	100.0	68.6	58.0	14.4	31.4
Aged 25 to 34	100.0	74.1	65.5	11.6	25.9
Aged 35 to 44	100.0	81.3	73.5	10.8	18.7
Aged 45 to 54	100.0	85.1	77.2	11.6	14.9
Aged 55 to 64	100.0	86.7	75.1	18.4	13.3
Aged 65 or older	100.0	99.2	60.6	95.4	0.8
PERCENT DISTRIBUTION BY AGE					
Total people	**100.0%**	**100.0%**	**100.0%**	**100.0%**	**100.0%**
Under age 18	25.4	26.7	24.4	27.7	18.0
Aged 18 to 24	9.6	7.8	8.2	5.1	19.1
Aged 25 to 34	13.5	11.9	13.0	5.8	22.2
Aged 35 to 44	14.9	14.4	16.1	5.9	17.7
Aged 45 to 54	14.4	14.6	16.3	6.1	13.7
Aged 55 to 64	10.1	10.4	11.2	6.9	8.6
Aged 65 or older	12.1	14.2	10.8	42.5	0.6

Note: Numbers may not add to total because some people have more than one type of health insurance coverage.
Source: Bureau of the Census, 2005 Current Population Survey, Internet site http://pubdb3.census.gov/macro/032005/health/h01_000.htm; calculations by New Strategist

Table 2.37 Private Health Insurance Coverage by Age, 2004

(number and percent distribution of people by age and private health insurance coverage status, 2004; numbers in thousands)

| | | with private health insurance | | | |
| | | total | employment based | | direct purchase |
	total	total	total	own	
Total people	**291,155**	**198,262**	**174,174**	**91,709**	**26,961**
Under age 18	73,821	48,462	44,892	237	4,166
Aged 18 to 24	27,972	16,229	12,966	5,122	1,495
Aged 25 to 34	39,307	25,765	24,027	18,151	2,266
Aged 35 to 44	43,350	31,883	29,824	21,335	2,773
Aged 45 to 54	41,960	32,414	30,088	22,141	3,215
Aged 55 to 64	29,532	22,174	19,872	14,907	3,066
Aged 65 or older	35,213	21,336	12,505	9,817	9,979
PERCENT DISTRIBUTION BY COVERAGE STATUS					
Total people	**100.0%**	**68.1%**	**59.8%**	**31.5%**	**9.3%**
Under age 18	100.0	65.6	60.8	0.3	5.6
Aged 18 to 24	100.0	58.0	46.4	18.3	5.3
Aged 25 to 34	100.0	65.5	61.1	46.2	5.8
Aged 35 to 44	100.0	73.5	68.8	49.2	6.4
Aged 45 to 54	100.0	77.2	71.7	52.8	7.7
Aged 55 to 64	100.0	75.1	67.3	50.5	10.4
Aged 65 or older	100.0	60.6	35.5	27.9	28.3
PERCENT DISTRIBUTION BY AGE					
Total people	**100.0%**	**100.0%**	**100.0%**	**100.0%**	**100.0%**
Under age 18	25.4	24.4	25.8	0.3	15.5
Aged 18 to 24	9.6	8.2	7.4	5.6	5.5
Aged 25 to 34	13.5	13.0	13.8	19.8	8.4
Aged 35 to 44	14.9	16.1	17.1	23.3	10.3
Aged 45 to 54	14.4	16.3	17.3	24.1	11.9
Aged 55 to 64	10.1	11.2	11.4	16.3	11.4
Aged 65 or older	12.1	10.8	7.2	10.7	37.0

Note: Numbers may not add to total because some people have more than one type of health insurance coverage.
Source: Bureau of the Census, 2005 Current Population Survey, Internet site http://pubdb3.census.gov/macro/032005/health/h01_000.htm; calculations by New Strategist

Table 2.38 Government Health Insurance Coverage by Age, 2004

(number and percent distribution of people by age and government health insurance coverage status, 2004; numbers in thousands)

	total	with government health insurance			
		total	Medicaid	Medicare	military
Total people	**291,155**	**79,086**	**37,514**	**39,745**	**10,680**
Under age 18	73,821	21,922	19,847	500	2,045
Aged 18 to 24	27,972	4,022	3,196	212	804
Aged 25 to 34	39,307	4,578	3,408	482	982
Aged 35 to 44	43,350	4,680	3,135	900	1,129
Aged 45 to 54	41,960	4,847	2,595	1,548	1,425
Aged 55 to 64	29,532	5,442	2,036	2,651	1,785
Aged 65 or older	35,213	33,595	3,297	33,452	2,509

PERCENT DISTRIBUTION BY COVERAGE STATUS

Total people	**100.0%**	**27.2%**	**12.9%**	**13.7%**	**3.7%**
Under age 18	100.0	29.7	26.9	0.7	2.8
Aged 18 to 24	100.0	14.4	11.4	0.8	2.9
Aged 25 to 34	100.0	11.6	8.7	1.2	2.5
Aged 35 to 44	100.0	10.8	7.2	2.1	2.6
Aged 45 to 54	100.0	11.6	6.2	3.7	3.4
Aged 55 to 64	100.0	18.4	6.9	9.0	6.0
Aged 65 or older	100.0	95.4	9.4	95.0	7.1

PERCENT DISTRIBUTION BY AGE

Total people	**100.0%**	**100.0%**	**100.0%**	**100.0%**	**100.0%**
Under age 18	25.4	27.7	52.9	1.3	19.1
Aged 18 to 24	9.6	5.1	8.5	0.5	7.5
Aged 25 to 34	13.5	5.8	9.1	1.2	9.2
Aged 35 to 44	14.9	5.9	8.4	2.3	10.6
Aged 45 to 54	14.4	6.1	6.9	3.9	13.3
Aged 55 to 64	10.1	6.9	5.4	6.7	16.7
Aged 65 or older	12.1	42.5	8.8	84.2	23.5

Note: Numbers may not add to total because some people have more than one type of health insurance coverage.
Source: Bureau of the Census, 2005 Current Population Survey, Internet site http://pubdb3.census.gov/macro/032005/health/ h01_000.htm; calculations by New Strategist

Table 2.39 Spending on Health Care by Age, 2003

(percent of people with health care expense, median expense per person, total expenses, and percent distribution of total expenses by source of payment, by age, 2003)

	total (thousands)	percent with expense	median expense per person	total expenses amount (millions)	total expenses percent distribution
Total people	**290,604**	**85.6%**	**$1,021**	**$895,527**	**100.0%**
Under age 18	72,996	86.4	425	80,187	9.0
Under age 1	3,639	91.4	483	7,314	0.8
Aged 1 to 5	19,490	91.2	363	20,908	2.3
Aged 6 to 11	24,522	85.5	395	20,348	2.3
Aged 12 to 17	25,345	82.8	546	31,617	3.5
Aged 18 to 24	27,156	74.6	561	39,654	4.4
Aged 25 to 29	20,425	76.3	703	37,357	4.2
Aged 30 to 34	19,850	79.7	777	36,581	4.1
Aged 35 to 44	43,710	82.6	928	114,425	12.8
Aged 45 to 64	69,768	89.6	1,892	297,040	33.2
Aged 65 or older	36,699	96.3	3,649	290,283	32.4

PERCENT DISTRIBUTION BY SOURCE OF PAYMENT

	total	out of pocket	private insurance	Medicare	Medicaid	other
Total people	**100.0%**	**19.6%**	**42.4%**	**19.9%**	**9.2%**	**8.9%**
Under age 18	100.0	20.5	50.3	–	22.6	6.3
Under age 1	100.0	4.7	47.8	–	37.3	10.2
Aged 1 to 5	100.0	11.9	56.2	–	23.7	7.7
Aged 6 to 11	100.0	22.6	48.9	–	24.1	4.2
Aged 12 to 17	100.0	28.5	47.9	–	17.5	5.7
Aged 18 to 24	100.0	20.0	52.0	–	20.9	6.9
Aged 25 to 29	100.0	19.2	56.2	–	14.5	9.0
Aged 30 to 34	100.0	20.3	59.5	–	12.0	5.9
Aged 35 to 44	100.0	17.7	50.1	–	10.6	18.6
Aged 45 to 64	100.0	20.8	57.2	–	7.2	8.1
Aged 65 or older	100.0	18.8	16.7	53.0	4.3	7.2

Note: "Other" insurance includes Department of Veterans Affairs (except Tricare), American Indian Health Service, state and local clinics, worker's compensation, homeowner's and automobile insurance, etc. "–" means not applicable or sample is too small to make a reliable estimate.
Source: Agency for Healthcare Research and Quality, Medical Expenditure Panel Survey, 2003, Internet site http://www.meps .ahrq.gov/CompendiumTables/TC_TOC.htm; calculations by New Strategist

Asthma and Allergies Affect Many Children

Boys are more likely than girls to have learning disabilities.

Asthma is a widespread problem among children. Twelve percent of the nation's 73 million children under age 18 have been diagnosed with asthma. Five percent had an asthma attack in the past year. Boys are more likely to have asthma than girls (15 versus 9 percent). The percentage of black children with asthma is nearly triple the Asian figure (17 versus 6 percent).

Nearly 5 million children (8 percent) have been diagnosed with a learning disability, and more than 4 million (7 percent) have attention deficit disorder. Boys are far more likely than girls to suffer from these conditions, accounting for 61 percent of those with learning disabilities and 71 percent of those with attention deficit disorder.

Among younger adults, lower back pain is the most common health problem, reported by 24 percent. The 18-to-44 age group accounts for the majority of Americans with asthma, migraines, and feelings of nervousness and restlessness.

■ The growing number of children with learning disabilities is a problem for the public schools.

Asthma is a big problem for the nation's children

(percent of people under age 18 diagnosed with asthma, by age, 2004)

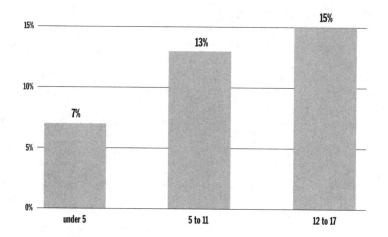

Table 2.40 Health Conditions among Children, 2004

(number of people under age 18 with selected health conditions, by type of condition, sex, age, race, and Hispanic origin, 2004; numbers in thousands)

| | total children | diagnosed with asthma | experienced in last 12 months | | | | ever told had[*] | | prescription medication taken regularly at least 3 months |
			asthma attack	hay fever	respiratory allergies	other allergies	learning disability	attention deficit hyperactivity disorder	
Total children	**73,067**	**8,890**	**3,975**	**6,725**	**8,410**	**9,151**	**4,881**	**4,527**	**9,627**
Sex									
Boys	37,351	5,524	2,497	3,769	4,648	4,434	2,989	3,194	5,757
Girls	35,715	3,366	1,478	2,956	3,762	4,727	1,892	1,333	3,870
Age									
Aged 0 to 4	19,983	1,454	781	904	1,613	2,878	202	151	1,475
Aged 5 to 11	28,110	3,653	1,710	2,742	3,434	3,500	2,063	1,822	3,840
Aged 12 to 17	24,974	3,782	1,484	3,079	3,363	2,773	2,615	2,553	4,313
Race and Hispanic origin									
Asian	2,726	171	61	141	104	299	46	38	162
Black	11,166	1,910	882	879	1,243	1,769	875	762	1,399
Hispanic	13,956	1,423	568	1,002	1,100	1,357	647	462	1,026
Non-Hispanic white	43,405	5,059	2,329	4,464	5,680	5,478	3,115	3,147	6,718

* *"Ever told" by a school representative or health professional. Data exclude children under age 3.*
Note: *Other allergies include food or digestive allergies, eczema, and other skin allergies.*
Source: *National Center for Health Statistics, Summary Health Statistics for U.S. Children: National Health Interview Survey, 2004, Series 10, No. 227, 2005, Internet site http://www.cdc.gov/nchs/nhis.htm*

Table 2.41 Percent of Children with Health Conditions, 2004

(percent of people under age 18 with selected health conditions, by sex, age, race, and Hispanic origin, 2004)

	total children	diagnosed with asthma	asthma attack	hay fever	respiratory allergies	other allergies	learning disability	attention deficit hyperactivity disorder	prescription medication taken regularly at least 3 months
			experienced in last 12 months					ever told had*	
Total children	100.0%	12.2%	5.4%	9.2%	11.6%	12.5%	8.0%	7.4%	13.2%
Sex									
Boys	100.0	14.8	6.7	10.1	12.5	11.9	9.5	10.2	15.5
Girls	100.0	9.4	4.1	8.3	10.6	13.2	6.3	4.4	10.8
Age									
Aged 0 to 4	100.0	7.3	3.9	4.5	8.1	14.4	2.5	1.8	7.4
Aged 5 to 11	100.0	13.0	6.1	9.8	12.3	12.5	7.4	6.5	13.7
Aged 12 to 17	100.0	15.2	5.9	12.4	13.5	11.1	10.5	10.2	17.3
Race and Hispanic origin									
Asian	100.0	6.2	2.2	5.0	3.7	11.5	1.9	1.6	6.0
Black	100.0	17.2	8.0	7.9	11.2	15.9	9.4	8.2	12.6
Hispanic	100.0	10.4	4.2	7.3	8.0	9.7	5.8	4.1	7.6
Non-Hispanic white	100.0	11.6	5.3	10.2	13.1	12.7	8.4	8.5	15.4

* *"Ever told" by a school representative or health professional. Data exclude children under age 3.*
Note: Other allergies include food or digestive allergies, eczema, and other skin allergies.
Source: National Center for Health Statistics, Summary Health Statistics for U.S. Children: National Health Interview Survey, 2004, Series 10, No. 227, 2005, Internet site http://www.cdc.gov/nchs/nhis.htm

Table 2.42 Distribution of Health Conditions among Children by Sex, Age, Race, and Hispanic Origin, 2004

(percent distribution of people under age 18 with health condition by sex, age, race, and Hispanic origin, 2004)

| | total children | diagnosed with asthma | experienced in last 12 months | | | | learning disability | ever told had* attention deficit hyperactivity disorder | prescription medication taken regularly at least 3 months |
			asthma attack	hay fever	respiratory allergies	other allergies			
Total children	100.0%	100.0%	100.0%	100.0%	100.0%	100.0%	100.0%	100.0%	100.0%
Sex									
Boys	51.1	62.1	62.8	56.0	55.3	48.5	61.2	70.6	59.8
Girls	48.9	37.9	37.2	44.0	44.7	51.7	38.8	29.4	40.2
Age									
Aged 0 to 4	27.3	16.4	19.6	13.4	19.2	31.5	4.1	3.3	15.3
Aged 5 to 11	38.5	41.1	43.0	40.8	40.8	38.2	42.3	40.2	39.9
Aged 12 to 17	34.2	42.5	37.3	45.8	40.0	30.3	53.6	56.4	44.8
Race and Hispanic origin									
Asian	3.7	1.9	1.5	2.1	1.2	3.3	0.9	0.8	1.7
Black	15.3	21.5	22.2	13.1	14.8	19.3	17.9	16.8	14.5
Hispanic	19.1	16.0	14.3	14.9	13.1	14.8	13.3	10.2	10.7
Non-Hispanic white	59.4	56.9	58.6	66.4	67.5	59.9	63.8	69.5	69.8

* *"Ever told" by a school representative or health professional. Data exclude children under age 3.*
Note: Other allergies include food or digestive allergies, eczema, and other skin allergies.
Source: National Center for Health Statistics, Summary Health Statistics for U.S. Children: National Health Interview Survey, 2004, Series 10, No. 227, 2005, Internet site http://www.cdc.gov/nchs/nhis.htm

Table 2.43 Health Conditions among People Aged 18 to 44, 2004

(number of people aged 18 or older and aged 18 to 44 with selected health conditions, by type of condition, 2004; numbers in thousands)

	total	aged 18 to 44		
		number	percent with condition	share of total
Total people	**215,191**	**110,417**	**100.0%**	**51.3%**
Selected circulatory diseases				
Heart disease, all types	24,666	4,953	4.5	20.1
Coronary	13,621	1,184	1.1	8.7
Hypertension	47,493	8,133	7.4	17.1
Stroke	5,519	510	0.5	9.2
Selected respiratory conditions				
Emphysema	3,576	309	0.3	8.6
Asthma				
Ever	21,300	10,959	9.9	51.5
Still	14,358	7,058	6.4	49.2
Hay fever	18,629	8,777	8.0	47.1
Sinusitis	30,789	13,976	12.7	45.4
Chronic bronchitis	9,047	3,483	3.2	38.5
Cancer, any	**15,024**	**2,046**	**1.9**	**13.6**
Breast cancer (men and women)	2,581	160	0.1	6.2
Cervical cancer	1,108	506	0.9	45.7
Prostate cancer	1,688	–	–	–
Other selected diseases and conditions				
Diabetes	15,126	2,173	2.0	14.4
Ulcers	14,828	4,956	4.5	33.4
Kidney disease	3,652	972	0.9	26.6
Liver disease	2,860	878	0.8	30.7
Arthritic diagnosis	46,515	8,841	8.0	19.0
Chronic joint symptoms	58,005	17,349	15.7	29.9
Migraines or severe headaches	32,923	20,279	18.4	61.6
Pain in neck	31,742	13,721	12.4	43.2
Pain in lower back	58,394	26,382	23.9	45.2
Pain in face or jaw	9,215	4,939	4.5	53.6
Selected sensory problems				
Hearing trouble	35,135	8,459	7.7	24.1
Vision trouble	19,086	5,624	5.1	29.5
Absence of all natural teeth	16,814	2,016	1.8	12.0

(continued)

		aged 18 to 44		
	total	number	percent with condition	share of total
Selected mental health problems				
Sadness	24,232	11,215	10.3%	46.3%
Hopelessness	13,259	6,570	6.1	49.6
Worthlessness	10,400	5,033	4.6	48.4
Everything is an effort	29,686	15,395	14.2	51.9
Nervousness	33,450	17,899	16.4	53.5
Restlessness	36,172	19,322	17.7	53.4

Note: The conditions shown are those that have ever been diagnosed by a doctor, except as noted. Hay fever, sinusitis, and chronic bronchitis have been diagnosed in the past twelve months. Kidney and liver disease have been diagnosed in the past twelve months and exclude kidney stones, bladder infections, and incontinence. Chronic joint symptoms are shown if the respondent had pain, aching, or stiffness in or around a joint (excluding back and neck) and the condition began more than three months ago. Migraines, pain in neck, lower back, face, or jaw are shown only if pain lasted a whole day or more. Hearing trouble is anyone saying they had at least "a little trouble." Vision trouble is anyone with "any trouble seeing" even when wearing glasses or contacts. Mental health problems are indicated if the person had the feeling during the past 30 days at least "some of the time." "–" means sample is too small to make a reliable estimate.
Source: National Center for Health Statistics, Summary Health Statistics for U.S. Adults: National Health Interview Survey, 2004, Series 10, No. 228, 2005, Internet site http://www.cdc.gov/nchs/nhis.htm; calculations by New Strategist

Nearly 3 Million Children Are Disabled

More than half have a mental disability.

Population surveys and censuses measure disability in many different ways. The Census Bureau's 2003 American Community Survey counted 2.8 million disabled children aged 5 to 15 and 1.3 million disabled 16-to-20-year-olds. The 62 percent majority of disabled children in the 5-to-15 age group have a mental disability. Among the disabled in the 16-to-20 age group, those with mental disabilities account for a smaller 36 percent.

Boys are more likely than girls to be classified as disabled. Among children aged 5 to 15, a substantial 7.9 percent of boys and 4.5 percent of girls have at least one disability. Among those with a mental disability, boys accounted for the 69 percent majority.

According to the Census Bureau's Current Population Survey, 5 percent of young adults aged 16 to 24 have a work disability—meaning they have a health problem that prevents them from working or limits the kind or amount of work they can do. This is less than half the 10 percent work disability rate for the entire working-age population, aged 16 to 64.

People with AIDS are sometimes counted among the disabled. Most of those diagnosed with AIDS were aged 35 or older at the time of diagnosis. Only 5 percent were under age 25.

■ The learning disabled account for many of the children with mental disabilities. Some will outgrow their disability as they mature.

Most disabled children have mental problems, often learning disabilities

(number of children aged 5 to 15 with one type of disability, by type, 2003)

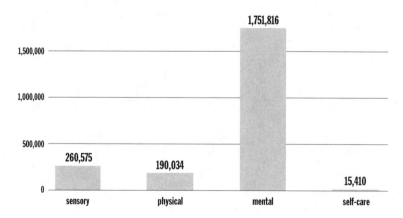

Table 2.44 Children with Disabilities, 2003

(number, percent, and percent distribution of people aged 5 to 15 with disabilities, by type of disability and sex, 2003)

	total	female	male
TOTAL CHILDREN AGED 5 TO 15	**44,973,893**	**21,957,548**	**23,016,345**
Number with disability	**2,805,605**	**984,429**	**1,821,176**
Percent with disability	**6.2%**	**4.5%**	**7.9%**
NUMBER WITH DISABILITY			
Total with any disability	**2,805,605**	**984,429**	**1,821,176**
With one type of disability	2,217,835	763,749	1,454,086
Sensory disability	260,575	122,245	138,330
Physical disability	190,034	94,845	95,189
Mental disability	1,751,816	540,075	1,211,741
Self-care disability	15,410	6,584	8,826
With two or more types of disabilities	587,770	220,680	367,090
PERCENT DISTRIBUTION OF DISABLED BY TYPE OF DISABILITY			
Total with any disability	**100.0%**	**100.0%**	**100.0%**
With one type of disability	79.1	77.6	79.8
Sensory disability	9.3	12.4	7.6
Physical disability	6.8	9.6	5.2
Mental disability	62.4	54.9	66.5
Self-care disability	0.5	0.7	0.5
With two or more types of disabilities	20.9	22.4	20.2
PERCENT DISTRIBUTION OF DISABLED BY SEX			
Total with any disability	**100.0%**	**35.1%**	**64.9%**
With one type of disability	100.0	34.4	65.6
Sensory disability	100.0	46.9	53.1
Physical disability	100.0	49.9	50.1
Mental disability	100.0	30.8	69.2
Self-care disability	100.0	42.7	57.3
With two or more types of disabilities	100.0	37.5	62.5

Note: People are considered to have a disability if they answered yes to questions regarding sensory disability: trouble seeing or hearing; physical disability: trouble walking, climbing stairs, reaching, lifting, or carrying; mental disability: difficulty learning, remembering, or concentrating; self-care disability: difficulty dressing, bathing, or getting around inside the home.
Source: Bureau of the Census, 2003 American Community Survey, Internet site http://www.census.gov/hhes/www/disability/ data_title.html#2003; calculations by New Strategist

Table 2.45 Young Adults with Disabilities, 2003

(number, percent, and percent distribution of people aged 16 to 20 with disabilities, by type of disability and sex, 2003)

	total	female	male
TOTAL ADULTS AGED 16 TO 20	**18,531,416**	**8,997,585**	**9,533,831**
Number with disability	**1,254,189**	**519,327**	**734,862**
Percent with disability	**6.8%**	**5.8%**	**7.7%**
NUMBER WITH DISABILITY			
Total with any disability	**1,254,189**	**519,327**	**734,862**
With one type of disability	762,930	308,950	453,980
Sensory disability	129,610	58,346	71,264
Physical disability	104,016	61,337	42,679
Mental disability	457,228	149,995	307,233
Self-care disability	3,721	2,168	1,553
Go outside home disability	14,033	7,421	6,612
Employment disability	54,322	29,683	24,639
With two or more types of disabilities	491,259	210,377	280,882
PERCENT DISTRIBUTION OF DISABLED BY TYPE OF DISABILITY			
Total with any disability	**100.0%**	**100.0%**	**100.0%**
With one type of disability	60.8	59.5	61.8
Sensory disability	10.3	11.2	9.7
Physical disability	8.3	11.8	5.8
Mental disability	36.5	28.9	41.8
Self-care disability	0.3	0.4	0.2
Go outside home disability	1.1	1.4	0.9
Employment disability	4.3	5.7	3.4
With two or more types of disabilities	39.2	40.5	38.2
PERCENT DISTRIBUTION OF DISABLED BY SEX			
Total with any disability	**100.0%**	**41.4%**	**58.6%**
With one type of disability	100.0	40.5	59.5
Sensory disability	100.0	45.0	55.0
Physical disability	100.0	59.0	41.0
Mental disability	100.0	32.8	67.2
Self-care disability	100.0	58.3	41.7
Go outside home disability	100.0	52.9	47.1
Employment disability	100.0	54.6	45.4
With two or more types of disabilities	100.0	42.8	57.2

Note: People are considered to have a disability if they answered yes to questions regarding sensory disability: trouble seeing or hearing; physical disability: trouble walking, climbing stairs, reaching, lifting, or carrying; mental disability: difficulty learning, remembering, or concentrating; self-care disability: difficulty dressing, bathing, or getting around inside the home; going outside the home disability: difficulty going outside the home alone to shop or visit a doctor's office; employment disability: difficulty working at a job or business.
Source: Bureau of the Census, 2003 American Community Survey, Internet site http://www.census.gov/hhes/www/disability/ data_title.html#2003; calculations by New Strategist

Table 2.46 People Aged 16 to 34 with a Work Disability, 2005

(number and percent of people aged 16 or older with a work disability, by selected age group, education, and severity of disability, 2005; numbers in thousands)

| | | with a work disability | | | | | |
| | | total | | not severe | | severe | |
	total	number	percent	number	percent	number	percent
Total aged 16 to 64	**190,023**	**19,656**	**10.3%**	**5,414**	**2.8%**	**14,243**	**7.5%**
Not a high school graduate	33,536	5,226	15.6	821	2.4	4,406	13.1
High school graduate	56,398	7,413	13.1	1,797	3.2	5,615	10.0
Associate's degree or some college	52,347	4,647	8.9	1,706	3.3	2,942	5.6
Bachelor's degree or more	47,743	2,370	5.0	1,090	2.3	1,280	2.7
Total aged 16 to 24	**36,589**	**1,709**	**4.7**	**510**	**1.4**	**1,199**	**3.3**
Not a high school graduate	14,685	833	5.7	228	1.6	605	4.1
High school graduate	8,453	563	6.7	147	1.7	417	4.9
Associate's degree or some college	11,108	286	2.6	123	1.1	163	1.5
Bachelor's degree or more	2,342	27	1.2	13	0.6	14	0.6
Total aged 25 to 34	**38,990**	**2,475**	**6.3**	**739**	**1.9**	**1,736**	**4.5**
Not a high school graduate	5,211	558	10.7	93	1.8	463	8.9
High school graduate	11,203	1,030	9.2	254	2.3	776	6.9
Associate's degree or some college	10,769	654	6.1	291	2.7	363	3.4
Bachelor's degree or more	11,806	233	2.0	100	0.8	134	1.1

Note: A person is considered to have a work disability if any of the following conditions are met:
1. Identified by the March supplement question "Does anyone in this household have a health problem or disability which prevents them from working or which limits the kind or amount of work they can do?"
2. Identified by the March supplement question "Is there anyone in this household who ever retired or left a job for health reasons?"
3. Identified by the core questionnaire as currently not in the labor force because of a disability.
4. Identified by the March supplement as a person who did not work at all in the previous year because of illness or disability.
5. Under 65 years old and covered by Medicare in previous year.
6. Under 65 years old and received Supplemental Security Income (SSI) in previous year.
7. Received VA disability income in previous year.
If one or more of conditions 3, 4, 5, or 6 are met, the person is considered to have a severe work disability.
Source: Bureau of the Census, 2005 Current Population Survey Annual Social and Economic Supplement, Internet site http://www.census.gov/hhes/www/disability/disabcps.html

Table 2.47 AIDS Cases by Age, through 2003

(cumulative number and percent distribution of AIDS cases by age at diagnosis through 2003)

	number	percent of total cases
Total cases	**929,985**	**100.0%**
Under age 13	9,419	1.0
Aged 13 to 14	891	0.1
Aged 15 to 24	37,599	4.0
Aged 25 to 34	311,137	33.5
Aged 35 to 44	365,432	39.3
Aged 45 to 54	148,347	16.0
Aged 55 to 64	43,451	4.7
Aged 65 or older	13,711	1.5

Source: National Center for Health Statistics, Health, United States, 2005, Internet site http://www.cdc.gov/nchs/hus.htm

Young Adults Are Least Likely to See a Doctor

People aged 15 to 24 visit doctors fewer than two times a year, on average.

In 2003, Americans visited physicians a total of 906 million times. People under age 25 accounted for 24 percent of physician visits. Children under age 15 visit a doctor an average of 2.4 times a year. Young adults aged 15 to 24 visit a doctor only 1.8 times a year. The 15-to-24 age group visits a doctor less often than any other in part because it is least likely to be covered by health insurance.

People under age 25 account for 35 percent of hospital outpatient visitors, with the largest share in the outpatient department because of an acute health problem. The under-25 age group accounts for an even bigger 37 percent share of visits to hospital emergency departments. This is the age group whose emergency visits are least likely to be deemed "emergent"—or a true emergency. Many head to the emergency room because they lack health insurance and have no other source of health care.

When people visiting a doctor or health care clinic are asked to rate the care they receive, fewer than half give it the highest rating (a 9 or 10 on a scale of 0 to 10). The proportion rating their experience a 9 or 10 rises with age to a peak of 58 percent among Medicare recipients (people aged 65 or older). Only 38 to 42 percent of people aged 18 to 29 give the health care they received the highest rating. The parents of children under age 18 rate their child's experience much more highly, with 66 percent giving it the highest rating.

■ Among children under age 15, boys visit doctors slightly more often than girls. This is the only age group in which males go to the doctor more frequently than females.

People aged 15 to 24 see doctors less frequently than any other age group

(average number of physician visits per person per year, by age, 2003)

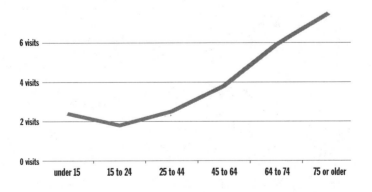

Table 2.48 Physician Office Visits by Sex and Age, 2003

(total number, percent distribution, and number of physician office visits per person per year, by sex and age, 2003; numbers in thousands)

	total	percent distribution	average visits per year
Total visits	**906,023**	**100.0%**	**3.2**
Under age 15	145,245	16.0	2.4
Aged 15 to 24	72,447	8.0	1.8
Aged 25 to 44	203,553	22.5	2.5
Aged 45 to 64	257,258	28.4	3.8
Aged 65 to 74	106,424	11.7	5.9
Aged 75 or older	121,096	13.4	7.5
Visits by females	**537,298**	**59.3**	**3.7**
Under age 15	67,442	7.4	2.3
Aged 15 to 24	46,705	5.2	2.3
Aged 25 to 44	136,881	15.1	3.3
Aged 45 to 64	153,417	16.9	4.4
Aged 65 to 74	60,449	6.7	6.1
Aged 75 or older	72,404	8.0	7.3
Visits by males	**368,724**	**40.7**	**2.6**
Under age 15	77,802	8.6	2.5
Aged 15 to 24	25,742	2.8	1.3
Aged 25 to 44	66,672	7.4	1.6
Aged 45 to 64	103,841	11.5	3.1
Aged 65 to 74	45,975	5.1	5.6
Aged 75 or older	48,692	5.4	7.8

Source: National Center for Health Statistics, National Ambulatory Medical Care Survey: 2003 Summary, Advance Data No. 365, 2005, Internet site http://www.cdc.gov/nchs/about/major/ahcd/adata.htm

Table 2.49 Hospital Outpatient Department Visits by Age and Reason, 2003

(number and percent distribution of visits to hospital outpatient departments by age and major reason for visit, 2003; numbers in thousands)

	total	major reason for visit					
		acute problem	chronic problem, routine	chronic problem, flare-up	pre- or post-surgery	preventive care	unknown
Total visits	**94,578**	**38,339**	**27,355**	**6,135**	**3,974**	**17,053**	**1,721**
Under age 15	21,822	10,354	4,762	1,273	581	4,423	427
Aged 15 to 24	11,521	4,847	2,007	436	280	3,783	168
Aged 25 to 44	24,784	10,812	5,839	1,332	1,003	5,449	348
Aged 45 to 64	23,307	8,123	8,894	2,053	1,394	2,388	454
Aged 65 to 74	7,077	2,070	3,236	588	412	598	173
Aged 75 or older	6,067	2,133	2,616	452	303	412	150
PERCENT DISTRIBUTION BY AGE							
Total visits	**100.0%**	**100.0%**	**100.0%**	**100.0%**	**100.0%**	**100.0%**	**100.0%**
Under age 15	23.1	27.0	17.4	20.7	14.6	25.9	24.8
Aged 15 to 24	12.2	12.6	7.3	7.1	7.0	22.2	9.8
Aged 25 to 44	26.2	28.2	21.3	21.7	25.2	32.0	20.2
Aged 45 to 64	24.6	21.2	32.5	33.5	35.1	14.0	26.4
Aged 65 to 74	7.5	5.4	11.8	9.6	10.4	3.5	10.1
Aged 75 or older	6.4	5.6	9.6	7.4	7.6	2.4	8.7
PERCENT DISTRIBUTION BY MAJOR REASON							
Total visits	**100.0%**	**40.5%**	**28.9%**	**6.5%**	**4.2%**	**18.0%**	**1.8%**
Under age 15	100.0	47.4	21.8	5.8	2.7	20.3	2.0
Aged 15 to 24	100.0	42.1	17.4	3.8	2.4	32.8	1.5
Aged 25 to 44	100.0	43.6	23.6	5.4	4.0	22.0	1.4
Aged 45 to 64	100.0	34.9	38.2	8.8	6.0	10.2	1.9
Aged 65 to 74	100.0	29.2	45.7	8.3	5.8	8.4	2.4
Aged 75 or older	100.0	35.2	43.1	7.5	5.0	6.8	2.5

Source: National Center for Health Statistics, National Hospital Ambulatory Medical Care Survey: 2003 Outpatient Department Summary, Advance Data No. 366, 2005, Internet site http://www.cdc.gov/nchs/about/major/ahcd/adata.htm; calculations by New Strategist

Table 2.50 Emergency Department Visits by Age and Urgency of Problem, 2003

(number of visits to emergency rooms and percent distribution by urgency of problem, by age, 2003; numbers in thousands)

	number	percent distribution	percent distribution by urgency of problem					
			total	emergent	urgent	semiurgent	nonurgent	unknown
Total visits	**113,903**	**100.0%**	**100.0%**	**15.2%**	**35.2%**	**20.0%**	**12.8%**	**16.7%**
Under age 15	24,733	21.7	100.0	10.8	33.7	22.3	15.5	17.7
Aged 15 to 24	17,731	15.6	100.0	11.9	34.6	22.0	15.1	16.5
Aged 25 to 44	32,906	28.9	100.0	13.3	35.8	20.9	13.8	16.2
Aged 45 to 64	20,992	18.4	100.0	17.7	35.7	18.3	11.5	16.9
Aged 65 to 74	7,153	6.3	100.0	24.5	36.3	15.3	7.2	16.6
Aged 75 or older	10,389	9.1	100.0	25.5	36.5	15.5	5.9	16.7

Note: Emergent is a status in which the patient should be seen in less than 15 minutes; urgent is a status in which the patient should be seen within 15 to 60 minutes; semiurgent is a status in which the patient should be seen within 61 to 120 minutes; nonurgent is a status in which the patient should be seen within 121 minutes to 24 hours; unknown denotes a visit with no mention of immediacy or triage or the patient was dead on arrival.
Source: National Center for Health Statistics, National Hospital Ambulatory Medical Care Survey: 2003 Emergency Department Summary, Advance Data No. 358, 2005, Internet site http://www.cdc.gov/nchs/about/major/ahcd/adata.htm

Table 2.51 Parents' Rating of Health Care Received by Children at Doctor's Office or Clinic, 2003

(number of children under age 18 visiting a doctor or health care clinic in past 12 months, and percent distribution by rating given by parents for health care received by children on a scale from 0 (worst) to 10 (best), 2003; children in thousands)

| | with health care visit | | rating | | |
	number	percent	9 to 10	7 to 8	0 to 6
Total children	**54,519**	**100.0%**	**66.4%**	**27.1%**	**6.4%**
Age					
Under age 1	2,356	100.0	73.9	20.6	4.9
Aged 1 to 5	16,995	100.0	67.5	26.4	6.1
Aged 6 to 11	17,470	100.0	67.2	26.1	6.5
Aged 12 to 14	9,339	100.0	63.9	29.8	6.4
Aged 15 to 17	8,359	100.0	63.4	29.1	7.0
Sex					
Female	26,964	100.0	67.1	26.9	5.8
Male	27,555	100.0	65.8	27.2	6.9
Race and Hispanic origin					
Asian, non-Hispanic	1,850	100.0	52.8	34.6	11.9
Black, non-Hispanic	7,805	100.0	67.1	24.1	8.7
Hispanic	9,070	100.0	66.4	26.5	6.9
White, non-Hispanic	34,328	100.0	67.2	27.3	5.3

Note: Numbers by race and Hispanic origin will not sum to total because not all races are shown and Hispanics may be of any race. Percentages will not sum to 100 because "don't know" and no response are not shown.
Source: Agency for Healthcare Research and Quality, Medical Expenditure Panel Survey, 2003, Internet site http://www.meps.ahrq.gov/CompendiumTables/TC_TOC.htm; calculations by New Strategist

Table 2.52 Rating of Health Care Received from Doctor's Office or Clinic, 2003

(number of people aged 18 or older visiting a doctor or health care clinic in past 12 months, and percent distribution by rating for health care received on a scale from 0 (worst) to 10 (best), by age, 2003; people in thousands)

| | with health care visit | | rating | | |
	number	percent	9 to 10	7 to 8	0 to 6
Total people	**147,294**	**100.0%**	**47.2%**	**37.8%**	**14.2%**
Aged 18 to 24	14,088	100.0	42.2	37.8	19.2
Aged 25 to 29	11,589	100.0	38.1	43.1	18.4
Aged 30 to 39	24,952	100.0	42.1	41.6	15.6
Aged 40 to 49	29,918	100.0	44.2	40.1	14.9
Aged 50 to 59	26,402	100.0	48.6	37.5	13.1
Aged 60 to 64	10,615	100.0	51.0	35.9	12.7
Aged 65 or older	29,730	100.0	57.7	31.2	10.1

Source: Agency for Healthcare Research and Quality, Medical Expenditure Panel Survey, 2003, Internet site http://www.meps.ahrq.gov/CompendiumTables/TC_TOC.htm; calculations by New Strategist

Among Children, Accidents Are the Leading Cause of Death

Homicide and suicide are important causes of death as well.

Once children are past infancy, accidents cause the largest share of deaths among children and young adults—which means a large portion of deaths in the age group are preventable. Among infants, congenital malformations are the leading cause of death.

In the 1-to-4 age group, accidents account for one-third of deaths, while congenital malformations rank second. Disturbingly, homicide is the third leading cause of death in the age group. Among 5-to-14-year-olds, accidents are the leading cause of death followed by cancer, congenital malformations, and homicide. In the 15-to-24 age group, accidents, homicide, and suicide top the list. Among 25-to-34-year-olds, accidents are still number one, but suicide is two and homicide three.

Life expectancy has been rising for decades thanks to the success of medical science at combating the ailments of childhood. In 2003, life expectancy at birth stood at 74.8 years for males and 80.1 years for females. At age 25, males have an average of 51 years of life remaining, while females average 56 years left.

■ As medical science tamed the ailments that once killed many infants and children, accidents have become a more important cause of death.

Newborn girls today can expect to live more than 80 years

(years of life remaining at birth and at age 25, by sex, 2003)

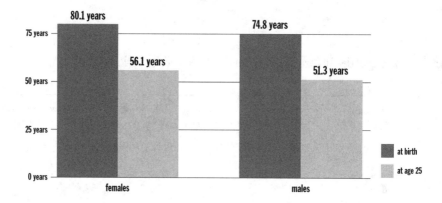

Table 2.53 Leading Causes of Death for Infants, 2002

(number and percent distribution of deaths accounted for by the ten leading causes of death for children under age 1, 2002)

		number	percent distribution
All causes		**28,034**	**100.0%**
1.	Congenital malformations, deformations, and chromosomal abnormalities	5,623	20.1
2.	Disorders relating to short gestation and low birthweight	4,637	16.5
3.	Sudden infant death syndrome	2,295	8.2
4.	Newborn affected by maternal complications of pregnancy	1,708	6.1
5.	Newborn affected by complications of placenta, cord, and membranes	1,028	3.7
6.	Accidents (unintentional injuries) (5)	946	3.4
7.	Respiratory distress syndrome	943	3.4
8.	Bacterial sepsis of newborn	749	2.7
9.	Diseases of the circulatory system	667	2.4
10.	Intrauterine hypoxia and birth asphyxia	583	2.1
All other causes		8,855	31.6

Note: Number in parentheses shows rank for all Americans if the cause of death is among the top fifteen.
Source: National Center for Health Statistics, Deaths: Final Data for 2002, National Vital Statistics Reports, Vol. 53, No. 5, 2004,
Internet site http://www.cdc.gov/nchs/products/pubs/pubd/nvsr/53/53-21.htm; calculations by New Strategist

Table 2.54 Leading Causes of Death for Children Aged 1 to 4, 2002

(number and percent distribution of deaths accounted for by the ten leading causes of death for children aged 1 to 4, 2002)

	number	percent distribution
All causes	**4,858**	**100.0%**
1. Accidents (unintentional injuries) (5)	1,641	33.8
2. Congenital malformations, deformations, and chromosomal abnormalities	530	10.9
3. Homicide (14)	423	8.7
4. Malignant neoplasms (cancer) (2)	402	8.3
5. Diseases of the heart (1)	165	3.4
6. Influenza and pneumonia (7)	110	2.3
7. Septicemia (10)	79	1.6
8. Chronic lower respiratory diseases	65	1.3
9. Certain conditions originating in the perinatal period	65	1.3
10. Benign neoplasms	60	1.2
All other causes	1,318	27.1

Note: Number in parentheses shows rank for all Americans if the cause of death is among the top fifteen.
Source: National Center for Health Statistics, Deaths: Final Data for 2002, National Vital Statistics Reports, Vol. 53, No. 5, 2004, Internet site http://www.cdc.gov/nchs/products/pubs/pubd/nvsr/53/53-21.htm; calculations by New Strategist

Table 2.55 Leading Causes of Death for Children Aged 5 to 14, 2002

(number and percent distribution of deaths accounted for by the ten leading causes of death for children aged 5 to 14, 2002)

	number	percent distribution
All causes	**7,150**	**100.0%**
1. Accidents (unintentional injuries) (5)	2,718	38.0
2. Malignant neoplasms (cancer) (2)	1,072	15.0
3. Congenital malformations, deformations	417	5.8
4. Homicide (14)	356	5.0
5. Suicide (11)	264	3.7
6. Diseases of the heart (1)	255	3.6
7. Chronic lower respiratory disease (4)	136	1.9
8. Septicemia (10)	95	1.3
9. Cerebrovascular diseases (3)	91	1.3
10. Influenza and pneumonia (7)	91	1.3
All other causes	1,655	23.1

Note: Number in parentheses shows rank for all Americans if the cause of death is among the top fifteen.
Source: National Center for Health Statistics, Deaths: Final Data for 2002, National Vital Statistics Reports, Vol. 53, No. 5, 2004, Internet site http://www.cdc.gov/nchs/products/pubs/pubd/nvsr/53/53-21.htm; calculations by New Strategist

Table 2.56 Leading Causes of Death for People Aged 15 to 24, 2002

(number and percent distribution of deaths accounted for by the ten leading causes of death for people aged 15 to 24, 2002)

		number	percent distribution
All causes		**33,046**	**100.0%**
1.	Accidents (unintentional injuries) (5)	15,412	46.6
2.	Homicide (14)	5,219	15.8
3.	Suicide (11)	4,010	12.1
4.	Malignant neoplasms (cancer) (2)	1,730	5.2
5.	Diseases of the heart (1)	1,022	3.1
6.	Congenital malformations, deformations	492	1.5
7.	Chronic lower respiratory disease (4)	192	0.6
8.	Human immunodeficiency virus infection	178	0.5
9.	Diabetes mellitus (6)	171	0.5
10.	Cerebrovascular diseases (3)	171	0.5
All other causes		4,449	13.5

Note: Number in parentheses shows rank for all Americans if the cause of death is among the top fifteen.
Source: National Center for Health Statistics, Deaths: Final Data for 2002, National Vital Statistics Reports, Vol. 53, No. 5, 2004, Internet site http://www.cdc.gov/nchs/products/pubs/pubd/nvsr/53/53-21.htm; calculations by New Strategist

Table 2.57 Leading Causes of Death for People Aged 25 to 34, 2002

(number and percent distribution of deaths accounted for by the ten leading causes of death for people aged 25 to 34, 2002)

		number	percent distribution
All causes		**41,355**	**100.0%**
1.	Accidents (unintentional injuries) (5)	12,569	30.4
2.	Suicide (11)	5,046	12.2
3.	Homicide (14)	4,489	10.9
4.	Malignant neoplasms (cancer) (2)	3,872	9.4
5.	Diseases of the heart (1)	3,165	7.7
6.	Human immunodeficiency virus infection	1,839	4.4
7.	Diabetes mellitus (6)	642	1.6
8.	Cerebrovascular diseases (3)	567	1.4
9.	Congenital malformations, deformations	475	1.1
10.	Chronic liver disease and cirrhosis (12)	374	0.9
All other causes		8,317	20.1

Note: Number in parentheses shows rank for all Americans if the cause of death is among the top fifteen.
Source: National Center for Health Statistics, Deaths: Final Data for 2002, National Vital Statistics Reports, Vol. 53, No. 5, 2004, Internet site http://www.cdc.gov/nchs/products/pubs/pubd/nvsr/53/53-21.htm; calculations by New Strategist

Table 2.58 Life Expectancy by Age and Sex, 2003

(years of life remaining at selected ages, by sex, 2003)

	total	females	males
At birth	77.6	80.1	74.8
Aged 1	77.1	79.6	74.4
Aged 5	73.2	75.7	70.5
Aged 10	68.2	70.8	65.6
Aged 15	63.3	65.8	60.7
Aged 20	58.5	60.9	55.9
Aged 25	53.8	56.1	51.3
Aged 30	49.0	51.2	46.6
Aged 35	44.3	46.4	41.9
Aged 40	39.6	41.7	37.3
Aged 45	35.0	37.0	32.8
Aged 50	30.6	32.5	28.5
Aged 55	26.4	28.0	24.4
Aged 60	22.3	23.8	20.5
Aged 65	18.5	19.8	16.8
Aged 70	15.0	16.1	13.5
Aged 75	11.8	12.7	10.6
Aged 80	9.1	9.7	8.1
Aged 85	6.9	7.2	6.1
Aged 90	5.1	5.3	4.5
Aged 95	3.8	4.0	3.4
Aged 100	2.9	3.0	2.7

Source: National Center for Health Statistics, Deaths: Preliminary Data for 2003, National Vital Statistics Report, Vol. 53, No. 15, 2005, Internet site http://www.cdc.gov/nchs/products/pubs/pubd/nvsr/53/53-21.htm; calculations by New Strategist

3

Housing

■ The nation's homeownership rate climbed by 5 percentage points between 1990 and 2005. The homeownership rate of householders under age 25 (Millennials were aged 28 and younger in 2005) rose much faster than average during those years, up 10 percentage points.

■ Although homeownership rates have been rising among young adults, the great majority are renters. Fully 74 percent of householders under age 25 rent their home, while only 26 percent are homeowners. Among 25-to-29-year-olds, the homeownership rate rises to 41 percent.

■ Among householders under age 25, only 39 percent of couples are homeowners. The figure is a higher 45 percent among male-headed families in the age group.

■ Sixty percent of householders under age 25 live in multi-unit buildings, as do 43 percent of householders aged 25 to 29.

■ Homeowning couples in the 25-to-29 age group have median monthly housing costs of $969. Costs peak for couples aged 30 to 44, at more than $1,000 per month.

■ Only 10 percent of people aged 30 or older moved between 2003 and 2004, but among people aged 20 to 29, the figure was a much higher 28 to 29 percent.

More Young Adults Are Homeowners

Householders under age 25 have seen their homeownership rate rise the most.

The nation's homeownership rate has climbed considerably since 1990, up by 5 percentage points to 68.9 percent in 2005. The homeownership rate of householders under age 25 (Millennials were aged 28 and younger in 2005) rose much faster than average, up 10 percentage points. Twenty-six percent of householders under age 25 were homeowners in 2005, up from 16 percent in 1990.

Behind the rise in the homeownership rate of young adults are low interest rates, and perhaps the financial help of their Boomer parents. Figuring that now is the time to get into the housing market, Boomers may be urging their children to invest in a starter home.

■ As housing prices rise, young adult homeowners will reap the rewards of their housing investment throughout their lives.

Homeownership grew the most for the youngest adults

(percentage point change in homeownership rate, by age of householder, 1990 to 2005)

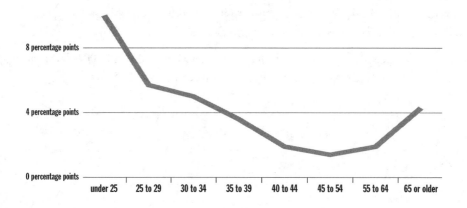

Table 3.1 Homeownership by Age of Householder, 1990 to 2005

(percentage of householders who own their home by age of householder, 1990 to 2005; percentage point change, 2000–05 and 1990–2005)

				percentage point change	
	2005	2000	1990	2000–05	1990–2005
Total households	**68.9%**	**67.4%**	**63.9%**	**1.5**	**5.0**
Under age 25	25.7	21.7	15.7	4.0	10.0
Aged 25 to 29	40.9	38.1	35.2	2.8	5.7
Aged 30 to 34	56.8	54.6	51.8	2.2	5.0
Aged 35 to 39	66.6	65.0	63.0	1.6	3.6
Aged 40 to 44	71.7	70.6	69.8	1.1	1.9
Aged 45 to 54	76.6	76.5	75.2	0.1	1.4
Aged 55 to 64	81.2	80.3	79.3	0.9	1.9
Aged 65 or older	80.6	80.4	76.3	0.2	4.3

Source: Bureau of the Census, Housing Vacancies and Homeownership Survey, Internet site http://www.census.gov/hhes/www/ housing/hvs/annual05/ann05t15.html; calculations by New Strategist

Homeownership Rises with Age

Most young adults are renters.

Although the homeownership rate has been rising among young adults, the great majority are renters. Fully 74 percent of householders under age 25 rent their home, while only 26 percent are homeowners. Among 25-to-29-year-olds, the homeownership rate rises to 41 percent.

The homeownership rate climbs steeply as people enter their thirties and forties. During the past two decades, Boomers have filled those age groups, fueling the real estate, construction, and home improvement industries. When the large Millennial generation enters its thirties and forties beginning in another few years, it will add more fuel to the fire under the housing market.

■ Millennials today are giving the rental market a boost as they inflate the young-adult age group.

Few young adults own their home

(percent distribution of householders under age 25 by homeownership status, 2005)

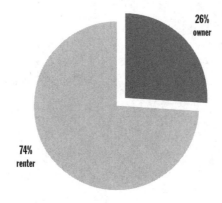

26%
owner

74%
renter

Table 3.2 Owners and Renters by Age of Householder, 2005

(number and percent distribution of householders by homeownership status, and owner and renter share of total, by age of householder, 2005; numbers in thousands)

	total	owners			renters		
		number	percent distribution	share of total	number	percent distribution	share of total
Total households	**108,231**	**74,553**	**100.0%**	**68.9%**	**33,678**	**100.0%**	**31.1%**
Under age 30	15,326	5,279	7.1	34.4	10,047	29.8	65.6
Under age 25	6,536	1,682	2.3	25.7	4,854	14.4	74.3
Aged 25 to 29	8,790	3,597	4.8	40.9	5,193	15.4	59.1
Aged 30 to 34	9,583	5,444	7.3	56.8	4,139	12.3	43.2
Aged 35 to 44	22,248	15,412	20.7	69.3	6,836	20.3	30.7
Aged 45 to 54	22,375	17,129	23.0	76.6	5,246	15.6	23.4
Aged 55 to 64	16,840	13,668	18.3	81.2	3,172	9.4	18.8
Aged 65 or older	21,859	17,622	23.6	80.6	4,237	12.6	19.4

Source: Bureau of the Census, Housing Vacancies and Homeownership Survey, Internet site http://www.census.gov/hhes/www/housing/hvs/annual05/ann05t15.html; calculations by New Strategist

Among Householders under Age 25, Few Married Couples Are Homeowners

Male-headed families are more likely to own a home.

Although married couples are much more likely to own a home than other household types, this is not true among the youngest adults. Among householders under age 25, only 39 percent of couples are homeowners. The figure is a higher 45 percent among male-headed families in the age group. Twenty-six percent of female-headed families under age 25 are homeowners, as are 14 to 18 percent of men and women who live alone.

The homeownership rate rises with age for every household type. The majority of couples are homeowners beginning in the 25-to-29 age group. Homeownership does not reach majority status until ages 40 or older for most other household types.

■ The homeownership of married couples quickly surpasses that of other household types because couples are most likely to have two incomes.

Among young adults, homeownership is highest for male-headed families

(percent of householders under age 25 who own their home, by household type, 2005)

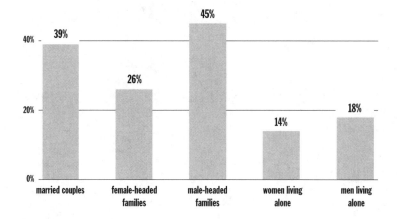

Table 3.3   Homeownership Rate by Age of Householder and Type of Household, 2005

(percent of households owning their home, by age of householder and type of household, 2005)

| | total | family households | | | people living alone | |
		married couples	female hh, no spouse present	male hh, no spouse present	females	males
Total households	**68.9%**	**84.2%**	**51.0%**	**59.1%**	**59.6%**	**50.3%**
Under age 25	25.7	39.1	25.7	44.6	13.6	17.8
Aged 25 to 29	40.9	58.5	23.6	38.9	26.0	30.2
Aged 30 to 34	56.8	72.6	32.2	49.7	37.0	37.5
Aged 35 to 39	66.6	81.7	44.6	55.4	45.0	45.5
Aged 40 to 44	71.7	85.5	52.9	62.7	51.6	47.6
Aged 45 to 49	75.0	88.5	60.1	67.4	53.9	52.2
Aged 50 to 54	78.3	90.6	65.8	72.4	60.2	53.6
Aged 55 to 59	80.6	91.4	68.5	73.1	66.8	58.4
Aged 60 to 64	81.9	92.3	71.3	75.7	69.7	61.3
Aged 65 or older	80.6	92.2	82.0	83.4	70.2	68.1

Source: Bureau of the Census, Housing Vacancies and Homeownership Survey, Internet site http://www.census.gov/hhes/www/housing/hvs/annual05/ann05t15.html; calculations by New Strategist

Most Blacks and Hispanics Are Not Homeowners

The homeownership rate is below 50 percent for those in their twenties and thirties.

The homeownership rate of blacks and Hispanics is well below average. The overall homeownership rate stood at 68.3 percent for all households in 2003 (the latest data available by race, Hispanic origin, and age). Among blacks, the rate was a smaller 47.6 percent. The Hispanic rate was an even lower 46.3 percent.

Homeownership rises above 50 percent for black householders in the 45-to-54 age group. Among Hispanics, the rate reaches 50 percent in the 35-to-44 age group. Homeownership peaks in the 75-or-older age group for both blacks and Hispanics.

■ Blacks are less likely to be homeowners because a smaller share of their households are headed by married couples.

Among Hispanics, homeownership reaches 50 percent in the 35-to-44 age group

(homeownership rate of householders under age 55, by race and Hispanic origin, 2003)

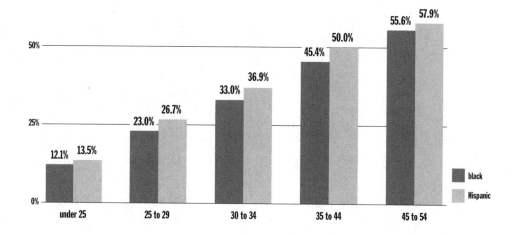

Table 3.4 Black and Hispanic Homeownership by Age, 2003

(percent of total, black, and Hispanic households owning their home, by age of householder, 2003)

	total	black	Hispanic
Total households	**68.3%**	**47.6%**	**46.3%**
Under age 25	20.9	12.1	13.5
Aged 25 to 29	41.1	23.0	26.7
Aged 30 to 34	55.3	33.0	36.9
Aged 35 to 44	68.4	45.4	50.0
Aged 45 to 54	76.3	55.6	57.9
Aged 55 to 64	81.1	63.9	63.5
Aged 65 to 74	82.3	66.1	60.5
Aged 75 or older	78.1	66.6	64.6

Note: Blacks include only those identifying themselves as being black alone. Hispanics may be of any race.
Source: Bureau of the Census, American Housing Survey for the United States: 2003, Current Housing Reports, Internet site http://www.census.gov/hhes/www/ahs.html; calculations by New Strategist

Few Young Adults Live in Single-Family Homes

The majority of the youngest adults live in apartment buildings.

Most American households (64 percent) live in detached, single-family homes. But there is great variation by age. While the majority of householders aged 30 or older live in this type of home, the figure is a minority among those under age 30. The under-30 age group accounts for only 7 percent of householders in single-family, detached homes.

Sixty percent of householders under age 25 live in multi-unit buildings, as do 43 percent of householders aged 25 to 29. The share drops to just 19 percent among those aged 30 or older. Householders under age 30 account for 28 percent of apartment dwellers.

Six percent of householders live in mobile homes, a proportion that does not vary much by age. Householders under age 30 account for 13 percent of mobile home householders.

■ As the number of young adults grows with the aging of the Millennial generation, the demand for apartments is likely to be strong.

Young adults are most likely to live in multi-unit buildings

(percent of households living in multi-unit buildings, by age of householder, 2003)

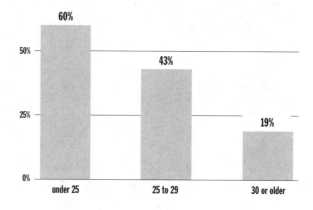

Table 3.5 Number of Units in Structure by Age of Householder, 2003

*(number and percent distribution of households by age of householder and number of units in structure, 2003;
numbers in thousands)*

	total	one, detached	one, attached	multi-unit dwellings total	2 to 4	5 to 9	10 to 19	20 to 49	50 or more	mobile homes
Total households	**105,842**	**67,753**	**6,272**	**24,963**	**8,474**	**5,135**	**4,468**	**3,294**	**3,592**	**6,854**
Under age 25	6,087	1,618	447	3,681	1,165	891	858	470	297	341
Aged 25 to 29	7,805	3,282	615	3,384	1,191	755	664	478	295	524
Aged 30 or older	91,950	62,852	5,210	17,898	6,117	3,488	2,947	2,346	3,000	5,989
Median age (years)	47	49	44	40	40	37	36	39	51	48

PERCENT DISTRIBUTION BY AGE OF HOUSEHOLDER

	total	one, detached	one, attached	multi-unit dwellings total	2 to 4	5 to 9	10 to 19	20 to 49	50 or more	mobile homes
Total households	**100.0%**	**100.0%**	**100.0%**	**100.0%**	**100.0%**	**100.0%**	**100.0%**	**100.0%**	**100.0%**	**100.0%**
Under age 25	5.8	2.4	7.1	14.7	13.7	17.4	19.2	14.3	8.3	5.0
Aged 25 to 29	7.4	4.8	9.8	13.6	14.1	14.7	14.9	14.5	8.2	7.6
Aged 30 or older	86.9	92.8	83.1	71.7	72.2	67.9	66.0	71.2	83.5	87.4

PERCENT DISTRIBUTION BY UNITS IN STRUCTURE

	total	one, detached	one, attached	multi-unit dwellings total	2 to 4	5 to 9	10 to 19	20 to 49	50 or more	mobile homes
Total households	**100.0%**	**64.0%**	**5.9%**	**23.6%**	**8.0%**	**4.9%**	**4.2%**	**3.1%**	**3.4%**	**6.5%**
Under age 25	100.0	26.6	7.3	60.5	19.1	14.6	14.1	7.7	4.9	5.6
Aged 25 to 29	100.0	42.0	7.9	43.4	15.3	9.7	8.5	6.1	3.8	6.7
Aged 30 or older	100.0	68.4	5.7	19.5	6.7	3.8	3.2	2.6	3.3	6.5

*Source: Bureau of the Census, American Housing Survey for the United States in 2003, Internet site http://www.census.gov/hhes/
www/housing/ahs/ahs03/ahs03.html; calculations by New Strategist*

Many Younger Homeowners Live in New Homes

Few older homeowners are in recently built homes.

New homes are the province of the young. Overall, only 6 percent of homeowners live in a new home—meaning one built in the past four years. The share is much greater among young homeowners, however. Thirteen percent of homeowners under age 25 live in a new home, as do 16 percent of those aged 25 to 29. In contrast, only 6 percent of homeowners aged 30 or older are in a new home. Older homeowners usually are in homes they have owned for many years. Even if new at the time they bought it, the home has aged along with its owner.

Overall, 3 percent of renters are in housing units built in the past four years. The proportion is a higher 5 percent among renters under age 25, but falls to 4 percent among those aged 25 to 29 and 3 percent among those aged 30 or older.

■ The large Millennial generation is likely to boost sales of new homes as its members reach adulthood.

Few homeowners aged 30 or older are in new homes

(percent of homeowners living in homes built in the past four years, by age of householder, 2003)

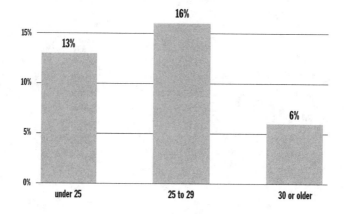

Table 3.6 Owners and Renters of New Homes by Age of Householder, 2003

(number of total occupied housing units, number and percent built in the past four years, and percent distribution of new units by housing tenure and age of householder, 2003; numbers in thousands)

		new homes		
	total	number	percent of total	percent distribution
Total households	**105,842**	**5,691**	**5.4%**	**100.0%**
Under age 25	6,087	385	6.3	6.8
Aged 25 to 29	7,805	677	8.7	11.9
Aged 30 or older	91,950	4,628	5.0	81.3
Total owner households	**72,238**	**4,673**	**6.5**	**100.0**
Under age 25	1,272	159	12.5	3.4
Aged 25 to 29	3,207	515	16.1	11.0
Aged 30 or older	67,759	3,998	5.9	85.6
Total renter households	**33,604**	**1,018**	**3.0**	**100.0**
Under age 25	4,815	226	4.7	22.2
Aged 25 to 29	4,598	162	3.5	15.9
Aged 30 or older	24,190	629	2.6	61.8

Source: Bureau of the Census, American Housing Survey for the United States in 2003, Internet site http://www.census.gov/hhes/ www/housing/ahs/ahs03/ahs03.html; calculations by New Strategist

Housing Costs Are Rising for Millennials

Costs are lowest among homeowners aged 65 or older.

Monthly housing costs for the average household in 2003 stood at a median of $684, including mortgage interest and utilities. For homeowners, median monthly housing cost was $717, and for renters the figure was a slightly smaller $651.

Among married-couple homeowners, housing costs are relatively low for those under age 25, a median of $779 per month. But costs rise sharply as couples age into their late twenties, in part because they buy bigger homes to make room for their growing families. Home-owning couples in the 25-to-29 age group have median monthly housing costs of $969. Costs peak for couples aged 30 to 44, at more than $1,000 per month.

Housing costs are lowest for married-couple homeowners aged 65 or older. For older renters, however, housing costs do not decline much with age. Among married householders aged 65 or older, homeowners paid a median of $398 for housing while renters paid a median of $661.

■ The financial advantages of homeownership grow as householders pay off their mortgages in middle and old age.

Housing costs rise steeply as couples age into their thirties

(median monthly housing costs for married couples, by age of householder, 2003)

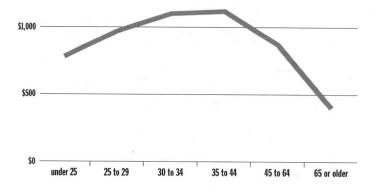

Table 3.7 Median Monthly Housing Costs of Married Couples by Age of Householder, 2003

(median monthly housing costs and indexed costs of married couples by age of householder and housing tenure, 2003)

	median monthly cost			indexed cost		
	total	owners	renters	total	owners	renters
TOTAL HOUSEHOLDS	**$684**	**$717**	**$651**	**100**	**105**	**95**
Married couples	**810**	**843**	**740**	**118**	**123**	**108**
Under age 25	688	779	653	101	114	95
Aged 25 to 29	825	969	700	121	142	102
Aged 30 to 34	954	1,100	756	139	161	111
Aged 35 to 44	1,023	1,117	792	150	163	116
Aged 45 to 64	852	869	763	125	127	112
Aged 65 or older	416	398	661	61	58	97

Note: Housing costs include utilities, mortgages, real estate taxes, property insurance, and regime fees.
Source: Bureau of the Census, American Housing Survey for the United States in 2003, Internet site http://www.census.gov/hhes/www/housing/ahs/ahs03/ahs03.html; calculations by New Strategist

The Homes of the Youngest Adults Are Below-Average in Value

Home values rise as young couples trade in their starter homes for more expensive models.

The median value of America's owned homes stood at $140,269 in 2003. Median home value is an even higher $157,610 among the nation's married couples. Home values peak among couples aged 35 to 44, with a median value of $170,314.

The value of the homes owned by married couples under age 25 is well below average ($113,675) because many have small starter homes. Among couples aged 25 to 29, median home value stood at $126,086 in 2003. After age 30, home values surge as families move into bigger homes with more room for children. The median value of the homes owned by couples aged 30 to 34 is above the married-couple average, at $155,125 in 2003. Seventeen percent own a home worth at least $300,000.

■ Home values have been rising steadily and are now significantly higher than the 2003 figures shown in this section.

Home values are highest for 35-to-44-year-old couples

(median value of homes owned by married couples, by age of householder, 2003)

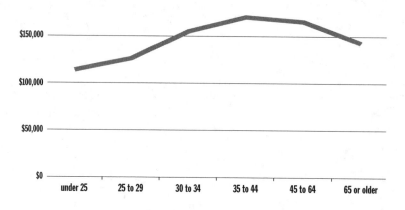

Table 3.8 Value of Homes Owned by Married Couples by Age of Householder, 2003

(total number of married-couple homeowners and percent distribution by value of home, median value of housing unit, and indexed median value, by age of householder, 2003)

	number (in 000s)	under $100,000	$100,000 to $149,999	$150,000 to $199,999	$200,000 to $249,999	$250,000 to $299,999	$300,000 or more	median value of home	indexed median value
TOTAL HOMEOWNERS	**72,238**	**24,630**	**14,266**	**9,989**	**6,358**	**4,561**	**12,434**	**$140,269**	**100**
Married couples	**44,684**	**12,562**	**8,767**	**6,655**	**4,382**	**3,214**	**9,103**	**157,610**	**112**
Under age 25	465	200	119	51	36	12	47	113,675	81
Aged 25 to 29	1,948	699	529	288	163	91	178	126,086	90
Aged 30 to 34	3,848	1,062	794	671	406	261	656	155,125	111
Aged 35 to 44	10,719	2,675	2,031	1,610	1,110	855	2,439	170,314	121
Aged 45 to 64	19,197	5,132	3,595	2,817	1,947	1,425	4,282	165,485	118
Aged 65 or older	8,506	2,796	1,701	1,218	720	570	1,501	142,851	102

Source: Bureau of the Census, American Housing Survey for the United States in 2003, Internet site http://www.census.gov/hhes/ www/housing/ahs/ahs03/ahs03.html; calculations by New Strategist

Twentysomethings Are Most Likely to Move

More than one in four move each year.

Young adults are far more likely than their elders to move from one home to another. Only 10 percent of people aged 30 or older moved between 2003 and 2004, but among people aged 20 to 29, the percentage was a much higher 28 to 29 percent. Children under age 18 are less likely to move than young adults because many parents try to stay put while their children are in school. Households with children aged 6 to 17 and none younger are less likely to move (12 percent) than those with preschoolers (25 percent).

Among twentysomething movers, most stay within the same county. Only 18 percent cross state lines. Among movers under age 30, as for all movers, housing is the primary reason for moving—such as buying a home or moving into a bigger home. Family is the second-most-important reason, and employment ranks only third. Many 20-to-24-year-olds move for "other" reasons, which includes graduating from college.

■ Americans are moving less than they once did. Several factors are behind the lower mobility rate, including the aging of the population, greater homeownership, and more dual-income couples.

Mobility rates are high among people aged 20 to 29

(percent of people who moved between March 2003 and March 2004, by age)

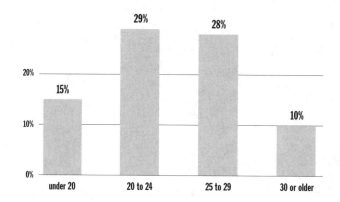

Table 3.9 Geographical Mobility by Age, 2003 to 2004

(total number and percent distribution of people aged 1 or older by mobility status between March 2003 and March 2004, by selected age groups; numbers in thousands)

		movers				
	total	total	same county	different county, same state	different state	abroad
Total, aged 1 or older	**284,367**	**38,995**	**22,551**	**7,842**	**7,330**	**1,272**
Total under age 30	116,499	22,859	13,514	4,590	4,006	749
Aged 1 to 4	16,026	3,324	2,109	600	542	73
Aged 5 to 9	19,636	3,105	1,914	625	490	76
Aged 10 to 14	21,176	2,663	1,613	509	481	60
Aged 15 to 17	12,829	1,418	849	263	257	49
Aged 18 to 19	7,485	1,218	666	282	232	38
Aged 20 to 24	20,339	5,882	3,343	1,281	1,038	220
Aged 25 to 29	19,008	5,249	3,020	1,030	966	233
Aged 30 or older	167,869	16,134	9,036	3,252	3,322	524
PERCENT DISTRIBUTION BY MOBILITY STATUS						
Total, aged 1 or older	**100.0%**	**13.7%**	**7.9%**	**2.8%**	**2.6%**	**0.4%**
Total under age 30	100.0	19.6	11.6	3.9	3.4	0.6
Aged 1 to 4	100.0	20.7	13.2	3.7	3.4	0.5
Aged 5 to 9	100.0	15.8	9.7	3.2	2.5	0.4
Aged 10 to 14	100.0	12.6	7.6	2.4	2.3	0.3
Aged 15 to 17	100.0	11.1	6.6	2.1	2.0	0.4
Aged 18 to 19	100.0	16.3	8.9	3.8	3.1	0.5
Aged 20 to 24	100.0	28.9	16.4	6.3	5.1	1.1
Aged 25 to 29	100.0	27.6	15.9	5.4	5.1	1.2
Aged 30 or older	100.0	9.6	5.4	1.9	2.0	0.3
PERCENT DISTRIBUTION OF MOVERS BY TYPE OF MOVE						
Total, aged 1 or older	–	**100.0%**	**57.8%**	**20.1%**	**18.8%**	**3.3%**
Total under age 30	–	100.0	59.1	20.1	17.5	3.3
Aged 1 to 4	–	100.0	63.4	18.1	16.3	2.2
Aged 5 to 9	–	100.0	61.6	20.1	15.8	2.4
Aged 10 to 14	–	100.0	60.6	19.1	18.1	2.3
Aged 15 to 17	–	100.0	59.9	18.5	18.1	3.5
Aged 18 to 19	–	100.0	54.7	23.2	19.0	3.1
Aged 20 to 24	–	100.0	56.8	21.8	17.6	3.7
Aged 25 to 29	–	100.0	57.5	19.6	18.4	4.4
Aged 30 or older	–	100.0	56.0	20.2	20.6	3.2

Note: "–" means not applicable.
Source: Bureau of the Census, Geographical Mobility: 2004, Detailed Tables, Internet site http://www.census.gov/population/www/socdemo/migrate/cps2004.html; calculations by New Strategist

Table 3.10 Mobility of Families with Children, 2003 to 2004

(total number and percent distribution of family householders aged 15 to 54 by mobility status and presence of own children under age 18 at home, March 2003 to March 2004; numbers in thousands)

			movers			
	total	total	same county	different county, same state	different state	abroad
Total family householders	**52,607**	**7,773**	**4,679**	**1,516**	**1,352**	**226**
No children <18	17,989	2,325	1,245	515	466	99
With children <18	34,618	5,447	3,434	1,001	885	127
Under age 6 only	8,320	2,059	1,309	351	348	51
Under age 6 and aged 6 to 17	7,167	1,188	745	232	181	30
Aged 6 to 17 only	19,131	2,200	1,380	418	356	46
PERCENT DISTRIBUTION BY MOBILITY STATUS						
Total family householders	**100.0%**	**14.8%**	**8.9%**	**2.9%**	**2.6%**	**0.4%**
No children <18	100.0	12.9	6.9	2.9	2.6	0.6
With children <18	100.0	15.7	9.9	2.9	2.6	0.4
Under age 6 only	100.0	24.7	15.7	4.2	4.2	0.6
Under age 6 and aged 6 to 17	100.0	16.6	10.4	3.2	2.5	0.4
Aged 6 to 17 only	100.0	11.5	7.2	2.2	1.9	0.2
PERCENT DISTRIBUTION OF MOVERS BY TYPE OF MOVE						
Total family householders	**–**	**100.0%**	**60.2%**	**19.5%**	**17.4%**	**2.9%**
No children <18	–	100.0	53.5	22.2	20.0	4.3
With children <18	–	100.0	63.0	18.4	16.2	2.3
Under age 6 only	–	100.0	63.6	17.0	16.9	2.5
Under age 6 and aged 6 to 17	–	100.0	62.7	19.5	15.2	2.5
Aged 6 to 17 only	–	100.0	62.7	19.0	16.2	2.1

Note: "–" means not applicable.
Source: Bureau of the Census, Geographical Mobility: 2004, Detailed Tables, Internet site http://www.census.gov/population/www/socdemo/migrate/cps2004.html; calculations by New Strategist

Table 3.11 Reason for Moving by Age, 2003 to 2004

(number and percent distribution of movers by primary reason for move between March 2003 and March 2004, by age; numbers in thousands)

	total	family reasons	employment reasons	housing reasons	other
Total movers	**38,995**	**9,475**	**6,624**	**20,577**	**2,319**
Under age 16	9,545	2,307	1,463	5,506	269
Aged 16 to 19	2,183	676	270	1,030	206
Aged 20 to 24	5,883	1,622	993	2,603	665
Aged 25 to 29	5,249	1,262	977	2,660	350
Aged 30 or older	16,136	3,607	2,922	8,779	828
Total movers	**100.0%**	**24.3%**	**17.0%**	**52.8%**	**5.9%**
Under age 16	100.0	24.2	15.3	57.7	2.8
Aged 16 to 19	100.0	31.0	12.4	47.2	9.4
Aged 20 to 24	100.0	27.6	16.9	44.2	11.3
Aged 25 to 29	100.0	24.0	18.6	50.7	6.7
Aged 30 or older	100.0	22.4	18.1	54.4	5.1

Note: "Other" includes to attend or leave college, change of climate, and health reasons.
Source: Bureau of the Census, Geographical Mobility: 2004, Detailed Tables, Internet site http://www.census.gov/population/ www/socdemo/migrate/cps2004.html; calculations by New Strategist

4

Income

■ The median income of the average household fell 4 percent between 2000 and 2004, after adjusting for inflation. Among householders under age 25 (Millennials were aged 10 to 27 in 2004), the decline was an even larger 10 percent.

■ Householders under age 25 had a median income of $27,586 in 2004, well below the $44,389 national median. Within the age group, black householders have the lowest incomes, while non-Hispanic whites have the highest incomes.

■ In most age groups, married couples are the most affluent household type. Among households headed by people under age 25, however, the median income of male-headed families is higher than that of married couples.

■ The median incomes of men and women under age 25 are low—$10,045 for men and $7,675 for women in 2004—because many in the age group are in college and few work full-time.

■ Children and young adults are much more likely to be poor than middle-aged or older adults. While 12.7 percent of all Americans were poor in 2004, the poverty rate among the Millennial generation was a larger 16.3 percent.

The Incomes of Millennial Householders Are below Their Peak

Young adults have gained ground since 1990, however.

The median income of the average household fell 4 percent between 2000 and 2004, after adjusting for inflation. Among householders under age 25 (Millennials were aged 10 to 27 in 2004), the decline was a much larger 10 percent. Householders aged 25 to 34 saw their median income decline by 7 percent. The recession of 2001 and the lackluster recovery limited the earnings of young adults, lowering their household income.

Despite the decline since 2000, the median income of householders under age 35 was higher in 2004 than in 1990, and the gain experienced by young adults exceeded that of the average household during those years. The median income of householders under age 25 was 9 percent greater in 2004 than in 1990, after adjusting for inflation. This compares with a 6 percent gain for the average household. The median income of households headed by 25-to-34-year-olds rose 7 percent between 1990 and 2004.

■ Because the Millennial generation is large, competition for jobs will be tough, limiting the income growth of young adults even when the labor market tightens.

Young adults have seen their incomes rise and fall

(median income of households headed by people under age 25, 1990, 2000, and 2004; in 2004 dollars)

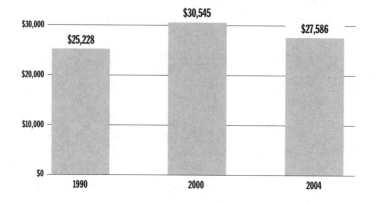

Table 4.1   Median Income of Households Headed by People under Age 35, 1990 to 2004

(median income of total households and households headed by people under age 35, 1990 to 2004; percent change for selected years; in 2004 dollars)

	total households	15 to 24	25 to 34
2004	$44,389	$27,586	$45,485
2003	44,482	27,780	45,982
2002	44,546	29,231	47,615
2001	45,062	30,088	48,105
2000	46,058	30,545	48,717
1999	46,129	28,505	47,709
1998	45,003	27,272	46,374
1997	43,430	26,504	44,802
1996	42,544	25,698	43,019
1995	41,943	25,822	42,713
1994	40,677	24,383	41,796
1993	40,217	24,888	40,269
1992	40,422	23,305	41,218
1991	40,746	24,768	41,714
1990	41,963	25,228	42,546
Percent change			
2000 to 2004	–3.6%	–9.7%	–6.6%
1990 to 2004	5.8	9.3	6.9

Source: Bureau of the Census, Current Population Survey Annual Social and Economic Supplements, Internet site http://www .census.gov/hhes//www/income/histinc/inchhtoc.html; calculations by New Strategist

Household Income Differs Sharply by Race and Hispanic Origin

Among householders under age 25, blacks have the lowest incomes.

Householders under age 25 had a median income of $27,586 in 2004, well below the $44,389 national median. Within the age group, black householders have the lowest incomes by far—a median of just $19,202. Non-Hispanic whites have the highest median household income, at $31,325. Among Asian households, median income is $28,001; the Hispanic median is $26,263.

Household income rises substantially in the 25-to-29 age group as young men and women marry and more households have two incomes. The median income of householders aged 25 to 29 is just below the national average at $41,722. Within the 25-to-29 age group, Asians have the highest median income, at $52,055.

■ Differences in household income among young adults by race and Hispanic origin are due to differences in household composition and educational attainment.

Asians and non-Hispanic whites have the highest incomes

(median income of householders under age 25, by race and Hispanic origin, 2004)

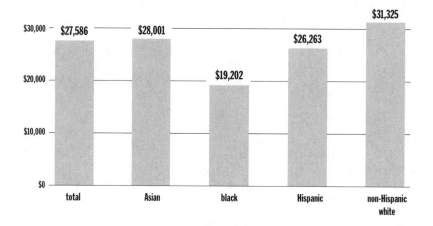

Table 4.2 Income of Households Headed by People under Age 30, 2004: Total Households

(number and percent distribution of total households and households headed by people under age 30, by household income, 2004; households in thousands as of 2005)

	total	15 to 24	25 to 29
Total households	**113,146**	**6,686**	**9,145**
Under $10,000	9,805	1,090	703
$10,000 to $19,999	14,754	1,274	982
$20,000 to $29,999	14,263	1,165	1,241
$30,000 to $39,999	12,641	1,000	1,365
$40,000 to $49,999	10,743	712	1,172
$50,000 to $59,999	9,229	451	919
$60,000 to $69,999	8,078	288	794
$70,000 to $79,999	6,457	199	527
$80,000 to $89,999	5,294	138	418
$90,000 to $99,999	4,068	81	236
$100,000 or more	17,814	288	790
Median income	$44,389	$27,586	$41,722
Total households	**100.0%**	**100.0%**	**100.0%**
Under $10,000	8.7	16.3	7.7
$10,000 to $19,999	13.0	19.1	10.7
$20,000 to $29,999	12.6	17.4	13.6
$30,000 to $39,999	11.2	15.0	14.9
$40,000 to $49,999	9.5	10.6	12.8
$50,000 to $59,999	8.2	6.7	10.0
$60,000 to $69,999	7.1	4.3	8.7
$70,000 to $79,999	5.7	3.0	5.8
$80,000 to $89,999	4.7	2.1	4.6
$90,000 to $99,999	3.6	1.2	2.6
$100,000 or more	15.7	4.3	8.6

Source: Bureau of the Census, 2005 Current Population Survey Annual Social and Economic Supplement, Internet site http:// pubdb3.census.gov/macro/032003/hhinc/new02_000.htm; calculations by New Strategist

Table 4.3 Income of Households Headed by People under Age 30, 2004: Asian Households

(number and percent distribution of total Asian households and Asian households headed by people under age 30, by household income, 2004; households in thousands as of 2005)

	total	15 to 24	25 to 29
Total Asian households	**4,360**	**274**	**427**
Under $10,000	331	48	27
$10,000 to $19,999	373	55	29
$20,000 to $29,999	405	41	45
$30,000 to $39,999	355	29	71
$40,000 to $49,999	420	30	32
$50,000 to $59,999	371	18	35
$60,000 to $69,999	315	13	34
$70,000 to $79,999	267	9	36
$80,000 to $89,999	236	5	30
$90,000 to $99,999	195	11	14
$100,000 or more	1,093	15	74
Median income	$57,475	$28,001	$52,055
Total Asian households	**100.0%**	**100.0%**	**100.0%**
Under $10,000	7.6	17.5	6.3
$10,000 to $19,999	8.6	20.1	6.8
$20,000 to $29,999	9.3	15.0	10.5
$30,000 to $39,999	8.1	10.6	16.6
$40,000 to $49,999	9.6	10.9	7.5
$50,000 to $59,999	8.5	6.6	8.2
$60,000 to $69,999	7.2	4.7	8.0
$70,000 to $79,999	6.1	3.3	8.4
$80,000 to $89,999	5.4	1.8	7.0
$90,000 to $99,999	4.5	4.0	3.3
$100,000 or more	25.1	5.5	17.3

Note: Asians include those identifying themselves as being Asian alone and those identifying themselves as being Asian in combination with one or more other races.
Source: Bureau of the Census, 2005 Current Population Survey Annual Social and Economic Supplement, Internet site http://pubdb3.census.gov/macro/032003/hhinc/new02_000.htm; calculations by New Strategist

Table 4.4 Income of Households Headed by People under Age 30, 2004: Black Households

(number and percent distribution of total black households and black households headed by people under age 30, by household income, 2004; households in thousands as of 2005)

	total	15 to 24	25 to 29
Total black households	**14,127**	**1,126**	**1,338**
Under $10,000	2,496	346	258
$10,000 to $19,999	2,334	237	236
$20,000 to $29,999	2,167	195	227
$30,000 to $39,999	1,799	133	189
$40,000 to $49,999	1,290	84	110
$50,000 to $59,999	922	38	88
$60,000 to $69,999	842	35	87
$70,000 to $79,999	578	14	47
$80,000 to $89,999	416	12	17
$90,000 to $99,999	341	6	31
$100,000 or more	941	26	47
Median income	$30,268	$19,202	$27,816
Total black households	**100.0%**	**100.0%**	**100.0%**
Under $10,000	17.7	30.7	19.3
$10,000 to $19,999	16.5	21.0	17.6
$20,000 to $29,999	15.3	17.3	17.0
$30,000 to $39,999	12.7	11.8	14.1
$40,000 to $49,999	9.1	7.5	8.2
$50,000 to $59,999	6.5	3.4	6.6
$60,000 to $69,999	6.0	3.1	6.5
$70,000 to $79,999	4.1	1.2	3.5
$80,000 to $89,999	2.9	1.1	1.3
$90,000 to $99,999	2.4	0.5	2.3
$100,000 or more	6.7	2.3	3.5

Note: Blacks include those identifying themselves as being black alone and those identifying themselves as being black in combination with one or more other races.
Source: Bureau of the Census, 2005 Current Population Survey Annual Social and Economic Supplement, Internet site http:// pubdb3.census.gov/macro/032003/hhinc/new02_000.htm; calculations by New Strategist

Table 4.5 Income of Households Headed by People under Age 30, 2004: Hispanic Households

(number and percent distribution of total Hispanic households and Hispanic households headed by people under age 30, by household income, 2004; households in thousands as of 2005)

	total	15 to 24	25 to 29
Total Hispanic households	**12,181**	**1,209**	**1,596**
Under $10,000	1,303	158	130
$10,000 to $19,999	1,957	240	258
$20,000 to $29,999	2,040	284	283
$30,000 to $39,999	1,631	155	268
$40,000 to $49,999	1,326	128	221
$50,000 to $59,999	1,018	84	130
$60,000 to $69,999	694	29	95
$70,000 to $79,999	562	46	71
$80,000 to $89,999	378	30	44
$90,000 to $99,999	293	16	23
$100,000 or more	980	37	73
Median income	$34,241	$26,263	$34,096
Total Hispanic households	**100.0%**	**100.0%**	**100.0%**
Under $10,000	10.7	13.1	8.1
$10,000 to $19,999	16.1	19.9	16.2
$20,000 to $29,999	16.7	23.5	17.7
$30,000 to $39,999	13.4	12.8	16.8
$40,000 to $49,999	10.9	10.6	13.8
$50,000 to $59,999	8.4	6.9	8.1
$60,000 to $69,999	5.7	2.4	6.0
$70,000 to $79,999	4.6	3.8	4.4
$80,000 to $89,999	3.1	2.5	2.8
$90,000 to $99,999	2.4	1.3	1.4
$100,000 or more	8.0	3.1	4.6

Source: Bureau of the Census, 2005 Current Population Survey Annual Social and Economic Supplement, Internet site http:// pubdb3.census.gov/macro/032003/hhinc/new02_000.htm; calculations by New Strategist

Table 4.6 Income of Households Headed by People under Age 30, 2004: Non-Hispanic White Households

(number and percent distribution of total non-Hispanic white households and non-Hispanic white households headed by people under age 30, by household income, 2004; households in thousands as of 2005)

	total	15 to 24	25 to 29
Total non-Hispanic white households	**81,445**	**4,002**	**5,710**
Under $10,000	5,593	519	283
$10,000 to $19,999	9,937	723	446
$20,000 to $29,999	9,578	651	671
$30,000 to $39,999	8,687	659	812
$40,000 to $49,999	7,623	469	798
$50,000 to $59,999	6,830	310	663
$60,000 to $69,999	6,131	210	576
$70,000 to $79,999	4,984	128	369
$80,000 to $89,999	4,203	84	327
$90,000 to $99,999	3,223	48	170
$100,000 or more	14,654	203	596
Median income	$48,977	$31,325	$47,929
Total non-Hispanic white households	**100.0%**	**100.0%**	**100.0%**
Under $10,000	6.9	13.0	5.0
$10,000 to $19,999	12.2	18.1	7.8
$20,000 to $29,999	11.8	16.3	11.8
$30,000 to $39,999	10.7	16.5	14.2
$40,000 to $49,999	9.4	11.7	14.0
$50,000 to $59,999	8.4	7.7	11.6
$60,000 to $69,999	7.5	5.2	10.1
$70,000 to $79,999	6.1	3.2	6.5
$80,000 to $89,999	5.2	2.1	5.7
$90,000 to $99,999	4.0	1.2	3.0
$100,000 or more	18.0	5.1	10.4

Note: Non-Hispanic whites are those identifying themselves as being white alone and not Hispanic.
Source: Bureau of the Census, 2005 Current Population Survey Annual Social and Economic Supplement, Internet site http:// pubdb3.census.gov/macro/032003/hhinc/new02_000.htm; calculations by New Strategist

Married Couples Have Above-Average Incomes

Among householders under age 25, however, the median income of male-headed families is slightly higher than that of married couples.

In most age groups, married couples are the most affluent household type. Among households headed by people under age 25, however, the $39,448 median income of male-headed families is higher than the $35,189 median of married couples. Female-headed families had a median household income of just $20,021, while women who live alone had the lowest incomes, a median of just $14,065.

Male-headed families often have more than one working adult in the household, which boosts their income. While most married couples also have more than one earner in the household, among young couples a relatively large proportion has a stay-at-home wife. Many of these couples have young children, and the wife is taking care of the kids rather than working outside the home—lowering household income.

In the 25-to-29 age group, the incomes of married couples soar as dual-earners become more common. The median income of married couples aged 25 to 29 stood at $51,858 in 2004, well above that of any other household type.

■ Young adult households are diverse and many have only one or even no earners, which limits their incomes.

Women who live alone have the lowest incomes

(median income of householders under age 25, by household type, 2004)

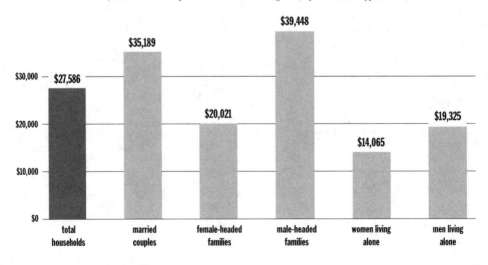

Table 4.7 Income of Households by Household Type, 2004: Aged 15 to 24

(number and percent distribution of households headed by people aged 15 to 24, by household income and house-hold type, 2004; households in thousands as of 2005)

| | | family households | | | nonfamily households | | | |
| | | | | | female householder | | male householder | |
	total	married couples	female hh, no spouse present	male hh, no spouse present	total	living alone	total	living alone
Total households headed by 15-to-24-year-olds	**6,686**	**1,411**	**1,437**	**785**	**1,497**	**756**	**1,555**	**746**
Under $10,000	1,090	77	373	54	322	270	263	188
$10,000 to $19,999	1,274	200	345	116	313	194	299	202
$20,000 to $29,999	1,165	268	233	111	252	157	302	183
$30,000 to $39,999	1,000	300	150	115	220	98	215	100
$40,000 to $49,999	712	217	97	94	136	24	166	31
$50,000 to $59,999	451	120	77	68	90	7	96	19
$60,000 to $69,999	288	75	52	44	62	2	56	3
$70,000 to $79,999	199	54	40	54	31	–	22	3
$80,000 to $89,999	138	37	16	35	23	–	27	1
$90,000 to $99,999	81	23	11	7	15	–	24	3
$100,000 or more	288	40	42	87	33	2	85	11
Median income	$27,586	$35,189	$20,021	$39,448	$25,270	$14,065	$26,132	$19,325
Total households headed by 15-to-24-year-olds	**100.0%**	**100.0%**	**100.0%**	**100.0%**	**100.0%**	**100.0%**	**100.0%**	**100.0%**
Under $10,000	16.3	5.5	26.0	6.9	21.5	35.7	16.9	25.2
$10,000 to $19,999	19.1	14.2	24.0	14.8	20.9	25.7	19.2	27.1
$20,000 to $29,999	17.4	19.0	16.2	14.1	16.8	20.8	19.4	24.5
$30,000 to $39,999	15.0	21.3	10.4	14.6	14.7	13.0	13.8	13.4
$40,000 to $49,999	10.6	15.4	6.8	12.0	9.1	3.2	10.7	4.2
$50,000 to $59,999	6.7	8.5	5.4	8.7	6.0	0.9	6.2	2.5
$60,000 to $69,999	4.3	5.3	3.6	5.6	4.1	0.3	3.6	0.4
$70,000 to $79,999	3.0	3.8	2.8	6.9	2.1	–	1.4	0.4
$80,000 to $89,999	2.1	2.6	1.1	4.5	1.5	–	1.7	0.1
$90,000 to $99,999	1.2	1.6	0.8	0.9	1.0	–	1.5	0.4
$100,000 or more	4.3	2.8	2.9	11.1	2.2	0.3	5.5	1.5

Note: "–" means number is less than 500, percentage is less than 0.05, or sample is too small to make a reliable estimate.
Source: Bureau of the Census, 2005 Current Population Survey Annual Social and Economic Supplement, Internet site http://pubdb3.census.gov/macro/032003/hhinc/new02_000.htm; calculations by New Strategist

Table 4.8 Income of Households by Household Type, 2004: Aged 25 to 29

(number and percent distribution of households headed by people aged 25 to 29, by income and household type, 2004; households in thousands as of 2005)

| | | family households | | | nonfamily households | | | |
	total	married couples	female hh, no spouse present	male hh, no spouse present	female householder total	female householder living alone	male householder total	male householder living alone
Total households headed by 25-to-29-year-olds	**9,145**	**3,930**	**1,435**	**626**	**1,302**	**899**	**1,852**	**1,113**
Under $10,000	703	94	328	19	159	138	103	97
$10,000 to $19,999	982	262	298	60	165	147	196	164
$20,000 to $29,999	1,241	417	258	68	218	186	279	211
$30,000 to $39,999	1,365	532	202	111	225	179	296	216
$40,000 to $49,999	1,172	543	106	72	175	127	275	149
$50,000 to $59,999	919	505	82	71	74	27	187	108
$60,000 to $69,999	794	436	50	74	111	41	121	47
$70,000 to $79,999	527	318	28	33	50	15	97	41
$80,000 to $89,999	418	249	13	28	46	15	80	23
$90,000 to $99,999	236	138	22	15	17	2	46	15
$100,000 or more	790	438	44	75	60	21	173	44
Median income	$41,722	$51,858	$23,254	$47,601	$34,100	$28,897	$41,194	$33,244
Total households headed by 25-to-29-year-olds	**100.0%**	**100.0%**	**100.0%**	**100.0%**	**100.0%**	**100.0%**	**100.0%**	**100.0%**
Under $10,000	7.7	2.4	22.9	3.0	12.2	15.4	5.6	8.7
$10,000 to $19,999	10.7	6.7	20.8	9.6	12.7	16.4	10.6	14.7
$20,000 to $29,999	13.6	10.6	18.0	10.9	16.7	20.7	15.1	19.0
$30,000 to $39,999	14.9	13.5	14.1	17.7	17.3	19.9	16.0	19.4
$40,000 to $49,999	12.8	13.8	7.4	11.5	13.4	14.1	14.8	13.4
$50,000 to $59,999	10.0	12.8	5.7	11.3	5.7	3.0	10.1	9.7
$60,000 to $69,999	8.7	11.1	3.5	11.8	8.5	4.6	6.5	4.2
$70,000 to $79,999	5.8	8.1	2.0	5.3	3.8	1.7	5.2	3.7
$80,000 to $89,999	4.6	6.3	0.9	4.5	3.5	1.7	4.3	2.1
$90,000 to $99,999	2.6	3.5	1.5	2.4	1.3	0.2	2.5	1.3
$100,000 or more	8.6	11.1	3.1	12.0	4.6	2.3	9.3	4.0

Source: Bureau of the Census, 2005 Current Population Survey Annual Social and Economic Supplement, Internet site http://pubdb3.census.gov/macro/032003/hhinc/new02_000.htm; calculations by New Strategist

Children in Married-Couple Families Are Better Off

Among families with children, married couples are far more affluent than single parents.

Many members of the Millennial generation (aged 10 to 27 in 2004) are children, and their financial well-being depends greatly on the type of household in which they live. Those living with married parents are far better off than those living in other household types.

Among households with children under age 18 at home, the median income of married couples stood at $68,104 in 2004. This compares with a median of $42,857 for male-headed families and just $26,469 for female-headed families. Nonfamily households with children (such as cohabiting couples in which the child is not related to the householder) had a relatively high median income of $47,228.

Married couples with children aged 6 to 17 and none younger have the highest incomes, a median of $74,490 in 2004. Thirty-one percent have incomes of $100,000 or more. The incomes of male- and female-headed families with school-aged children also surpass the incomes of those with preschoolers. Most householders with school-aged children are in their peak earning years, which accounts for their above-average incomes. Female-headed families with preschoolers have the lowest incomes—a median of just $16,660 in 2004.

■ Black children have a higher poverty rate than non-Hispanic white children because they are much less likely to live in married-couple families.

Single-parent families have the lowest incomes

(median income of families with children under age 18 at home, by family type, 2004)

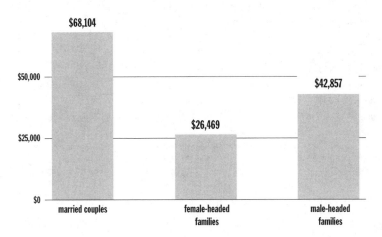

Table 4.9 Income of Households with Children under Age 18 by Household Type, 2004

(number and percent distribution of households with children under age 18 at home, by household income and household type, 2004; households in thousands as of 2005)

	total	family households married couples	family households female-headed families	family households male-headed families	nonfamily households
Total households with children	**40,214**	**27,485**	**9,709**	**2,591**	**428**
Under $10,000	2,484	510	1,806	145	24
$10,000 to $19,999	3,404	1,242	1,840	282	41
$20,000 to $29,999	4,120	1,953	1,747	365	54
$30,000 to $39,999	4,188	2,447	1,307	385	52
$40,000 to $49,999	3,868	2,586	905	322	56
$50,000 to $59,999	3,692	2,780	610	262	42
$60,000 to $69,999	3,324	2,615	450	228	33
$70,000 to $79,999	2,859	2,340	350	144	25
$80,000 to $89,999	2,299	1,979	160	140	19
$90,000 to $99,999	1,886	1,649	149	66	22
$100,000 or more	8,088	7,386	389	251	63
Median income	$55,036	$68,104	$26,469	$42,857	$47,228

DISTRIBUTION BY HOUSEHOLD INCOME

Total households with children	**100.0%**	**100.0%**	**100.0%**	**100.0%**	**100.0%**
Under $10,000	6.2	1.9	18.6	5.6	5.6
$10,000 to $19,999	8.5	4.5	19.0	10.9	9.6
$20,000 to $29,999	10.2	7.1	18.0	14.1	12.6
$30,000 to $39,999	10.4	8.9	13.5	14.9	12.1
$40,000 to $49,999	9.6	9.4	9.3	12.4	13.1
$50,000 to $59,999	9.2	10.1	6.3	10.1	9.8
$60,000 to $69,999	8.3	9.5	4.6	8.8	7.7
$70,000 to $79,999	7.1	8.5	3.6	5.6	5.8
$80,000 to $89,999	5.7	7.2	1.6	5.4	4.4
$90,000 to $99,999	4.7	6.0	1.5	2.5	5.1
$100,000 or more	20.1	26.9	4.0	9.7	14.7

Source: Bureau of the Census, 2005 Current Population Survey Annual Social and Economic Supplement, Internet site http://pubdb3.census.gov/macro/032005/hhinc/new04_000.htm; calculations by New Strategist

Table 4.10 Household Income of Married-Couple Families with Children under Age 18, 2004

(number and percent distribution of total married-couple households and those with related children under age 18 at home, by household income and age of children, 2004; households in thousands as of 2005)

		with one or more children			
	total	total	all under 6	some under 6, some 6 to 17	all 6 to 17
Total married-couple families	**58,118**	**27,412**	**6,728**	**5,982**	**14,702**
Under $10,000	1,402	516	144	137	235
$10,000 to $19,999	3,607	1,247	375	370	502
$20,000 to $29,999	5,402	1,971	593	546	831
$30,000 to $39,999	5,591	2,443	690	683	1,072
$40,000 to $49,999	5,440	2,581	695	620	1,266
$50,000 to $59,999	5,581	2,766	696	655	1,415
$60,000 to $69,999	5,048	2,612	611	579	1,422
$70,000 to $79,999	4,564	2,334	544	492	1,299
$80,000 to $89,999	3,829	1,971	458	356	1,158
$90,000 to $99,999	3,147	1,632	363	310	956
$100,000 or more	14,508	7,337	1,558	1,235	4,544
Median income	$63,630	$67,898	$62,200	$59,566	$74,490

DISTRIBUTION BY HOUSEHOLD INCOME

Total married-couple families	**100.0%**	**100.0%**	**100.0%**	**100.0%**	**100.0%**
Under $10,000	2.4	1.9	2.1	2.3	1.6
$10,000 to $19,999	6.2	4.5	5.6	6.2	3.4
$20,000 to $29,999	9.3	7.2	8.8	9.1	5.7
$30,000 to $39,999	9.6	8.9	10.3	11.4	7.3
$40,000 to $49,999	9.4	9.4	10.3	10.4	8.6
$50,000 to $59,999	9.6	10.1	10.3	10.9	9.6
$60,000 to $69,999	8.7	9.5	9.1	9.7	9.7
$70,000 to $79,999	7.9	8.5	8.1	8.2	8.8
$80,000 to $89,999	6.6	7.2	6.8	6.0	7.9
$90,000 to $99,999	5.4	6.0	5.4	5.2	6.5
$100,000 or more	25.0	26.8	23.2	20.6	30.9

Source: Bureau of the Census, 2005 Current Population Survey Annual Social and Economic Supplement, Internet site http:// pubdb3.census.gov/macro/032005/faminc/new03_000.htm; calculations by New Strategist

Table 4.11 Household Income of Female-Headed Families with Children under Age 18, 2004

(number and percent distribution of total female-headed households and those with related children under age 18 at home, by household income and age of children, 2004; households in thousands as of 2005)

	total	with one or more children total	all under 6	some under 6, some 6 to 17	all 6 to 17
Total female-headed families	**14,009**	**9,721**	**2,111**	**1,855**	**5,755**
Under $10,000	2,509	2,141	712	525	904
$10,000 to $19,999	2,604	1,981	475	436	1,070
$20,000 to $29,999	2,509	1,819	347	299	1,174
$30,000 to $39,999	1,898	1,290	198	251	843
$40,000 to $49,999	1,341	812	125	145	540
$50,000 to $59,999	959	532	104	55	374
$60,000 to $69,999	718	354	43	58	254
$70,000 to $79,999	462	271	29	36	208
$80,000 to $89,999	292	135	25	8	102
$90,000 to $99,999	200	115	15	20	80
$100,000 or more	515	269	39	23	207
Median income	$26,964	$23,428	$16,660	$18,922	$27,118

DISTRIBUTION BY HOUSEHOLD INCOME

Total female-headed families	**100.0%**	**100.0%**	**100.0%**	**100.0%**	**100.0%**
Under $10,000	17.9	22.0	33.7	28.3	15.7
$10,000 to $19,999	18.6	20.4	22.5	23.5	18.6
$20,000 to $29,999	17.9	18.7	16.4	16.1	20.4
$30,000 to $39,999	13.5	13.3	9.4	13.5	14.6
$40,000 to $49,999	9.6	8.4	5.9	7.8	9.4
$50,000 to $59,999	6.8	5.5	4.9	3.0	6.5
$60,000 to $69,999	5.1	3.6	2.0	3.1	4.4
$70,000 to $79,999	3.3	2.8	1.4	1.9	3.6
$80,000 to $89,999	2.1	1.4	1.2	0.4	1.8
$90,000 to $99,999	1.4	1.2	0.7	1.1	1.4
$100,000 or more	3.7	2.8	1.8	1.2	3.6

Source: Bureau of the Census, 2005 Current Population Survey Annual Social and Economic Supplement, Internet site http:// pubdb3.census.gov/macro/032005/faminc/new03_000.htm; calculations by New Strategist

Table 4.12 Household Income of Male-Headed Families with Children under Age 18, 2004

(number and percent distribution of total male-headed households and those with related children under age 18 at home, by household income and age of children, 2004; households in thousands as of 2005)

		with one or more children			
	total	total	all under 6	some under 6, some 6 to 17	all 6 to 17
Total male-headed families	**4,893**	**2,577**	**697**	**339**	**1,541**
Under $10,000	345	203	82	32	91
$10,000 to $19,999	610	387	147	57	180
$20,000 to $29,999	708	416	116	59	243
$30,000 to $39,999	763	411	109	68	234
$40,000 to $49,999	614	317	82	34	201
$50,000 to $59,999	439	231	44	27	159
$60,000 to $69,999	368	160	34	14	111
$70,000 to $79,999	233	112	29	13	71
$80,000 to $89,999	210	103	10	8	84
$90,000 to $99,999	123	49	7	4	39
$100,000 or more	479	186	36	26	125
Median income	$40,293	$36,394	$30,241	$33,449	$40,801

DISTRIBUTION BY HOUSEHOLD INCOME

Total male-headed families	**100.0%**	**100.0%**	**100.0%**	**100.0%**	**100.0%**
Under $10,000	7.1	7.9	11.8	9.4	5.9
$10,000 to $19,999	12.5	15.0	21.1	16.8	11.7
$20,000 to $29,999	14.5	16.1	16.6	17.4	15.8
$30,000 to $39,999	15.6	15.9	15.6	20.1	15.2
$40,000 to $49,999	12.5	12.3	11.8	10.0	13.0
$50,000 to $59,999	9.0	9.0	6.3	8.0	10.3
$60,000 to $69,999	7.5	6.2	4.9	4.1	7.2
$70,000 to $79,999	4.8	4.3	4.2	3.8	4.6
$80,000 to $89,999	4.3	4.0	1.4	2.4	5.5
$90,000 to $99,999	2.5	1.9	1.0	1.2	2.5
$100,000 or more	9.8	7.2	5.2	7.7	8.1

Source: Bureau of the Census, 2005 Current Population Survey Annual Social and Economic Supplement, Internet site http:// pubdb3.census.gov/macro/032005/faminc/new03_000.htm; calculations by New Strategist

Young Adults Have Seen Incomes Decline Since 2000

But their incomes are higher than they were in 1990.

Between 2000 and 2004, men under age 25 saw their median income fall 4 percent, after adjusting for inflation. Women under age 25 experienced a 5 percent decline in median income during those years. The recession of 2001 and the lackluster recovery were behind the decline. In 2004, men under age 25 had a median income of $10,045, while women in the age group had a median income of $7,675.

Despite the decline since 2000, the median income of young men and women was substantially greater in 2004 than in 1990. For men aged 15 to 24, median income grew 13 percent during those years, after adjusting for inflation. For those aged 25 to 34, income expanded a much smaller 3 percent. Among women aged 15 to 24, median income rose 12 percent between 1990 and 2004. For those aged 25 to 34, median income increased by an even larger 25 percent.

■ The median income of men and women under age 25 is low because many are going to school and working part-time or not at all. As these young adults earn their degree, their incomes will rise.

The incomes of young men and women are low because many work part-time

(median income of people under age 25, by sex, 2004)

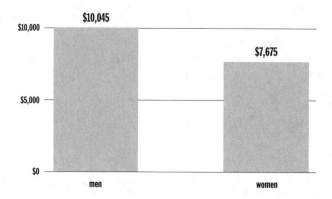

Table 4.13   Median Income of Men under Age 35, 1990 to 2004

(median income of men aged 15 or older and under age 35, 1990 to 2004; percent change for selected years; in 2004 dollars)

	total men	15 to 24	25 to 34
2004	$30,513	$10,045	$30,984
2003	30,735	10,229	31,383
2002	30,712	10,128	32,223
2001	31,054	9,925	32,557
2000	31,089	10,471	33,185
1999	30,937	9,465	33,299
1998	30,660	9,479	32,541
1997	29,590	8,765	30,510
1996	28,570	8,343	30,182
1995	27,771	8,509	29,060
1994	27,384	8,886	28,501
1993	27,165	8,276	28,227
1992	26,989	8,308	28,364
1991	27,684	8,495	29,207
1990	28,439	8,856	29,981
Percent change			
2000 to 2004	–1.9%	–4.1%	–6.6%
1990 to 2004	7.3	13.4	3.3

Source: Bureau of the Census, data from the Current Population Survey Annual Demographic Supplements, Internet site http:// www.census.gov/hhes/income/histinc/p08ar.html; calculations by New Strategist

Table 4.14 Median Income of Women under Age 35, 1990 to 2004

(median income of women aged 15 or older and under age 35, 1990 to 2004; percent change for selected years; in 2004 dollars)

	total women	15 to 24	25 to 34
2004	$17,629	$7,675	$22,009
2003	17,723	7,635	22,583
2002	17,659	7,964	22,740
2001	17,729	7,968	22,914
2000	17,619	8,073	23,088
1999	17,347	7,570	21,886
1998	16,700	7,562	21,130
1997	16,082	7,443	20,711
1996	15,361	7,050	19,639
1995	14,930	6,536	19,149
1994	14,456	6,944	18,765
1993	14,220	6,888	18,007
1992	14,136	6,821	17,985
1991	14,169	7,029	17,534
1990	14,112	6,870	17,643
Percent change			
2000 to 2004	0.1%	–4.9%	–4.7%
1990 to 2004	24.9	11.7	24.7

Source: Bureau of the Census, data from the Current Population Survey Annual Demographic Supplements, Internet site http://www.census.gov/hhes/income/histinc/p08ar.html; calculations by New Strategist

The Incomes of Millennial Men Are Low

Their incomes are low because few work full-time.

The median income of men under age 25 stood at just $10,045 in 2004 (Millennials were aged 10 to 27 in 2004). Behind the low figure is the fact that few men in the age group work full-time—only 22 percent are full-time workers versus 54 percent of all men aged 16 or older. A much larger 68 percent of men aged 25 to 29 work full-time, and their incomes are a higher $27,400.

Among men under age 25, Hispanics have the highest median income ($12,234) because they are most likely to work full-time. Among the 30 percent with full-time jobs, median income was $18,499 in 2004. Only 15 percent of Asian men under age 25 work full-time because most are in college, which explains their modest median income of $9,650. The median income of non-Hispanic white men under age 25 is a slightly smaller $9,475 because they, too, are likely to be in college—only 22 percent work full-time. Black men under age 25 have the lowest income, just $7,641 in 2004. Only 16 percent of black men under age 25 work full-time.

■ Men's incomes rise steeply as they enter their late twenties and the majority gets full-time jobs.

Among young men, Hispanics have the highest incomes

(median income of men under age 25, by race and Hispanic origin, 2004)

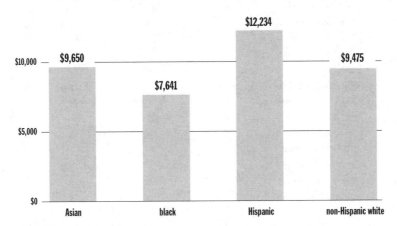

Table 4.15 Income of Men under Age 30, 2004: Total Men

(number and percent distribution of men aged 16 or older and under age 30 by income, 2004; median income by work status, and percent working year-round, full-time; men in thousands as of 2005)

	total	15 to 24	25 to 29
TOTAL MEN	**111,686**	**20,790**	**9,825**
Without income	**9,909**	**6,587**	**551**
With income	**101,777**	**14,203**	**9,274**
Under $10,000	15,853	7,079	1,054
$10,000 to $19,999	18,096	3,432	1,833
$20,000 to $29,999	15,898	2,015	2,140
$30,000 to $39,999	13,391	971	1,629
$40,000 to $49,999	10,283	352	1,113
$50,000 to $59,999	7,376	158	613
$60,000 to $69,999	5,208	49	304
$70,000 to $79,999	3,767	40	240
$80,000 to $89,999	2,574	14	98
$90,000 to $99,999	1,881	14	57
$100,000 or more	7,452	78	193
Median income of men with income	$30,513	$10,045	$27,400
Median income of full-time workers	41,667	21,750	32,082
Percent working full-time	53.8%	22.3%	67.8%
TOTAL MEN	**100.0%**	**100.0%**	**100.0%**
Without income	**8.9**	**31.7**	**5.6**
With income	**91.1**	**68.3**	**94.4**
Under $10,000	14.2	34.1	10.7
$10,000 to $19,999	16.2	16.5	18.7
$20,000 to $29,999	14.2	9.7	21.8
$30,000 to $39,999	12.0	4.7	16.6
$40,000 to $49,999	9.2	1.7	11.3
$50,000 to $59,999	6.6	0.8	6.2
$60,000 to $69,999	4.7	0.2	3.1
$70,000 to $79,999	3.4	0.2	2.4
$80,000 to $89,999	2.3	0.1	1.0
$90,000 to $99,999	1.7	0.1	0.6
$100,000 or more	6.7	0.4	2.0

Source: Bureau of the Census, 2005 Current Population Survey Annual Social and Economic Supplement, Internet site http:// pubdb3.census.gov/macro/032005/perinc/new01_000.htm; calculations by New Strategist

Table 4.16 Income of Men under Age 30, 2004: Asian Men

(number and percent distribution of Asian men aged 16 or older and under age 30 by income, 2004; median income by work status, and percent working year-round, full-time; men in thousands as of 2005)

	total	15 to 24	25 to 29
TOTAL ASIAN MEN	**5,038**	**927**	**526**
Without income	**654**	**422**	**57**
With income	**4,384**	**505**	**469**
Under $10,000	695	256	70
$10,000 to $19,999	679	127	77
$20,000 to $29,999	607	49	96
$30,000 to $39,999	535	42	61
$40,000 to $49,999	388	15	44
$50,000 to $59,999	352	14	48
$60,000 to $69,999	205	1	11
$70,000 to $79,999	194	0	21
$80,000 to $89,999	154	0	14
$90,000 to $99,999	123	0	5
$100,000 or more	450	0	21
Median income of men with income	$32,419	$9,650	$28,951
Median income of full-time workers	46,429	26,040	38,311
Percent working full-time	57.1%	15.0%	59.7%
TOTAL ASIAN MEN	**100.0%**	**100.0%**	**100.0%**
Without income	**13.0**	**45.5**	**10.8**
With income	**87.0**	**54.5**	**89.2**
Under $10,000	13.8	27.6	13.3
$10,000 to $19,999	13.5	13.7	14.6
$20,000 to $29,999	12.0	5.3	18.3
$30,000 to $39,999	10.6	4.5	11.6
$40,000 to $49,999	7.7	1.6	8.4
$50,000 to $59,999	7.0	1.5	9.1
$60,000 to $69,999	4.1	0.1	2.1
$70,000 to $79,999	3.9	0.0	4.0
$80,000 to $89,999	3.1	0.0	2.7
$90,000 to $99,999	2.4	0.0	1.0
$100,000 or more	8.9	0.0	4.0

Note: Asians are those identifying themselves as being Asian alone and those identifying themselves as being Asian in combination with one or more other races.
Source: Bureau of the Census, 2005 Current Population Survey Annual Social and Economic Supplement, Internet site http:// pubdb3.census.gov/macro/032005/perinc/new01_000.htm; calculations by New Strategist

Table 4.17 Income of Men under Age 30, 2004: Black Men

(number and percent distribution of black men aged 16 or older and under age 30 by income, 2004; median income by work status, and percent working year-round, full-time; men in thousands as of 2005)

	total	15 to 24	25 to 29
TOTAL BLACK MEN	**12,609**	**3,039**	**1,238**
Without income	**2,273**	**1,430**	**168**
With income	**10,336**	**1,609**	**1,070**
Under $10,000	2,363	897	184
$10,000 to $19,999	2,115	365	249
$20,000 to $29,999	1,889	209	288
$30,000 to $39,999	1,456	75	182
$40,000 to $49,999	896	23	76
$50,000 to $59,999	594	23	40
$60,000 to $69,999	314	6	9
$70,000 to $79,999	211	2	18
$80,000 to $89,999	99	2	5
$90,000 to $99,999	120	2	4
$100,000 or more	280	4	14
Median income of men with income	$22,740	$7,641	$23,163
Median income of full-time workers	31,724	20,207	26,597
Percent working full-time	46.2%	15.9%	56.5%
TOTAL BLACK MEN	**100.0%**	**100.0%**	**100.0%**
Without income	**18.0**	**47.1**	**13.6**
With income	**82.0**	**52.9**	**86.4**
Under $10,000	18.7	29.5	14.9
$10,000 to $19,999	16.8	12.0	20.1
$20,000 to $29,999	15.0	6.9	23.3
$30,000 to $39,999	11.5	2.5	14.7
$40,000 to $49,999	7.1	0.8	6.1
$50,000 to $59,999	4.7	0.8	3.2
$60,000 to $69,999	2.5	0.2	0.7
$70,000 to $79,999	1.7	0.1	1.5
$80,000 to $89,999	0.8	0.1	0.4
$90,000 to $99,999	1.0	0.1	0.3
$100,000 or more	2.2	0.1	1.1

Note: Blacks are those identifying themselves as being black alone and those identifying themselves as being black in combination with one or more other races.
Source: Bureau of the Census, 2005 Current Population Survey Annual Social and Economic Supplement, Internet site http:// pubdb3.census.gov/macro/032005/perinc/new01_000.htm; calculations by New Strategist

Table 4.18 Income of Men under Age 30, 2004: Hispanic Men

(number and percent distribution of Hispanic men aged 16 or older and under age 30 by income, 2004; median income by work status, and percent working year-round, full-time; men in thousands as of 2005)

	total	15 to 24	25 to 29
TOTAL HISPANIC MEN	**15,223**	**3,711**	**2,177**
Without income	**1,968**	**1,369**	**131**
With income	**13,255**	**2,342**	**2,046**
Under $10,000	2,239	895	229
$10,000 to $19,999	3,700	846	613
$20,000 to $29,999	2,823	396	561
$30,000 to $39,999	1,725	129	306
$40,000 to $49,999	1,027	45	166
$50,000 to $59,999	616	10	75
$60,000 to $69,999	370	5	43
$70,000 to $79,999	198	6	21
$80,000 to $89,999	130	2	7
$90,000 to $99,999	88	2	4
$100,000 or more	336	6	22
Median income of men with income	$21,559	$12,234	$21,816
Median income of full-time workers	26,921	18,499	24,521
Percent working full-time	58.4%	29.6%	70.2%
TOTAL HISPANIC MEN	**100.0%**	**100.0%**	**100.0%**
Without income	**12.9**	**36.9**	**6.0**
With income	**87.1**	**63.1**	**94.0**
Under $10,000	14.7	24.1	10.5
$10,000 to $19,999	24.3	22.8	28.2
$20,000 to $29,999	18.5	10.7	25.8
$30,000 to $39,999	11.3	3.5	14.1
$40,000 to $49,999	6.7	1.2	7.6
$50,000 to $59,999	4.0	0.3	3.4
$60,000 to $69,999	2.4	0.1	2.0
$70,000 to $79,999	1.3	0.2	1.0
$80,000 to $89,999	0.9	0.1	0.3
$90,000 to $99,999	0.6	0.1	0.2
$100,000 or more	2.2	0.2	1.0

Source: Bureau of the Census, 2005 Current Population Survey Annual Social and Economic Supplement, Internet site http://pubdb3.census.gov/macro/032005/perinc/new01_000.htm; calculations by New Strategist

Table 4.19 Income of Men under Age 30, 2004: Non-Hispanic White Men

(number and percent distribution of non-Hispanic white men aged 16 or older and under age 30 by income, 2004; median income by work status, and percent working year-round, full-time; men in thousands as of 2005)

	total	15 to 24	25 to 29
TOTAL NON-HISPANIC WHITE MEN	**77,680**	**12,913**	**5,800**
Without income	**4,912**	**3,326**	**185**
With income	**72,768**	**9,587**	**5,615**
Under $10,000	10,326	4,938	554
$10,000 to $19,999	11,441	2,084	877
$20,000 to $29,999	10,426	1,337	1,177
$30,000 to $39,999	9,557	704	1,071
$40,000 to $49,999	7,868	259	829
$50,000 to $59,999	5,717	112	443
$60,000 to $69,999	4,268	33	235
$70,000 to $79,999	3,137	32	180
$80,000 to $89,999	2,160	10	72
$90,000 to $99,999	1,535	10	44
$100,000 or more	6,334	68	136
Median income of men with income	$33,652	$9,475	$31,348
Median income of full-time workers	46,986	23,328	36,477
Percent working full-time	54.0%	22.1%	70.3%
TOTAL NON-HISPANIC WHITE MEN	**100.0%**	**100.0%**	**100.0%**
Without income	**6.3**	**25.8**	**3.2**
With income	**93.7**	**74.2**	**96.8**
Under $10,000	13.3	38.2	9.6
$10,000 to $19,999	14.7	16.1	15.1
$20,000 to $29,999	13.4	10.4	20.3
$30,000 to $39,999	12.3	5.5	18.5
$40,000 to $49,999	10.1	2.0	14.3
$50,000 to $59,999	7.4	0.9	7.6
$60,000 to $69,999	5.5	0.3	4.1
$70,000 to $79,999	4.0	0.2	3.1
$80,000 to $89,999	2.8	0.1	1.2
$90,000 to $99,999	2.0	0.1	0.8
$100,000 or more	8.2	0.5	2.3

Note: Non-Hispanic whites are those identifying themselves as being white alone and not Hispanic.
Source: Bureau of the Census, 2005 Current Population Survey Annual Social and Economic Supplement, Internet site http://pubdb3.census.gov/macro/032005/perinc/new01_000.htm; calculations by New Strategist

The Incomes of Young Women Are Low

Incomes are low because few women under age 25 work full-time.

The median income of women under age 25 is even lower than that of their male counter-parts, standing at just $7,675 in 2004. Behind the low figures for both men and women is the fact that few in the age group work full-time. Only 16 percent of women under age 25 work full-time compared with 36 percent of all women aged 16 or older. Among those who work full-time, median income was $20,602, well below the $32,101 median of all women who work full-time. Median income rises to $21,349 among women aged 25 to 29, with 46 percent working full-time.

Among women under age 25, Asians are least likely to work full-time (11 percent) because they are most likely to attend college. The median income of Asian women under age 25 was just $7,738 in 2004. The median income of non-Hispanic white women in the age group is about the same ($7,705), although a larger share (17 percent) has a full-time job. The figure is similar for black women, who have a median income of $6,946. Just 15 percent of black women under age 25 work full-time. Among women under age 25, Hispanics have the highest income, a median of $8,717 in 2004. Hispanic women do not retain this lead, however. By age 25 to 29, the incomes of Hispanic women are below those of Asians, blacks, and non-Hispanics whites.

■ Young women are more likely to be in school than young men, and many work only part-time or not at all. Their incomes will rise as they gain the credentials to advance in the job market.

Among the youngest women, Hispanics have the highest incomes

(median income of women under age 25, by race and Hispanic origin, 2004)

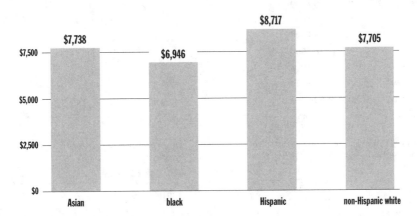

Table 4.20 Income of Women under Age 30, 2004: Total Women

(number and percent distribution of women aged 16 or older and under age 30 by income, 2004; median income by work status, and percent working year-round, full-time; women in thousands as of 2005)

	total	15 to 24	25 to 29
TOTAL WOMEN	**118,739**	**20,273**	**9,674**
Without income	**15,370**	**6,676**	**1,406**
With income	**103,369**	**13,597**	**8,268**
Under $10,000	31,885	7,849	2,020
$10,000 to $19,999	23,868	3,259	1,789
$20,000 to $29,999	16,588	1,513	1,753
$30,000 to $39,999	11,583	605	1,297
$40,000 to $49,999	7,048	212	717
$50,000 to $59,999	4,128	93	286
$60,000 to $69,999	2,818	27	175
$70,000 to $79,999	1,737	18	73
$80,000 to $89,999	1,099	6	51
$90,000 to $99,999	675	2	39
$100,000 or more	1,939	14	69
Median income of women with income	$17,629	$7,675	$21,349
Median income of full-time workers	32,101	20,602	30,267
Percent working full-time	35.7%	16.1%	46.3%
TOTAL WOMEN	**100.0%**	**100.0%**	**100.0%**
Without income	**12.9**	**32.9**	**14.5**
With income	**87.1**	**67.1**	**85.5**
Under $10,000	26.9	38.7	20.9
$10,000 to $19,999	20.1	16.1	18.5
$20,000 to $29,999	14.0	7.5	18.1
$30,000 to $39,999	9.8	3.0	13.4
$40,000 to $49,999	5.9	1.0	7.4
$50,000 to $59,999	3.5	0.5	3.0
$60,000 to $69,999	2.4	0.1	1.8
$70,000 to $79,999	1.5	0.1	0.8
$80,000 to $89,999	0.9	0.0	0.5
$90,000 to $99,999	0.6	0.0	0.4
$100,000 or more	1.6	0.1	0.7

Source: Bureau of the Census, 2005 Current Population Survey Annual Social and Economic Supplement, Internet site http://pubdb3.census.gov/macro/032005/perinc/new01_000.htm; calculations by New Strategist

Table 4.21 Income of Women under Age 30, 2004: Asian Women

(number and percent distribution of Asian women aged 16 or older and under age 30 by income, 2004; median income by work status, and percent working year-round, full-time; women in thousands as of 2005)

	total	15 to 24	25 to 29
TOTAL ASIAN WOMEN	**5,484**	**913**	**598**
Without income	**1,176**	**405**	**152**
With income	**4,308**	**508**	**446**
Under $10,000	1,338	280	127
$10,000 to $19,999	762	116	60
$20,000 to $29,999	610	55	72
$30,000 to $39,999	483	27	73
$40,000 to $49,999	338	15	32
$50,000 to $59,999	230	8	25
$60,000 to $69,999	168	2	16
$70,000 to $79,999	111	5	14
$80,000 to $89,999	79	0	6
$90,000 to $99,999	39	0	5
$100,000 or more	151	0	12
Median income of women with income	$20,618	$7,738	$24,581
Median income of full-time workers	36,491	24,430	35,661
Percent working full-time	37.5%	11.3%	38.8%
TOTAL ASIAN WOMEN	**100.0%**	**100.0%**	**100.0%**
Without income	**21.4**	**44.4**	**25.4**
With income	**78.6**	**55.6**	**74.6**
Under $10,000	24.4	30.7	21.2
$10,000 to $19,999	13.9	12.7	10.0
$20,000 to $29,999	11.1	6.0	12.0
$30,000 to $39,999	8.8	3.0	12.2
$40,000 to $49,999	6.2	1.6	5.4
$50,000 to $59,999	4.2	0.9	4.2
$60,000 to $69,999	3.1	0.2	2.7
$70,000 to $79,999	2.0	0.5	2.3
$80,000 to $89,999	1.4	0.0	1.0
$90,000 to $99,999	0.7	0.0	0.8
$100,000 or more	2.8	0.0	2.0

Note: Asians are those identifying themselves as being Asian alone and those identifying themselves as being Asian in combination with one or more other races.
Source: Bureau of the Census, 2005 Current Population Survey Annual Social and Economic Supplement, Internet site http:// pubdb3.census.gov/macro/032005/perinc/new01_000.htm; calculations by New Strategist

Table 4.22 Income of Women under Age 30, 2004: Black Women

(number and percent distribution of black women aged 16 or older and under age 30 by income, 2004; median income by work status, and percent working year-round, full-time; women in thousands as of 2005)

	total	15 to 24	25 to 29
TOTAL BLACK WOMEN	**15,365**	**3,257**	**1,459**
Without income	**2,380**	**1,273**	**160**
With income	**12,985**	**1,984**	**1,299**
Under $10,000	4,147	1,223	351
$10,000 to $19,999	2,946	400	303
$20,000 to $29,999	2,390	245	295
$30,000 to $39,999	1,571	66	183
$40,000 to $49,999	759	15	94
$50,000 to $59,999	415	18	25
$60,000 to $69,999	308	9	23
$70,000 to $79,999	176	6	12
$80,000 to $89,999	80	2	6
$90,000 to $99,999	55	0	4
$100,000 or more	137	0	6
Median income of women with income	$17,369	$6,946	$19,801
Median income of full-time workers	29,191	21,548	27,676
Percent working full-time	39.7%	14.6%	47.4%
TOTAL BLACK WOMEN	**100.0%**	**100.0%**	**100.0%**
Without income	**15.5**	**39.1**	**11.0**
With income	**84.5**	**60.9**	**89.0**
Under $10,000	27.0	37.5	24.1
$10,000 to $19,999	19.2	12.3	20.8
$20,000 to $29,999	15.6	7.5	20.2
$30,000 to $39,999	10.2	2.0	12.5
$40,000 to $49,999	4.9	0.5	6.4
$50,000 to $59,999	2.7	0.6	1.7
$60,000 to $69,999	2.0	0.3	1.6
$70,000 to $79,999	1.1	0.2	0.8
$80,000 to $89,999	0.5	0.1	0.4
$90,000 to $99,999	0.4	0.0	0.3
$100,000 or more	0.9	0.0	0.4

Note: Blacks are those identifying themselves as being black alone and those identifying themselves as being black in combination with one or more other races.
Source: Bureau of the Census, 2005 Current Population Survey Annual Social and Economic Supplement, Internet site http:// pubdb3.census.gov/macro/032005/perinc/new01_000.htm; calculations by New Strategist

Table 4.23 Income of Women under Age 30, 2004: Hispanic Women

(number and percent distribution of Hispanic women aged 16 or older and under age 30 by income, 2004; median income by work status, and percent working year-round, full-time; women in thousands as of 2005)

	total	15 to 24	25 to 29
TOTAL HISPANIC WOMEN	**14,381**	**3,342**	**1,771**
Without income	**3,992**	**1,598**	**495**
With income	**10,389**	**1,744**	**1,276**
Under $10,000	3,702	964	384
$10,000 to $19,999	2,880	477	365
$20,000 to $29,999	1,732	209	260
$30,000 to $39,999	944	49	149
$40,000 to $49,999	493	30	63
$50,000 to $59,999	232	5	23
$60,000 to $69,999	143	5	20
$70,000 to $79,999	101	2	5
$80,000 to $89,999	41	0	3
$90,000 to $99,999	29	0	1
$100,000 or more	95	0	3
Median income of women with income	$14,425	$8,717	$16,216
Median income of full-time workers	24,255	18,470	22,713
Percent working full-time	32.9%	15.2%	39.0%
TOTAL HISPANIC WOMEN	**100.0%**	**100.0%**	**100.0%**
Without income	**27.8**	**47.8**	**28.0**
With income	**72.2**	**52.2**	**72.0**
Under $10,000	25.7	28.8	21.7
$10,000 to $19,999	20.0	14.3	20.6
$20,000 to $29,999	12.0	6.3	14.7
$30,000 to $39,999	6.6	1.5	8.4
$40,000 to $49,999	3.4	0.9	3.6
$50,000 to $59,999	1.6	0.1	1.3
$60,000 to $69,999	1.0	0.1	1.1
$70,000 to $79,999	0.7	0.1	0.3
$80,000 to $89,999	0.3	0.0	0.2
$90,000 to $99,999	0.2	0.0	0.1
$100,000 or more	0.7	0.0	0.2

Source: Bureau of the Census, 2005 Current Population Survey Annual Social and Economic Supplement, Internet site http:// pubdb3.census.gov/macro/032005/perinc/new01_000.htm; calculations by New Strategist

Table 4.24 Income of Women under Age 30, 2004: Non-Hispanic White Women

(number and percent distribution of non-Hispanic white women aged 16 or older and under age 30 by income, 2004; median income by work status, and percent working year-round, full-time; women in thousands as of 2005)

	total	15 to 24	25 to 29
TOTAL NON-HISPANIC WHITE WOMEN	**82,544**	**12,596**	**5,816**
Without income	**7,734**	**3,377**	**600**
With income	**74,810**	**9,219**	**5,216**
Under $10,000	22,391	5,291	1,157
$10,000 to $19,999	17,037	2,216	1,046
$20,000 to $29,999	11,753	1,009	1,111
$30,000 to $39,999	8,487	457	884
$40,000 to $49,999	5,402	147	532
$50,000 to $59,999	3,223	58	213
$60,000 to $69,999	2,180	10	116
$70,000 to $79,999	1,346	9	42
$80,000 to $89,999	895	4	39
$90,000 to $99,999	549	2	29
$100,000 or more	1,547	14	49
Median income of women with income	$18,379	$7,705	$23,014
Median income of full-time workers	34,878	20,720	31,695
Percent working full-time	35.3%	17.2%	48.8%
TOTAL NON-HISPANIC WHITE WOMEN	**100.0%**	**100.0%**	**100.0%**
Without income	**9.4**	**26.8**	**10.3**
With income	**90.6**	**73.2**	**89.7**
Under $10,000	27.1	42.0	19.9
$10,000 to $19,999	20.6	17.6	18.0
$20,000 to $29,999	14.2	8.0	19.1
$30,000 to $39,999	10.3	3.6	15.2
$40,000 to $49,999	6.5	1.2	9.1
$50,000 to $59,999	3.9	0.5	3.7
$60,000 to $69,999	2.6	0.1	2.0
$70,000 to $79,999	1.6	0.1	0.7
$80,000 to $89,999	1.1	0.0	0.7
$90,000 to $99,999	0.7	0.0	0.5
$100,000 or more	1.9	0.1	0.8

Note: Non-Hispanic whites are those identifying themselves as being white alone and not Hispanic.
Source: Bureau of the Census, 2005 Current Population Survey Annual Social and Economic Supplement, Internet site http://pubdb3.census.gov/macro/032005/perinc/new01_000.htm; calculations by New Strategist

Jobs Are the Most Important Source of Income for Young Adults

A substantial proportion receives educational grants and scholarships.

Earnings are the most common source of income for young adults. Eighty-three to 84 percent of men and women aged 15 to 24 received wage or salary income from an employer in 2004.

The second-most-common source of income for young adults is interest. Twenty-seven to 28 percent of people under age 25 receive interest income, although those receiving it collected an average of less than $500 in 2004.

A substantial 13 percent of men and 19 percent of women under age 25 receive educational assistance. On average, women collected $5,144 and men a larger $6,187 in educational grants and scholarships in 2004, accounting for a substantial portion of the income of many young adults. Educational assistance is a less-important, but still significant, source of income among 25-to-34-year-olds.

■ Earnings from employment will always be the primary source of income for young adults. For many, however, educational support is significant.

Educational assistance counts among young adults

(percent of people under age 35 receiving educational assistance, by sex, 2004)

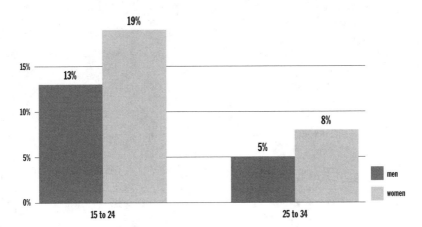

Table 4.25 Sources of Income for Men Aged 15 to 24, 2004

(number and percent distribution of men aged 15 to 24 with income and average income for those with income, by selected sources of income, 2004; people in thousands as of 2005; ranked by percentage receiving source)

	number	percent distribution	average income
Men aged 15 to 24 with income	**14,203**	**100.0%**	**$14,352**
Earnings	12,123	85.4	14,800
Wages and salary	11,861	83.5	14,764
Nonfarm self-employment	474	3.3	7,730
Farm self-employment	179	1.3	3,617
Property income	4,140	29.1	821
Interest	3,873	27.3	494
Dividends	779	5.5	1,348
Rents, royalties, estates or trusts	82	0.6	5,261
Educational assistance	1,835	12.9	6,187
Scholarships only	764	5.4	6,748
Pell grant only	347	2.4	2,661
Other government only	233	1.6	5,318
Other only	139	1.0	6,413
Combinations	352	2.5	8,937
Unemployment compensation	288	2.0	2,214
Social Security	432	3.0	5,670
Financial assistance from other household	367	2.6	8,116
SSI (Supplemental Security Income)	314	2.2	5,752
Child support	108	0.8	3,369
Public assistance	90	0.6	2,646
Workers' compensation	71	0.5	–
Retirement income	58	0.4	–
Disability benefits	38	0.3	–
Survivor benefits	34	0.2	–
Veterans' benefits	21	0.1	–
Alimony	5	0.0	–
Pension income	4	0.0	–
Other income	27	0.2	–

Note: "–" means sample is too small to make a reliable estimate.
Source: Bureau of the Census, 2005 Current Population Survey Annual Social and Economic Supplement, Internet site http:// pubdb3.census.gov/macro/032005/perinc/new09_000.htm; calculations by New Strategist

Table 4.26 Sources of Income for Men Aged 25 to 34, 2004

(number and percent distribution of men aged 25 to 34 with income and average income for those with income, by selected sources of income, 2004; men in thousands as of 2005; ranked by percentage receiving source)

	number	percent with income	average income
Total men aged 25 to 34 with income	**18,724**	**100.0%**	**$37,324**
Earnings	17,900	95.6	37,516
Wages and salary	17,061	91.1	37,660
Nonfarm self-employment	1,260	6.7	21,076
Farm self-employment	229	1.2	10,835
Property income	7,400	39.5	1,249
Interest	6,974	37.2	572
Dividends	2,198	11.7	1,301
Rents, royalties, estates or trusts	492	2.6	4,867
Educational assistance	924	4.9	6,294
Unemployment compensation	864	4.6	4,009
SSI (Supplemental Security Income)	306	1.6	5,481
Social Security	301	1.6	7,586
Workers' compensation	203	1.1	6,414
Financial assistance from other household	168	0.9	5,099
Retirement income	134	0.7	9,859
Veterans' benefits	121	0.6	7,426
Disability benefits	78	0.4	8,816
Child support	51	0.3	–
Pension income	47	0.3	–
Public assistance	38	0.2	–
Survivor benefits	34	0.2	–
Other income	24	0.1	–
Alimony	1	0.0	–

Note: "–" means sample is too small to make a reliable estimate.
Source: Bureau of the Census, 2005 Current Population Survey Annual Social and Economic Supplement, Internet site http:// pubdb3.census.gov/macro/032005/perinc/new08_000.htm; calculations by New Strategist

Table 4.27 Sources of Income for Women Aged 15 to 24, 2004

(number and percent distribution of women aged 15 to 24 with income and average income for those with income, by selected sources of income, 2004; people in thousands as of 2005; ranked by percentage receiving source)

	number	percent distribution	average
Women aged 15 to 24 with income	**13,597**	**100.0%**	**$11,157**
Earnings	11,379	83.7	10,970
Wages and salary	11,283	83.0	10,906
Nonfarm self-employment	296	2.2	5,741
Farm self-employment	123	0.9	681
Property income	4,073	30.0	572
Interest	3,868	28.4	443
Dividends	663	4.9	660
Rents, royalties, estates or trusts	91	0.7	1,987
Educational assistance	2,534	18.6	5,144
Scholarships only	932	6.9	5,737
Pell grant only	566	4.2	2,784
Other government only	268	2.0	4,257
Other only	171	1.3	5,612
Combinations	597	4.4	6,720
Financial assistance from other household	534	3.9	6,037
Public assistance	473	3.5	2,487
Child support	452	3.3	3,091
Social Security	425	3.1	6,517
SSI (Supplemental Security Income)	267	2.0	5,332
Unemployment compensation	211	1.6	2,587
Retirement income	76	0.6	8,396
Workers' compensation	55	0.4	–
Survivor benefits	45	0.3	–
Disability benefits	40	0.3	–
Veterans' benefits	18	0.1	–
Alimony	8	0.1	–
Pension income	2	0.0	–
Other income	47	0.3	–

Note: "–" means sample is too small to make a reliable estimate.
Source: Bureau of the Census, 2005 Current Population Survey Annual Social and Economic Supplement, Internet site http:// pubdb3.census.gov/macro/032005/perinc/new09_000.htm; calculations by New Strategist

Table 4.28 Sources of Income for Women Aged 25 to 34, 2004

(number and percent distribution of women aged 25 to 34 with income and average income for those with income, by selected sources of income, 2004; women in thousands as of 2005; ranked by percentage receiving source)

	number	percent with income	average income
Total women aged 25 to 34 with income	**17,023**	**100.0%**	**$26,117**
Earnings	14,843	87.2	27,679
Wages and salary	14,353	84.3	27,762
Nonfarm self-employment	866	5.1	13,106
Farm self-employment	158	0.9	6,459
Property income	7,584	44.6	831
Interest	7,205	42.3	410
Dividends	1,924	11.3	1,117
Rents, royalties, estates or trusts	410	2.4	2,922
Child support	1,702	10.0	3,928
Educational assistance	1,306	7.7	5,450
Unemployment compensation	670	3.9	3,143
Public assistance	551	3.2	3,419
SSI (Supplemental Security Income)	404	2.4	6,337
Social Security	377	2.2	7,581
Financial assistance from other household	237	1.4	4,793
Retirement income	164	1.0	8,776
Workers' compensation	139	0.8	4,001
Disability benefits	89	0.5	5,313
Pension income	57	0.3	–
Survivor benefits	37	0.2	–
Veterans' benefits	36	0.2	–
Alimony	24	0.1	–
Other income	53	0.3	–

Note: "–" means sample is too small to make a reliable estimate.
Source: Bureau of the Census, 2005 Current Population Survey Annual Social and Economic Supplement, Internet site http://pubdb3.census.gov/macro/032005/perinc/new08_000.htm; calculations by New Strategist

Children Have the Highest Poverty Rate

The Millennial generation accounts for more than one-third of the nation's poor.

Children and young adults are much more likely to be poor than middle-aged or older adults. While 12.7 percent of Americans were poor in 2004, the poverty rate among the Millennial generation (people aged 10 to 27 in 2004) was a larger 16.3 percent. Millennials account for 35 percent of the nation's poor. Twenty-eight percent of black and 23 percent of Hispanic Millennials are poor, while the poverty rate is just 11 percent among non-Hispanic whites and 13 percent among Asians in the age group. Non-Hispanic whites account for a 42 percent minority of the Millennial poor.

Children under age 18 living in families headed by married couples are much less likely to be poor than those in single-parent families. Only 9 percent of children in married-couple families are poor versus 42 percent of those in female-headed families. The poverty rate is even higher among black and Hispanic children living in single-parent families, 49 to 52 percent of whom are poor.

■ Poverty rates for Millennials are well above average because many live in female-headed families—the poorest household type. Until single parenthood becomes less common, poverty among the young will remain stubbornly high.

The nation's young are most likely to be poor

(percent of people living below poverty level, by age, 2004)

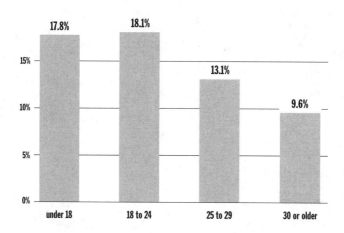

Table 4.29 People below Poverty Level by Age, Race, and Hispanic Origin, 2004

(number, percent, and percent distribution of people below poverty level by age, race, and Hispanic origin, 2004; people in thousands as of 2005)

	total	Asian	black	Hispanic	non-Hispanic white
NUMBER IN POVERTY					
Total people	**36,997**	**1,303**	**9,393**	**9,132**	**16,870**
Millennials (10 to 27)	11,966	454	3,263	3,098	5,079
Under age 18	13,027	334	4,050	4,103	4,508
Aged 18 to 24	5,068	214	1,154	1,119	2,520
Aged 25 to 29	2,558	103	642	744	1,058
Aged 30 or older	16,348	654	3,547	3,169	8,784
PERCENT IN POVERTY					
Total people	**12.7%**	**9.9%**	**24.7%**	**21.9%**	**8.6%**
Millennials (10 to 27)	16.3	13.4	28.3	23.5	11.3
Under age 18	17.8	9.8	33.2	28.9	10.5
Aged 18 to 24	18.1	17.1	27.8	22.6	14.5
Aged 25 to 29	13.1	9.2	23.8	18.8	9.1
Aged 30 or older	9.6	8.7	18.7	17.0	7.1
PERCENT DISTRIBUTION OF POOR BY AGE					
Total people	**100.0%**	**100.0%**	**100.0%**	**100.0%**	**100.0%**
Millennials (10 to 27)	32.3	34.8	34.7	33.9	30.1
Under age 18	35.2	25.6	43.1	44.9	26.7
Aged 18 to 24	13.7	16.4	12.3	12.3	14.9
Aged 25 to 29	6.9	7.9	6.8	8.1	6.3
Aged 30 or older	44.2	50.2	37.8	34.7	52.1
PERCENT DISTRIBUTION OF POOR BY RACE AND HISPANIC ORIGIN					
Total people	**100.0%**	**3.5%**	**25.4%**	**24.7%**	**45.6%**
Millennials (10 to 27)	100.0	3.8	27.3	25.9	42.4
Under age 18	100.0	2.6	31.1	31.5	34.6
Aged 18 to 24	100.0	4.2	22.8	22.1	49.7
Aged 25 to 29	100.0	4.0	25.1	29.1	41.4
Aged 30 or older	100.0	4.0	21.7	19.4	53.7

Note: Numbers will not add to total because Asians and blacks include those identifying themselves as being of the race alone and those identifying themselves as being of the race in combination with one or more other races, because Hispanics may be of any race, and because not all races are shown. Non-Hispanic whites include only those identifying themselves as being white alone and not Hispanic.
Source: Bureau of the Census, 2005 Current Population Survey Annual Social and Economic Supplement, Internet site http:// pubdb3.census.gov/macro/032005/pov/new34_100.htm; calculations by New Strategist

Table 4.30 Children under Age 18 in Poverty by Family Type, Race, and Hispanic Origin, 2004

(number, percent, and percent distribution of children under age 18 in families with incomes below poverty level by family type, race, and Hispanic origin, 2004; children in thousands as of 2005)

	total	Asian	black	Hispanic	non-Hispanic white
NUMBER OF CHILDREN IN POVERTY					
All family types	**12,479**	**320**	**3,957**	**3,997**	**4,182**
Married-couple families	4,583	200	618	1,978	1,748
Female householder, no spouse present	7,140	82	3,139	1,839	2,109
Male householder, no spouse present	756	38	199	180	325
PERCENT OF CHILDREN IN POVERTY					
All family types	**17.3%**	**9.5%**	**32.9%**	**28.6%**	**9.9%**
Married-couple families	8.9	7.1	12.7	20.7	5.2
Female householder, no spouse present	41.8	21.6	48.9	51.8	31.5
Male householder, no spouse present	19.1	19.7	27.5	20.7	15.1
PERCENT DISTRIBUTION OF POOR CHILDREN BY TYPE OF FAMILY					
All family types	**100.0%**	**100.0%**	**100.0%**	**100.0%**	**100.0%**
Married-couple families	36.7	62.5	15.6	49.5	41.8
Female householder, no spouse present	57.2	25.6	79.3	46.0	50.4
Male householder, no spouse present	6.1	11.9	5.0	4.5	7.8
PERCENT DISTRIBUTION OF POOR CHILDREN BY RACE AND HISPANIC ORIGIN					
All family types	**100.0%**	**2.6%**	**31.7%**	**32.0%**	**33.5%**
Married-couple families	100.0	4.4	13.5	43.2	38.1
Female householder, no spouse present	100.0	1.1	44.0	25.8	29.5
Male householder, no spouse present	100.0	5.0	26.3	23.8	43.0

Note: Numbers will not add to total because Asians and blacks include those identifying themselves as being of the race alone and those identifying themselves as being of the race in combination with one or more other races, because Hispanics may be of any race, and because not all races are shown. Non-Hispanic whites include only those identifying themselves as being white alone and not Hispanic.

Source: Bureau of the Census, 2005 Current Population Survey Annual Social and Economic Supplement, Internet site http:// pubdb3.census.gov/macro/032005/pov/new03_100.htm; calculations by New Strategist

5

Labor Force

■ The percentage of men and women under age 30 who are in the labor force fell sharply between 2000 and 2005. The decline was particularly steep among teenagers.

■ Fifteen percent of the nation's workers are under age 25 and one in four is under age 30. Among the nation's unemployed, 33 percent are under age 25 and 46 percent are under age 30.

■ Nearly one-third of black men aged 18 to 19 were unemployed in 2005. In contrast, only 13 percent of Asian men in the age group were unemployed.

■ Workers under age 30 account for 65 percent of cashiers, 63 percent of food preparation workers, 59 percent of athletes, and 54 percent of construction laborers.

■ Among the nation's 2 million minimum-wage workers, more than half (51 percent) are under age 25 and nearly two out of three (62 percent) are under age 30.

■ Between 2005 and 2014, the Millennial generation will fill the 25-to-34 age group. The number of workers aged 25 to 34 will expand by 13 percent, adding more than 4 million to the labor force.

■ For young Millennials, working parents are the norm. Sixty-one percent of married couples with children under age 18 are dual earners.

Fewer Young Adults Are at Work

Labor force participation rate has fallen sharply among young men and women.

The percentage of men and women under age 30 who are in the labor force fell sharply between 2000 and 2005. The decline was particularly steep among teenagers. In 2005, only 31 percent of men aged 16 to 17 were in the labor force, fully 10 percentage points less than the 41 percent of 2000. Among their female counterparts, labor force participation fell from 42 to 34 percent during those years. The labor force participation rate is also down substantially among men and women in their twenties.

The weak economy of the past few years is the primary factor behind young adults' declining labor force participation rate. Another factor is the increasing proportion of high school graduates who go to college. In a tight labor market, many college students may not even bother to look for a job.

■ When the U.S. labor market begins to grow again, the labor force participation rate of teenagers is likely to rise.

A shrinking share of young adults are in the labor force

(percent of people aged 20 to 24 in the labor force, by sex, 2000 and 2005)

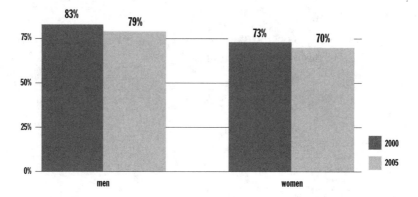

Table 5.1 Labor Force Participation Rate by Sex and Age, 1990 to 2005

(civilian labor force participation rate of people aged 16 or older, by sex and age, 1990 to 2005; percentage point change, 2000–2005 and 1990–2005)

				percentage point change	
	2005	2000	1990	2000–05	1990–2005
Men aged 16 or older	**73.3%**	**74.8%**	**76.4%**	**−1.5**	**−3.1**
Aged 16 to 17	30.5	40.9	43.5	−10.4	−13.0
Aged 18 to 19	57.9	65.0	67.1	−7.1	−9.2
Aged 20 to 24	79.1	82.6	84.4	−3.5	−5.3
Aged 25 to 29	90.8	92.5	93.7	−1.7	−2.9
Aged 30 to 34	92.7	94.2	94.5	−1.5	−1.8
Aged 35 to 39	92.6	93.2	94.8	−0.6	−2.2
Aged 40 to 44	91.6	92.1	93.9	−0.5	−2.3
Aged 45 to 49	89.3	90.2	92.2	−0.9	−2.9
Aged 50 to 54	85.9	86.8	88.8	−0.9	−2.9
Aged 55 to 59	77.6	77.0	79.9	0.6	−2.3
Aged 60 to 64	58.0	54.9	55.5	3.1	2.5
Aged 65 or older	19.8	17.7	16.3	2.1	3.5
Women aged 16 or older	**59.3**	**59.9**	**57.5**	**−0.6**	**1.8**
Aged 16 to 17	33.9	40.8	41.7	−6.9	−7.8
Aged 18 to 19	55.9	61.3	60.3	−5.4	−4.4
Aged 20 to 24	70.1	73.1	71.3	−3.0	−1.2
Aged 25 to 29	74.0	76.7	73.6	−2.7	0.4
Aged 30 to 34	73.9	75.5	73.3	−1.6	0.6
Aged 35 to 39	74.6	75.7	75.5	−1.1	−0.9
Aged 40 to 44	76.8	78.7	77.5	−1.9	−0.7
Aged 45 to 49	77.7	79.1	74.7	−1.4	3.0
Aged 50 to 54	74.0	74.1	66.9	−0.1	7.1
Aged 55 to 59	65.6	61.4	55.3	4.2	10.3
Aged 60 to 64	45.8	40.2	35.5	5.6	10.3
Aged 65 or older	11.5	9.4	8.6	2.1	2.9

Source: Bureau of Labor Statistics, Public Query Data Tool, Internet site http://www.bls.gov/data; and 2005 Current Population Survey, Internet site http://www.bls.gov/cps/home.htm; calculations by New Strategist

Labor Force Rate Is Low among Teens

More than half of 18-to-19-year-olds are in the labor force, however.

Fifteen percent of the nation's workers are under age 25 and more than one in four is under age 30. As the large Millennial generation fills the young-adult age group, the number of younger workers is rising. Restraining this growth, however, is higher education. Only 57 percent of 18-to-19-year-olds are in the labor force, in large part because many in the age group are attending college, which limits their work options. Among 20-to-24-year-olds, labor force participation rises to 75 percent. Until age 20 to 24, there is little difference in labor force participation by sex.

Fully 33 percent of the nation's unemployed are under age 25, and 46 percent are under age 30. While the unemployment rate stood at 5.1 percent among all workers in 2005, it was a much higher 19.2 percent among 16-to-17-year-olds, 14.9 percent among 18-to-19-year-olds, and 8.8 percent among 20-to-24-year-olds.

■ Young adults are much more likely to be unemployed than older workers because they are more often between jobs as they look for the right position and because entry-level workers are more likely to be let go during layoffs.

Few teens are in the labor force

(labor force participation rate of people under age 30, by age, 2005)

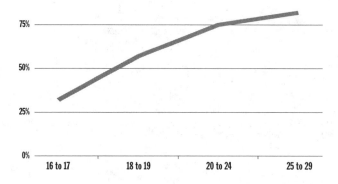

Table 5.2　Employment Status by Sex and Age, 2005

(number and percent of people aged 16 or older in the civilian labor force by sex and age, 2005; numbers in thousands)

	civilian noninstitutional population	civilian labor force			unemployed	
		total	percent of population	employed	number	percent of labor force
Total, aged 16 or older	**226,082**	**149,320**	**66.0%**	**141,730**	**7,591**	**5.1%**
Aged 16 to 17	8,778	2,825	32.2	2,284	541	19.2
Aged 18 to 19	7,619	4,339	56.9	3,694	645	14.9
Aged 20 to 24	20,276	15,127	74.6	13,792	1,335	8.8
Aged 25 to 29	19,484	16,049	82.4	15,116	933	5.8
Aged 30 to 64	134857	116888	86.7	101750	3953	3.4
Aged 65 or older	35,068	5,278	15.1	5,094	184	3.5
Men, aged 16 or older	**109,151**	**80,033**	**73.3**	**75,973**	**4,059**	**5.1**
Aged 16 to 17	4,481	1,368	30.5	1,067	300	21.9
Aged 18 to 19	3,836	2,222	57.9	1,855	367	16.5
Aged 20 to 24	10,181	8,054	79.1	7,279	775	9.6
Aged 25 to 29	9,744	8,843	90.8	8,363	480	5.4
Aged 30 to 64	65,965	56,587	85.8	54,553	2,034	3.6
Aged 65 or older	14,944	2,959	19.8	2,857	102	3.4
Women, aged 16 or older	**116,931**	**69,288**	**59.3**	**65,757**	**3,531**	**5.1**
Aged 16 to 17	4,297	1,457	33.9	1,217	240	16.5
Aged 18 to 19	3,784	2,117	55.9	1,838	278	13.1
Aged 20 to 24	10,095	7,073	70.1	6,513	560	7.9
Aged 25 to 29	9,740	7,206	74.0	6,753	453	6.3
Aged 30 to 64	68,890	49,115	71.3	47,197	1,919	3.9
Aged 65 or older	20,125	2,319	11.5	2,238	82	3.5

Source: Bureau of Labor Statistics, 2005 Current Population Survey, Internet site http://www.bls.gov/cps/home.htm; calculations by New Strategist

Asian and Black Teens Are Least Likely to Work

Young black men are most likely to be unemployed.

Among teenagers, the labor force participation rate is higher for Hispanics and whites than for Asians or blacks. While 62 percent of Hispanic men and 61 percent of white men aged 18 to 19 are in the labor force, the figure is just 48 percent among blacks and 36 percent among Asians. The pattern is the same for women, with white and Hispanic 18-to-19-year-olds more likely to be in the labor force than Asian or black women in the age group. The differences are pronounced in the 20-to-24 age group as well. Among Asian men aged 20 to 24, only 65 percent are in the labor force. Among blacks, the figure is 70 percent. The labor force participation rates of white and Hispanic men in the age group are a much higher 81 and 84 percent, respectively. Behind the low labor force participation rate of young Asian men is their college attendance.

Unemployment is much higher for black teens than it is for Asians, Hispanics, or whites. Nearly one-third of black men aged 18 to 19 are unemployed—meaning they want a job but cannot find one. In contrast, only 13 percent of Asian men in the age group are unemployed. Among women aged 18 to 19, the comparable unemployment figures are 26 percent for blacks and 6 percent for Asians.

■ Some black men have so much difficulty finding a job that they drop out of the labor force altogether.

Nearly one-third of black men aged 18 to 19 are unemployed

(percent of men aged 18 to 19 who are unemployed, by race and Hispanic origin, 2005)

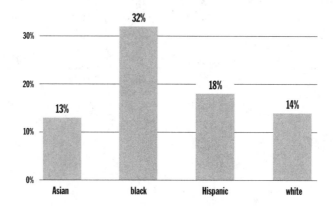

Table 5.3 Employment Status of Men by Race, Hispanic Origin, and Age, 2005

(number and percent of men aged 16 or older in the civilian labor force by race, Hispanic origin, and age, 2005; numbers in thousands)

	civilian noninstitutional population	civilian labor force total	percent of population	employed	unemployed number	percent of labor force
ASIAN MEN						
Total aged 16 or older	**4,679**	**3,500**	**74.8%**	**3,359**	**141**	**4.0%**
Aged 16 to 17	168	27	16.1	21	7	25.9
Aged 18 to 19	150	54	36.0	47	7	13.0
Aged 20 to 24	428	279	65.2	254	25	9.0
Aged 25 to 29	518	438	84.6	416	23	5.3
Aged 30 to 64	2,941	2,609	88.7	2,532	77	3.0
Aged 65 or older	474	94	19.8	91	3	3.2
BLACK MEN						
Total aged 16 or older	**11,882**	**7,998**	**67.3**	**7,155**	**844**	**10.6**
Aged 16 to 17	682	139	20.4	76	63	45.3
Aged 18 to 19	541	260	48.1	178	82	31.5
Aged 20 to 24	1,341	940	70.1	748	192	20.4
Aged 25 to 29	1,175	987	84.0	871	116	11.8
Aged 30 to 64	6,995	5,477	78.3	5,100	377	6.9
Aged 65 or older	1,148	196	17.1	182	14	7.1
HISPANIC MEN						
Total aged 16 or older	**14,962**	**11,985**	**80.1**	**11,337**	**647**	**5.4**
Aged 16 to 17	730	179	24.5	137	42	23.5
Aged 18 to 19	646	398	61.6	328	70	17.6
Aged 20 to 24	1,956	1,645	84.1	1,511	134	8.1
Aged 25 to 29	2,167	2,015	93.0	1,923	92	4.6
Aged 30 to 64	8,509	7,557	88.8	7,256	300	4.0
Aged 65 or older	953	192	20.1	183	9	4.7
WHITE MEN						
Total aged 16 or older	**90,027**	**66,694**	**74.1**	**63,763**	**2,931**	**4.4**
Aged 16 to 17	3,464	1,162	33.5	942	220	18.9
Aged 18 to 19	3,006	1,826	60.7	1,566	260	14.2
Aged 20 to 24	8,057	6,562	81.4	6,041	522	8.0
Aged 25 to 29	7,765	7,165	92.3	6,844	322	4.5
Aged 30 to 64	54,612	47,347	86.7	45,821	1,526	3.2
Aged 65 or older	13,123	2,631	20.0	2,550	81	3.1

Note: People who selected more than one race are not included. Hispanics may be of any race.
Source: Bureau of Labor Statistics, 2005 Current Population Survey, Internet site http://www.bls.gov/cps/home.htm; calculations by New Strategist

Table 5.4 Employment Status of Women by Race, Hispanic Origin, and Age, 2005

(number and percent of women aged 16 or older in the civilian labor force by race, Hispanic origin, and age, 2005; numbers in thousands)

	civilian noninstitutional population	civilian labor force			unemployed	
		total	percent of population	employed	number	percent of labor force
ASIAN WOMEN						
Total aged 16 or older	**5,163**	**3,002**	**58.1%**	**2,885**	**118**	**3.9%**
Aged 16 to 17	161	32	19.9	28	3	9.4
Aged 18 to 19	137	47	34.3	45	3	6.4
Aged 20 to 24	439	260	59.2	250	10	3.8
Aged 25 to 29	560	362	64.6	343	19	5.2
Aged 30 to 64	3,246	2,225	68.5	2,145	80	3.6
Aged 65 or older	619	76	12.3	74	2	2.6
BLACK WOMEN						
Total aged 16 or older	**14,635**	**9,014**	**61.6**	**8,158**	**856**	**9.5**
Aged 16 to 17	659	140	21.2	88	52	37.1
Aged 18 to 19	598	265	44.3	194	70	26.4
Aged 20 to 24	1,494	1,017	68.1	852	166	16.3
Aged 25 to 29	1,414	1,087	76.9	958	129	11.9
Aged 30 to 64	8,649	6,297	72.8	5,873	425	6.7
Aged 65 or older	1,819	207	11.4	193	14	6.8
HISPANIC WOMEN						
Total aged 16 or older	**14,172**	**7,839**	**55.3**	**7,295**	**544**	**6.9**
Aged 16 to 17	685	152	22.2	116	36	23.7
Aged 18 to 19	628	310	49.4	266	43	13.9
Aged 20 to 24	1,692	1,005	59.4	912	93	9.3
Aged 25 to 29	1,787	1,094	61.2	1,011	83	7.6
Aged 30 to 64	8,091	5,159	63.8	4,877	283	5.5
Aged 65 or older	1,289	119	9.2	113	6	5.0
WHITE WOMEN						
Total aged 16 or older	**94,419**	**55,605**	**58.9**	**53,186**	**2,419**	**4.4**
Aged 16 to 17	3,304	1,228	37.2	1,057	172	14.0
Aged 18 to 19	2,915	1,733	59.5	1,540	193	11.1
Aged 20 to 24	7,814	5,546	71.0	5,190	356	6.4
Aged 25 to 29	7,490	5,559	74.2	5,272	287	5.2
Aged 30 to 64	55,462	39,546	71.3	38,197	1,348	3.4
Aged 65 or older	17,433	1,993	11.4	1,930	63	3.2

Note: People who selected more than one race are not included. Hispanics may be of any race.
Source: Bureau of Labor Statistics, 2005 Current Population Survey, Internet site http://www.bls.gov/cps/home.htm; calculations by New Strategist

Most Couples under Age 30 Are Dual Earners

The husband is the sole support of only 31 percent of young couples.

Dual incomes are the norm among married couples. Both husband and wife are in the labor force in 55 percent of the nation's couples. In another 23 percent, the husband is the only worker. Not far behind are the 17 percent of couples in which neither spouse is in the labor force. The wife is the sole worker among 6 percent of couples.

Sixty-three percent of couples under age 30 are dual earners. The proportion is just 35 percent among the few married couples under age 20, but leaps to 58 percent among those aged 20 to 24, and rises to 65 percent among those aged 25 to 29. The proportion peaks among couples aged 40 to 54 because their children are grown and wives are more likely to work. The dual-earner share falls to just 47 percent among couples aged 55 to 64, in part because of early retirement.

■ The proportion of couples in which the husband is the sole earner is highest among the youngest adults because many wives are at home with newborns.

Dual earners dominate married couples under age 55

(percent of married couples in which both husband and wife are in the labor force, by age, 2004)

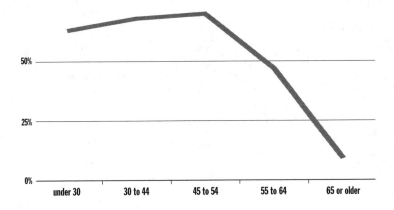

Table 5.5 Labor Force Status of Married-Couple Family Groups by Age of Reference Person, 2004

(number and percent distribution of married-couple family groups by age of reference person and labor force status of husband and wife, 2004; numbers in thousands)

		husband and/or wife in labor force			neither husband nor wife in labor force
	total	husband and wife	husband only	wife only	
Total married-couple family groups	**59,064**	**32,199**	**13,328**	**3,771**	**9,766**
Under age 30	5,526	3,463	1,738	178	150
Under age 20	79	28	41	3	8
Aged 20 to 24	1,516	874	541	52	50
Aged 25 to 29	3,931	2,561	1,156	123	92
Aged 30 to 44	19,762	13,443	5,398	591	332
Aged 45 to 54	13,793	9,701	2,847	795	451
Aged 55 to 64	10,013	4,741	2,274	1,257	1,741
Aged 65 or older	9,970	853	1,073	953	7,092
PERCENT DISTRIBUTION					
Total married-couple family groups	**100.0%**	**54.5%**	**22.6%**	**6.4%**	**16.5%**
Under age 30	100.0	62.7	31.5	3.2	2.7
Under age 20	100.0	35.4	51.9	3.8	10.1
Aged 20 to 24	100.0	57.7	35.7	3.4	3.3
Aged 25 to 29	100.0	65.1	29.4	3.1	2.3
Aged 30 to 44	100.0	68.0	27.3	3.0	1.7
Aged 45 to 54	100.0	70.3	20.6	5.8	3.3
Aged 55 to 64	100.0	47.3	22.7	12.6	17.4
Aged 65 or older	100.0	8.6	10.8	9.6	71.1

Source: Bureau of the Census, 2004 Current Population Survey Annual Demographic Supplement, Internet site http://www .census.gov/population/www/socdemo/hh-fam/cps2004.html; calculations by New Strategist

The Youngest Workers Dominate Many Entry-Level Positions

They account for the majority of food preparation workers.

Among the 142 million employed Americans in 2005, just over 50 million, or 36 percent, were under age 35. In some occupations, however, workers under age 35 account for a disproportionate share. While workers under age 35 are only 21 percent of the nation's managers, they are 75 percent of waiters and waitresses.

One in four employed 16-to-19-year-olds works in a food preparation and serving occupation. The figure declines with age to 5 percent among workers aged 25 to 34. Another 24 percent of workers aged 16 to 19 are in sales occupations, a share that falls to 10 percent among workers aged 25 to 34. Workers under age 35 account for 65 percent of cashiers, 63 percent of food preparation workers, 59 percent of athletes, and 54 percent of laborers. Most young adults will move out of these entry-level positions as they earn educational credentials and gain job experience.

■ Young adults account for a large share of workers in occupations with considerable public contact. Employers should train young adults to relate well to middle aged and older people if they want customers to come back for more.

Many occupations are dominated by young adults

(percent of workers under age 35, by occupation, 2005)

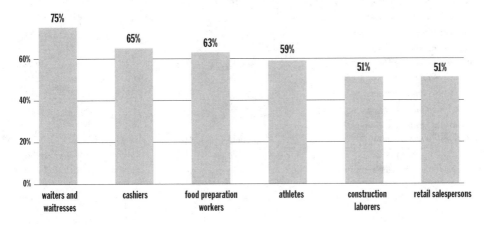

Table 5.6 Occupations of Workers under Age 35, 2005

(number of employed workers aged 16 or older, median age of workers, and number of workers under age 35, by occupation, 2005; numbers in thousands)

	total	median age	16 to 19	20 to 24	25 to 34
TOTAL WORKERS	**141,730**	**40.7**	**5,978**	**13,792**	**30,680**
Management and professional occupations	**49,245**	**43.1**	**355**	**2,587**	**10,890**
Management, business and financial operations	20,450	44.3	58	775	3,959
Management	14,685	45.1	45	448	2,520
Business and financial operations	5,765	42.1	13	327	1,439
Professional and related occupations	28,795	42.2	297	1,812	6,931
Computer and mathematical	3,246	39.4	15	189	1,061
Architecture and engineering	2,793	42.3	14	162	637
Life, physical, and social sciences	1,406	41.6	11	101	364
Community and social services	2,138	44.0	17	115	482
Legal	1,614	43.9	2	51	354
Education, training, and library	8,114	43.0	111	574	1,837
Arts, design, entertainment, sports, and media	2,736	40.5	94	252	674
Health care practitioner and technician	6,748	42.9	33	368	1,522
Service occupations	**23,133**	**36.9**	**2,275**	**3,410**	**4,904**
Health care support	3,092	38.4	98	447	739
Protective service	2,894	40.6	97	211	714
Food preparation and serving	7,374	28.6	1,477	1,658	1,507
Building and grounds cleaning and maintenance	5,241	41.5	258	491	978
Personal care and service	4,531	38.6	344	603	966
Sales and office occupations	**35,962**	**39.9**	**2,247**	**4,393**	**7,211**
Sales and related occupations	16,433	39.1	1,417	2,105	3,167
Office and administrative support	19,529	40.5	830	2,288	4,044
Natural resources, construction, and maintenance occupations	**15,348**	**38.9**	**465**	**1,710**	**3,878**
Farming, fishing, and forestry	976	36.8	91	140	215
Construction and extraction	9,145	38.0	273	1,106	2,482
Installation, maintenance, and repair	5,226	40.8	102	464	1,181
Production, transportation, and material-moving occupations	**18,041**	**41.0**	**636**	**1,692**	**3,796**
Production	9,378	41.5	221	811	1,976
Transportation and material moving	8,664	40.5	415	881	1,820

Source: Bureau of Labor Statistics, unpublished data from the 2005 Current Population Survey; calculations by New Strategist

Table 5.7　Distribution of Workers under Age 35 by Occupation, 2005

(percent distribution of employed people aged 16 or older and under age 35 by occupation, 2005)

	total	16 to 19	20 to 24	25 to 34
TOTAL WORKERS	**100.0%**	**4.2%**	**9.7%**	**21.6%**
Management and professional occupations	**100.0**	**0.7**	**5.3**	**22.1**
Management, business and financial operations	100.0	0.3	3.8	19.4
Management	100.0	0.3	3.1	17.2
Business and financial operations	100.0	0.2	5.7	25.0
Professional and related occupations	100.0	1.0	6.3	24.1
Computer and mathematical	100.0	0.5	5.8	32.7
Architecture and engineering	100.0	0.5	5.8	22.8
Life, physical, and social sciences	100.0	0.8	7.2	25.9
Community and social services	100.0	0.8	5.4	22.5
Legal	100.0	0.1	3.2	21.9
Education, training, and library	100.0	1.4	7.1	22.6
Arts, design, entertainment, sports, and media	100.0	3.4	9.2	24.6
Health care practitioner and technician	100.0	0.5	5.5	22.6
Service occupations	**100.0**	**9.8**	**14.7**	**21.2**
Health care support	100.0	3.2	14.5	23.9
Protective service	100.0	3.4	7.3	24.7
Food preparation and serving	100.0	20.0	22.5	20.4
Building and grounds cleaning and maintenance	100.0	4.9	9.4	18.7
Personal care and service	100.0	7.6	13.3	21.3
Sales and office occupations	**100.0**	**6.2**	**12.2**	**20.1**
Sales and related occupations	100.0	8.6	12.8	19.3
Office and administrative support	100.0	4.3	11.7	20.7
Natural resources, construction, maintenance occupations	**100.0**	**3.0**	**11.1**	**25.3**
Farming, fishing, and forestry	100.0	9.3	14.3	22.0
Construction and extraction	100.0	3.0	12.1	27.1
Installation, maintenance, and repair	100.0	2.0	8.9	22.6
Production, transportation, material-moving occupations	**100.0**	**3.5**	**9.4**	**21.0**
Production	100.0	2.4	8.6	21.1
Transportation and material moving	100.0	4.8	10.2	21.0

Source: Calculations by New Strategist based on Bureau of Labor Statistics' unpublished 2005 Current Population Survey data

Table 5.8 Share of Workers under Age 35 by Occupation, 2005

(percent distribution of total employed and employed under age 35, by occupation, 2005)

	total	16 to 19	20 to 24	25 to 34
TOTAL WORKERS	100.0%	100.0%	100.0%	100.0%
Management and professional occupations	**34.7**	**5.9**	**18.8**	**35.5**
Management, business and financial operations	14.4	1.0	5.6	12.9
Management	10.4	0.8	3.2	8.2
Business and financial operations	4.1	0.2	2.4	4.7
Professional and related occupations	20.3	5.0	13.1	22.6
Computer and mathematical	2.3	0.3	1.4	3.5
Architecture and engineering	2.0	0.2	1.2	2.1
Life, physical, and social sciences	1.0	0.2	0.7	1.2
Community and social services	1.5	0.3	0.8	1.6
Legal	1.1	0.0	0.4	1.2
Education, training, and library	5.7	1.9	4.2	6.0
Arts, design, entertainment, sports, and media	1.9	1.6	1.8	2.2
Health care practitioner and technician	4.8	0.6	2.7	5.0
Service occupations	**16.3**	**38.1**	**24.7**	**16.0**
Health care support	2.2	1.6	3.2	2.4
Protective service	2.0	1.6	1.5	2.3
Food preparation and serving	5.2	24.7	12.0	4.9
Building and grounds cleaning and maintenance	3.7	4.3	3.6	3.2
Personal care and service	3.2	5.8	4.4	3.1
Sales and office occupations	**25.4**	**37.6**	**31.9**	**23.5**
Sales and related occupations	11.6	23.7	15.3	10.3
Office and administrative support	13.8	13.9	16.6	13.2
Natural resources, construction, maintenance occupations	**10.8**	**7.8**	**12.4**	**12.6**
Farming, fishing, and forestry	0.7	1.5	1.0	0.7
Construction and extraction	6.5	4.6	8.0	8.1
Installation, maintenance, and repair	3.7	1.7	3.4	3.8
Production, transportation, material-moving occupations	**12.7**	**10.6**	**12.3**	**12.4**
Production	6.6	3.7	5.9	6.4
Transportation and material moving	6.1	6.9	6.4	5.9

Source: Calculations by New Strategist based on Bureau of Labor Statistics' unpublished 2005 Current Population Survey data

Table 5.9 Workers under Age 35 by Detailed Occupation, 2005

(number of employed workers aged 16 or older, median age, and number and percent under age 35, by selected detailed occupation, 2005; numbers in thousands)

	total workers	median age	aged 16 to 19		aged 20 to 24		aged 25 to 34	
			number	percent of total	number	percent of total	number	percent of total
TOTAL WORKERS	**141,730**	**40.7**	**5,978**	**4.2%**	**13,792**	**9.7%**	**30,680**	**21.6%**
Chief executives	1,644	49.3	2	0.1	7	0.4	138	8.4
Legislators	17	54.2	–	–	1	5.9	1	5.9
Marketing and sales managers	798	41.2	1	0.1	32	4.0	198	24.8
Computer and information systems managers	351	42.5	–	–	7	2.0	68	19.4
Financial managers	1,045	42.2	2	0.2	46	4.4	241	23.1
Human resources managers	272	43.6	–	–	8	2.9	58	21.3
Farmers and ranchers	195	48.5	2	1.0	5	2.6	23	11.8
Education administrators	805	47.3	3	0.4	25	3.1	119	14.8
Food service managers	929	39.9	13	1.4	91	9.8	232	25.0
Medical and health services managers	470	47.8	–	–	4	0.9	65	13.8
Accountants and auditors	1,683	41.7	5	0.3	85	5.1	440	26.1
Computer scientists and systems analysts	745	40.6	1	0.1	38	5.1	222	29.8
Computer programmers	581	39.6	3	0.5	34	5.9	179	30.8
Computer software engineers	832	39.3	2	0.2	40	4.8	272	32.7
Architects	235	45.3	–	–	6	2.6	57	24.3
Civil engineers	319	43.3	–	–	17	5.3	72	22.6
Electrical engineers	352	42.1	–	–	12	3.4	75	21.3
Mechanical engineers	318	42.2	–	–	16	5.0	76	23.9
Medical scientists	125	37.6	–	–	9	7.2	46	36.8
Psychologists	188	50.7	–	–	2	1.1	27	14.4
Social workers	670	42.9	2	0.3	31	4.6	183	27.3
Clergy	435	48.2	–	–	20	4.6	53	12.2
Lawyers	961	45.4	1	0.1	6	0.6	183	19.0
Postsecondary teachers	1,185	45.1	5	0.4	87	7.3	254	21.4
Preschool and kindergarten teachers	719	38.2	13	1.8	95	13.2	206	28.7
Elementary and middle school teachers	2,616	43.1	3	0.1	128	4.9	674	25.8
Secondary school teachers	1,136	44.1	1	0.1	44	3.9	295	26.0
Librarians	214	50.3	1	0.5	10	4.7	26	12.1
Teacher assistants	947	42.6	30	3.2	85	9.0	131	13.8
Artists	234	44.0	3	1.3	10	4.3	54	23.1
Actors	41	34.7	3	7.3	7	17.1	10	24.4
Athletes	273	31.0	47	17.2	54	19.8	59	21.6
Editors	150	41.8	–	–	12	8.0	38	25.3
Writers and authors	178	47.5	–	–	8	4.5	32	18.0
Dentists	164	48.2	–	–	–	–	29	17.7
Pharmacists	248	42.6	–	–	14	5.6	71	28.6
Physicians and surgeons	830	44.9	–	–	4	0.5	164	19.8
Registered nurses	2,416	44.6	2	0.1	87	3.6	462	19.1
Physical therapists	177	39.9	–	–	6	3.4	57	32.2
Licensed practical nurses	510	43.8	1	0.2	29	5.7	107	21.0
Nursing, psychiatric, and home health aides	1,900	39.4	54	2.8	272	14.3	423	22.3

(continued)

	total workers	median age	aged 16 to 19		aged 20 to 24		aged 25 to 34	
			number	percent of total	number	percent of total	number	percent of total
Firefighters	243	38.2	1	0.4%	13	5.3%	85	35.0%
Police and sheriff's patrol officers	677	39.2	1	0.1	30	4.4	233	34.4
Security guards, gaming surveillance officers	814	42.5	14	1.7	94	11.5	175	21.5
Chefs and head cooks	317	37.5	8	2.5	39	12.3	93	29.3
Cooks	1,838	32.9	269	14.6	322	17.5	407	22.1
Food preparation workers	664	27.6	164	24.7	137	20.6	119	17.9
Waiters and waitresses	1,927	24.4	395	20.5	639	33.2	407	21.1
Janitors and building cleaners	2,074	43.2	118	5.7	179	8.6	320	15.4
Maids and housekeeping cleaners	1,382	42.2	37	2.7	99	7.2	255	18.5
Grounds maintenance workers	1,187	36.1	96	8.1	185	15.6	290	24.4
Hairdressers, hair stylists, cosmetologists	738	39.5	12	1.6	87	11.8	179	24.3
Child care workers	1,329	36.8	158	11.9	185	13.9	277	20.8
Cashiers	3,075	25.8	832	27.1	687	22.3	485	15.8
Retail salespersons	3,248	34.5	411	12.7	648	20.0	591	18.2
Insurance sales agents	531	44.7	3	0.6	30	5.6	113	21.3
Securities, commodities, and financial services sales agents	392	39.7	3	0.8	35	8.9	110	28.1
Sales representatives, wholesale and manufacturing	1,379	42.7	17	1.2	62	4.5	291	21.1
Real estate brokers and sales agents	995	47.5	8	0.8	51	5.1	147	14.8
Bookkeeping, accounting, auditing clerks	1,456	45.0	16	1.1	89	6.1	254	17.4
Customer service representatives	1,833	35.8	115	6.3	288	15.7	502	27.4
Receptionists and information clerks	1,376	36.9	135	9.8	240	17.4	273	19.8
Stock clerks and order fillers	1,461	32.4	200	13.7	295	20.2	289	19.8
Secretaries and administrative assistants	3,499	44.0	41	1.2	256	7.3	619	17.7
Miscellaneous agricultural workers	698	34.5	82	11.7	111	15.9	163	23.4
Carpenters	1,797	37.4	46	2.6	233	13.0	517	28.8
Construction laborers	1,491	34.6	90	6.0	250	16.8	422	28.3
Automotive service technicians, mechanics	954	38.6	22	2.3	118	12.4	223	23.4
Miscellaneous assemblers and fabricators	1,107	39.8	35	3.2	121	10.9	265	23.9
Machinists	420	44.7	3	0.7	18	4.3	76	18.1
Aircraft pilots and flight engineers	121	44.9	–	–	2	1.7	21	17.4
Driver/sales workers and truck drivers	3,409	42.4	53	1.6	231	6.8	726	21.3
Freight, stock, material movers, hand laborers	1,806	33.1	224	12.4	317	17.6	429	23.8

Note: "–" means number is less than 500 or sample is too small to make a reliable estimate.
Source: Bureau of Labor Statistics, unpublished tables from the 2005 Current Population Survey; calculations by New Strategist

The Youngest Workers Are Mostly Part-Timers

Among 20-to-24-year-olds, however, most work full-time.

Among people aged 16 or older in the civilian labor force, 11 percent of men and 25 percent of women work part-time. Among 16- and 17-year-olds workers, however, 83 percent of men and 89 percent of women hold part-time jobs. Most are high school students with after-school jobs in such places as fast-food restaurants.

Among 18-to-19-year-olds in the labor force, the 61 percent majority of women works part-time but the 51 percent majority of men works full-time. Women in the age group are more likely than their male counterparts to work part-time because they are more likely to be in college.

Among 20-to-24-year-old workers in the labor force, the majority of both men and women has a full-time job. Nevertheless, a substantial 21 percent of men and 34 percent of women work part-time. In the 25-to-34 age group, only 6 percent of male workers and 19 percent of female workers are part-timers.

■ As more high school graduates go to college, part-time work is becoming increasingly important in the educational plans of young adults.

Part-time work is common among teens

(percent of people aged 16 to 24 in the civilian labor force who work part-time, by sex, 2005)

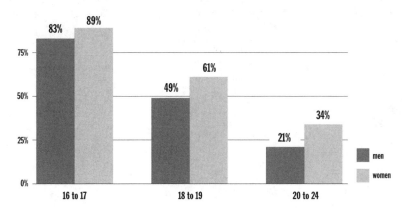

Table 5.10 Full- and Part-Time Workers by Age and Sex, 2005

(number and percent distribution of employed people aged 16 or older in the civilian labor force by age, sex, and employment status, 2005; numbers in thousands)

	men			women		
	total	full-time	part-time	total	full-time	part-time
Total employed	**80,033**	**71,302**	**8,731**	**69,288**	**51,890**	**17,398**
Aged 16 to 17	1,368	237	1,131	1,457	166	1,291
Aged 18 to 19	2,222	1,143	1,079	2,117	820	1,297
Aged 20 to 24	8,054	6,324	1,730	7,073	4,684	2,389
Aged 25 to 34	17,837	16,785	1,052	14,503	11,695	2,808
Aged 35 or older	50,552	46,813	3,739	44,137	34,524	9,613

PERCENT DISTRIBUTION BY AGE

	men			women		
Total employed	**100.0%**	**100.0%**	**100.0%**	**100.0%**	**100.0%**	**100.0%**
Aged 16 to 17	1.7	0.3	13.0	2.1	0.3	7.4
Aged 18 to 19	2.8	1.6	12.4	3.1	1.6	7.5
Aged 20 to 24	10.1	8.9	19.8	10.2	9.0	13.7
Aged 25 to 34	22.3	23.5	12.0	20.9	22.5	16.1
Aged 35 or older	63.2	65.7	42.8	63.7	66.5	55.3

PERCENT DISTRIBUTION BY EMPLOYMENT STATUS

	men			women		
Total employed	**100.0%**	**89.1%**	**10.9%**	**100.0%**	**74.9%**	**25.1%**
Aged 16 to 17	100.0	17.3	82.7	100.0	11.4	88.6
Aged 18 to 19	100.0	51.4	48.6	100.0	38.7	61.3
Aged 20 to 24	100.0	78.5	21.5	100.0	66.2	33.8
Aged 25 to 34	100.0	94.1	5.9	100.0	80.6	19.4
Aged 35 or older	100.0	92.6	7.4	100.0	78.2	21.8

Source: Unpublished data from the 2005 Current Population Survey, Bureau of Labor Statistics; calculations by New Strategist

Few Millennials Are Self-Employed

Self-employment rises with age and experience.

Although many teens and young adults may dream of being their own boss, few are able to do so. Among the nation's 142 million employed workers, only 7.4 percent are self-employed. Among workers under age 25, the figure ranges from 1 to 2 percent. It rises to 5.3 percent among those aged 25 to 34.

As people age, the percentage of the self-employed rises. Nine percent of workers aged 35 or older are self-employed. Self-employment increases with age because it takes years of experience to gain marketable skills.

■ Self-employment is becoming a more difficult proposition for Americans because the cost of buying private health insurance can be prohibitive, especially for those starting businesses.

Self-employment rises with age

(percent of workers who are self-employed, by age, 2005)

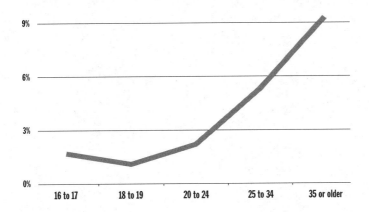

Table 5.11 Self-Employed Workers by Sex and Age, 2005

(number of employed workers aged 16 or older, number and percent who are self-employed, and percent distribution of self-employed, by age, 2005; numbers in thousands)

	total	self-employed number	self-employed percent	percent distribution
Total workers aged 16 or older	**141,729**	**10,464**	**7.4%**	**100.0%**
Aged 16 to 17	2,284	38	1.7	0.4
Aged 18 to 19	3,693	41	1.1	0.4
Aged 20 to 24	13,792	310	2.2	3.0
Aged 25 to 34	30,680	1,612	5.3	15.4
Aged 35 or older	91,282	8,463	9.3	80.9
Total men aged 16 or older	**75,973**	**6,632**	**8.7**	**100.0**
Aged 16 to 17	1,068	26	2.4	0.4
Aged 18 to 19	1,855	29	1.6	0.4
Aged 20 to 24	7,278	220	3.0	3.3
Aged 25 to 34	16,993	991	5.8	14.9
Aged 35 or older	48,780	5,367	11.0	80.9
Total women aged 16 or older	**65,757**	**3,832**	**5.8**	**100.0**
Aged 16 to 17	1,216	11	0.9	0.3
Aged 18 to 19	1,839	12	0.7	0.3
Aged 20 to 24	6,513	91	1.4	2.4
Aged 25 to 34	13,687	622	4.5	16.2
Aged 35 or older	42,501	3,096	7.3	80.8

Source: Bureau of Labor Statistics, 2005 Current Population Survey, Internet site http://www.bls.gov/cps/home.htm; calculations by New Strategist

Few Young Adults Have Alternative Work Arrangements

But the young are more likely than average to be on-call workers.

Among the nation's 15 million alternative workers, only about 1.2 million (8.5 percent) are under age 25. The Bureau of Labor Statistics defines alternative workers as independent contractors, on-call workers (such as substitute teachers), temporary-help agency workers, and people who work for contract firms (such as lawn or janitorial service companies).

Among all age groups, the most popular alternative work arrangement is independent contracting—which includes most of the self-employed. Among the nation's alternative workers, 70 percent are independent contractors. But independent contractors account for only 35 percent of alternative workers under age 25. A larger 39 percent are on-call workers—such as substitute teachers and construction workers supplied by union hiring halls. People under age 25 are more likely than average to be on-call workers.

The percentage of workers with alternative work arrangements rises with age as independent contracting becomes more popular. Twelve percent of workers aged 35 or older have an alternative work arrangement, and 9 percent are independent contractors.

■ Older workers have more skills and experience, which makes it easier for them to earn a living by self-employment.

Few young workers are independent contractors

(percent of employed workers who are independent contractors, by age, 2005)

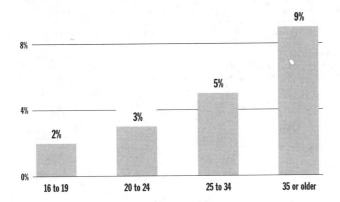

Table 5.12 Alternative Work Arrangements by Age, 2005

(number and percent distribution of employed people aged 16 or older by age and work arrangement, 2005; numbers in thousands)

	total employed	total in traditional arrangements	alternative workers				
			total	independent contractors	on-call workers	temporary-help agency workers	workers provided by contract firms
Total people	**138,952**	**123,843**	**14,826**	**10,342**	**2,454**	**1,217**	**813**
Aged 16 to 19	5,510	5,194	262	89	133	33	7
Aged 20 to 24	13,114	12,055	1,000	356	355	202	87
Aged 25 to 34	30,103	27,427	2,622	1,520	535	362	205
Aged 35 or older	90,225	79,167	10,942	8,377	1,430	621	514

PERCENT DISTRIBUTION BY ALTERNATIVE WORK STATUS

Total people	**100.0%**	**89.1%**	**10.7%**	**7.4%**	**1.8%**	**0.9%**	**0.6%**
Aged 16 to 19	100.0	94.3	4.8	1.6	2.4	0.6	0.1
Aged 20 to 24	100.0	91.9	7.6	2.7	2.7	1.5	0.7
Aged 25 to 34	100.0	91.1	8.7	5.0	1.8	1.2	0.7
Aged 35 or older	100.0	87.7	12.1	9.3	1.6	0.7	0.6

PERCENT DISTRIBUTION BY AGE

Total people	**100.0%**	**100.0%**	**100.0%**	**100.0%**	**100.0%**	**100.0%**	**100.0%**
Aged 16 to 19	4.0	4.2	1.8	0.9	5.4	2.7	0.9
Aged 20 to 24	9.4	9.7	6.7	3.4	14.5	16.6	10.7
Aged 25 to 34	21.7	22.1	17.7	14.7	21.8	29.7	25.2
Aged 35 or older	64.9	63.9	73.8	81.0	58.3	51.0	63.2

Note: Numbers may not add to total because the total employed include day laborers, an alternative arrangement not shown separately, and a small number of workers were both "on call" and "provided by contract firms." Independent contractors are workers who obtain customers on their own to provide a product or service, including the self-employed. On-call workers are in a pool of workers who are called to work only as needed, such as substitute teachers and construction workers supplied by a union hiring hall. Temporary-help agency workers are those who said they are paid by a temporary-help agency. Workers provided by contract firms are those employed by a company that provides employees or their services under contract, such as security, landscaping, and computer programming.
Source: Bureau of Labor Statistics, Contingent and Alternative Employment Arrangements, February 2005, Internet site http:// www.bls.gov/news.release/conemp.t05.htm; calculations by New Strategist

Many Workers Have Flexible Schedules

Young women are more likely than young men to have a flexible schedule.

Twenty-seven percent of the nation's wage and salary workers have a flexible work schedule—meaning they can vary the time they begin or end work, according to the Bureau of Labor Statistics. Among young adults, women are more likely than men to have a flexible work schedule.

Males aged 16 to 24 are least likely to have a flexible work schedule. Only 20 to 21 percent of men in the age group who work full-time have a flexible schedule versus 28 percent of all men who work full-time. Among their female counterparts, a larger 26 to 29 percent have a flexible schedule.

Fifteen percent of wage and salary workers do not work a regular daytime schedule. The youngest workers are most likely to be shift workers—22 percent of those aged 20 to 24 work the evening, night, or other shift, with evening being most common. The percentage of workers who do not have a regular daytime schedule falls to 15 percent in the 25-to-34 age group.

■ Younger workers are less likely to work a regular daytime shift because many are students in school during the day.

Many young adults do not work a regular daytime shift

(percent of full-time wage and salary workers who do not work a regular, daytime shift, by age, 2004)

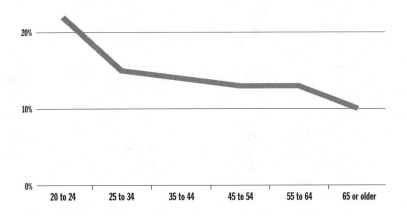

Table 5.13 Workers with Flexible Work Schedules by Sex and Age, 2004

(total number of full-time wage and salary workers aged 16 or older and number and percent with flexible work schedules, by sex and age, 2004; numbers in thousands)

	total	with flexible schedules number	with flexible schedules percent
Total full-time wage and salary workers	**99,778**	**27,411**	**27.5%**
Aged 16 to 19	1,427	336	23.5
Aged 20 to 24	9,004	2,058	22.9
Aged 25 to 34	24,640	6,902	28.0
Aged 35 or older	64,707	18,114	28.0
Total men	**56,412**	**15,853**	**28.1**
Aged 16 to 19	903	185	20.5
Aged 20 to 24	5,147	1,065	20.7
Aged 25 to 34	14,358	4,051	28.2
Aged 35 or older	36,004	10,553	29.3
Total women	**43,366**	**11,558**	**26.7**
Aged 16 to 19	524	151	28.8
Aged 20 to 24	3,856	993	25.8
Aged 25 to 34	10,283	2,851	27.7
Aged 35 or older	28,703	7,561	26.3

Note: Flexible schedules are those that allow workers to vary the time they begin or end work.
Source: Bureau of Labor Statistics, Workers on Flexible and Shift Schedules, Internet site http://www.bls.gov/news.release/flex
.t01.htm

Table 5.14 Workers by Age and Shift Usually Worked, 2004

(total number of full-time wage and salary workers aged 20 or older and percent distribution by age and shift usually worked, 2004; numbers in thousands)

	total workers number	total workers percent	regular daytime schedule	shift schedule total	evening shift	night shift	rotating shift	employer-arranged irregular shift	split or other shift
Total aged 20 or older	98,351	100.0%	84.9%	14.6%	4.6%	3.2%	2.5%	3.0%	1.2%
Aged 20 to 24	9,004	100.0	76.8	22.3	8.8	3.7	3.3	4.6	1.8
Aged 25 to 34	24,640	100.0	84.1	15.2	5.0	3.4	2.7	2.8	1.3
Aged 35 to 44	26,766	100.0	85.4	14.1	4.1	3.2	2.5	3.1	1.1
Aged 45 to 54	24,855	100.0	86.8	12.8	3.6	3.2	2.3	2.5	1.2
Aged 55 to 64	11,745	100.0	87.1	12.5	3.8	2.6	2.0	3.0	1.1
Aged 65 or older	1,341	100.0	88.8	10.3	3.5	1.8	1.4	2.9	0.7

Source: Bureau of Labor Statistics, Workers on Flexible and Shift Schedules, Internet site http://www.bls.gov/news.release/flex
.t04.htm

Most Minimum-Wage Workers Are Teens and Young Adults

Nearly two out of three are under age 30.

Among the nation's 74 million workers who are paid hourly rates, only 2 million (3 percent) make minimum wage or less, according to the Bureau of Labor Statistics. Of those 2 million workers, more than half (51 percent) are under age 25 and nearly two out of three (62 percent) are under age 30.

One in four minimum-wage workers (25 percent) is aged 16 to 19. Another 26 percent are aged 20 to 24. Among workers paid hourly rates in the 16-to-19 age group, 9 percent earn minimum wage or less. Among those in the 20-to-24 age group, 5 percent earn minimum wage or less.

■ Younger workers are most likely to earn minimum wage or less because many are in entry-level jobs.

Teens and young adults account for the majority of minimum-wage workers

(percent distribution of workers making minimum wage or less, by age, 2004)

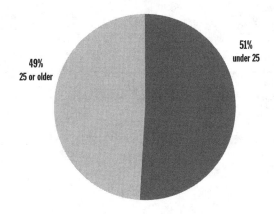

49%
25 or older

51%
under 25

Table 5.15 Workers Earning Minimum Wage by Age, 2004

(number and percent distribution of workers paid hourly rates at or below minimum wage, by age, 2004; numbers in thousands)

	total paid hourly rates	at or below minimum wage		
		total	at $5.15/hour	below $5.15/hour
Total aged 16 or older	**73,939**	**2,003**	**520**	**1,483**
Under age 30	24,623	1,246	305	941
Aged 16 to 19	5,433	497	168	329
Aged 20 to 24	10,741	523	103	420
Aged 25 to 29	8,449	226	34	192
Aged 30 or older	49,314	755	214	541
PERCENT DISTRIBUTION BY AGE				
Total aged 16 or older	**100.0%**	**100.0%**	**100.0%**	**100.0%**
Under age 30	33.3	62.2	58.7	63.5
Aged 16 to 19	7.3	24.8	32.3	22.2
Aged 20 to 24	14.5	26.1	19.8	28.3
Aged 25 to 29	11.4	11.3	6.5	12.9
Aged 30 or older	66.7	37.7	41.2	36.5
PERCENT DISTRIBUTION BY WAGE STATUS				
Total aged 16 or older	**100.0%**	**2.7%**	**0.7%**	**2.0%**
Under age 30	100.0	5.1	1.2	3.8
Aged 16 to 19	100.0	9.1	3.1	6.1
Aged 20 to 24	100.0	4.9	1.0	3.9
Aged 25 to 29	100.0	2.7	0.4	2.3
Aged 30 or older	100.0	1.5	0.4	1.1

Source: Bureau of Labor Statistics, Characteristics of Minimum Wage Workers, 2004, Internet site http://www.bls.gov/cps/minwage2004.htm; calculations by New Strategist

Few Millennials Are Represented by a Union

Men are more likely than women to be represented by a union.

Union representation has fallen sharply over the past few decades. In 2005, only 14 percent of employed wage and salary workers were represented by a union.

The percentage of workers represented by a union peaks in the 45-to-64 age group at 18 percent. Men are more likely than women to be represented by a union because men are more likely to work in manufacturing—the traditional stronghold of labor unions. In fact, the decline of labor unions is partly the result of the shift in jobs from manufacturing to services. Among workers under age 25, only 6 percent of men and 4 percent of women are represented by a union.

■ Union representation may rise along with workers' concerns about the cost of health care coverage.

Few workers are represented by a union

(percent of employed wage and salary workers who are represented by unions, by age, 2005)

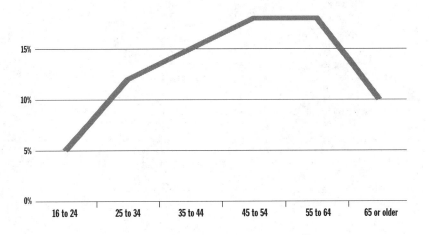

Table 5.16 Union Representation by Sex and Age, 2005

(number and percent of employed wage and salary workers aged 16 or older by union representation status, sex, and age, 2005; numbers in thousands)

	total employed	represented by unions	
		number	percent
Total aged 16 or older	**125,889**	**17,223**	**13.7%**
Aged 16 to 24	19,283	1,019	5.3
Aged 25 to 34	28,450	3,368	11.8
Aged 35 to 44	30,654	4,579	14.9
Aged 45 to 54	28,714	5,158	18.0
Aged 55 to 64	15,158	2,732	18.0
Aged 65 or older	3,631	366	10.1
Men aged 16 or older	**65,466**	**9,597**	**14.7**
Aged 16 to 24	9,860	603	6.1
Aged 25 to 34	15,559	1,915	12.3
Aged 35 to 44	16,196	2,582	15.9
Aged 45 to 54	14,421	2,849	19.8
Aged 55 to 64	7,606	1,458	19.2
Aged 65 or older	1,824	190	10.4
Women aged 16 or older	**60,423**	**7,626**	**12.6**
Aged 16 to 24	9,423	417	4.4
Aged 25 to 34	12,891	1,454	11.3
Aged 35 to 44	14,457	1,997	13.8
Aged 45 to 54	14,293	2,309	16.2
Aged 55 to 64	7,552	1,274	16.9
Aged 65 or older	1,806	176	9.8

Note: Workers represented by unions are either members of a labor union or similar employee association or workers who report no union affiliation but whose jobs are covered by a union or an employee association contract.
Source: Bureau of Labor Statistics, 2005 Current Population Survey, Internet site http://www.bls.gov/cps/home.htm

The Millennial Generation Will Expand the Labor Force

The number of workers aged 25 to 34 will increase substantially during the coming decade.

Between 2005 and 2014, the Millennial generation will fill the 25-to-34 age group (the oldest Millennials turn 37 in 2014). The number of workers aged 25 to 34 will expand by 13 percent between 2005 and 2014, adding more than 4 million to the labor force, according to the Bureau of Labor Statistics. At the same time, the number of workers aged 35 to 44 will fall by 7 percent as the small Generation X fills the age group. The labor force participation rates of men and women aged 25 to 34 are projected to increase during the coming decade, while younger adults should see a decline in labor force participation as more go to college.

The number of older workers is projected to soar during the coming decade. The Bureau of Labor Statistics projects a 59 percent increase in the number of workers aged 60 or older between 2005 and 2014 as the large Baby-Boom generation fills the older age groups.

■ The projected decline in the labor force participation rate of teenagers may be due in part to competition from their Boomer grandparents. Many older Americans will be vying for part-time jobs to supplement their meager retirement income.

The number of workers aged 25 to 34 will increase, while the number aged 35 to 44 will decline

(percent change in number of workers, by age, 2005–14)

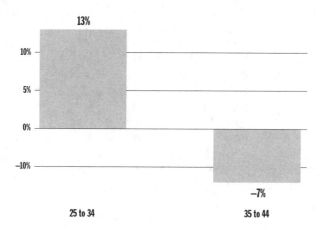

Table 5.17 Projections of the Labor Force by Sex and Age, 2005 and 2014

(number and percent of people aged 16 or older in the civilian labor force by sex and age, 2005 and 2014; percent change in number and percentage point change in participation rate, 2005–14; numbers in thousands)

	number			participation rate		
	2005	2014	percent change	2005	2014	percentage point change
Total labor force	**149,132**	**162,100**	**8.7%**	**66.0%**	**65.6%**	**–0.4**
Total men in labor force	**80,040**	**86,194**	**7.7**	**73.3**	**71.8**	**–1.5**
Aged 16 to 17	1,319	961	–27.1	30.1	23.4	–6.7
Aged 18 to 19	2,272	2,096	–7.7	57.9	53.7	–4.2
Aged 20 to 21	3,010	3,029	0.6	73.6	71.3	–2.3
Aged 22 to 24	5,078	5,304	4.5	82.8	80.6	–2.2
Aged 25 to 29	8,968	10,200	13.7	91.7	94.1	2.4
Aged 30 to 34	9,122	10,365	13.6	93.7	96.5	2.8
Aged 35 to 39	9,401	9,027	–4.0	92.7	92.0	–0.7
Aged 40 to 44	10,043	9,040	–10.0	91.0	89.5	–1.5
Aged 45 to 54	17,954	18,355	2.2	87.3	86.6	–0.7
Aged 55 to 64	9,975	13,022	30.5	68.8	68.7	–0.1
Aged 65 or older	2,898	4,795	65.5	19.4	24.6	5.2
Total women in labor force	**69,092**	**75,906**	**9.9**	**59.1**	**59.7**	**0.6**
Aged 16 to 17	1,432	1,173	–18.1	32.8	28.4	–4.4
Aged 18 to 19	2,098	2,013	–4.1	55.8	53.7	–2.1
Aged 20 to 21	2,673	2,565	–4.0	57.9	53.8	–4.1
Aged 22 to 24	4,463	5,018	12.4	81.0	83.9	2.9
Aged 25 to 29	7,140	8,073	13.1	73.5	75.2	1.7
Aged 30 to 34	7,295	8,116	11.3	74.1	75.6	1.5
Aged 35 to 39	7,730	7,395	–4.3	74.4	74.2	–0.2
Aged 40 to 44	8,741	7,882	–9.8	76.7	76.6	–0.1
Aged 45 to 54	16,278	17,172	5.5	75.7	78.1	2.4
Aged 55 to 64	8,936	12,606	41.1	57.0	61.9	4.9
Aged 65 or older	2,307	3,892	68.7	11.5	15.9	4.4

Note: Figures for 2005 are slightly different from those shown elsewhere in this chapter because they are projections rather than estimates.
Source: Bureau of Labor Statistics, Projected Labor Force Data, Internet site http://www.bls.gov/emp/emplab1.htm; calculations by New Strategist

Most Children Have Working Parents

For the Millennial and post-Millennial generations, working mothers are the norm.

Among women with children under age 18, fully 70 percent were in the labor force in 2004 (the Millennial generation was aged 10 to 27 in that year). Forty-nine percent of women with children under age 18 are employed full-time. Even among women with infants, 53 percent are in the labor force—most with full-time jobs.

In 61 percent of married couples with children under age 18, both husband and wife are employed. Seventy-two percent of women heading single-parent families have jobs, as do 84 percent of men who head single-parent families.

Because most parents work, the 61 percent majority of children aged 0 to 6 and not yet in kindergarten are in nonparental care—including 85 percent of children whose mother works 35 or more hours per week. The largest share of preschoolers (34 percent) are in center-based programs, while 23 percent are cared for by a relative and 16 percent by a nonrelative.

■ Day care is the norm for the Millennial generation while mom and dad are at work.

For most children in married-couple families, mom is at work

(percent of families with children under age 18, by family type and parents' labor force status, 2004)

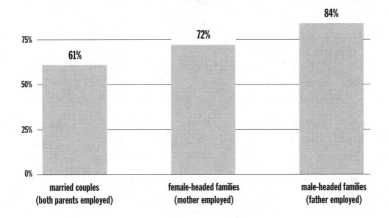

Table 5.18 Labor Force Status of Parents with Children under Age 18, 2004

(number and percent distribution of people aged 16 or older with own children under age 18 by family type, labor force status, and age of children, 2004; numbers in thousands)

		with children under age 18	
	total	aged 6 to 17, none younger	under age 6
NUMBER			
Married couples	**25,175**	**13,806**	**11,369**
One or both parents employed	24,424	13,381	11,044
Mother employed	16,557	10,089	6,468
Both parents employed	15,257	9,269	5,988
Mother employed, not father	1,300	820	481
Father employed, not mother	7,867	3,292	4,575
Neither parent employed	751	425	326
Female-headed families	**8,161**	**5,040**	**3,122**
Mother employed	5,875	3,884	1,991
Mother not employed	2,286	1,156	1,131
Male-headed families	**2,043**	**1,250**	**793**
Father employed	1,713	1,043	671
Father not employed	330	207	122
PERCENT DISTRIBUTION			
Married couples	**100.0%**	**100.0%**	**100.0%**
One or both parents employed	97.0	96.9	97.1
Mother employed	65.8	73.1	56.9
Both parents employed	60.6	67.1	52.7
Mother employed, not father	5.2	5.9	4.2
Father employed, not mother	31.2	23.8	40.2
Neither parent employed	3.0	3.1	2.9
Female-headed families	**100.0**	**100.0**	**100.0**
Mother employed	72.0	77.1	63.8
Mother not employed	28.0	22.9	36.2
Male-headed families	**100.0**	**100.0**	**100.0**
Father employed	83.8	83.4	84.6
Father not employed	16.2	16.6	15.4

Source: Bureau of Labor Statistics, Employment Characteristics of Families, Internet site http://www.bls.gov/news.release/famee.t04.htm

Table 5.19 Labor Force Status of Women by Presence of Children, 2004

(number and percent distribution of women by labor force status and presence and age of own children under age 18 at home, 2004; numbers in thousands)

| | civilian population | civilian labor force | | | | not in labor force |
| | | total | employed | | | |
			total	full-time	part-time	
Total women	**115,646**	**68,421**	**64,728**	**48,074**	**16,655**	**47,225**
No children under age 18	79,160	42,740	40,467	30,110	10,357	36,420
With children under age 18	36,486	25,681	24,261	17,964	6,298	10,805
Children aged 6 to 17, none younger	20,277	15,666	14,957	11,473	3,485	4,611
Children under age 6	16,210	10,014	9,304	6,491	2,813	6,196
Children under age 3	9,345	5,377	4,964	3,360	1,604	3,968
Children under age 1	3,259	1,725	1,575	1,035	540	1,534
Total women	**100.0%**	**59.2%**	**56.0%**	**41.6%**	**14.4%**	**40.8%**
No children under age 18	100.0	54.0	51.1	38.0	13.1	46.0
With children under age 18	100.0	70.4	66.5	49.2	17.3	29.6
Children aged 6 to 17, none younger	100.0	77.3	73.8	56.6	17.2	22.7
Children under age 6	100.0	61.8	57.4	40.0	17.4	38.2
Children under age 3	100.0	57.5	53.1	36.0	17.2	42.5
Children under age 1	100.0	52.9	48.3	31.8	16.6	47.1

Source: Bureau of Labor Statistics, Employment Characteristics of Families, Internet site http://www.bls.gov/news.release/ famee.t05.htm and http://www.bls.gov/news.release/famee.t06.htm

Table 5.20 Child Care Experiences of Children through Age 6, 2001

(percent of children aged 0 to 6 and not yet in kindergarten by type of care arrangement and child and family characteristics, 2001)

| | parental care only | nonparental care | | | |
| | | total | care in home | | center-based program |
			by a relative	by a nonrelative	
Total children aged 0 to 6, not in kindergarten	**39%**	**61%**	**23%**	**16%**	**34%**
Age					
Aged 0 to 2	48	52	23	18	17
Aged 3 to 6	26	74	22	14	56
Race and Hispanic origin					
Black, non-Hispanic	26	75	34	14	41
Hispanic	53	47	23	12	20
White, non-Hispanic	38	62	20	19	35
Other, non-Hispanic	35	65	23	15	37
Poverty status					
Below poverty level	46	54	26	10	27
At or above poverty level	37	63	22	18	35
Mother's educational attainment					
Less than high school	56	44	21	9	21
High school graduate	43	58	26	14	28
Vocational/technical or some college	37	64	25	16	36
College graduate	32	69	17	23	42
Mother's employment status					
Works 35 or more hours per week	15	85	33	26	42
Works fewer than 35 hours per week	29	71	32	20	36
Looking for work	57	43	16	9	25
Not in the labor force	68	32	6	5	24

Source: America's Children: Key National Indicators of Well-Being, 2005, Federal Interagency Forum on Child and Family Statistics, Internet site http://www.childstats.gov/americaschildren/

Living Arrangements

■ People younger than age 30 headed only 14 percent of the nation's 113 million households in 2005 (Millennials were aged 11 to 28 in that year).

■ The living arrangements of young adults depend greatly on their race and Hispanic origin. Married couples account for fully 41 percent of households headed by Hispanics under age 30 but for only 16 percent of black households in the age group.

■ Fifty-two percent of black and 54 percent of Hispanic householders under age 30 have children under age 18 at home. This compares with a smaller 33 percent of non-Hispanic whites and only 21 percent of Asians in the age group.

■ The proportion of children living with two parents ranges from a low of 35 percent among black children to a high of 82 percent among Asian children.

■ Among the nation's households with children, 89 percent include only biological children. A substantial 11 percent include step- or adopted children.

■ The majority of men and women under age 30 have never married. Among men aged 20 to 24, fully 86 percent are single. The figure is 75 percent among their female counterparts.

The Millennial Generation Heads Few Households

Only 14 percent of households are headed by people under age 30.

People younger than age 30 headed only 14 percent of the nation's 113 million households in 2005 (Millennials were aged 11 to 28 in that year). Young adults are slow to establish their own households because many are in college and still financially dependent on their parents. In addition, entry-level pay has fallen over the past few decades as inflation has eroded the minimum wage. Consequently, few young adults can afford to strike out on their own.

Households headed by young adults are extremely diverse. Married couples account for the 34 percent plurality of households headed by people under age 30. Fully 22 percent are men and women who live alone, while another 18 percent are female-headed families. Seventeen percent of householders under age 30 live with nonrelatives, many of them cohabiting with romantic partners. Nine percent of householders under age 30 are male-headed families, including 12 percent of households headed by people under age 25—the largest share held by this household type among all age groups.

■ The diversity of young adults' living arrangement makes it difficult for marketers, politicians, and community organizations to reach them.

Households headed by young adults are diverse

(percent distribution of households headed by people under age 30, by type, 2005)

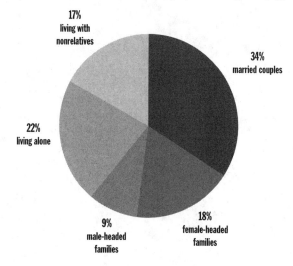

17%
living with
nonrelatives

34%
married couples

22%
living alone

9%
male-headed
families

18%
female-headed
families

Table 6.1 Households Headed by People under Age 30 by Household Type, 2005: Total Households

(number and percent distribution of total households and households headed by people under age 30, by household type, 2005; numbers in thousands)

	total	aged 15 to 29		
		total	15 to 24	25 to 29
TOTAL HOUSEHOLDS	113,146	15,831	6,686	9,145
Family households	**77,010**	**9,624**	**3,633**	**5,991**
Married couples	58,109	5,341	1,411	3,930
Female householder, no spouse present	14,009	2,872	1,437	1,435
Male householder, no spouse present	4,893	1,411	785	626
Nonfamily households	**36,136**	**6,206**	**3,052**	**3,154**
Female householder	19,792	2,799	1,497	1,302
Living alone	17,207	1,655	756	899
Male householder	16,344	3,407	1,555	1,852
Living alone	12,652	1,859	746	1,113
PERCENT DISTRIBUTION BY TYPE				
TOTAL HOUSEHOLDS	100.0%	100.0%	100.0%	100.0%
Family households	**68.1**	**60.8**	**54.3**	**65.5**
Married couples	51.4	33.7	21.1	43.0
Female householder, no spouse present	12.4	18.1	21.5	15.7
Male householder, no spouse present	4.3	8.9	11.7	6.8
Nonfamily households	**31.9**	**39.2**	**45.6**	**34.5**
Female householder	17.5	17.7	22.4	14.2
Living alone	15.2	10.5	11.3	9.8
Male householder	14.4	21.5	23.3	20.3
Living alone	11.2	11.7	11.2	12.2
PERCENT DISTRIBUTION BY AGE				
TOTAL HOUSEHOLDS	100.0%	14.0%	5.9%	8.1%
Family households	**100.0**	**12.5**	**4.7**	**7.8**
Married couples	100.0	9.2	2.4	6.8
Female householder, no spouse present	100.0	20.5	10.3	10.2
Male householder, no spouse present	100.0	28.8	16.0	12.8
Nonfamily households	**100.0**	**17.2**	**8.4**	**8.7**
Female householder	100.0	14.1	7.6	6.6
Living alone	100.0	9.6	4.4	5.2
Male householder	100.0	20.8	9.5	11.3
Living alone	100.0	14.7	5.9	8.8

Source: Bureau of the Census, 2005 Current Population Survey, Annual Social and Economic Supplement, Internet site http://pubdb3.census.gov/macro/032005/hhinc/new02_000.htm

Young Adult Households Differ by Race and Hispanic Origin

A large share of the nation's young married couples are Hispanic.

Non-Hispanic whites account for the 61 percent majority of householders under age 30, but the figure varies greatly by type of household. Non-Hispanic whites account for 69 percent of nonfamily householders under age 30, but for only 42 percent of female-headed families in the age group. Among married couples under age 30, Hispanics head 21 percent and blacks just 7 percent.

Female-headed families account for the 39 percent plurality of black households headed by young adults. In contrast only 12 percent of Asian and non-Hispanic white households under age 30 are female-headed families. Married couples account for the 41 percent plurality of households headed by Hispanic young adults, but for only 16 percent of black households in the age group.

Among young adults, nonfamilies (people who live alone or with nonrelatives) account for 44 percent of households headed by non-Hispanic whites and 45 percent of households headed by Asians. In contrast, they account for only 24 percent of households headed by Hispanics and 36 percent of those headed by blacks.

■ Young adults have differing wants and needs depending on their living arrangements.

Hispanic young adults are least likely to live alone

(percent of householders under age 30 who live alone, by race and Hispanic origin, 2005)

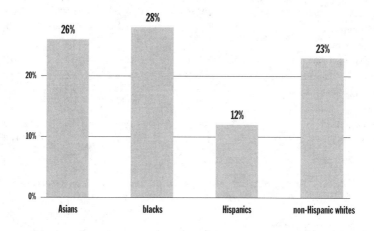

Table 6.2 Households Headed by People under Age 30 by Household Type, Race, and Hispanic Origin, 2005

(number and percent distribution of households headed by people under age 30, by household type, race, and Hispanic origin, 2005; numbers in thousands)

	total	Asian	black	Hispanic	non-Hispanic white
TOTAL HOUSEHOLDERS					
UNDER AGE 30	**15,831**	**701**	**2,464**	**2,805**	**9,712**
Family households	**9,624**	**387**	**1,585**	**2,121**	**5,456**
Married couples	5,341	195	398	1,138	3,569
Female householder, no spouse present	2,872	85	965	589	1,209
Male householder, no spouse present	1,411	107	222	393	678
Nonfamily households	**6,206**	**315**	**879**	**684**	**4,255**
Female householder	2,799	149	519	212	1,884
Living alone	1,655	94	418	141	979
Male householder	3,407	166	360	472	2,371
Living alone	1,859	90	265	204	1,277
PERCENT DISTRIBUTION BY RACE AND HISPANIC ORIGIN					
TOTAL HOUSEHOLDERS					
UNDER AGE 30	**100.0%**	**4.4%**	**15.6%**	**17.7%**	**61.3%**
Family households	**100.0**	**4.0**	**16.5**	**22.0**	**56.7**
Married couples	100.0	3.7	7.5	21.3	66.8
Female householder, no spouse present	100.0	3.0	33.6	20.5	42.1
Male householder, no spouse present	100.0	7.6	15.7	27.9	48.1
Nonfamily households	**100.0**	**5.1**	**14.2**	**11.0**	**68.6**
Female householder	100.0	5.3	18.5	7.6	67.3
Living alone	100.0	5.7	25.3	8.5	59.2
Male householder	100.0	4.9	10.6	13.9	69.6
Living alone	100.0	4.8	14.3	11.0	68.7

Note: Numbers will not add to total because Asians and blacks include those identifying themselves as being of the respective race alone and those identifying themselves as being of the race in combination with other races. Non-Hispanic whites include only those identifying themselves as being white alone and not Hispanic. Hispanics may be of any race.
Source: Bureau of the Census, 2005 Current Population Survey, Annual Social and Economic Supplement, Internet site http://pubdb3.census.gov/macro/032005/hhinc/new02_000.htm; calculations by New Strategist

Table 6.3 Households Headed by People under Age 30 by Household Type, 2005: Asian Households

(number and percent distribution of total households headed by Asians and households headed by Asians under age 30, by household type, 2005; numbers in thousands)

	total	aged 15 to 29 total	15 to 24	25 to 29
TOTAL ASIAN HOUSEHOLDS	**4,360**	**701**	**274**	**427**
Family households	**3,295**	**387**	**143**	**244**
Married couples	2,649	195	32	163
Female householder, no spouse present	385	85	49	36
Male householder, no spouse present	261	107	62	45
Nonfamily households	**1,065**	**315**	**132**	**183**
Female householder	558	149	68	81
Living alone	463	94	38	56
Male householder	507	166	64	102
Living alone	372	90	28	62
PERCENT DISTRIBUTION BY TYPE				
TOTAL ASIAN HOUSEHOLDS	**100.0%**	**100.0%**	**100.0%**	**100.0%**
Family households	**75.6**	**55.2**	**52.2**	**57.1**
Married couples	60.8	27.8	11.7	38.2
Female householder, no spouse present	8.8	12.1	17.9	8.4
Male householder, no spouse present	6.0	15.3	22.6	10.5
Nonfamily households	**24.4**	**44.9**	**48.2**	**42.9**
Female householder	12.8	21.3	24.8	19.0
Living alone	10.6	13.4	13.9	13.1
Male householder	11.6	23.7	23.4	23.9
Living alone	8.5	12.8	10.2	14.5
PERCENT DISTRIBUTION BY AGE				
TOTAL ASIAN HOUSEHOLDS	**100.0%**	**16.1%**	**6.3%**	**9.8%**
Family households	**100.0**	**11.7**	**4.3**	**7.4**
Married couples	100.0	7.4	1.2	6.2
Female householder, no spouse present	100.0	22.1	12.7	9.4
Male householder, no spouse present	100.0	41.0	23.8	17.2
Nonfamily households	**100.0**	**29.6**	**12.4**	**17.2**
Female householder	100.0	26.7	12.2	14.5
Living alone	100.0	20.3	8.2	12.1
Male householder	100.0	32.7	12.6	20.1
Living alone	100.0	24.2	7.5	16.7

Note: Asians include those identifying themselves as being of the race alone and those identifying themselves as being of the race in combination with other races.
Source: Bureau of the Census, 2005 Current Population Survey, Annual Social and Economic Supplement, Internet site http:// pubdb3.census.gov/macro/032005/hhinc/new02_000.htm; calculations by New Strategist

Table 6.4   Households Headed by People under Age 30 by Household Type, 2005: Black Households

(number and percent distribution of total households headed by blacks and households headed by blacks under age 30, by household type, 2005; numbers in thousands)

	total	aged 15 to 29 total	15 to 24	25 to 29
TOTAL BLACK HOUSEHOLDS	**14,127**	**2,464**	**1,126**	**1,338**
Family households	**9,109**	**1,585**	**705**	**880**
Married couples	4,272	398	110	288
Female householder, no spouse present	4,084	965	472	493
Male householder, no spouse present	754	222	123	99
Nonfamily households	**5,018**	**879**	**421**	**458**
Female householder	2,863	519	255	264
Living alone	2,599	418	199	219
Male householder	2,155	360	166	194
Living alone	1,833	265	107	158
PERCENT DISTRIBUTION BY TYPE				
TOTAL BLACK HOUSEHOLDS	**100.0%**	**100.0%**	**100.0%**	**100.0%**
Family households	**64.5**	**64.3**	**62.6**	**65.8**
Married couples	30.2	16.2	9.8	21.5
Female householder, no spouse present	28.9	39.2	41.9	36.8
Male householder, no spouse present	5.3	9.0	10.9	7.4
Nonfamily households	**35.5**	**35.7**	**37.4**	**34.2**
Female householder	20.3	21.1	22.6	19.7
Living alone	18.4	17.0	17.7	16.4
Male householder	15.3	14.6	14.7	14.5
Living alone	13.0	10.8	9.5	11.8
PERCENT DISTRIBUTION BY AGE				
TOTAL BLACK HOUSEHOLDS	**100.0%**	**17.4%**	**8.0%**	**9.5%**
Family households	**100.0**	**17.4**	**7.7**	**9.7**
Married couples	100.0	9.3	2.6	6.7
Female householder, no spouse present	100.0	23.6	11.6	12.1
Male householder, no spouse present	100.0	29.4	16.3	13.1
Nonfamily households	**100.0**	**17.5**	**8.4**	**9.1**
Female householder	100.0	18.1	8.9	9.2
Living alone	100.0	16.1	7.7	8.4
Male householder	100.0	16.7	7.7	9.0
Living alone	100.0	14.5	5.8	8.6

Note: Blacks include those identifying themselves as being of the race alone and those identifying themselves as being of the race in combination with other races.
Source: Bureau of the Census, 2005 Current Population Survey, Annual Social and Economic Supplement, Internet site http:// pubdb3.census.gov/macro/032005/hhinc/new02_000.htm; calculations by New Strategist

Table 6.5 Households Headed by People under Age 30 by Household Type, 2005: Hispanic Households

(number and percent distribution of total households headed by Hispanics and households headed by Hispanics under age 30, by household type, 2005; numbers in thousands)

	total	aged 15 to 29 total	15 to 24	25 to 29
TOTAL HISPANIC HOUSEHOLDS	12,181	2,805	1,209	1,596
Family households	**9,537**	**2,121**	**884**	**1,237**
Married couples	6,367	1,138	351	787
Female householder, no spouse present	2,240	589	286	303
Male householder, no spouse present	930	393	246	147
Nonfamily households	**2,644**	**684**	**325**	**359**
Female householder	1,177	212	116	96
Living alone	981	141	67	74
Male householder	1,467	472	209	263
Living alone	941	204	82	122
PERCENT DISTRIBUTION BY TYPE				
TOTAL HISPANIC HOUSEHOLDS	100.0%	100.0%	100.0%	100.0%
Family households	**78.3**	**75.6**	**73.1**	**77.5**
Married couples	52.3	40.6	29.0	49.3
Female householder, no spouse present	18.4	21.0	23.7	19.0
Male householder, no spouse present	7.6	14.0	20.3	9.2
Nonfamily households	**21.7**	**24.4**	**26.9**	**22.5**
Female householder	9.7	7.6	9.6	6.0
Living alone	8.1	5.0	5.5	4.6
Male householder	12.0	16.8	17.3	16.5
Living alone	7.7	7.3	6.8	7.6
PERCENT DISTRIBUTION BY AGE				
TOTAL HISPANIC HOUSEHOLDS	100.0%	23.0%	9.9%	13.1%
Family households	**100.0**	**22.2**	**9.3**	**13.0**
Married couples	100.0	17.9	5.5	12.4
Female householder, no spouse present	100.0	26.3	12.8	13.5
Male householder, no spouse present	100.0	42.3	26.5	15.8
Nonfamily households	**100.0**	**25.9**	**12.3**	**13.6**
Female householder	100.0	18.0	9.9	8.2
Living alone	100.0	14.4	6.8	7.5
Male householder	100.0	32.2	14.2	17.9
Living alone	100.0	21.7	8.7	13.0

Source: Bureau of the Census, 2005 Current Population Survey, Annual Social and Economic Supplement, Internet site http:// pubdb3.census.gov/macro/032005/hhinc/new02_000.htm; calculations by New Strategist

Table 6.6 Households Headed by People under Age 30 by Household Type, 2005: Non-Hispanic White Households

(number and percent distribution of total households headed by non-Hispanic whites under age 30, by household type, 2005; numbers in thousands)

		aged 15 to 29		
	total	total	15 to 24	25 to 29
TOTAL NON-HISPANIC WHITE HOUSEHOLDS	81,445	9,712	4,002	5,710
Family households	**54,383**	**5,456**	**1,862**	**3,594**
Married couples	44,296	3,569	898	2,671
Female householder, no spouse present	7,200	1,209	611	598
Male householder, no spouse present	2,888	678	353	325
Nonfamily households	**27,062**	**4,255**	**2,139**	**2,116**
Female householder	15,052	1,884	1,034	850
Living alone	13,053	979	442	537
Male householder	12,009	2,371	1,105	1,266
Living alone	9,349	1,277	522	755
PERCENT DISTRIBUTION BY TYPE				
TOTAL NON-HISPANIC WHITE HOUSEHOLDS	100.0%	100.0%	100.0%	100.0%
Family households	**66.8**	**56.2**	**46.5**	**62.9**
Married couples	54.4	36.7	22.4	46.8
Female householder, no spouse present	8.8	12.4	15.3	10.5
Male householder, no spouse present	3.5	7.0	8.8	5.7
Nonfamily households	**33.2**	**43.8**	**53.4**	**37.1**
Female householder	18.5	19.4	25.8	14.9
Living alone	16.0	10.1	11.0	9.4
Male householder	14.7	24.4	27.6	22.2
Living alone	11.5	13.1	13.0	13.2
PERCENT DISTRIBUTION BY AGE				
TOTAL NON-HISPANIC WHITE HOUSEHOLDS	100.0%	11.9%	4.9%	7.0%
Family households	**100.0**	**10.0**	**3.4**	**6.6**
Married couples	100.0	8.1	2.0	6.0
Female householder, no spouse present	100.0	16.8	8.5	8.3
Male householder, no spouse present	100.0	23.5	12.2	11.3
Nonfamily households	**100.0**	**15.7**	**7.9**	**7.8**
Female householder	100.0	12.5	6.9	5.6
Living alone	100.0	7.5	3.4	4.1
Male householder	100.0	19.7	9.2	10.5
Living alone	100.0	13.7	5.6	8.1

Note: Non-Hispanic whites include only those identifying themselves as being white alone and not Hispanic.
Source: Bureau of the Census, 2005 Current Population Survey, Annual Social and Economic Supplement, Internet site http://pubdb3.census.gov/macro/032005/hhinc/new02_000.htm; calculations by New Strategist

The Households of Young Adults Are of Average Size

Between two and three people live in the average household headed by someone under age 30.

Households headed by people under age 30 are home to an average of 2.43 to 2.91 people—close to the national average of 2.57 people. Because so many young adults live alone or with nonrelatives, they average fewer than one child per household.

Household size grows as householders age through their thirties. It peaks among householders aged 35 to 39—at 3.28 people—because this age group is most likely to have at least one child at home. As householders age into their forties and fifties, the nest empties and household size shrinks.

■ As young adults marry and have children, the nest will become increasingly crowded, fueling the real estate and home furnishings industries.

Among householders under age 30, average household size is less than three people

(average household size by age of householder, 2004)

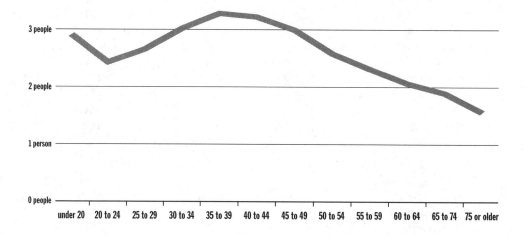

Table 6.7 Average Size of Household by Age of Householder, 2004

(number of households, average number of people per household, and average number of people under age 18 per household, by age of householder, 2004; number of households in thousands)

	number	average number of people	average number of people under age 18
Total households	**112,000**	**2.57**	**0.66**
Under age 20	837	2.91	0.84
Aged 20 to 24	5,772	2.43	0.55
Aged 25 to 29	8,738	2.66	0.85
Aged 30 to 34	10,421	3.02	1.21
Aged 35 to 39	10,997	3.28	1.42
Aged 40 to 44	12,224	3.22	1.22
Aged 45 to 49	12,360	2.99	0.82
Aged 50 to 54	10,778	2.58	0.41
Aged 55 to 59	9,504	2.31	0.23
Aged 60 to 64	7,320	2.06	0.14
Aged 65 to 74	11,499	1.89	0.08
Aged 75 or older	11,550	1.56	0.03

Source: Bureau of the Census, Current Population Survey Annual Social and Economic Supplement, America's Families and Living Arrangements: 2004, detailed tables, Internet site http://www.census.gov/population/www/socdemo/hh-fam/cps2004.html

A Minority of Young Adult Households include Children

Most black and Hispanic householders under age 30 have children at home, however.

Among all households headed by people under age 30, only 39 percent include children under age 18. The figure is a higher 65 percent for married-couple householders in the age group, and an even higher 80 percent for female-headed families.

The percentage of households that include children under age 18 varies greatly by race and Hispanic origin. Fifty-two percent of black and 54 percent of Hispanic householders under age 30 have children under age 18 at home. This compares with a smaller 33 percent of non-Hispanic whites and only 21 percent of Asians in the age group. Regardless of race or Hispanic origin, the majority of young married couples have children under age 18 at home.

■ The lifestyles of young adults are diverse, ranging from students with class schedules to parents with family and work schedules.

Few households headed by Asians under age 30 include children

(percent of householders under age 30 with children under age 18 at home, by race and Hispanic origin, 2004)

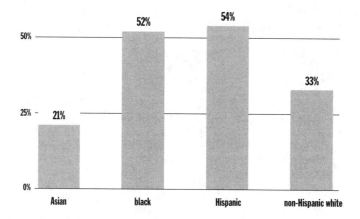

Table 6.8 Households by Type, Age of Householder, and Presence of Children, 2004: Total Households

(total number of households and number and percent with own children under age 18 at home, by household type and age of householder, 2004; numbers in thousands)

	total	with own children under age 18	
		number	percent
Total households	**112,000**	**35,944**	**32.1%**
Under age 30	15,347	6,003	39.1
Aged 15 to 19	837	150	17.9
Aged 20 to 24	5,772	1,830	31.7
Aged 25 to 29	8,738	4,023	46.0
Aged 30 to 34	10,421	6,223	59.7
Aged 35 to 54	46,359	22,428	48.4
Aged 55 or older	39,873	1,292	3.2
Married couples	**57,719**	**25,793**	**44.7**
Under age 30	5,195	3,352	64.5
Aged 15 to 19	57	43	75.4
Aged 20 to 24	1,359	786	57.8
Aged 25 to 29	3,779	2,523	66.8
Aged 30 to 34	5,794	4,469	77.1
Aged 35 to 54	27,084	16,919	62.5
Aged 55 or older	19,646	1,054	5.4
Female family householder, no spouse present	**13,781**	**8,221**	**59.7**
Under age 30	2,797	2,226	79.6
Aged 15 to 19	264	89	33.7
Aged 20 to 24	1,134	890	78.5
Aged 25 to 29	1,399	1,247	89.1
Aged 30 to 34	1,560	1,441	92.4
Aged 35 to 54	6,334	4,403	69.5
Aged 55 or older	3,090	151	4.9
Male family householder, no spouse present	**4,716**	**1,931**	**40.9**
Under age 30	1,307	426	32.6
Aged 15 to 19	223	19	8.5
Aged 20 to 24	551	155	28.1
Aged 25 to 29	533	252	47.3
Aged 30 to 34	492	313	63.6
Aged 35 to 54	2,041	1,106	54.2
Aged 55 or older	874	86	9.8

Source: Bureau of the Census, Current Population Survey Annual Social and Economic Supplement, America's Families and Living Arrangements: 2004, detailed tables, Internet site http://www.census.gov/population/www/socdemo/hh-fam/cps2004.html; calculations by New Strategist

Table 6.9 Households by Type, Age of Householder, and Presence of Children, 2004: Asian Households

(total number of Asian households and number and percent with own children under age 18 at home, by household type and age of householder, 2004; numbers in thousands)

	total	with own children under age 18	
		number	percent
Total Asian households	**4,235**	**1,711**	**40.4%**
Under age 30	696	146	21.0
Aged 15 to 19	46	4	8.7
Aged 20 to 24	240	25	10.4
Aged 25 to 29	410	117	28.5
Aged 30 to 34	602	308	51.2
Aged 35 to 54	1,850	1,181	63.8
Aged 55 or older	1,087	74	6.8
Married couples	**2,574**	**1,462**	**56.8**
Under age 30	206	105	51.0
Aged 15 to 19	2	2	100.0
Aged 20 to 24	35	17	48.6
Aged 25 to 29	169	86	50.9
Aged 30 to 34	370	256	69.2
Aged 35 to 54	1,337	1,031	77.1
Aged 55 or older	660	69	10.5
Female family householder, no spouse present	**378**	**196**	**51.9**
Under age 30	83	29	34.9
Aged 15 to 19	13	–	–
Aged 20 to 24	38	5	13.2
Aged 25 to 29	32	24	75.0
Aged 30 to 34	48	38	79.2
Aged 35 to 54	190	125	65.8
Aged 55 or older	58	4	6.9
Male family householder, no spouse present	**241**	**53**	**22.0**
Under age 30	105	12	11.4
Aged 15 to 19	14	2	14.3
Aged 20 to 24	55	3	5.5
Aged 25 to 29	36	7	19.4
Aged 30 to 34	35	15	42.9
Aged 35 to 54	62	25	40.3
Aged 55 or older	39	2	5.1

Note: Asians include those identifying themselves as being of the race alone and those identifying themselves as being of the race in combination with other races. "–" means number is less than 500 or sample is too small to make a reliable estimate.
Source: Bureau of the Census, Current Population Survey Annual Social and Economic Supplement, America's Families and Living Arrangements: 2004, detailed tables, Internet site http://www.census.gov/population/www/socdemo/hh-fam/cps2004.html; calculations by New Strategist

Table 6.10 Households by Type, Age of Householder, and Presence of Children, 2004: Black Households

(total number of black households and number and percent with own children under age 18 at home, by household type and age of householder, 2004; numbers in thousands)

	total	with own children under age 18	
		number	percent
Total black households	**13,969**	**5,104**	**36.5%**
Under age 30	2,432	1,266	52.1
Aged 15 to 19	164	37	22.6
Aged 20 to 24	969	484	49.9
Aged 25 to 29	1,299	745	57.4
Aged 30 to 34	1,526	966	63.3
Aged 35 to 54	6,100	2,702	44.3
Aged 55 or older	3,912	170	4.3
Married couples	**4,259**	**2,102**	**49.4**
Under age 30	408	309	75.7
Aged 15 to 19	3	1	33.3
Aged 20 to 24	116	84	72.4
Aged 25 to 29	289	224	77.5
Aged 30 to 34	481	387	80.5
Aged 35 to 54	2,152	1,301	60.5
Aged 55 or older	1,217	104	8.5
Female family householder, no spouse present	**4,067**	**2,640**	**64.9**
Under age 30	987	854	86.5
Aged 15 to 19	79	31	39.2
Aged 20 to 24	412	360	87.4
Aged 25 to 29	496	463	93.3
Aged 30 to 34	563	529	94.0
Aged 35 to 54	1,809	1,213	67.1
Aged 55 or older	708	44	6.2
Male family householder, no spouse present	**804**	**362**	**45.0**
Under age 30	247	102	41.3
Aged 15 to 19	37	4	10.8
Aged 20 to 24	101	39	38.6
Aged 25 to 29	109	59	54.1
Aged 30 to 34	80	49	61.3
Aged 35 to 54	333	188	56.5
Aged 55 or older	143	23	16.1

Note: Blacks include those identifying themselves as being of the race alone and those identifying themselves as being of the race in combination with other races.
Source: Bureau of the Census, Current Population Survey Annual Social and Economic Supplement, America's Families and Living Arrangements: 2004, detailed tables, Internet site http://www.census.gov/population/www/socdemo/hh-fam/cps2004.html; calculations by New Strategist

Table 6.11 Households by Type, Age of Householder, and Presence of Children, 2004: Hispanic Households

(total number of Hispanic households and number and percent with own children under age 18 at home, by household type and age of householder, 2004; numbers in thousands)

	total	with own children under age 18	
		number	percent
Total Hispanic households	**11,692**	**5,837**	**49.9%**
Under age 30	2,641	1,418	53.7
Aged 15 to 19	197	41	20.8
Aged 20 to 24	965	443	45.9
Aged 25 to 29	1,479	934	63.2
Aged 30 to 34	1,702	1,226	72.0
Aged 35 to 54	5,008	3,011	60.1
Aged 55 or older	2,342	183	7.8
Married couples	**6,227**	**4,086**	**65.6**
Under age 30	1,107	891	80.5
Aged 15 to 19	24	19	79.2
Aged 20 to 24	340	253	74.4
Aged 25 to 29	743	619	83.3
Aged 30 to 34	1,011	884	87.4
Aged 35 to 54	2,932	2,165	73.8
Aged 55 or older	1,176	146	12.4
Female family householder, no spouse present	**2,138**	**1,422**	**66.5**
Under age 30	549	418	76.1
Aged 15 to 19	59	16	27.1
Aged 20 to 24	205	151	73.7
Aged 25 to 29	285	251	88.1
Aged 30 to 34	287	269	93.7
Aged 35 to 54	982	706	71.9
Aged 55 or older	319	30	9.4
Male family householder, no spouse present	**908**	**329**	**36.2**
Under age 30	366	109	29.8
Aged 15 to 19	70	6	8.6
Aged 20 to 24	151	38	25.2
Aged 25 to 29	145	65	44.8
Aged 30 to 34	142	74	52.1
Aged 35 to 54	317	140	44.2
Aged 55 or older	83	6	7.2

Source: Bureau of the Census, Current Population Survey Annual Social and Economic Supplement, America's Families and Living Arrangements: 2004, detailed tables, Internet site http://www.census.gov/population/www/socdemo/hh-fam/cps2004.html; calculations by New Strategist

Table 6.12 Households by Type, Age of Householder, and Presence of Children, 2004: Non-Hispanic White Households

(total number of non-Hispanic white households and number and percent with own children under age 18 at home, by household type and age of householder, 2004; numbers in thousands)

	total	with own children under age 18	
		number	percent
Total non-Hispanic white households	**81,149**	**23,040**	**28.4%**
Under age 30	9,459	3,110	32.9
Aged 15 to 19	420	64	15.2
Aged 20 to 24	3,559	863	24.2
Aged 25 to 29	5,480	2,183	39.8
Aged 30 to 34	6,508	3,679	56.5
Aged 35 to 54	33,000	15,397	46.7
Aged 55 or older	32,181	853	2.7
Married couples	**44,197**	**17,961**	**40.6**
Under age 30	3,449	2,026	58.7
Aged 15 to 19	27	19	70.4
Aged 20 to 24	878	439	50.0
Aged 25 to 29	2,544	1,568	61.6
Aged 30 to 34	3,887	2,905	74.7
Aged 35 to 54	20,438	12,304	60.2
Aged 55 or older	16,422	726	4.4
Female family householder, no spouse present	**7,115**	**3,927**	**55.2**
Under age 30	1,153	900	78.1
Aged 15 to 19	108	37	34.3
Aged 20 to 24	462	358	77.5
Aged 25 to 29	583	505	86.6
Aged 30 to 34	656	600	91.5
Aged 35 to 54	3,326	2,353	70.7
Aged 55 or older	1,979	74	3.7
Male family householder, no spouse present	**2,711**	**1,152**	**42.5**
Under age 30	568	184	32.4
Aged 15 to 19	104	8	7.7
Aged 20 to 24	236	66	28.0
Aged 25 to 29	228	110	48.2
Aged 30 to 34	233	173	74.2
Aged 35 to 54	1,309	741	56.6
Aged 55 or older	602	54	9.0

Note: Non-Hispanic whites include only those identifying themselves as being white alone and not Hispanic.
Source: Bureau of the Census, Current Population Survey Annual Social and Economic Supplement, America's Families and Living Arrangements: 2004, detailed tables, Internet site http://www.census.gov/population/www/socdemo/hh-fam/cps2004.html; calculations by New Strategist

One-Third of Young Adult Households include Preschoolers

The proportion with toddlers is well above average.

The majority of young adults go to college after high school, postponing marriage and family until their midtwenties. Consequently, a 39 percent minority of householders under age 30 has children under age 18 at home.

But young-adult households are more likely than the average household to include preschoolers. While 14 percent of all households include children under age 6, the proportion is 34 percent among householders under age 30. Similarly, while only 8 percent of all households include children under age 3, the figure is a much higher 23 percent among young adults. Nine percent of householders under age 30 have infants at home.

■ While most young adults postpone childbearing, others establish independent households because they have children.

Young adult households are more likely than average to include preschoolers

(percent of total households and households headed by people under age 30 that include children under age 6, 2004)

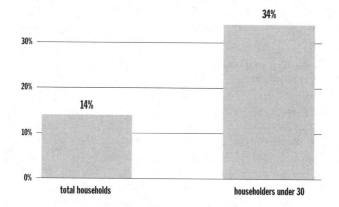

Table 6.13 Households by Presence and Age of Children and Age of Householder, 2004

(number and percent distribution of households by presence and age of own children at home, by age of children and age of householder, 2004; numbers in thousands)

	total	under age 30 total	15 to 19	20 to 24	25 to 29	30 to 34	35 or older
Total households	**112,000**	**15,347**	**837**	**5,772**	**8,738**	**10,421**	**86,232**
With children of any age	46,253	6,043	160	1,840	4,043	6,256	33,955
Under age 25	41,544	6,035	160	1,840	4,035	6,242	29,267
Under age 18	35,944	6,003	150	1,830	4,023	6,223	23,720
Under age 12	26,118	5,938	143	1,821	3,974	5,854	14,326
Under age 6	15,614	5,214	128	1,702	3,384	4,194	6,207
Under age 3	8,954	3,570	109	1,303	2,158	2,564	2,822
Under age 1	3,057	1,398	56	547	795	834	825
Aged 12 to 17	16,960	269	12	31	226	1,509	15,182

PERCENT DISTRIBUTION BY AGE OF CHILD

	total	under age 30 total	15 to 19	20 to 24	25 to 29	30 to 34	35 or older
Total households	**100.0%**	**100.0%**	**100.0%**	**100.0%**	**100.0%**	**100.0%**	**100.0%**
With children of any age	41.3	39.4	19.1	31.9	46.3	60.0	39.4
Under age 25	37.1	39.3	19.1	31.9	46.2	59.9	33.9
Under age 18	32.1	39.1	17.9	31.7	46.0	59.7	27.5
Under age 12	23.3	38.7	17.1	31.5	45.5	56.2	16.6
Under age 6	13.9	34.0	15.3	29.5	38.7	40.2	7.2
Under age 3	8.0	23.3	13.0	22.6	24.7	24.6	3.3
Under age 1	2.7	9.1	6.7	9.5	9.1	8.0	1.0'
Aged 12 to 17	15.1	1.8	1.4	0.5	2.6	14.5	17.6

PERCENT DISTRIBUTION BY AGE OF HOUSEHOLDER

	total	under age 30 total	15 to 19	20 to 24	25 to 29	30 to 34	35 or older
Total households	**100.0%**	**13.7%**	**0.7%**	**5.2%**	**7.8%**	**9.3%**	**77.0%**
With children of any age	100.0	13.1	0.3	4.0	8.7	13.5	73.4
Under age 25	100.0	14.5	0.4	4.4	9.7	15.0	70.4
Under age 18	100.0	16.7	0.4	5.1	11.2	17.3	66.0
Under age 12	100.0	22.7	0.5	7.0	15.2	22.4	54.9
Under age 6	100.0	33.4	0.8	10.9	21.7	26.9	39.8
Under age 3	100.0	39.9	1.2	14.6	24.1	28.6	31.5
Under age 1	100.0	45.7	1.8	17.9	26.0	27.3	27.0
Aged 12 to 17	100.0	1.6	0.1	0.2	1.3	8.9	89.5

Source: Bureau of the Census, Current Population Survey Annual Social and Economic Supplement, America's Families and Living Arrangements: 2004, detailed tables, Internet site http://www.census.gov/population/www/socdemo/hh-fam/cps2004.html; calculations by New Strategist

Most Young Couples Have One or Two Children

Ten percent have three or more.

Smaller families have been growing in popularity for decades. Most Americans now consider two children the ideal number. Among married couples under age 30, the 54 percent majority has one or two children. But a substantial 10 percent have three or more. Among female-headed families in the age group, an even larger 15 percent have three or more children.

Among couples aged 20 to 24, the largest share (42 percent) do not yet have children. Twenty-nine percent have one child under age 18 at home, 21 percent have two, and 8 percent have three or more. Among couples aged 25 to 29, a still substantial 33 percent do not have children in the household, while 28 percent have one child; another 28 percent have two children, and 11 percent have three or more.

■ The percentage of couples with three or more children in the household reaches 19 percent in the 30-to-34 age group.

Among married couples under age 30, only 36 percent do not have children

(percent of married couples under age 30 by number of children under age 18 at home, 2004)

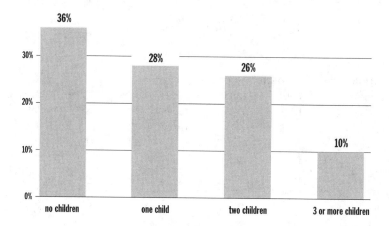

Table 6.14 Married Couples by Presence and Number of Children and Age of Householder, 2004

(number and percent distribution of married couples by presence and number of own children under age 18 at home, by age of householder, 2004; numbers in thousands)

	total	under age 30				30 to 34	35 or older
		total	15 to 19	20 to 24	25 to 29		
Total married couples	**57,719**	**5,195**	**57**	**1,359**	**3,779**	**5,794**	**46,730**
Without children under18	31,926	1,845	15	574	1,256	1,325	28,757
With children under 18	25,792	3,353	43	786	2,524	4,470	17,971
One child	9,763	1,473	28	391	1,054	1,419	6,871
Two children	10,481	1,347	15	288	1,044	1,954	7,181
Three children	4,073	377	–	84	293	780	2,916
Four or more children	1,475	156	–	23	133	317	1,003
PERCENT DISTRIBUTION							
Total married couples	**100.0%**	**100.0%**	**100.0%**	**100.0%**	**100.0%**	**100.0%**	**100.0%**
Without children under18	55.3	35.5	26.3	42.2	33.2	22.9	61.5
With children under 18	44.7	64.5	75.4	57.8	66.8	77.1	38.5
One child	16.9	28.4	49.1	28.8	27.9	24.5	14.7
Two children	18.2	25.9	26.3	21.2	27.6	33.7	15.4
Three children	7.1	7.3	–	6.2	7.8	13.5	6.2
Four or more children	2.6	3.0	–	1.7	3.5	5.5	2.1

Note: "–" means number is less than 500 or sample is too small to make a reliable estimate.
Source: Bureau of the Census, Current Population Survey Annual Social and Economic Supplement, America's Families and Living Arrangements: 2004, detailed tables, Internet site http://www.census.gov/population/www/socdemo/hh-fam/cps2004.html; calculations by New Strategist

Table 6.15 Female-Headed Families by Presence and Number of Children and Age of Householder, 2004

(number and percent distribution of female-headed families by presence and number of own children under age 18 at home, by age of householder, 2004; numbers in thousands)

	total	under age 30				30 to 34	35 or older
		total	15 to 19	20 to 24	25 to 29		
Total female-headed families	**13,781**	**2,797**	**264**	**1,134**	**1,399**	**1,560**	**9,424**
Without children under18	5,560	570	175	244	151	120	4,870
With children under 18	8,221	2,226	89	890	1,247	1,441	4,555
One child	4,055	1,073	82	489	502	511	2,472
Two children	2,665	731	5	282	444	489	1,446
Three children	1,046	281	2	85	194	280	484
Four or more children	455	141	–	34	107	161	153
PERCENT DISTRIBUTION							
Total female-headed families	**100.0%**	**100.0%**	**100.0%**	**100.0%**	**100.0%**	**100.0%**	**100.0%**
Without children under18	40.3	20.4	66.3	21.5	10.8	7.7	51.7
With children under 18	59.7	79.6	33.7	78.5	89.1	92.4	48.3
One child	29.4	38.4	31.1	43.1	35.9	32.8	26.2
Two children	19.3	26.1	1.9	24.9	31.7	31.3	15.3
Three children	7.6	10.0	0.8	7.5	13.9	17.9	5.1
Four or more children	3.3	5.0	–	3.0	7.6	10.3	1.6

Note: "–" means number is less than 500 or sample is too small to make a reliable estimate.
Source: Bureau of the Census, Current Population Survey Annual Social and Economic Supplement, America's Families and Living Arrangements: 2004, detailed tables, Internet site http://www.census.gov/population/www/socdemo/hh-fam/cps2004.html; calculations by New Strategist

Table 6.16 Male-Headed Families by Presence and Number of Children and Age of Householder, 2004

(number and percent distribution of male-headed families by presence and number of own children under age 18 at home, by age of householder, 2004; numbers in thousands)

	total	under age 30 total	15 to 19	20 to 24	25 to 29	30 to 34	35 or older
Total male-headed families	**4,716**	**1,307**	**223**	**551**	**533**	**492**	**2,915**
Without children under 18	2,786	884	205	397	282	179	1,723
With children under 18	1,931	424	19	154	251	313	1,192
One child	1,146	274	12	98	164	181	691
Two children	550	96	3	43	50	99	354
Three children	180	48	–	13	35	26	105
Four or more children	55	6	4	–	2	7	42
PERCENT DISTRIBUTION							
Total male-headed families	**100.0%**	**100.0%**	**100.0%**	**100.0%**	**100.0%**	**100.0%**	**100.0%**
Without children under 18	59.1	67.6	91.9	72.1	52.9	36.4	59.1
With children under 18	40.9	32.4	8.5	27.9	47.1	63.6	40.9
One child	24.3	21.0	5.4	17.8	30.8	36.8	23.7
Two children	11.7	7.3	1.3	7.8	9.4	20.1	12.1
Three children	3.8	3.7	–	2.4	6.6	5.3	3.6
Four or more children	1.2	0.5	1.8	–	0.4	1.4	1.4

Note: "–" means number is less than 500 or sample is too small to make a reliable estimate.
Source: Bureau of the Census, Current Population Survey Annual Social and Economic Supplement, America's Families and Living Arrangements: 2004, detailed tables, Internet site http://www.census.gov/population/www/socdemo/hh-fam/cps2004.html; calculations by New Strategist

Half of Black Children Live with Mother Only

Only 14 percent of Asian children live only with mom.

Among the nation's 73 million children, 68 percent live with two parents. The proportion of those who live with two parents stands at a high of 82 percent among Asian children. The figure is a lower 77 percent among non-Hispanic white children and a still lower 65 percent among Hispanic children. Only 35 percent of black children live with two parents.

Eighty percent of children under age 18 share their home with a sibling. The largest share (40 percent) has just one sibling living at home with them. Only 16 percent of children have parents under age 30, while the 59 percent majority has parents in the 30-to-44 age group. Twenty-six percent of children under age 18 have a parent with a college degree, and 53 percent have a parent with college experience.

■ Children who live with only one parent are more likely to be poor than those living with two parents

Asian children are most likely to live with two parents

(percent of children under age 18 who live with two parents, by race and Hispanic origin, 2004)

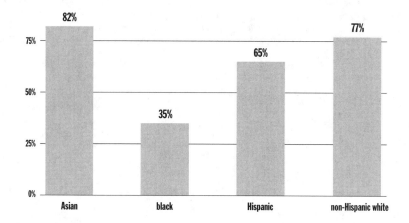

Table 6.17 Living Arrangements of Children by Race and Hispanic Origin, 2004

(number and percent distribution of children under age 18 by living arrangement and race and Hispanic origin of child, 2004; numbers in thousands)

	total	Asian	black	Hispanic	non-Hispanic white
Total children	**73,205**	**3,314**	**12,277**	**13,752**	**43,262**
Living with two parents	49,603	2,706	4,340	8,886	33,251
Living with mother only	17,072	449	6,153	3,489	6,894
Living with father only	3,402	80	688	731	1,844
Living with neither parent	3,128	79	1,096	646	1,274
PERCENT DISTRIBUTION BY LIVING ARRANGEMENT					
Total children	**100.0%**	**100.0%**	**100.0%**	**100.0%**	**100.0%**
Living with two parents	67.8	81.7	35.4	64.6	76.9
Living with mother only	23.3	13.5	50.1	25.4	15.9
Living with father only	4.6	2.4	5.6	5.3	4.3
Living with neither parent	4.3	2.4	8.9	4.7	2.9
PERCENT DISTRIBUTION BY RACE AND HISPANIC ORIGIN					
Total children	**100.0%**	**4.5%**	**16.8%**	**18.8%**	**59.1%**
Living with two parents	100.0	5.5	8.7	17.9	67.0
Living with mother only	100.0	2.6	36.0	20.4	40.4
Living with father only	100.0	2.4	20.2	21.5	54.2
Living with neither parent	100.0	2.5	35.0	20.7	40.7

Note: Numbers will not add to total because Asians and blacks include those identifying themselves as being of the respective race alone and those identifying themselves as being of the race in combination with other races. Non-Hispanic whites include only those identifying themselves as being white alone and not Hispanic. Hispanics may be of any race.
Source: Bureau of the Census, Current Population Survey Annual Social and Economic Supplement, America's Families and Living Arrangements: 2004, detailed tables, Internet site http://www.census.gov/population/www/socdemo/hh-fam/cps2004.html; calculations by New Strategist

Table 6.18 Children under Age 18 by Selected Characteristics, 2004

(number and percent distribution of children under age 18 by selected characteristics, 2004; numbers in thousands)

	number	percent distribution
Total children under age 18	**73,205**	**100.0%**
Sex of child		
Female	35,869	49.0
Male	37,336	51.0
Age of child		
Under age 1	3,913	5.3
Aged 1 to 2	8,087	11.0
Aged 3 to 5	11,793	16.1
Aged 6 to 8	11,674	15.9
Aged 9 to 11	12,432	17.0
Aged 12 to 14	12,807	17.5
Aged 15 to 17	12,499	17.1
Number of siblings in household		
None	14,835	20.3
One	29,010	39.6
Two	18,209	24.9
Three or more	11,152	15.2
Age of parent		
Under age 20	404	0.6
Aged 20 to 24	3,590	4.9
Aged 25 to 29	7,791	10.6
Aged 30 to 34	12,909	17.6
Aged 35 to 39	15,598	21.3
Aged 40 to 44	14,723	20.1
Aged 45 to 49	9,536	13.0
Aged 50 to 54	3,569	4.9
Aged 55 or older	1,957	2.7
No parents present	3,128	4.3
Education of parent		
Not a high school graduate	10,775	14.7
High school graduate	20,370	27.8
Some college or associate's degree	19,942	27.2
Bachelor's degree	12,647	17.3
Professional or graduate degree	6,343	8.7
No parents present	3,128	4.3

Source: Bureau of the Census, Current Population Survey Annual Social and Economic Supplement, America's Families and Living Arrangements: 2004, detailed tables, Internet site http://www.census.gov/population/www/socdemo/hh-fam/cps2004.html; calculations by New Strategist

Many Households Have Step- or Adopted Children

Householders with adopted children are better educated and have higher incomes.

Among the nation's 45 million households with children of the householder present, 89 percent include only biological children. A substantial 11 percent include step- or adopted children—7 percent include stepchildren and 4 percent include adopted children.

Adopted children are less likely to be white than biological or stepchildren. While 71 percent of biological children are white, the figure is just 64 percent among adopted children. Seventeen percent of adopted children are of a different race than the householder.

Adopted children live in households with higher incomes than biological or stepchildren. Similarly, the educational level of the parents of adopted children is significantly higher than those of other children—33 percent of their parents have at least a college degree.

Adopted children are more likely to be disabled than biological or stepchildren. Among children aged 5 to 17, 12 percent of adopted children have at least one disability versus only 5 percent of biological children and 7 percent of stepchildren. The 53 percent majority of adopted children are female, but among those with disabilities, the 59 percent majority are males.

Thirteen percent of adopted children are foreign-born. Among foreign-born adopted children, the most common country of origin is Korea, which accounts for 24 percent of the total. Russia accounts for another 10 percent.

■ The high divorce rate and fertility problems caused by delayed childbearing are creating more diverse families.

More than one in ten households include step- or adopted children

(percent distribution of households with children under age 18 by relationship of child to householder, 2000)

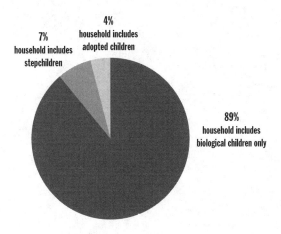

7%
household includes
stepchildren

4%
household includes
adopted children

89%
household includes
biological children only

Table 6.19 Households by Relationship of Children in Household to Householder, 2000 Census

(number and percent distribution of households by presence of biological, step-, and adopted children of any age, 2000; numbers in thousands)

	number	percent distribution
Total households with children of householder present	**45,490**	**100.0%**
HOUSEHOLDS BY TYPE OF CHILDREN PRESENT		
Total households with children of householder	**45,490**	**100.0**
Biological children only	40,658	89.4
Other relationships	4,832	10.6
Biological children and stepchildren	1,660	3.6
Stepchildren only	1,485	3.3
Adopted children only	817	1.8
Adopted and biological children	808	1.8
Biological children, adopted children, stepchildren	32	0.1
Adopted and stepchildren	30	0.1
HOUSEHOLDS BY NUMBER OF ADOPTED CHILDREN PRESENT		
Total households with adopted children	**1,687**	**100.0**
One adopted child	1,383	82.0
Two adopted children	248	14.7
Three or more adopted children	56	3.3

Source: Adopted Children and Stepchildren: 2000, Census 2000 Special Reports, CENSR-GRV, 2003, Internet site http://www .census.gov/population/www/cen2000/phc-t21.html

Table 6.20 Biological, Step-, and Adopted Children by Race and Hispanic Origin of Householder, 2000 Census

(number and percent distribution of biological, step-, and adopted children of the householder by race and Hispanic origin, 2000; numbers in thousands)

	total	biological	step	adopted
Race of child				
Total children under age 18	**64,652**	**59,774**	**3,292**	**1,586**
American Indian alone	663	598	40	26
Asian alone	2,225	2,069	39	117
Black alone	8,568	7,911	403	254
White alone	45,859	42,359	2,482	1,018
Other race	7,337	6,837	329	172
Hispanic origin of child				
Total children under age 18	**64,652**	**59,774**	**3,292**	**1,586**
Hispanic	9,814	9,720	479	216
Non-Hispanic white	42,413	37,958	2,262	918
Child and householder race/Hispanic difference				
Total children under age 18	**64,652**	**59,774**	**3,292**	**1,586**
Child is different race than householder	4,638	4,011	356	271
Child is different Hispanic origin than householder	1,708	1,385	218	105
PERCENT DISTRIBUTION BY RACE/HISPANIC ORIGIN				
Race of child				
Total children under age 18	**100.0%**	**100.0%**	**100.0%**	**100.0%**
American Indian alone	1.0	1.0	1.2	1.6
Asian alone	3.4	3.5	1.2	7.4
Black alone	13.3	13.2	12.2	16.0
White alone	70.9	70.9	75.4	64.2
Other race	11.3	11.4	10.0	10.8
Hispanic origin of child				
Total children under age 18	**100.0**	**100.0**	**100.0**	**100.0**
Hispanic	15.2	16.3	14.6	13.6
Non-Hispanic white	65.6	63.5	68.7	57.9
Child and householder race/Hispanic difference				
Total children under age 18	**100.0**	**100.0**	**100.0**	**100.0**
Child is different race than householder	7.2	6.7	10.8	17.1
Child is different Hispanic origin than householder	2.6	2.3	6.6	6.6

Source: Adopted Children and Stepchildren: 2000, Census 2000 Special Reports, CENSR-GRV, 2003, Internet site http://www .census.gov/population/www/cen2000/phc-t21.html; calculations by New Strategist

Table 6.21 Biological, Step-, and Adopted Children by Household Income, 2000 Census

(number and percent distribution of biological, step-, and adopted children of the householder by household income, 1999; children in thousands as of 2000)

	total	biological	step	adopted
Total children under 18	**64,652**	**59,774**	**3,292**	**1,586**
$0 or less	692	662	15	15
$1 to $9,999	3,774	3,625	78	71
$10,000 to $14,999	2,907	2,768	87	51
$15,000 to $24,999	6,785	6,366	290	129
$25,000 to $34,999	7,508	6,935	418	156
$35,000 to $49,999	11,006	10,062	690	254
$50,000 to $74,999	14,693	13,413	905	376
$75,000 to $99,000	7,905	7,255	426	224
$100,000 to $149,999	5,795	5,351	262	183
$150,000 to $199,999	1,657	1,538	63	56
$200,000 or more	1,929	1,799	59	71
Median household income	$49,528	$48,200	$50,900	$56,138

PERCENT DISTRIBUTION BY HOUSEHOLD INCOME

Total children under 18	**100.0%**	**100.0%**	**100.0%**	**100.0%**
$0 or less	1.1	1.1	0.5	0.9
$1 to $9,999	5.8	6.1	2.4	4.5
$10,000 to $14,999	4.5	4.6	2.7	3.2
$15,000 to $24,999	10.5	10.7	8.8	8.1
$25,000 to $34,999	11.6	11.6	12.7	9.8
$35,000 to $49,999	17.0	16.8	21.0	16.0
$50,000 to $74,999	22.7	22.4	27.5	23.7
$75,000 to $99,000	12.2	12.1	12.9	14.1
$100,000 to $149,999	9.0	9.0	7.9	11.5
$150,000 to $199,999	2.6	2.6	1.9	3.5
$200,000 or more	3.0	3.0	1.8	4.5

Source: Adopted Children and Stepchildren: 2000, Census 2000 Special Reports, CENSR-GRV, 2003, Internet site http://www .census.gov/population/www/cen2000/phc-t21.html; calculations by New Strategist

Table 6.22 Biological, Step-, and Adopted Children by Education of Householder, 2000 Census

(number and percent distribution of biological, step-, and adopted children of the householder by educational attainment of householder, 2000; numbers in thousands)

	total	biological	step	adopted
Total children under age 18	**64,652**	**59,774**	**3,292**	**1,586**
Less than high school	11,536	10,742	568	227
High school graduate	17,300	15,808	1,133	359
Some college	19,315	17,769	1,075	471
Bachelor's degree or more	16,501	15,455	517	530
Bachelor's degree	10,274	9,631	354	288
Graduate or professional school degree	6,227	5,824	162	241

PERCENT DISTRIBUTION BY EDUCATIONAL ATTAINMENT OF HOUSEHOLDER

	total	biological	step	adopted
Total children under age 18	**100.0%**	**100.0%**	**100.0%**	**100.0%**
Less than high school	17.8	18.0	17.3	14.3
High school graduate	26.8	26.4	34.4	22.6
Some college	29.9	29.7	32.6	29.7
Bachelor's degree or more	25.5	25.9	15.7	33.4
Bachelor's degree	15.9	16.1	10.8	18.2
Graduate or professional school degree	9.6	9.7	4.9	15.2

Source: Adopted Children and Stepchildren: 2000, Census 2000 Special Reports, CENSR-GRV, 2003, Internet site http://www .census.gov/population/www/cen2000/phc-t21.html; calculations by New Strategist

Table 6.23 Biological, Step-, and Adopted Children by Disability Status, 2000 Census

(number and percent distribution of biological, step-, and adopted children of the householder by disability status, 2000; numbers in thousands)

	total	biological	step	adopted
Total children aged 5 to 17	**48,098**	**43,740**	**3,078**	**1,279**
At least one disability	2,643	2,279	214	150
Sensory disability	458	405	34	19
Physical disability	402	361	22	20
Mental disability	2,076	1,768	175	133
Self-care disability	469	418	30	21
Multiple disabilities	525	463	34	27

PERCENT DISTRIBUTION BY DISABILITY STATUS

	total	biological	step	adopted
Total children aged 5 to 17	**100.0%**	**100.0%**	**100.0%**	**100.0%**
At least one disability	5.5	5.2	6.9	11.8
Sensory disability	1.0	0.9	1.1	1.5
Physical disability	0.8	0.8	0.7	1.5
Mental disability	4.3	4.0	5.7	10.4
Self-care disability	1.0	1.0	1.0	1.6
Multiple disabilities	1.1	1.1	1.1	2.1

Source: Adopted Children and Stepchildren: 2000, Census 2000 Special Reports, CENSR-GRV, 2003, Internet site http://www .census.gov/population/www/cen2000/phc-t21.html; calculations by New Strategist

Table 6.24 Adopted Children under Age 18 by Race, Hispanic Origin, Disability Status, and Sex, 2000

(number and percent distribution of adopted children under age 18 by race, Hispanic origin, disability status, and sex, 2000; numbers in thousands)

	number			percent distribution		
	total	female	male	total	female	male
Total adopted children of householder	**1,586**	**835**	**751**	**100.0%**	**52.7%**	**47.3%**
Race of child						
American Indian alone	26	13	13	100.0	50.9	49.1
Asian alone	117	74	43	100.0	63.0	37.0
Black alone	254	132	122	100.0	51.9	48.1
White alone	1,018	528	490	100.0	51.9	48.1
Other race	172	89	82	100.0	52.0	48.0
Hispanic origin of child						
Hispanic	216	113	102	100.0	52.5	47.5
Non-Hispanic white	918	476	442	100.0	51.8	48.2
Disability status						
Children Aged 5 to 17	**1,279**	**668**	**611**	**100.0**	**52.2**	**47.8**
At least one disability	150	61	89	100.0	40.9	59.1
Sensory disability	19	9	10	100.0	48.7	51.3
Physical disability	20	9	11	100.0	45.0	55.0
Mental disability	133	52	81	100.0	39.2	60.8
Self-care disability	21	10	11	100.0	49.2	50.8
Multiple disabilities	27	12	15	100.0	44.2	55.8

Source: Adopted Children and Stepchildren: 2000, Census 2000 Special Reports, CENSR-GRV, 2003, Internet site http://www .census.gov/population/www/cen2000/phc-t21.html; calculations by New Strategist

Table 6.25 Adopted Children by Place of Birth, 2000 Census

(number and percent distribution of adopted children under age 18 by place of birth, 2000; numbers in thousands)

	number	percent
Total adopted children of householder	**1,586**	**100.0%**
Native-born	1,387	87.4
Foreign-born	199	12.6
Foreign-born	**199**	**100.0**
Europe	37	18.5
Russia	20	9.9
Romania	6	3.1
Ukraine	2	1.2
Asia	98	49.4
China	21	10.6
India	8	3.9
Korea	48	23.9
Phillippines	6	3.2
Vietnam	4	2.2
Africa	3	1.6
Latin America	58	29.2
Central America	32	16.3
Guatemala	7	3.7
Mexico	18	9.1
El Salvador	2	1.1
South America	20	10.2
Colombia	7	3.5
North America	2	0.8

Source: Adopted Children and Stepchildren: 2000, Census 2000 Special Reports, CENSR-GRV, 2003, Internet site http://www.census.gov/population/www/cen2000/phc-t21.html; calculations by New Strategist

Most Young Men Live with Their Parents

Few head their own households.

Among people under age 30, 51 percent of men and 44 percent of women live with their parents. These figures include college students living in dormitories because they are considered dependents. Not surprisingly, the proportion of young adults who live with their parents falls with age—more slowly for men than for women. Among men aged 20 to 24, 48 percent still live with their parents, a figure that drops to 19 percent in the 25-to-29 age group. Among women aged 20 to 24, 37 percent live with their parents, as do 11 percent of those aged 25 to 29.

Living with nonrelatives, either roommates or romantic partners, is just as common as living with a spouse for men under age 30. Fifteen percent of men under age 30 live with their spouse and 15 percent live with nonrelatives. Among women, 22 percent live with their spouse and 13 percent live with nonrelatives.

■ With more young adults pursuing a college degree, the dependency of childhood has stretched well into the twentysomething years.

Many young adults live with their parents

(percent of people aged 15 to 29 who live with their parents, by sex and age, 2004)

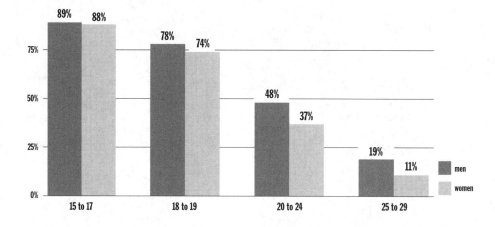

Table 6.26 Living Arrangements of Men by Age, 2004

(number and percent distribution of men aged 15 or older by living arrangement and age, 2004; numbers in thousands)

	total	aged 15 to 29					30 or older
		total	15 to 17	18 to 19	20 to 24	25 to 29	
NUMBER							
Total men	**110,048**	**30,104**	**6,404**	**3,923**	**10,242**	**9,535**	**79,946**
Married-couple householder or spouse	57,719	4,483	14	27	1,080	3,362	53,236
Other householder	20,852	4,611	87	284	1,925	2,315	16,240
Male family householder	4,716	1,307	83	140	551	533	3,407
Living alone	12,562	1,873	2	81	686	1,104	10,689
Living with nonrelatives	3,574	1,431	2	63	688	678	2,144
Nonhouseholder	31,477	21,010	6,304	3,611	7,237	3,858	10,466
Child of householder	18,936	15,459	5,686	3,071	4,938	1,764	3,477
Other relative of householder	5,575	2,370	473	303	871	723	3,206
Living with nonrelatives	6,965	3,181	145	237	1,428	1,371	3,783
PERCENT DISTRIBUTION BY LIVING ARRANGEMENT							
Total men	**100.0%**	**100.0%**	**100.0%**	**100.0%**	**100.0%**	**100.0%**	**100.0%**
Married-couple householder or spouse	52.4	14.9	0.2	0.7	10.5	35.3	66.6
Other householder	18.9	15.3	1.4	7.2	18.8	24.3	20.3
Male family householder	4.3	4.3	1.3	3.6	5.4	5.6	4.3
Living alone	11.4	6.2	0.0	2.1	6.7	11.6	13.4
Living with nonrelatives	3.2	4.8	0.0	1.6	6.7	7.1	2.7
Nonhouseholder	28.6	69.8	98.4	92.0	70.7	40.5	13.1
Child of householder	17.2	51.4	88.8	78.3	48.2	18.5	4.3
Other relative of householder	5.1	7.9	7.4	7.7	8.5	7.6	4.0
Living with nonrelatives	6.3	10.6	2.3	6.0	13.9	14.4	4.7
PERCENT DISTRIBUTION BY AGE							
Total men	**100.0%**	**27.4%**	**5.8%**	**3.6%**	**9.3%**	**8.7%**	**72.6%**
Married-couple householder or spouse	100.0	7.8	0.0	0.0	1.9	5.8	92.2
Other householder	100.0	22.1	0.4	1.4	9.2	11.1	77.9
Male family householder	100.0	27.7	1.8	3.0	11.7	11.3	72.2
Living alone	100.0	14.9	0.0	0.6	5.5	8.8	85.1
Living with nonrelatives	100.0	40.0	0.1	1.8	19.3	19.0	60.0
Nonhouseholder	100.0	66.7	20.0	11.5	23.0	12.3	33.2
Child of householder	100.0	81.6	30.0	16.2	26.1	9.3	18.4
Other relative of householder	100.0	42.5	8.5	5.4	15.6	13.0	57.5
Living with nonrelatives	100.0	45.7	2.1	3.4	20.5	19.7	54.3

Source: Bureau of the Census, Current Population Survey Annual Social and Economic Supplement, America's Families and Living Arrangements: 2004, detailed tables, Internet site http://www.census.gov/population/www/socdemo/hh-fam/cps2004.html; calculations by New Strategist

Table 6.27 Living Arrangements of Women by Age, 2004

(number and percent distribution of women aged 15 or older by living arrangement and age, 2004; numbers in thousands)

	total	aged 15 to 29					30 or older
		total	15 to 17	18 to 19	20 to 24	25 to 29	
NUMBER							
Total women	**117,295**	**29,488**	**6,417**	**3,552**	**10,059**	**9,460**	**87,808**
Married-couple householder or spouse	57,719	6,478	22	101	1,901	4,454	51,242
Other householder	33,428	5,540	109	299	2,489	2,643	27,889
Female family householder	13,781	2,798	105	159	1,135	1,399	10,984
Living alone	17,024	1,607	2	61	699	845	15,417
Living with nonrelatives	2,623	1,135	2	79	655	399	1,488
Nonhouseholder	26,147	17,472	6,285	3,152	5,671	2,364	8,677
Child of householder	14,863	13,030	5,648	2,635	3,693	1,054	1,836
Other relative of householder	5,926	1,704	460	258	612	374	4,222
Living with nonrelatives	5,358	2,738	177	259	1,366	936	2,619
PERCENT DISTRIBUTION BY LIVING ARRANGEMENT							
Total women	**100.0%**	**100.0%**	**100.0%**	**100.0%**	**100.0%**	**100.0%**	**100.0%**
Married-couple householder or spouse	49.2	22.0	0.3	2.8	18.9	47.1	58.4
Other householder	28.5	18.8	1.7	8.4	24.7	27.9	31.8
Female family householder	11.7	9.5	1.6	4.5	11.3	14.8	12.5
Living alone	14.5	5.4	0.0	1.7	6.9	8.9	17.6
Living with nonrelatives	2.2	3.8	0.0	2.2	6.5	4.2	1.7
Nonhouseholder	22.3	59.3	97.9	88.7	56.4	25.0	9.9
Child of householder	12.7	44.2	88.0	74.2	36.7	11.1	2.1
Other relative of householder	5.1	5.8	7.2	7.3	6.1	4.0	4.8
Living with nonrelatives	4.6	9.3	2.8	7.3	13.6	9.9	3.0
PERCENT DISTRIBUTION BY AGE							
Total women	**100.0%**	**25.1%**	**5.5%**	**3.0%**	**8.6%**	**8.1%**	**74.9%**
Married-couple householder or spouse	100.0	11.2	0.0	0.2	3.3	7.7	88.8
Other householder	100.0	16.6	0.3	0.9	7.4	7.9	83.4
Female family householder	100.0	20.3	0.8	1.2	8.2	10.2	79.7
Living alone	100.0	9.4	0.0	0.4	4.1	5.0	90.6
Living with nonrelatives	100.0	43.3	0.1	3.0	25.0	15.2	56.7
Nonhouseholder	100.0	66.8	24.0	12.1	21.7	9.0	33.2
Child of householder	100.0	87.7	38.0	17.7	24.8	7.1	12.4
Other relative of householder	100.0	28.8	7.8	4.4	10.3	6.3	71.2
Living with nonrelatives	100.0	51.1	3.3	4.8	25.5	17.5	48.9

Source: Bureau of the Census, Current Population Survey Annual Social and Economic Supplement, America's Families and Living Arrangements: 2004, detailed tables, Internet site http://www.census.gov/population/www/socdemo/hh-fam/cps2004.html; calculations by New Strategist

Among Young Adults, the Married Are a Minority

Most women are single until their late twenties, men until their early thirties.

The majority of men and women under age 30 have never married. Among men aged 20 to 24, fully 86 percent are single. The figure is 75 percent among their female counterparts. The percentage of women who have never married drops sharply in the 25-to-29 age group, to just 41 percent. But the 57 percent majority of men aged 25 to 29 are still single. For men, the proportion who have ever married surpasses 50 percent in the 30-to-34 age group.

Marital patterns do not vary much by race and Hispanic origin. The percentage of women who have never married falls below 50 percent in the 25-to-29 age group for Asians, Hispanics, and non-Hispanic whites. Among black women and all men regardless of race or Hispanic origin, the proportion who have never married does not fall below 50 percent until the 30-to-34 age group.

■ The great diversity in the living arrangements of young adults is the consequence of postponed marriages.

Most women have married by age 25 to 29, while most men are still single

(percent of people aged 25 to 29 who have never married, by sex, 2004)

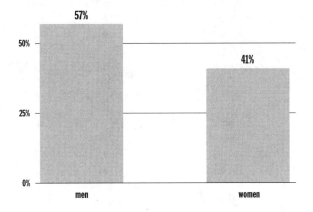

Table 6.28 Marital Status by Sex and Age, 2004: Total People

(number and percent distribution of people aged 15 or older by sex, age, and current marital status, 2004; numbers in thousands)

	total	never married	married	separated or divorced	widowed
NUMBER					
Total men	**110,048**	**35,885**	**60,724**	**10,791**	**2,648**
Under age 30	30,104	24,437	5,003	647	15
Aged 15 to 17	6,404	6,324	27	47	5
Aged 18 to 19	3,923	3,868	37	18	–
Aged 20 to 24	10,242	8,850	1,255	134	2
Aged 25 to 29	9,535	5,395	3,684	448	8
Aged 30 or older	79,946	11,448	55,719	10,144	2,631
Total women	**117,295**	**29,975**	**60,616**	**15,558**	**11,146**
Under age 30	29,488	21,147	7,086	1,195	60
Aged 15 to 17	6,417	6,320	33	56	7
Aged 18 to 19	3,552	3,391	127	34	–
Aged 20 to 24	10,059	7,581	2,180	288	11
Aged 25 to 29	9,460	3,855	4,746	817	42
Aged 30 or older	87,808	8,828	53,531	14,364	11,088
PERCENT DISTRIBUTION					
Total men	**100.0%**	**32.6%**	**55.2%**	**9.8%**	**2.4%**
Under age 30	100.0	81.2	16.6	2.1	0.0
Aged 15 to 17	100.0	98.8	0.4	0.7	0.1
Aged 18 to 19	100.0	98.6	0.9	0.5	–
Aged 20 to 24	100.0	86.4	12.3	1.3	0.0
Aged 25 to 29	100.0	56.6	38.6	4.7	0.1
Aged 30 or older	100.0	14.3	69.7	12.7	3.3
Total women	**100.0**	**25.6**	**51.7**	**13.3**	**9.5**
Under age 30	100.0	71.7	24.0	4.1	0.2
Aged 15 to 17	100.0	98.5	0.5	0.9	0.1
Aged 18 to 19	100.0	95.5	3.6	1.0	–
Aged 20 to 24	100.0	75.4	21.7	2.9	0.1
Aged 25 to 29	100.0	40.8	50.2	8.6	0.4
Aged 30 or older	100.0	10.1	61.0	16.4	12.6

Note: "–" means number is less than 500 or sample is too small to make a reliable estimate.
Source: Bureau of the Census, Current Population Survey Annual Social and Economic Supplement, America's Families and Living Arrangements: 2004, detailed tables, Internet site http://www.census.gov/population/www/socdemo/hh-fam/cps2004.html; calculations by New Strategist

Table 6.29 Marital Status by Sex and Age, 2004: Asians

(number and percent distribution of Asians aged 15 or older by sex, age, and current marital status, 2004; numbers in thousands)

	total	never married	married	separated or divorced	widowed
NUMBER					
Total Asian men	**4,874**	**1,752**	**2,842**	**213**	**68**
Under age 30	1,477	1,248	217	12	0
Aged 15 to 17	281	278	0	3	–
Aged 18 to 19	169	166	1	2	–
Aged 20 to 24	488	449	37	2	–
Aged 25 to 29	539	355	179	5	–
Aged 30 or older	3,398	504	2,624	200	68
Total Asian women	**5,247**	**1,327**	**3,197**	**377**	**346**
Under age 30	1,432	988	418	17	8
Aged 15 to 17	281	277	1	2	–
Aged 18 to 19	114	110	4	0	–
Aged 20 to 24	486	382	99	3	2
Aged 25 to 29	551	219	314	12	6
Aged 30 or older	3,816	340	2,779	359	338
PERCENT DISTRIBUTION					
Total Asian men	**100.0%**	**35.9%**	**58.3%**	**4.4%**	**1.4%**
Under age 30	100.0	84.5	14.7	0.8	0.0
Aged 15 to 17	100.0	98.9	0.0	1.1	–
Aged 18 to 19	100.0	98.2	0.6	1.2	–
Aged 20 to 24	100.0	92.0	7.6	0.4	–
Aged 25 to 29	100.0	65.9	33.2	0.9	–
Aged 30 or older	100.0	14.8	77.2	5.9	2.0
Total Asian women	**100.0**	**25.3**	**60.9**	**7.2**	**6.6**
Under age 30	100.0	69.0	29.2	1.2	0.6
Aged 15 to 17	100.0	98.6	0.4	0.7	–
Aged 18 to 19	100.0	96.5	3.5	0.0	–
Aged 20 to 24	100.0	78.6	20.4	0.6	0.4
Aged 25 to 29	100.0	39.7	57.0	2.2	1.1
Aged 30 or older	100.0	8.9	72.8	9.4	8.9

Note: Asians include those identifying themselves as being of the race alone and those identifying themselves as being of the race in combination with other races. "–" means number is less than 500 or sample is too small to make a reliable estimate.
Source: Bureau of the Census, Current Population Survey Annual Social and Economic Supplement, America's Families and Living Arrangements: 2004, detailed tables, Internet site http://www.census.gov/population/www/socdemo/hh-fam/cps2004.html; calculations by New Strategist

Table 6.30 Marital Status by Sex and Age, 2004: Blacks

(number and percent distribution of blacks aged 15 or older by sex, age, and current marital status, 2004; numbers in thousands)

	total	never married	married	separated or divorced	widowed
NUMBER					
Total black men	**12,330**	**5,795**	**4,689**	**1,535**	**312**
Under age 30	4,131	3,661	385	83	–
Aged 15 to 17	1,063	1,056	3	3	–
Aged 18 to 19	533	527	2	3	–
Aged 20 to 24	1,387	1,242	123	22	–
Aged 25 to 29	1,148	836	257	55	0
Aged 30 or older	8,200	2,135	4,305	1,450	313
Total black women	**15,110**	**6,417**	**4,587**	**2,715**	**1,390**
Under age 30	4,610	3,835	604	163	7
Aged 15 to 17	1,111	1,091	4	16	–
Aged 18 to 19	514	497	8	8	–
Aged 20 to 24	1,564	1,348	169	45	2
Aged 25 to 29	1,421	899	423	94	5
Aged 30 or older	10,499	2,583	3,981	2,553	1,383
PERCENT DISTRIBUTION					
Total black men	**100.0%**	**47.0%**	**38.0%**	**12.4%**	**2.5%**
Under age 30	100.0	88.6	9.3	2.0	–
Aged 15 to 17	100.0	99.3	0.3	0.3	–
Aged 18 to 19	100.0	98.9	0.4	0.6	–
Aged 20 to 24	100.0	89.5	8.9	1.6	–
Aged 25 to 29	100.0	72.8	22.4	4.8	0.0
Aged 30 or older	100.0	26.0	52.5	17.7	3.8
Total black women	**100.0**	**42.5**	**30.4**	**18.0**	**9.2**
Under age 30	100.0	83.2	13.1	3.5	0.2
Aged 15 to 17	100.0	98.2	0.4	1.4	–
Aged 18 to 19	100.0	96.7	1.6	1.6	–
Aged 20 to 24	100.0	86.2	10.8	2.9	0.1
Aged 25 to 29	100.0	63.3	29.8	6.6	0.4
Aged 30 or older	100.0	24.6	37.9	24.3	13.2

Note: Blacks include those identifying themselves as being of the race alone and those identifying themselves as being of the race in combination with other races. "–" means number is less than 500 or sample is too small to make a reliable estimate.
Source: Bureau of the Census, Current Population Survey Annual Social and Economic Supplement, America's Families and Living Arrangements: 2004, detailed tables, Internet site http://www.census.gov/population/www/socdemo/hh-fam/cps2004.html; calculations by New Strategist

Table 6.31 Marital Status by Sex and Age, 2004: Hispanics

(number and percent distribution of Hispanics aged 15 or older by sex, age, and current marital status, 2004; numbers in thousands)

	total	never married	married	separated or divorced	widowed
NUMBER					
Total Hispanic men	**14,640**	**6,003**	**7,248**	**1,199**	**190**
Under age 30	5,749	4,385	1,243	119	1
Aged 15 to 17	958	944	6	6	–
Aged 18 to 19	695	674	15	7	–
Aged 20 to 24	2,009	1,630	357	22	–
Aged 25 to 29	2,087	1,137	865	84	1
Aged 30 or older	8,891	1,619	6,005	1,079	189
Total Hispanic women	**13,878**	**4,306**	**6,987**	**1,825**	**761**
Under age 30	5,002	3,248	1,531	217	5
Aged 15 to 17	1,010	992	11	7	–
Aged 18 to 19	578	516	49	12	–
Aged 20 to 24	1,684	1,118	510	55	1
Aged 25 to 29	1,730	622	961	143	4
Aged 30 or older	8,875	1,058	5,456	1,607	755
PERCENT DISTRIBUTION					
Total Hispanic men	**100.0%**	**41.0%**	**49.5%**	**8.2%**	**1.3%**
Under age 30	100.0	76.3	21.6	2.1	0.0
Aged 15 to 17	100.0	98.5	0.6	0.6	–
Aged 18 to 19	100.0	97.0	2.2	1.0	–
Aged 20 to 24	100.0	81.1	17.8	1.1	–
Aged 25 to 29	100.0	54.5	41.4	4.0	0.0
Aged 30 or older	100.0	18.2	67.5	12.1	2.1
Total Hispanic women	**100.0**	**31.0**	**50.3**	**13.2**	**5.5**
Under age 30	100.0	64.9	30.6	4.3	0.1
Aged 15 to 17	100.0	98.2	1.1	0.7	–
Aged 18 to 19	100.0	89.3	8.5	2.1	–
Aged 20 to 24	100.0	66.4	30.3	3.3	0.1
Aged 25 to 29	100.0	36.0	55.5	8.3	0.2
Aged 30 or older	100.0	11.9	61.5	18.1	8.5

Note: "–" means number is less than 500 or sample is too small to make a reliable estimate.
Source: Bureau of the Census, Current Population Survey Annual Social and Economic Supplement, America's Families and Living Arrangements: 2004, detailed tables, Internet site http://www.census.gov/population/www/socdemo/hh-fam/cps2004.html; calculations by New Strategist

Table 6.32 Marital Status by Sex and Age, 2004: Non-Hispanic Whites

(number and percent distribution of non-Hispanic whites aged 15 or older by sex, age, and current marital status, 2004; numbers in thousands)

	total	never married	married	separated or divorced	widowed
NUMBER					
Total non-Hispanic white men	**77,192**	**22,000**	**45,438**	**7,710**	**2,045**
Under age 30	18,514	14,940	3,135	423	14
Aged 15 to 17	4,045	3,990	17	32	5
Aged 18 to 19	2,505	2,482	17	5	–
Aged 20 to 24	6,292	5,457	746	87	2
Aged 25 to 29	5,672	3,011	2,355	299	7
Aged 30 or older	58,678	7,060	42,301	7,288	2,031
Total non-Hispanic white women	**82,115**	**17,683**	**45,380**	**10,484**	**8,567**
Under age 30	18,189	12,880	4,496	773	39
Aged 15 to 17	3,936	3,883	16	30	7
Aged 18 to 19	2,319	2,240	64	14	–
Aged 20 to 24	6,234	4,661	1,386	180	6
Aged 25 to 29	5,700	2,096	3,030	549	26
Aged 30 or older	63,926	4,802	40,882	9,713	8,530
PERCENT DISTRIBUTION					
Total non-Hispanic white men	**100.0%**	**28.5%**	**58.9%**	**10.0%**	**2.6%**
Under age 30	100.0	80.7	16.9	2.3	0.1
Aged 15 to 17	100.0	98.6	0.4	0.8	0.1
Aged 18 to 19	100.0	99.1	0.7	0.2	–
Aged 20 to 24	100.0	86.7	11.9	1.4	0.0
Aged 25 to 29	100.0	53.1	41.5	5.3	0.1
Aged 30 or older	100.0	12.0	72.1	12.4	3.5
Total non-Hispanic white women	**100.0**	**21.5**	**55.3**	**12.8**	**10.4**
Under age 30	100.0	70.8	24.7	4.2	0.2
Aged 15 to 17	100.0	98.7	0.4	0.8	0.2
Aged 18 to 19	100.0	96.6	2.8	0.6	–
Aged 20 to 24	100.0	74.8	22.2	2.9	0.1
Aged 25 to 29	100.0	36.8	53.2	9.6	0.5
Aged 30 or older	100.0	7.5	64.0	15.2	13.3

Note: Non-Hispanic whites include only those identifying themselves as being white alone and not Hispanic. "–" means number is less than 500 or sample is too small to make a reliable estimate.
Source: Bureau of the Census, Current Population Survey Annual Social and Economic Supplement, America's Families and Living Arrangements: 2004, detailed tables, Internet site http://www.census.gov/population/www/socdemo/hh-fam/cps2004.html; calculations by New Strategist

Population

■ The Millennial generation numbers nearly 75 million people, a figure that includes everyone born between 1977 and 1994 (aged 11 to 28 in 2005). Millennials account for 25 percent of the total population.

■ America's children and young adults are more diverse than middle-aged or older people. Non-Hispanic whites account for 67 percent of all Americans, a smaller 61 percent of Millennials, and just 57 percent of children under age 11.

■ While 12 percent of Americans are foreign-born, the proportion is a smaller 7 percent among people under age 30. The figure climbs to an above-average 14 percent among those aged 20 to 24 and peaks at 20 percent among 25-to-29-year-olds.

■ The diversity of Millennials varies greatly by state of residence. In Maine, New Hampshire, South Dakota, Vermont, and West Virginia, at least 90 percent of Millennials are non-Hispanic white. But in California, the most populous state, the figure is just 35 percent.

■ Because of immigration and higher fertility rates, Hispanics outnumber blacks among Millennials in 26 of the 50 states.

Millennials Are the Second-Largest Generation

They are right behind the Baby Boom in size.

The Millennial generation numbers nearly 75 million people, a figure that includes every-one born between 1977 and 1994 (aged 11 to 28 in 2005). Millennials account for 25 percent of the total population, which makes them the second-largest generation. Boomers, the parents of many Millennials, numbered 78 million in 2005 and accounted for 26 percent of the population.

Between 2000 and 2005, Millennials entirely filled the 20-to-24 age group. During those years, the number of 20-to-24-year-olds grew 10 percent, twice as fast as the 5 percent gain for the overall population. The number of 25-to-29-year-olds grew 2 percent as Millennials began to replace the small Generation X in the age group.

In the 15 years between 2005 and 2020, Millennials will enter their late twenties and thirties. As they do, the number of people aged 25-to-39 will increase by 11 percent. The overall size of the Millennial generation will reach almost 80 million because of immigra-tion. By 2020, in fact, Millennials will outnumber Boomers by 9 million. But they may not be the largest generation in that year either. The post-Millennial population (which includes generations not yet named) will account for a substantial 34 percent of the U.S. population in 2020.

■ Millennials are bringing renewed attention to the youth market because of their numbers and because their Boomer parents demand it.

The number of people aged 25 to 39 will grow by 11 percent between 2005 and 2020

(percent change in number of people by age, 2005–20)

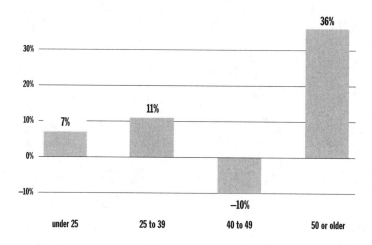

Table 7.1 Population by Age and Generation, 2005

(number and percent distribution of people by age and generation, 2005; numbers in thousands)

	number	percent distribution
Total people	**295,507**	**100.0%**
Under age 5	20,495	6.9
Aged 5 to 9	19,467	6.6
Aged 10 to 29	82,586	27.9
Aged 10 to 14	20,838	7.1
Aged 15 to 19	21,172	7.2
Aged 20 to 24	20,823	7.0
Aged 25 to 29	19,753	6.7
Aged 30 to 34	19,847	6.7
Aged 35 to 39	20,869	7.1
Aged 40 to 44	22,735	7.7
Aged 45 to 49	22,453	7.6
Aged 50 to 54	19,983	6.8
Aged 55 to 59	17,359	5.9
Aged 60 to 64	13,017	4.4
Aged 65 to 69	10,123	3.4
Aged 70 to 74	8,500	2.9
Aged 75 to 79	7,376	2.5
Aged 80 to 84	5,576	1.9
Aged 85 or older	5,120	1.7
Total people	**295,507**	**100.0**
Post-Millennial (under age 11)	43,978	14.9
Millennial (aged 11 to 28)	74,775	25.3
Generation X (aged 29 to 40)	48,985	16.6
Baby Boom (aged 41 to 59)	78,056	26.4
Older Americans (aged 60 or older)	49,713	16.8

Source: Bureau of the Census, State Interim Population Projections by Age and Sex: 2004–2030, Internet site http://www.census .gov/population/www/projections/projectionsagesex.html; calculations by New Strategist

Table 7.2 Population by Age and Sex, 2005

(number of people by age and sex, and sex ratio by age, 2005; numbers in thousands)

	total	female	male	sex ratio
Total people	**295,507**	**150,394**	**145,113**	**96**
Under age 5	20,495	10,024	10,471	104
Aged 5 to 9	19,467	9,512	9,954	105
Aged 10 to 29	82,586	40,381	42,205	105
Aged 10 to 14	20,838	10,167	10,670	105
Aged 15 to 19	21,172	10,310	10,862	105
Aged 20 to 24	20,823	10,166	10,657	105
Aged 25 to 29	19,753	9,737	10,016	103
Aged 30 to 34	19,847	9,860	9,987	101
Aged 35 to 39	20,869	10,420	10,449	100
Aged 40 to 44	22,735	11,452	11,282	99
Aged 45 to 49	22,453	11,377	11,076	97
Aged 50 to 54	19,983	10,212	9,771	96
Aged 55 to 59	17,359	8,944	8,415	94
Aged 60 to 64	13,017	6,814	6,203	91
Aged 65 to 69	10,123	5,412	4,712	87
Aged 70 to 74	8,500	4,697	3,804	81
Aged 75 to 79	7,376	4,282	3,094	72
Aged 80 to 84	5,576	3,459	2,117	61
Aged 85 or older	5,120	3,548	1,572	44

Note: The sex ratio is the number of males per 100 females.
Source: Bureau of the Census, State Interim Population Projections by Age and Sex: 2004–2030, Internet site http://www.census
.gov/population/www/projections/projectionsagesex.html; calculations by New Strategist

Table 7.3 Population by Age, 2000 and 2005

(number of people by age, April 1, 2000, and July 1, 2005; percent change 2000–05; numbers in thousands)

	2000	2005	percent change
Total people	**281,422**	**295,507**	**5.0%**
Under age 5	19,176	20,495	6.9
Aged 5 to 9	20,550	19,467	–5.3
Aged 10 to 14	20,528	20,838	1.5
Aged 15 to 19	20,220	21,172	4.7
Aged 20 to 24	18,964	20,823	9.8
Aged 25 to 29	19,381	19,753	1.9
Aged 30 to 34	20,510	19,847	–3.2
Aged 35 to 39	22,707	20,869	–8.1
Aged 40 to 44	22,442	22,735	1.3
Aged 45 to 49	20,092	22,453	11.7
Aged 50 to 54	17,586	19,983	13.6
Aged 55 to 59	13,469	17,359	28.9
Aged 60 to 64	10,805	13,017	20.5
Aged 65 to 69	9,534	10,123	6.2
Aged 70 to 74	8,857	8,500	–4.0
Aged 75 to 79	7,416	7,376	–0.5
Aged 80 to 84	4,945	5,576	12.7
Aged 85 or older	4,240	5,120	20.8

Source: Bureau of the Census, State Interim Population Projections by Age and Sex: 2004–2030, Internet site http://www.census.gov/population/www/projections/projectionsagesex.html; calculations by New Strategist

Table 7.4 Population by Age, 2005 to 2020

(number of people by age, 2005 to 2020; percent change, 2005–20; numbers in thousands)

	2005	2010	2015	2020	percent change 2005–20
Total people	**295,507**	**308,936**	**322,366**	**335,805**	**13.6%**
Under age 5	20,495	21,426	22,358	22,932	11.9
Aged 5 to 9	19,467	20,706	21,623	22,564	15.9
Aged 10 to 14	20,838	19,767	20,984	21,914	5.2
Aged 15 to 19	21,172	21,336	20,243	21,478	1.4
Aged 20 to 24	20,823	21,676	21,810	20,751	–0.3
Aged 25 to 29	19,753	21,375	22,195	22,361	13.2
Aged 30 to 34	19,847	20,271	21,858	22,704	14.4
Aged 35 to 39	20,869	20,137	20,543	22,143	6.1
Aged 40 to 44	22,735	20,984	20,250	20,673	–9.1
Aged 45 to 49	22,453	22,654	20,926	20,219	–9.9
Aged 50 to 54	19,983	22,173	22,376	20,702	3.6
Aged 55 to 59	17,359	19,507	21,649	21,876	26.0
Aged 60 to 64	13,017	16,679	18,761	20,856	60.2
Aged 65 to 69	10,123	12,172	15,621	17,618	74.0
Aged 70 to 74	8,500	9,097	10,987	14,161	66.6
Aged 75 to 79	7,376	7,186	7,761	9,450	28.1
Aged 80 to 84	5,576	5,665	5,600	6,134	10.0
Aged 85 or older	5,120	6,123	6,822	7,269	42.0

Source: Bureau of the Census, State Interim Population Projections by Age and Sex: 2004–2030, Internet site http://www.census .gov/population/www/projections/projectionsagesex.html; calculations by New Strategist

Table 7.5 Population by Generation, 2005 and 2020

(number and percent distribution of people by generation, 2005 and 2020; percent change in number, 2005–20; numbers in thousands)

	2005			2020		percent change
	number	percent distribution		number	percent distribution	2005–20
Total people	**295,507**	**100.0%**	**Total people**	**335,805**	**100.0%**	**13.6%**
Post-Millennial (under 11)	43,978	14.9	Post-Millennial (under 26)	113,942	33.9	159.1
Millennial (11 to 28)	74,775	25.3	Millennial (26 to 43)	79,639	23.7	6.5
Generation X (29 to 40)	48,985	16.6	Generation X (44 to 55)	49,219	14.7	0.5
Baby Boom (41 to 59)	78,056	26.4	Baby Boom (56 to 74)	70,151	20.9	–10.1
Older Americans (60+)	49,713	16.8	Older Americans (75+)	22,853	6.8	–54.0

Source: Bureau of the Census, State Interim Population Projections by Age and Sex: 2004–2030, Internet site http://www.census .gov/population/www/projections/projectionsagesex.html; calculations by New Strategist

The Nation's Children and Young Adults Are Diverse

Hispanics outnumber blacks among Millennials.

America's children and young adults are much more diverse than middle-aged or older people. While non-Hispanic whites account for 67 percent of all Americans, their share is a smaller 61 percent among Millennials, who were aged 11 to 28 in 2005. Among children under age 11, non-Hispanic whites account for only 57 percent of the population.

Among Millennials, Hispanics account for a larger share of the population than blacks—18 percent are Hispanic and 15 percent are black. Among children under age 11, Hispanics outnumber blacks by an even larger margin—21 to 15 percent. Among both Hispanics and blacks, Millennials are the largest generation, outnumbering Boomers. Among Asians and non-Hispanic whites, Boomers outnumber Millennials.

■ Racial and ethnic differences between young and old may divide the nation in the years ahead as older non-Hispanic whites attempt to govern young Hispanics, blacks, and Asians.

Minorities account for a large share of children and young adults

(minority share of population by generation, 2005)

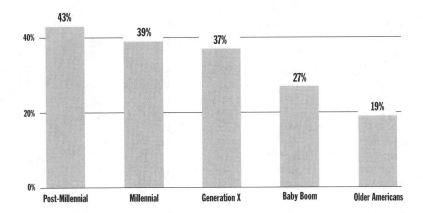

Table 7.6 Population by Age, Race, and Hispanic Origin, 2005

(number and percent distribution of people by age, race, and Hispanic origin, 2005; numbers in thousands)

	total	Asian	black	Hispanic	non-Hispanic white
Total people	**295,507**	**12,419**	**38,056**	**41,801**	**198,451**
Under age 5	20,495	833	3,113	4,397	11,528
Aged 5 to 9	19,467	763	2,941	3,892	11,330
Aged 10 to 29	82,586	3,484	12,523	14,814	50,100
Aged 10 to 14	20,838	787	3,332	3,853	12,370
Aged 15 to 19	21,172	815	3,306	3,576	13,013
Aged 20 to 24	20,823	898	3,078	3,604	12,836
Aged 25 to 29	19,753	985	2,807	3,781	11,881
Aged 30 to 34	19,847	1,190	2,678	3,666	12,060
Aged 35 to 39	20,869	1,117	2,732	3,297	13,480
Aged 40 to 44	22,735	1,033	2,892	2,926	15,606
Aged 45 to 49	22,453	948	2,736	2,375	16,113
Aged 50 to 54	19,983	828	2,276	1,823	14,812
Aged 55 to 59	17,359	685	1,788	1,393	13,289
Aged 60 to 64	13,017	480	1,250	978	10,161
Aged 65 to 69	10,123	370	972	745	7,931
Aged 70 to 74	8,500	275	767	571	6,811
Aged 75 to 79	7,376	200	591	433	6,097
Aged 80 to 84	5,576	125	407	275	4,733
Aged 85 or older	5,120	87	390	216	4,398

PERCENT DISTRIBUTION BY RACE AND HISPANIC ORIGIN

Total people	**100.0%**	**4.2%**	**12.9%**	**14.1%**	**67.2%**
Under age 5	100.0	4.1	15.2	21.5	56.2
Aged 5 to 9	100.0	3.9	15.1	20.0	58.2
Aged 10 to 29	100.0	4.2	15.2	17.9	60.7
Aged 10 to 14	100.0	3.8	16.0	18.5	59.4
Aged 15 to 19	100.0	3.8	15.6	16.9	61.5
Aged 20 to 24	100.0	4.3	14.8	17.3	61.6
Aged 25 to 29	100.0	5.0	14.2	19.1	60.1
Aged 30 to 34	100.0	6.0	13.5	18.5	60.8
Aged 35 to 39	100.0	5.4	13.1	15.8	64.6
Aged 40 to 44	100.0	4.5	12.7	12.9	68.6
Aged 45 to 49	100.0	4.2	12.2	10.6	71.8
Aged 50 to 54	100.0	4.1	11.4	9.1	74.1
Aged 55 to 59	100.0	3.9	10.3	8.0	76.6
Aged 60 to 64	100.0	3.7	9.6	7.5	78.1
Aged 65 to 69	100.0	3.7	9.6	7.4	78.3
Aged 70 to 74	100.0	3.2	9.0	6.7	80.1
Aged 75 to 79	100.0	2.7	8.0	5.9	82.7
Aged 80 to 84	100.0	2.2	7.3	4.9	84.9
Aged 85 or older	100.0	1.7	7.6	4.2	85.9

Note: Numbers will not add to total because Asians and blacks include those who identified themselves as being of the race respective alone and those who identified themselves as being of the race in combination with one or more other races, and because Hispanics may be of any race. Non-Hispanic whites include only those who identified themselves as white alone and not Hispanic.
Source: Bureau of the Census, U.S. Interim Projections by Age, Sex, Race, and Hispanic Origin, Internet site http://www.census .gov/ipc/www/usinterimproj/; calculations by New Strategist

Table 7.7 Population by Generation, Race, and Hispanic Origin, 2005

(number and percent distribution of people by generation, race, and Hispanic origin, 2005; numbers in thousands)

	total	Asian	black	Hispanic	non-Hispanic white
Total people	**295,507**	**12,419**	**38,056**	**41,801**	**198,451**
Post-Millennial (under age 11)	43,978	1,751	6,680	9,058	25,223
Millennial (aged 11 to 28)	74,775	3,114	11,375	13,287	45,488
Generation X (aged 29 to 40)	48,985	2,735	6,522	8,353	30,772
Baby Boom (aged 41 to 59)	78,056	3,280	9,101	7,885	56,836
Older Americans (aged 60 or older)	49,713	1,538	4,377	3,218	40,132

PERCENT DISTRIBUTION BY RACE AND HISPANIC ORIGIN

	total	Asian	black	Hispanic	non-Hispanic white
Total people	**100.0%**	**4.2%**	**12.9%**	**14.1%**	**67.2%**
Post-Millennial (under age 11)	100.0	4.0	15.2	20.6	57.4
Millennial (aged 11 to 28)	100.0	4.2	15.2	17.8	60.8
Generation X (aged 29 to 40)	100.0	5.6	13.3	17.1	62.8
Baby Boom (aged 41 to 59)	100.0	4.2	11.7	10.1	72.8
Older Americans (aged 60 or older)	100.0	3.1	8.8	6.5	80.7

PERCENT DISTRIBUTION BY GENERATION

	total	Asian	black	Hispanic	non-Hispanic white
Total people	**100.0%**	**100.0%**	**100.0%**	**100.0%**	**100.0%**
Post-Millennial (under age 11)	14.9	14.1	17.6	21.7	12.7
Millennial (aged 11 to 28)	25.3	25.1	29.9	31.8	22.9
Generation X (aged 29 to 40)	16.6	22.0	17.1	20.0	15.5
Baby Boom (aged 41 to 59)	26.4	26.4	23.9	18.9	28.6
Older Americans (aged 60 or older)	16.8	12.4	11.5	7.7	20.2

Note: Numbers will not add to total because Asians and blacks include those who identified themselves as being of the respective race alone and those who identified themselves as being of the race in combination with one or more other races, and because Hispanics may be of any race. Non-Hispanic whites include only those who identified themselves as being white alone and not Hispanic.
Source: Bureau of the Census, U.S. Interim Projections by Age, Sex, Race, and Hispanic Origin, Internet site http://www.census.gov/ipc/www/usinterimproj/; calculations by New Strategist

Few Children Are Foreign-Born

But many young adults were born in another country.

While 12 percent of all Americans are foreign-born, the proportion is a far lower 7 percent among people under age 30. The figure is only 2 percent among children under age 5 and climbs with age to an above-average 14 percent among those aged 20 to 24. It peaks at 20 percent among 25-to-29-year-olds. A large share of 20-to-29-year-olds are foreign-born because young adults migrate to the United States in search of job opportunities. Among the nearly 7 million 20-to-29-year-olds who are from a foreign country, only 19 percent are naturalized citizens.

Among the foreign-born in the 20-to-29 age group, nearly 52 percent were born in Central America (which includes Mexico in these statistics). Another 20 percent were born in Asia. Only 8 percent are from Europe.

■ The foreign-born population adds to the diversity of young adults. Because most are not citizens, however, they lack political power.

Among foreign-born young adults, most are from Latin America

(percent distribution of the foreign-born aged 20 to 29 by region of birth, 2004)

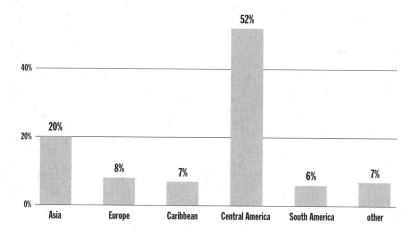

Table 7.8 Population by Age and Citizenship Status, 2004

(number and percent distribution of people by age and citizenship status, 2004; numbers in thousands)

			foreign-born		
	total	native born	total	naturalized citizen	not a citizen
Total people	**288,280**	**254,037**	**34,244**	**13,128**	**21,116**
Under age 30	101,404	94,687	6,717	1,125	5,592
Under age 5	19,932	19,597	334	75	259
Aged 5 to 9	19,646	18,938	709	81	628
Aged 10 to 14	21,118	20,005	1,113	138	975
Aged 15 to 19	20,369	18,692	1,677	286	1,391
Aged 20 to 24	20,339	17,455	2,884	545	2,339
Aged 25 to 29	19,008	15,257	3,751	711	3,040
Aged 30 or older	167,871	144,093	23,776	11,291	12,485
PERCENT DISTRIBUTION BY CITIZENSHIP STATUS					
Total people	**100.0%**	**88.1%**	**11.9%**	**4.6%**	**7.3%**
Under age 30	100.0	93.4	6.6	1.1	5.5
Under age 5	100.0	98.3	1.7	0.4	1.3
Aged 5 to 9	100.0	96.4	3.6	0.4	3.2
Aged 10 to 14	100.0	94.7	5.3	0.7	4.6
Aged 15 to 19	100.0	91.8	8.2	1.4	6.8
Aged 20 to 24	100.0	85.8	14.2	2.7	11.5
Aged 25 to 29	100.0	80.3	19.7	3.7	16.0
Aged 30 or older	100.0	85.8	14.2	6.7	7.4
PERCENT DISTRIBUTION BY AGE					
Total people	**100.0%**	**100.0%**	**100.0%**	**100.0%**	**100.0%**
Under age 30	35.2	37.3	19.6	8.6	26.5
Under age 5	6.9	7.7	1.0	0.6	1.2
Aged 5 to 9	6.8	7.5	2.1	0.6	3.0
Aged 10 to 14	7.3	7.9	3.3	1.1	4.6
Aged 15 to 19	7.1	7.4	4.9	2.2	6.6
Aged 20 to 24	7.1	6.9	8.4	4.2	11.1
Aged 25 to 29	6.6	6.0	11.0	5.4	14.4
Aged 30 or older	58.2	56.7	69.4	86.0	59.1

Source: Bureau of the Census, Foreign-Born Population of the United States, Current Population Survey, March 2004, Internet site http://www.census.gov/population/www/socdemo/foreign/ppl-176.html#cit; calculations by New Strategist

Table 7.9 Foreign-Born Population by Age and World Region of Birth, 2004

(number and percent distribution of people by age, foreign-born status, and region of birth, 2004; numbers in thousands)

	total	total	Asia	Europe	total	Caribbean	Central America	South America	other
		foreign-born			Latin America				
Total people	**288,280**	**34,244**	**8,685**	**4,661**	**18,314**	**3,323**	**12,924**	**2,066**	**2,584**
Under age 30	101,404	10,468	2,123	928	6,615	764	5,178	674	804
Under age 5	19,932	334	86	37	181	13	142	26	32
Aged 5 to 9	19,646	709	123	62	461	37	364	60	62
Aged 10 to 14	21,118	1,113	216	124	674	97	502	75	100
Aged 15 to 19	20,369	1,677	355	164	1,019	179	732	108	138
Aged 20 to 24	20,339	2,884	539	247	1,890	189	1,523	179	209
Aged 25 to 29	19,008	3,751	804	294	2,390	249	1,915	226	263
Aged 30 or older	167,871	23,776	6,562	3,734	11,699	2,560	7,745	1,392	1,782

PERCENT DISTRIBUTION OF FOREIGN-BORN BY REGION OF BIRTH

	total	total	Asia	Europe	total	Caribbean	Central America	South America	other
Total people	–	**100.0%**	**25.4%**	**13.6%**	**53.5%**	**9.7%**	**37.7%**	**6.0%**	**7.5%**
Under age 30	–	100.0	20.3	8.9	63.2	7.3	49.5	6.4	7.7
Under age 5	–	100.0	25.7	11.1	54.2	3.9	42.5	7.8	9.6
Aged 5 to 9	–	100.0	17.3	8.7	65.0	5.2	51.3	8.5	8.7
Aged 10 to 14	–	100.0	19.4	11.1	60.6	8.7	45.1	6.7	9.0
Aged 15 to 19	–	100.0	21.2	9.8	60.8	10.7	43.6	6.4	8.2
Aged 20 to 24	–	100.0	18.7	8.6	65.5	6.6	52.8	6.2	7.2
Aged 25 to 29	–	100.0	21.4	7.8	63.7	6.6	51.1	6.0	7.0
Aged 30 or older	–	100.0	27.6	15.7	49.2	10.8	32.6	5.9	7.5

PERCENT DISTRIBUTION BY AGE

	total	total	Asia	Europe	total	Caribbean	Central America	South America	other
Total people	**100.0%**	**100.0%**	**100.0%**	**100.0%**	**100.0%**	**100.0%**	**100.0%**	**100.0%**	**100.0%**
Under age 30	35.2	30.6	24.4	19.9	36.1	23.0	40.1	32.6	31.1
Under age 5	6.9	1.0	1.0	0.8	1.0	0.4	1.1	1.3	1.2
Aged 5 to 9	6.8	2.1	1.4	1.3	2.5	1.1	2.8	2.9	2.4
Aged 10 to 14	7.3	3.3	2.5	2.7	3.7	2.9	3.9	3.6	3.9
Aged 15 to 19	7.1	4.9	4.1	3.5	5.6	5.4	5.7	5.2	5.3
Aged 20 to 24	7.1	8.4	6.2	5.3	10.3	5.7	11.8	8.7	8.1
Aged 25 to 29	6.6	11.0	9.3	6.3	13.1	7.5	14.8	10.9	10.2
Aged 30 or older	58.2	69.4	75.6	80.1	63.9	77.0	59.9	67.4	69.0

Note: Central America includes Mexico in these statistics. "–" means not applicable.
Source: Bureau of the Census, Foreign Born Population of the United States, Current Population Survey, March 2004, Internet site http://www.census.gov/population/www/socdemo/foreign/ppl-176.html#cit; calculations by New Strategist

Among Immigrants in 2004, Young Adults Count

More than one-third of immigrants in 2004 were Millennials.

In 2004, more than 900,000 immigrants were admitted to the U.S., and nearly 350,000 of them were aged 10 to 29 (Millennials were aged 10 to 27 in that year). Many immigrants to the United States are young adults looking for job opportunities.

Immigrants are most likely to be aged 25 to 39. This 15-year age group accounted for 40 percent of immigrants in 2004 to the U.S. The under-25 age group accounts for a smaller 32 percent of immigrants, while only 28 percent are aged 40 or older.

■ Because most immigrants are children or young adults, immigration has a much greater impact on the diversity of young Americans than on the middle-aged or older populations.

Forty percent of immigrants in 2004 were aged 25 to 39

(percent distribution of immigrants by age, 2004)

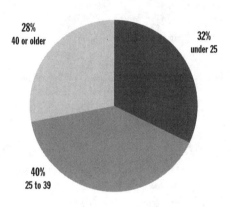

Table 7.10 Immigrants by Age, 2004

(number and percent distribution of immigrants by age, 2004)

	number	percent distribution
Total immigrants	**946,142**	**100.0%**
Under age 1	7,807	0.8
Aged 1 to 4	22,932	2.4
Aged 5 to 9	48,181	5.1
Aged 10 to 29	347,574	36.7
Aged 10 to 14	58,821	6.2
Aged 15 to 19	78,069	8.3
Aged 20 to 24	86,278	9.1
Aged 25 to 29	124,406	13.1
Aged 30 to 34	143,921	15.2
Aged 35 to 39	107,251	11.3
Aged 40 to 44	76,404	8.1
Aged 45 to 49	55,223	5.8
Aged 50 to 54	39,661	4.2
Aged 55 to 59	30,037	3.2
Aged 60 to 64	23,829	2.5
Aged 65 to 74	32,346	3.4
Aged 75 or older	10,936	1.2

Note: Numbers may not sum to total because "age not stated" is not shown.
Source: Office of Immigration Statistics, 2004 Yearbook of Immigration Statistics, Internet site http://uscis.gov/graphics/shared/statistics/yearbook/YrBk04Im.htm; calculations by New Strategist

Many Americans Do Not Speak English at Home

Most are Spanish speakers, but many also speak English.

Nearly 50 million Americans speak a language other than English at home, according to the Census Bureau's 2004 American Community Survey—19 percent of the population aged 5 or older. Among those who do not speak English at home, 61 percent speak Spanish.

The percentage of Americans who do not speak English at home does not vary much by age—19 percent of school children, 20 percent of working-age adults, and 13 percent of the elderly. But the languages spoken by each age group at home do vary by age. Fully 71 percent of children aged 5 to 17 who do not speak English at home are Spanish speakers. The proportion is a smaller 61 percent among adults aged 18 to 64, and falls to just 43 percent among people aged 65 or older. Thirty-seven percent of the elderly who do not speak English at home speak another Indo-European language, and 17 percent speak an Asian language.

Among school children, most of those who do not speak English at home are able to speak English "very well." Only 29 percent of the Spanish speakers aged 5 to 17, for example, cannot speak English very well. Among working-age adults, a much larger 53 percent of the Spanish speakers cannot speak English very well. Among people aged 65 or older, most of those who speak Spanish or an Asian language at home cannot speak English very well.

■ The language barrier is a bigger problem for adults than for school children.

Few children who speak Spanish at home cannot speak English "very well"

(percent of people aged 5 or older who speak Spanish at home and do not speak English "very well," by age, 2004)

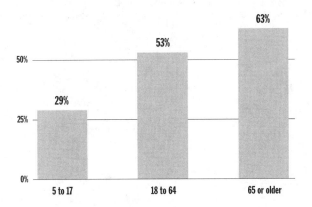

Table 7.11 Language Spoken at Home by Age, 2004

(number and percent distribution of people aged 5 or older who speak a language other than English at home by language spoken at home and ability to speak English "very well," by age, 2004; numbers in thousands)

	total		aged 5 to 17		aged 18 to 64		aged 65 or older	
	number	percent distribution	number	percent distribution	number	percent distribution	number	percent distribution
Total, aged 5 or older	**265,683**	**100.0%**	**52,916**	**100.0%**	**178,562**	**100.0%**	**34,205**	**100.0%**
Speak only English at home	216,050	81.3	42,939	81.1	143,420	80.3	29,691	86.8
Speak a language other than English at home	49,633	18.7	9,977	18.9	35,142	19.7	4,514	13.2
Speak English less than "very well"	22,305	8.4	2,774	5.2	16,944	9.5	2,587	7.6
Total who speak a language other than English at home	**49,633**	**100.0**	**9,977**	**100.0**	**35,142**	**100.0**	**4,514**	**100.0**
Speak Spanish at home	30,522	61.5	7,103	71.2	21,498	61.2	1,921	42.6
Speak other Indo-European language at home	9,634	19.4	1,440	14.4	6,530	18.6	1,664	36.9
Speak Asian or Pacific Island language at home	7,614	15.3	1,116	11.2	5,730	16.3	769	17.0
Speak other language at home	1,863	3.8	318	3.2	1,384	3.9	161	3.6
Speak Spanish at home	**30,522**	**100.0**	**7,103**	**100.0**	**21,498**	**100.0**	**1,921**	**100.0**
Speak English less than "very well"	14,637	48.0	2,075	29.2	11,358	52.8	1,203	62.6
Speak other Indo-European language at home	**9,634**	**100.0**	**1,440**	**100.0**	**6,530**	**100.0**	**1,664**	**100.0**
Speak English less than "very well"	3,317	34.4	341	23.6	2,237	34.3	740	44.4
Speak Asian or Pacific Island language at home	**7,614**	**100.0**	**1,116**	**100.0**	**5,730**	**100.0**	**769**	**100.0**
Speak English less than "very well"	3,807	50.0	306	27.4	2,932	51.2	569	74.0
Speak other language at home	**1,863**	**100.0**	**318**	**100.0**	**1,384**	**100.0**	**161**	**100.0**
Speak English less than "very well"	545	29.3	53	16.6	417	30.1	75	46.7

Source: Bureau of the Census, 2004 American Community Survey Data Profile, Internet site http://factfinder.census.gov/servlet/ DatasetMainPageServlet?_program=ACS&_submenuId=datasets_2&_lang=en&_ts=; calculations by New Strategist

The Largest Share of Millennials Lives in the South

Millennials account for 31 percent of Utah's population, but only 23 percent of the population of Vermont.

The South is home to the largest share of the population and, consequently, to the largest share of Millennials. The Census Bureau's 2004 American Community Survey found 36 percent of Millennials living in the South, where they account for 25 percent of the population.

The diversity of Millennials varies greatly by state of residence. In Maine, New Hampshire, South Dakota, Vermont, and West Virginia, at least 90 percent of Millennials are non-Hispanic white. But in California, the most populous state, the figure is just 35 percent. In Texas, only 42 percent of Millennials are non-Hispanic white. Hawaii, New Mexico, and the District of Columbia also have minority majorities in the Millennial generation.

Because of immigration and higher fertility rates, Hispanics outnumber blacks among Millennials in 26 of the 50 states. In California, 44 percent of Millennials are Hispanic (a greater share than the 35 percent non-Hispanic whites), 11 percent are Asian, and 7 percent are black. In other states with large Hispanic populations, such as Texas and Florida, Hispanics also greatly outnumber blacks among Millennials.

■ Although Millennials are more diverse in some states than others, racial and ethnic diversity influences youth culture everywhere.

In California, diversity is the rule among children and young adults

(percent distribution of Millennials in California by race and Hispanic origin, 2004)

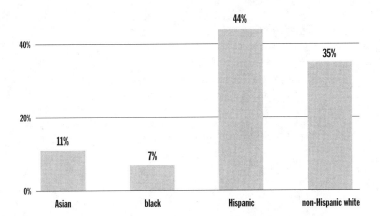

Table 7.12 Population by Age and Region, 2004

(number and percent distribution of people by age and region of residence, 2004; numbers in thousands)

	total	Northeast	Midwest	South	West
Total people	**285,692**	**52,865**	**63,910**	**103,021**	**65,896**
Under age 30	117,929	20,322	26,259	42,787	28,561
Under age 5	20,008	3,360	4,318	7,418	4,912
Aged 5 to 9	19,659	3,418	4,375	7,124	4,743
Aged 10 to 14	21,085	3,804	4,691	7,509	5,080
Aged 15 to 19	19,078	3,347	4,338	6,833	4,561
Aged 20 to 24	19,328	3,219	4,389	7,048	4,672
Aged 25 to 29	18,771	3,175	4,148	6,856	4,593
Aged 30 or older	167,762	32,543	37,651	60,234	37,335

PERCENT DISTRIBUTION BY AGE

	total	Northeast	Midwest	South	West
Total people	**100.0%**	**100.0%**	**100.0%**	**100.0%**	**100.0%**
Under age 30	41.3	38.4	41.1	41.5	43.3
Under age 5	7.0	6.4	6.8	7.2	7.5
Aged 5 to 9	6.9	6.5	6.8	6.9	7.2
Aged 10 to 14	7.4	7.2	7.3	7.3	7.7
Aged 15 to 19	6.7	6.3	6.8	6.6	6.9
Aged 20 to 24	6.8	6.1	6.9	6.8	7.1
Aged 25 to 29	6.6	6.0	6.5	6.7	7.0
Aged 30 or older	58.7	61.6	58.9	58.5	56.7

PERCENT DISTRIBUTION BY REGION

	total	Northeast	Midwest	South	West
Total people	**100.0%**	**18.5%**	**22.4%**	**36.1%**	**23.1%**
Under age 30	100.0	17.2	22.3	36.3	24.2
Under age 5	100.0	16.8	21.6	37.1	24.6
Aged 5 to 9	100.0	17.4	22.3	36.2	24.1
Aged 10 to 14	100.0	18.0	22.2	35.6	24.1
Aged 15 to 19	100.0	17.5	22.7	35.8	23.9
Aged 20 to 24	100.0	16.7	22.7	36.5	24.2
Aged 25 to 29	100.0	16.9	22.1	36.5	24.5
Aged 30 or older	100.0	19.4	22.4	35.9	22.3

Source: Bureau of the Census, 2004 American Community Survey, Internet site http://factfinder.census.gov/servlet/ DatasetMainPageServlet?_program=ACS&_lang=en&_ts=143547961449; calculations by New Strategist

Table 7.13 Population by Generation and Region, 2004

(number and percent distribution of people by generation and region of residence, 2004; numbers in thousands)

	total	Northeast	Midwest	South	West
Total people	**285,692**	**52,865**	**63,910**	**103,021**	**65,896**
Post-Millennial (under age 10)	39,667	6,778	8,693	14,542	9,655
Millennial (aged 10 to 27)	70,753	12,274	15,907	25,503	17,069
Generation X (aged 28 to 39)	48,123	8,908	10,445	17,334	11,437
Baby Boom (aged 40 to 58)	77,079	14,885	17,457	27,503	17,235
Older Americans (aged 59 or older)	50,069	10,020	11,409	18,140	10,500
PERCENT DISTRIBUTION BY GENERATION					
Total people	**100.0%**	**100.0%**	**100.0%**	**100.0%**	**100.0%**
Post-Millennial (under age 10)	13.9	12.8	13.6	14.1	14.7
Millennial (aged 10 to 27)	24.8	23.2	24.9	24.8	25.9
Generation X (aged 28 to 39)	16.8	16.9	16.3	16.8	17.4
Baby Boom (aged 40 to 58)	27.0	28.2	27.3	26.7	26.2
Older Americans (aged 59 or older)	17.5	19.0	17.9	17.6	15.9
PERCENT DISTRIBUTION BY REGION					
Total people	**100.0%**	**18.5%**	**22.4%**	**36.1%**	**23.1%**
Post-Millennial (under age 10)	100.0	17.1	21.9	36.7	24.3
Millennial (aged 10 to 27)	100.0	17.3	22.5	36.0	24.1
Generation X (aged 28 to 39)	100.0	18.5	21.7	36.0	23.8
Baby Boom (aged 40 to 58)	100.0	19.3	22.6	35.7	22.4
Older Americans (aged 59 or older)	100.0	20.0	22.8	36.2	21.0

Source: Bureau of the Census, 2004 American Community Survey, Internet site http://factfinder.census.gov/servlet/ DatasetMainPageServlet?_program=ACS&_lang=en&_ts=143547961449; calculations by New Strategist

Table 7.14 Post-Millennial Generation by Region, Race, and Hispanic Origin, 2004

(number and percent distribution of people under age 10 by region of residence, race, and Hispanic origin, 2004; numbers in thousands)

	total under 10	Asian	black	Hispanic	non-Hispanic white
United States	**39,667**	**1,565**	**5,819**	**8,254**	**22,565**
Northeast	6,778	350	965	1,032	4,280
Midwest	8,693	203	1,114	776	6,288
South	14,542	316	3,261	2,725	7,804
West	9,655	695	478	3,721	4,193
PERCENT DISTRIBUTION BY RACE AND HISPANIC ORIGIN					
United States	**100.0%**	**3.9%**	**14.7%**	**20.8%**	**56.9%**
Northeast	100.0	5.2	14.2	15.2	63.1
Midwest	100.0	2.3	12.8	8.9	72.3
South	100.0	2.2	22.4	18.7	53.7
West	100.0	7.2	5.0	38.5	43.4
PERCENT DISTRIBUTION BY REGION					
United States	**100.0%**	**100.0%**	**100.0%**	**100.0%**	**100.0%**
Northeast	17.1	22.4	16.6	12.5	19.0
Midwest	21.9	13.0	19.1	9.4	27.9
South	36.7	20.2	56.0	33.0	34.6
West	24.3	44.4	8.2	45.1	18.6

Note: Blacks and Asians are those who identify themselves as being of the respective race alone. Non-Hispanic whites are those who identify themselves as being white alone and not Hispanic. Numbers will not sum to total because Hispanics may be of any race and not all races are shown.
Source: Bureau of the Census, 2004 American Community Survey, Internet site http://factfinder.census.gov/servlet/ DatasetMainPageServlet?_program=ACS&_lang=en&_ts=143547961449; calculations by New Strategist

Table 7.15 Millennial Generation by Region, Race, and Hispanic Origin, 2004

(number and percent distribution of people aged 10 to 27 by region of residence, race, and Hispanic origin, 2004; numbers in thousands)

	total 10 to 27	Asian	black	Hispanic	non-Hispanic white
United States	**70,753**	**2,886**	**10,056**	**12,771**	**43,155**
Northeast	12,274	579	1,678	1,721	8,141
Midwest	15,907	375	1,890	1,177	12,123
South	25,503	581	5,609	4,213	14,564
West	17,069	1,351	879	5,660	8,327
PERCENT DISTRIBUTION BY RACE AND HISPANIC ORIGIN					
United States	**100.0%**	**4.1%**	**14.2%**	**18.1%**	**61.0%**
Northeast	100.0	4.7	13.7	14.0	66.3
Midwest	100.0	2.4	11.9	7.4	76.2
South	100.0	2.3	22.0	16.5	57.1
West	100.0	7.9	5.2	33.2	48.8
PERCENT DISTRIBUTION BY REGION					
United States	**100.0%**	**100.0%**	**100.0%**	**100.0%**	**100.0%**
Northeast	17.3	20.1	16.7	13.5	18.9
Midwest	22.5	13.0	18.8	9.2	28.1
South	36.0	20.1	55.8	33.0	33.7
West	24.1	46.8	8.7	44.3	19.3

Note: Blacks and Asians are those identifying themselves as being of the respective race alone. Non-Hispanic whites are those identifying themselves as being white alone and not Hispanic. Numbers will not sum to total because Hispanics may be of any race and not all races are shown.
Source: Bureau of the Census, 2004 American Community Survey, Internet site http://factfinder.census.gov/servlet/ DatasetMainPageServlet?_program=ACS&_lang=en&_ts=143547961449; calculations by New Strategist

Table 7.16 State Populations by Age, 2004

(number of people under age 30 by state of residence, 2004; numbers in thousands)

	total population	under age 30						
		total	under 5	5 to 9	10 to 14	15 to 19	20 to 24	25 to 29
United States	**285,692**	**117,929**	**20,008**	**19,659**	**21,085**	**19,078**	**19,328**	**18,771**
Alabama	4,415	1,799	296	277	336	286	314	291
Alaska	636	290	49	47	56	57	44	36
Arizona	5,634	2,482	452	425	426	378	405	396
Arkansas	2,676	1,105	182	171	205	176	193	179
California	35,055	15,325	2,639	2,600	2,779	2,437	2,435	2,435
Colorado	4,499	1,935	337	303	342	293	329	330
Connecticut	3,389	1,273	209	225	257	215	186	181
Delaware	805	317	54	50	57	50	55	51
District of Columbia	518	202	35	29	29	17	35	57
Florida	16,990	6,402	1,087	1,052	1,165	1,070	1,056	971
Georgia	8,581	3,738	667	648	623	578	614	608
Hawaii	1,227	482	87	76	85	79	78	77
Idaho	1,360	607	108	96	105	101	107	90
Illinois	12,391	5,225	893	881	931	820	852	848
Indiana	6,059	2,559	429	434	471	409	416	399
Iowa	2,851	1,133	179	185	195	191	203	181
Kansas	2,653	1,120	185	190	189	187	186	182
Kentucky	4,031	1,612	264	271	278	258	267	274
Louisiana	4,381	1,902	317	312	333	321	334	285
Maine	1,279	456	69	71	88	86	76	65
Maryland	5,422	2,179	371	393	390	361	350	315
Massachusetts	6,201	2,349	392	397	426	361	371	402
Michigan	9,859	4,033	656	697	732	690	655	604
Minnesota	4,959	2,031	335	321	368	339	339	329
Mississippi	2,805	1,221	210	196	215	202	208	190
Missouri	5,586	2,267	371	367	397	380	395	356
Montana	902	350	55	52	62	67	62	54
Nebraska	1,697	714	121	114	123	116	126	114
Nevada	2,301	966	170	168	171	146	145	165
New Hampshire	1,262	473	74	80	94	88	72	65
New Jersey	8,503	3,305	564	582	653	552	493	462
New Mexico	1,863	795	132	134	136	140	132	119
New York	18,634	7,352	1,241	1,210	1,323	1,186	1,171	1,221
North Carolina	8,270	3,380	596	574	601	503	526	580
North Dakota	610	245	35	36	40	42	48	45
Ohio	11,154	4,465	727	756	807	745	738	692
Oklahoma	3,412	1,423	244	230	239	222	253	236
Oregon	3,514	1,408	225	231	246	230	241	235
Pennsylvania	11,958	4,496	719	753	847	759	743	676
Rhode Island	1,037	401	61	64	76	60	71	70

(continued)

	total population	under age 30						
		total	under 5	5 to 9	10 to 14	15 to 19	20 to 24	25 to 29
South Carolina	4,060	1,653	272	278	293	265	278	269
South Dakota	741	312	52	49	54	53	55	49
Tennessee	5,748	2,289	386	381	387	364	381	389
Texas	21,912	10,020	1,842	1,687	1,721	1,590	1,593	1,588
Utah	2,349	1,262	234	202	192	179	229	226
Vermont	601	217	31	37	40	41	35	33
Virginia	7,224	2,899	497	479	518	463	477	466
Washington	6,063	2,461	393	379	446	418	426	399
West Virginia	1,770	645	99	94	121	108	116	107
Wisconsin	5,351	2,156	335	345	385	367	375	349
Wyoming	493	198	31	30	34	35	39	30

Source: Bureau of the Census, 2004 American Community Survey, Internet site http://factfinder.census.gov/servlet/ DatasetMainPageServlet?_program=ACS&_lang=en&_ts=143547961449; calculations by New Strategist

Table 7.17 Distribution of State Populations by Age, 2004

(percent distribution of people by state of residence and age, 2004)

	total population	under age 30						
		total	under 5	5 to 9	10 to 14	15 to 19	20 to 24	25 to 29
United States	**100.0%**	**41.3%**	**7.0%**	**6.9%**	**7.4%**	**6.7%**	**6.8%**	**6.6%**
Alabama	100.0	40.8	6.7	6.3	7.6	6.5	7.1	6.6
Alaska	100.0	45.6	7.7	7.4	8.9	9.0	6.9	5.6
Arizona	100.0	44.0	8.0	7.5	7.6	6.7	7.2	7.0
Arkansas	100.0	41.3	6.8	6.4	7.6	6.6	7.2	6.7
California	100.0	43.7	7.5	7.4	7.9	7.0	6.9	6.9
Colorado	100.0	43.0	7.5	6.7	7.6	6.5	7.3	7.3
Connecticut	100.0	37.5	6.2	6.6	7.6	6.3	5.5	5.3
Delaware	100.0	39.4	6.7	6.2	7.1	6.3	6.8	6.4
District of Columbia	100.0	39.1	6.7	5.6	5.7	3.4	6.7	11.0
Florida	100.0	37.7	6.4	6.2	6.9	6.3	6.2	5.7
Georgia	100.0	43.6	7.8	7.5	7.3	6.7	7.2	7.1
Hawaii	100.0	39.3	7.1	6.2	7.0	6.4	6.3	6.3
Idaho	100.0	44.6	7.9	7.0	7.7	7.4	7.9	6.6
Illinois	100.0	42.2	7.2	7.1	7.5	6.6	6.9	6.8
Indiana	100.0	42.2	7.1	7.2	7.8	6.7	6.9	6.6
Iowa	100.0	39.7	6.3	6.5	6.8	6.7	7.1	6.3
Kansas	100.0	42.2	7.0	7.2	7.1	7.1	7.0	6.8
Kentucky	100.0	40.0	6.6	6.7	6.9	6.4	6.6	6.8
Louisiana	100.0	43.4	7.2	7.1	7.6	7.3	7.6	6.5
Maine	100.0	35.6	5.4	5.5	6.9	6.7	6.0	5.1
Maryland	100.0	40.2	6.8	7.2	7.2	6.7	6.4	5.8
Massachusetts	100.0	37.9	6.3	6.4	6.9	5.8	6.0	6.5
Michigan	100.0	40.9	6.6	7.1	7.4	7.0	6.6	6.1
Minnesota	100.0	41.0	6.8	6.5	7.4	6.8	6.8	6.6
Mississippi	100.0	43.5	7.5	7.0	7.7	7.2	7.4	6.8
Missouri	100.0	40.6	6.6	6.6	7.1	6.8	7.1	6.4
Montana	100.0	38.8	6.1	5.7	6.9	7.4	6.8	6.0
Nebraska	100.0	42.1	7.1	6.7	7.2	6.8	7.4	6.7
Nevada	100.0	42.0	7.4	7.3	7.4	6.4	6.3	7.2
New Hampshire	100.0	37.5	5.9	6.3	7.5	6.9	5.7	5.2
New Jersey	100.0	38.9	6.6	6.8	7.7	6.5	5.8	5.4
New Mexico	100.0	42.7	7.1	7.2	7.3	7.5	7.1	6.4
New York	100.0	39.5	6.7	6.5	7.1	6.4	6.3	6.6
North Carolina	100.0	40.9	7.2	6.9	7.3	6.1	6.4	7.0
North Dakota	100.0	40.2	5.8	5.9	6.5	6.8	7.9	7.4
Ohio	100.0	40.0	6.5	6.8	7.2	6.7	6.6	6.2
Oklahoma	100.0	41.7	7.2	6.7	7.0	6.5	7.4	6.9
Oregon	100.0	40.1	6.4	6.6	7.0	6.5	6.9	6.7
Pennsylvania	100.0	37.6	6.0	6.3	7.1	6.3	6.2	5.7
Rhode Island	100.0	38.7	5.9	6.1	7.3	5.7	6.9	6.7

(continued)

	total population	under age 30						
		total	under 5	5 to 9	10 to 14	15 to 19	20 to 24	25 to 29
South Carolina	100.0%	40.7%	6.7%	6.8%	7.2%	6.5%	6.8%	6.6%
South Dakota	100.0	42.0	7.0	6.6	7.3	7.1	7.4	6.6
Tennessee	100.0	39.8	6.7	6.6	6.7	6.3	6.6	6.8
Texas	100.0	45.7	8.4	7.7	7.9	7.3	7.3	7.2
Utah	100.0	53.7	10.0	8.6	8.2	7.6	9.7	9.6
Vermont	100.0	36.1	5.2	6.1	6.6	6.8	5.8	5.6
Virginia	100.0	40.1	6.9	6.6	7.2	6.4	6.6	6.5
Washington	100.0	40.6	6.5	6.2	7.4	6.9	7.0	6.6
West Virginia	100.0	36.4	5.6	5.3	6.8	6.1	6.5	6.1
Wisconsin	100.0	40.3	6.3	6.5	7.2	6.9	7.0	6.5
Wyoming	100.0	40.3	6.2	6.0	6.9	7.1	7.9	6.1

Source: Bureau of the Census, 2004 American Community Survey, Internet site http://factfinder.census.gov/servlet/ DatasetMainPageServlet?_program=ACS&_lang=en&_ts=143547961449; calculations by New Strategist

Table 7.18 State Populations by Generation, 2004

(number of people by state of residence and generation, 2004; numbers in thousands)

	total population	post-Millennial (under age 10)	Millennial (10 to 27)	Generation X (28 to 39)	Baby Boom (40 to 58)	Older Americans (59 or older)
United States	**285,692**	**39,667**	**70,753**	**48,123**	**77,079**	**50,069**
Alabama	4,415	573	1,110	719	1,186	827
Alaska	636	96	179	100	192	69
Arizona	5,634	877	1,447	938	1,358	1,014
Arkansas	2,676	353	680	423	702	518
California	35,055	5,239	9,111	6,258	9,068	5,379
Colorado	4,499	640	1,162	812	1,229	655
Connecticut	3,389	434	766	559	986	644
Delaware	805	104	193	136	222	151
District of Columbia	518	64	116	112	132	94
Florida	16,990	2,140	3,874	2,633	4,479	3,865
Georgia	8,581	1,315	2,180	1,627	2,228	1,232
Hawaii	1,227	163	288	196	337	243
Idaho	1,360	204	367	209	357	223
Illinois	12,391	1,774	3,112	2,151	3,262	2,091
Indiana	6,059	864	1,535	984	1,614	1,062
Iowa	2,851	364	697	439	791	561
Kansas	2,653	375	672	427	709	470
Kentucky	4,031	535	968	672	1,122	734
Louisiana	4,381	630	1,159	687	1,172	733
Maine	1,279	140	290	195	399	255
Maryland	5,422	764	1,289	906	1,545	917
Massachusetts	6,201	789	1,399	1,108	1,777	1,128
Michigan	9,859	1,353	2,438	1,618	2,714	1,735
Minnesota	4,959	655	1,244	827	1,394	838
Mississippi	2,805	406	739	448	728	485
Missouri	5,586	739	1,386	891	1,528	1,043
Montana	902	106	222	127	269	177
Nebraska	1,697	235	433	267	457	305
Nevada	2,301	338	562	421	597	384
New Hampshire	1,262	154	293	205	389	221
New Jersey	8,503	1,146	1,975	1,440	2,398	1,545
New Mexico	1,863	267	480	288	500	328
New York	18,634	2,451	4,413	3,262	5,083	3,426
North Carolina	8,270	1,170	1,978	1,451	2,233	1,438
North Dakota	610	71	156	87	175	120
Ohio	11,154	1,483	2,705	1,787	3,104	2,075
Oklahoma	3,412	474	854	529	923	632
Oregon	3,514	456	858	600	957	643
Pennsylvania	11,958	1,472	2,754	1,873	3,371	2,487
Rhode Island	1,037	124	249	174	291	198

(continued)

	total population	post-Millennial (under age 10)	Millennial (10 to 27)	Generation X (28 to 39)	Baby Boom (40 to 58)	Older Americans (59 or older)
South Carolina	4,060	549	996	660	1,120	734
South Dakota	741	101	191	110	199	141
Tennessee	5,748	767	1,366	988	1,582	1,046
Texas	21,912	3,529	5,856	3,820	5,576	3,132
Utah	2,349	436	736	387	507	284
Vermont	601	68	135	93	189	115
Virginia	7,224	976	1,737	1,245	2,044	1,221
Washington	6,063	772	1,530	1,031	1,716	1,014
West Virginia	1,770	193	409	277	508	384
Wisconsin	5,351	680	1,336	857	1,510	968
Wyoming	493	60	126	70	149	88

Source: Bureau of the Census, 2004 American Community Survey, Internet site http://factfinder.census.gov/servlet/
DatasetMainPageServlet?_program=ACS&_lang=en&_ts=143547961449; calculations by New Strategist

Table 7.19 Distribution of State Populations by Generation, 2004

(percent distribution of people by state of residence and generation, 2004)

	total population	post-Millennial (under age 10)	Millennial (10 to 27)	Generation X (28 to 39)	Baby Boom (40 to 58)	Older Americans (59 or older)
United States	**100.0%**	**13.9%**	**24.8%**	**16.8%**	**27.0%**	**17.5%**
Alabama	100.0	13.0	25.1	16.3	26.9	18.7
Alaska	100.0	15.2	28.2	15.7	30.2	10.8
Arizona	100.0	15.6	25.7	16.7	24.1	18.0
Arkansas	100.0	13.2	25.4	15.8	26.2	19.4
California	100.0	14.9	26.0	17.9	25.9	15.3
Colorado	100.0	14.2	25.8	18.0	27.3	14.6
Connecticut	100.0	12.8	22.6	16.5	29.1	19.0
Delaware	100.0	12.9	23.9	16.8	27.6	18.8
District of Columbia	100.0	12.3	22.4	21.7	25.6	18.1
Florida	100.0	12.6	22.8	15.5	26.4	22.7
Georgia	100.0	15.3	25.4	19.0	26.0	14.4
Hawaii	100.0	13.3	23.5	16.0	27.5	19.8
Idaho	100.0	15.0	27.0	15.4	26.3	16.4
Illinois	100.0	14.3	25.1	17.4	26.3	16.9
Indiana	100.0	14.3	25.3	16.2	26.6	17.5
Iowa	100.0	12.8	24.4	15.4	27.7	19.7
Kansas	100.0	14.1	25.3	16.1	26.7	17.7
Kentucky	100.0	13.3	24.0	16.7	27.8	18.2
Louisiana	100.0	14.4	26.5	15.7	26.8	16.7
Maine	100.0	11.0	22.6	15.2	31.2	19.9
Maryland	100.0	14.1	23.8	16.7	28.5	16.9
Massachusetts	100.0	12.7	22.6)	17.9	28.7	18.2
Michigan	100.0	13.7	24.7	16.4	27.5	17.6
Minnesota	100.0	13.2	25.1	16.7	28.1	16.9
Mississippi	100.0	14.5	26.3	16.0	25.9	17.3
Missouri	100.0	13.2	24.8	15.9	27.3	18.7
Montana	100.0	11.8	24.6	14.1	29.8	19.6
Nebraska	100.0	13.8	25.5	15.7	26.9	18.0
Nevada	100.0	14.7	24.4	18.3	25.9	16.7
New Hampshire	100.0	12.2	23.2	16.3	30.8	17.5
New Jersey	100.0	13.5	23.2	16.9	28.2	18.2
New Mexico	100.0	14.3	25.8	15.5	26.8	17.6
New York	100.0	13.2	23.7	17.5	27.3	18.4
North Carolina	100.0	14.1	23.9	17.5	27.0	17.4
North Dakota	100.0	11.6	25.6	14.3	28.8	19.6
Ohio	100.0	13.3	24.3	16.0	27.8	18.6
Oklahoma	100.0	13.9	25.0	15.5	27.0	18.5
Oregon	100.0	13.0	24.4	17.1	27.2	18.3
Pennsylvania	100.0	12.3	23.0	15.7	28.2	20.8
Rhode Island	100.0	12.0	24.0	16.8	28.0	19.1

(continued)

	total population	post-Millennial (under age 10)	Millennial (10 to 27)	Generation X (28 to 39)	Baby Boom (40 to 58)	Older Americans (59 or older)
South Carolina	100.0%	13.5%	24.5%	16.3%	27.6%	18.1%
South Dakota	100.0	13.6	25.7	14.8	26.8	19.1
Tennessee	100.0	13.3	23.8	17.2	27.5	18.2
Texas	100.0	16.1	26.7	17.4	25.4	14.3
Utah	100.0	18.6	31.3	16.5	21.6	12.1
Vermont	100.0	11.3	22.5	15.4	31.5	19.1
Virginia	100.0	13.5	24.0	17.2	28.3	16.9
Washington	100.0	12.7	25.2	17.0	28.3	16.7
West Virginia	100.0	10.9	23.1	15.7	28.7	21.7
Wisconsin	100.0	12.7	25.0	16.0	28.2	18.1
Wyoming	100.0	12.2	25.6	14.1	30.2	17.8

Source: Bureau of the Census, 2004 American Community Survey, Internet site http://factfinder.census.gov/servlet/ DatasetMainPageServlet?_program=ACS&_lang=en&_ts=143547961449; calculations by New Strategist

Table 7.20 Post-Millennial Generation by State, Race, and Hispanic Origin, 2004

(number and percent distribution of people under age 10 by state of residence, race, and Hispanic origin, 2004; numbers in thousands)

| | number | | | | percent distribution | | | | |
	total under 10	Asian	black	Hispanic	non-Hispanic white	total	Asian	black	Hispanic	non-Hispanic white
United States	**39,667**	**1,565**	**5,819**	**8,254**	**22,565**	**100.0%**	**3.9%**	**14.7%**	**20.8%**	**56.9%**
Alabama	573	7	174	20	360	100.0	1.2	30.4	3.4	62.9
Alaska	96	4	4	7	54	100.0	4.3	4.3	7.4	56.2
Arizona	877	19	30	368	388	100.0	2.2	3.4	41.9	44.3
Arkansas	353	2	69	26	246	100.0	0.5	19.6	7.5	69.6
California	5,239	518	340	2,574	1,603	100.0	9.9	6.5	49.1	30.6
Colorado	640	13	30	185	394	100.0	2.1	4.7	28.8	61.5
Connecticut	434	16	51	71	286	100.0	3.6	11.8	16.3	65.9
Delaware	104	3	26	10	61	100.0	3.2	25.5	9.9	58.6
District of Columbia	64	1	45	6	11	100.0	1.2	70.6	9.8	16.6
Florida	2,140	43	465	504	1,081	100.0	2.0	21.7	23.5	50.5
Georgia	1,315	28	442	120	689	100.0	2.1	33.6	9.1	52.4
Hawaii	163	51	2	25	26	100.0	30.9	1.3	15.2	15.9
Idaho	204	1	–	31	162	100.0	0.5	–	15.1	79.6
Illinois	1,774	67	304	369	989	100.0	3.8	17.2	20.8	55.8
Indiana	864	11	81	61	680	100.0	1.3	9.3	7.0	78.8
Iowa	364	6	11	26	311	100.0	1.6	2.9	7.1	85.6
Kansas	375	7	22	37	289	100.0	1.9	5.8	10.0	77.0
Kentucky	535	4	44	16	454	100.0	0.8	8.2	2.9	84.8
Louisiana	630	8	255	18	333	100.0	1.3	40.6	2.9	52.8
Maine	140	1	2	3	129	100.0	0.9	1.3	2.0	92.0
Maryland	764	35	249	53	399	100.0	4.6	32.6	7.0	52.2
Massachusetts	789	36	59	104	563	100.0	4.6	7.5	13.1	71.4
Michigan	1,353	33	239	79	952	100.0	2.4	17.7	5.8	70.4
Minnesota	655	29	46	44	502	100.0	4.5	7.1	6.8	76.5
Mississippi	406	1	184	9	207	100.0	0.2	45.3	2.2	51.0
Missouri	739	11	103	30	566	100.0	1.5	14.0	4.1	76.7
Montana	106	–	–	4	86	100.0	–	–	3.6	80.8
Nebraska	235	3	11	30	180	100.0	1.2	4.6	12.6	76.8
Nevada	338	17	18	118	162	100.0	5.2	5.3	34.8	48.0
New Hampshire	154	4	2	6	138	100.0	2.4	1.5	3.6	90.2
New Jersey	1,146	90	177	224	623	100.0	7.9	15.4	19.6	54.3
New Mexico	267	2	7	147	79	100.0	0.9	2.5	55.1	29.4
New York	2,451	156	465	513	1,286	100.0	6.4	19.0	21.0	52.5
North Carolina	1,170	19	285	122	702	100.0	1.7	24.3	10.5	60.0
North Dakota	71	0	–	2	61	100.0	0.4	–	2.2	85.9
Ohio	1,483	19	229	47	1,141	100.0	1.3	15.4	3.1	76.9
Oklahoma	474	5	46	54	297	100.0	1.1	9.6	11.4	62.7
Oregon	456	21	11	79	325	100.0	4.5	2.3	17.2	71.3
Pennsylvania	1,472	42	197	87	1,105	100.0	2.9	13.4	5.9	75.1
Rhode Island	124	4	11	23	85	100.0	3.3	9.1	18.3	68.5

(continued)

	number					percent distribution				
	total under 10	Asian	black	Hispanic	non-Hispanic white	total	Asian	black	Hispanic	non-Hispanic white
South Carolina	549	5	193	22	320	100.0%	1.0%	35.1%	4.0%	58.3%
South Dakota	101	1	1	3	90	100.0	1.2	1.1	3.1	88.7
Tennessee	767	9	162	37	539	100.0	1.2	21.2	4.8	70.2
Texas	3,529	99	406	1,626	1,323	100.0	2.8	11.5	46.1	37.5
Utah	436	7	5	59	352	100.0	1.6	1.0	13.5	80.6
Vermont	68	1	–	1	64	100.0	1.1	–	1.0	94.2
Virginia	976	46	211	80	602	100.0	4.7	21.7	8.2	61.7
Washington	772	41	32	120	512	100.0	5.3	4.2	15.6	66.3
West Virginia	193	1	5	2	182	100.0	0.3	2.4	1.0	93.9
Wisconsin	680	14	67	50	526	100.0	2.1	9.8	7.3	77.4
Wyoming	60	1	1	6	51	100.0	0.8	1.0	9.6	84.0

Note: Blacks and Asians are those identified as being of the respective race alone. Non-Hispanic whites are those identifying themselves as being white alone and not Hispanic. Numbers will not sum to total because Hispanics may be of any race and not all races are shown. "–" means sample is too small to make a reliable estimate.
Source: Bureau of the Census, 2004 American Community Survey, Internet site http://factfinder.census.gov/servlet/ DatasetMainPageServlet?_program=ACS&_lang=en&_ts=143547961449; calculations by New Strategist

Table 7.21 Millennial Generation by State, Race, and Hispanic Origin, 2004

(number and percent distribution of people aged 10 to 27 by state, race, and Hispanic origin, 2004; numbers in thousands)

| | number | | | | | percent distribution | | | | |
	total 10 to 27	Asian	black	Hispanic	non-Hispanic white	total	Asian	black	Hispanic	non-Hispanic white
United States	**70,753**	**2,886**	**10,056**	**12,771**	**43,155**	**100.0%**	**4.1%**	**14.2%**	**18.1%**	**61.0%**
Alabama	1,110	8	350	31	707	100.0	0.8	31.5	2.8	63.7
Alaska	179	8	6	10	110	100.0	4.5	3.6	5.8	61.1
Arizona	1,447	26	50	524	731	100.0	1.8	3.5	36.2	50.5
Arkansas	680	10	132	41	482	100.0	1.5	19.4	6.0	70.9
California	9,111	1,014	613	3,969	3,234	100.0	11.1	6.7	43.6	35.5
Colorado	1,162	32	55	282	763	100.0	2.7	4.7	24.2	65.6
Connecticut	766	22	92	113	522	100.0	2.9	12.1	14.7	68.2
Delaware	193	5	45	16	124	100.0	2.6	23.4	8.6	64.1
District of Columbia	116	4	66	14	30	100.0	3.4	57.1	12.1	25.9
Florida	3,874	80	782	863	2,088	100.0	2.1	20.2	22.3	53.9
Georgia	2,180	61	725	187	1,181	100.0	2.8	33.2	8.6	54.2
Hawaii	288	97	7	31	53	100.0	33.7	2.3	10.9	18.6
Idaho	367	6	–	42	309	100.0	1.5	–	11.5	84.2
Illinois	3,112	126	552	570	1,825	100.0	4.0	17.7	18.3	58.7
Indiana	1,535	17	150	91	1,240	100.0	1.1	9.7	5.9	80.8
Iowa	697	9	21	37	619	100.0	1.3	3.0	5.3	88.8
Kansas	672	15	40	50	545	100.0	2.3	5.9	7.4	81.1
Kentucky	968	7	75	28	847	100.0	0.8	7.7	2.9	87.5
Louisiana	1,159	18	431	32	661	100.0	1.5	37.2	2.8	57.0
Maine	290	3	2	5	272	100.0	0.9	0.7	1.6	94.1
Maryland	1,289	59	406	95	698	100.0	4.6	31.5	7.4	54.2
Massachusetts	1,399	72	108	149	1,048	100.0	5.1	7.8	10.7	74.9
Michigan	2,438	55	398	117	1,813	100.0	2.2	16.3	4.8	74.4
Minnesota	1,244	61	60	54	1,034	100.0	4.9	4.9	4.3	83.1
Mississippi	739	2	327	13	392	100.0	0.3	44.2	1.7	53.0
Missouri	1,386	14	187	48	1,110	100.0	1.0	13.5	3.5	80.1
Montana	222	–	–	6	190	100.0	–	–	2.8	85.6
Nebraska	433	7	17	37	361	100.0	1.5	3.9	8.6	83.2
Nevada	562	26	51	169	291	100.0	4.6	9.1	30.1	51.9
New Hampshire	293	5	3	8	272	100.0	1.8	0.9	2.8	92.8
New Jersey	1,975	133	306	374	1,127	100.0	6.7	15.5	18.9	57.1
New Mexico	480	6	15	236	163	100.0	1.2	3.2	49.2	34.0
New York	4,413	278	810	882	2,411	100.0	6.3	18.4	20.0	54.6
North Carolina	1,978	34	492	160	1,238	100.0	1.7	24.9	8.1	62.6
North Dakota	156	1	–	3	136	100.0	0.9	–	1.8	87.3
Ohio	2,705	40	367	79	2,181	100.0	1.5	13.6	2.9	80.6
Oklahoma	854	13	64	70	577	100.0	1.5	7.5	8.2	67.5
Oregon	858	26	16	116	661	100.0	3.0	1.9	13.5	77.0
Pennsylvania	2,754	57	338	151	2,179	100.0	2.1	12.3	5.5	79.1
Rhode Island	249	9	18	38	180	100.0	3.5	7.4	15.2	72.2

(continued)

	number				percent distribution				
	total 10 to 27	Asian	black	Hispanic	non-Hispanic white	total	Asian	black	Hispanic	non-Hispanic white
South Carolina	996	11	338	44	589	100.0%	1.1%	33.9%	4.4%	59.1%
South Dakota	191	2	2	5	173	100.0	0.8	1.1	2.4	90.5
Tennessee	1,366	17	265	58	999	100.0	1.3	19.4	4.2	73.1
Texas	5,856	173	708	2,425	2,465	100.0	3.0	12.1	41.4	42.1
Utah	736	14	6	88	609	100.0	1.9	0.8	11.9	82.7
Vermont	135	1	–	2	129	100.0	1.1	–	1.4	95.1
Virginia	1,737	75	388	133	1,102	100.0	4.3	22.3	7.7	63.5
Washington	1,530	96	58	175	1,106	100.0	6.3	3.8	11.4	72.3
West Virginia	409	2	15	3	384	100.0	0.4	3.6	0.7	94.0
Wisconsin	1,336	30	96	87	1,087	100.0	2.2	7.2	6.5	81.3
Wyoming	126	1	1	12	107	100.0	1.0	1.1	9.4	84.5

Note: Blacks and Asians are those who identify themselves as being of the respective race alone. Non-Hispanic whites are those who identify themselves as being white alone and not Hispanic. Numbers will not sum to total because Hispanics may be of any race and not all races are shown. "–" means sample is too small to make a reliable estimate.
Source: Bureau of the Census, 2004 American Community Survey, Internet site http://factfinder.census.gov/servlet/ DatasetMainPageServlet?_program=ACS&_lang=en&_ts=143547961449; calculations by New Strategist

8

Spending

■ Households headed by people under age 30 spent only 1 percent more in 2004 than they did in 2000 as the recession and lackluster recovery took their toll.

■ The incomes of young adults are well below average, and so is their spending. Householders under age 30 spent $32,018 in 2004, just 74 percent as much as the average household.

■ The spending of married couples with preschoolers rose by a small 0.6 percent to $55,981 between 2000 and 2004, after adjusting for inflation. This household type reined in its spending on many products and services as the cost of health insurance and other necessities climbed.

■ Married couples with school-aged children rank among the most-affluent households in the nation. But they are cautious spenders. In 2004, they spent $60,578, only 2 percent more than in 2000 after adjusting for inflation.

■ Married couples with children aged 18 or older at home spent an average of $64,162 in 2004, up 7 percent from what they spent in 2000, after adjusting for inflation. Much of their spending boost was devoted to health insurance and education.

■ Single parents with children under age 18 at home spent 3 percent more in 2004 than in 2000, after adjusting for inflation. This household type spent an enormous 42 percent more for health insurance in 2004 than in 2000.

Millennial Spending Has Grown Slowly

Spending by the youngest householders grew by only 1 percent between 2000 and 2004.

The average household boosted its spending by 4 percent between 2000 and 2004, after adjusting for inflation. Households headed by people under age 30, most of them members of the Millennial generation (aged 10 to 27 in 2004), spent $32,018 in 2004. This amount was only $441 more than they spent in 2000, an indication of the toll taken by the recession of 2001 and the lackluster recovery.

Householders under age 30 cut their spending on many items between 2000 and 2004. Among the losers were new and used cars and trucks, fees and admissions to entertainment events, household furnishings and equipment, and gifts for nonhousehold members. Householders under age 30 boosted their spending on a variety of items as well, including food away from home, alcoholic beverages, mortgage interest, women's clothes, and health insurance.

Many householders under age 30 are in college. Their spending on education rose 27 percent between 2000 and 2004 thanks to rising tuition costs. Despite their pursuit of higher education, young adults are not big on reading. Their spending on reading material fell 27 percent between 2000 and 2004—a troubling trend for the print media.

■ Householders under age 30 are a diverse mix of single parents, people living alone, and friends living together. Their spending patterns reflect this diversity.

Young adults are spending more on some items

(percent change in spending by householders under age 30, 2000 to 2004; in 2004 dollars)

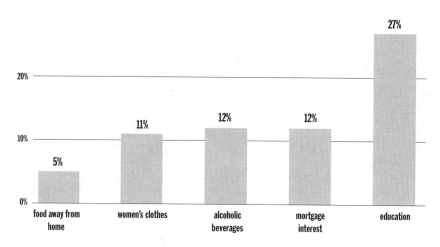

Table 8.1 Average Spending of Householders under Age 30, 2000 and 2004

(average annual spending of total consumer units and consumer units headed by people under age 30, 2000 and 2004; percent change, 2000–04; in 2004 dollars)

	total consumer units			under age 30		
	2004	2000	percent change 2000–04	2004	2000	percent change 2000–04
Number of consumer units (in 000s)	116,282	109,367	6.3%	18,107	16,787	7.9%
Average before-tax income	$54,453	$48,975	11.2	$34,712	$32,978	5.3
Average annual spending	43,395	41,731	4.0	32,018	31,577	1.4
FOOD	**5,781**	**5,658**	**2.2**	**4,506**	**4,408**	**2.2**
Food at home	**3,347**	**3,314**	**1.0**	**2,395**	**2,390**	**0.2**
Cereals and bakery products	461	497	−7.2	328	346	−5.1
Cereals and cereal products	154	171	−10.0	125	134	−6.6
Bakery products	307	326	−5.8	203	212	−4.1
Meats, poultry, fish, and eggs	880	872	0.9	640	615	4.0
Beef	265	261	1.5	195	191	2.2
Pork	181	183	−1.2	129	120	7.9
Other meats	108	111	−2.5	70	80	−12.6
Poultry	156	159	−1.9	134	124	8.1
Fish and seafood	128	121	6.1	79	76	4.4
Eggs	42	37	12.6	33	26	25.4
Dairy products	371	356	4.1	260	256	1.7
Fresh milk and cream	144	144	0.2	112	109	3.1
Other dairy products	226	212	6.8	149	147	1.4
Fruits and vegetables	561	571	−1.8	380	386	−1.6
Fresh fruits	187	179	4.6	120	115	4.2
Fresh vegetables	183	174	4.9	121	118	2.1
Processed fruits	110	126	−12.8	81	89	−8.8
Processed vegetables	82	92	−11.0	58	64	−8.8
Other food at home	1,075	1,017	5.7	788	789	−0.1
Sugar and other sweets	128	128	−0.3	81	93	−13.1
Fats and oils	89	91	−2.2	59	61	−3.9
Miscellaneous foods	527	479	9.9	402	396	1.5
Nonalcoholic beverages	290	274	5.8	229	213	7.6
Food prepared by household on trips	41	44	−6.6	16	25	−36.6
Food away from home	**2,434**	**2,344**	**3.8**	**2,111**	**2,018**	**4.6**
ALCOHOLIC BEVERAGES	**459**	**408**	**12.5**	**508**	**454**	**11.9**
HOUSING	**13,918**	**13,513**	**3.0**	**10,292**	**10,233**	**0.6**
Shelter	**7,998**	**7,803**	**2.5**	**6,341**	**6,326**	**0.2**
Owned dwellings	5,324	5,048	5.5	2,183	1,909	14.4
Mortgage interest and charges	2,936	2,895	1.4	1,477	1,318	12.0
Property taxes	1,391	1,249	11.3	442	366	20.6
Maintenance, repairs, insurance, other expenses	997	905	10.2	264	224	18.0

	total consumer units			under age 30		
	2004	2000	percent change 2000–04	2004	2000	percent change 2000–04
Rented dwellings	$2,201	$2,231	–1.3%	$3,942	$4,123	–4.4%
Other lodging	473	524	–9.8	216	294	–26.5
Utilities, fuels, public services	**2,927**	**2,730**	**7.2**	**1,954**	**1,869**	**4.5**
Natural gas	424	337	25.9	221	185	19.2
Electricity	1,064	999	6.5	697	669	4.2
Fuel oil and other fuels	121	106	13.7	43	41	6.0
Telephone services	990	962	2.9	823	813	1.3
Water and other public services	327	325	0.7	170	161	5.4
Household services	**753**	**750**	**0.4**	**482**	**491**	**–1.9**
Personal services	300	358	–16.1	291	361	–19.4
Other household services	453	393	15.4	191	129	47.6
Housekeeping supplies	**594**	**529**	**12.4**	**373**	**348**	**7.3**
Laundry and cleaning supplies	149	144	3.7	106	94	12.4
Other household products	290	248	17.0	155	159	–2.5
Postage and stationery	155	138	12.1	112	94	18.7
Household furnishings and equipment	**1,646**	**1,699**	**–3.1**	**1,142**	**1,200**	**–4.8**
Household textiles	158	116	35.9	82	86	–4.2
Furniture	417	429	–2.8	347	369	–5.8
Floor coverings	52	48	7.7	21	20	6.4
Major appliances	204	207	–1.6	128	132	–2.8
Small appliances, misc. housewares	105	95	10.0	80	70	14.0
Miscellaneous household equipment	711	802	–11.3	485	523	–7.3
APPAREL AND SERVICES	**1,816**	**2,036**	**–10.8**	**1,714**	**1,759**	**–2.6**
Men and boys	**406**	**483**	**–15.9**	**353**	**420**	**–16.0**
Men, aged 16 or older	317	377	–16.0	291	351	–17.1
Boys, aged 2 to 15	89	105	–15.5	62	69	–10.3
Women and girls	**739**	**795**	**–7.1**	**614**	**563**	**9.1**
Women, aged 16 or older	631	666	–5.2	555	500	11.0
Girls, aged 2 to 15	108	129	–16.6	59	63	–5.6
Children under age 2	**79**	**90**	**–12.2**	**149**	**149**	**–0.1**
Footwear	**329**	**376**	**–12.6**	**329**	**373**	**–11.8**
Other apparel products and services	**264**	**292**	**–9.5**	**269**	**256**	**5.3**
TRANSPORTATION	**7,801**	**8,136**	**–4.1**	**6,541**	**7,164**	**–8.7**
Vehicle purchases	**3,397**	**3,749**	**–9.4**	**2,996**	**3,582**	**–16.4**
Cars and trucks, new	1,748	1,761	–0.7	1,138	1,401	–18.8
Cars and trucks, used	1,582	1,941	–18.5	1,815	2,101	–13.6
Gasoline and motor oil	**1,598**	**1,416**	**12.8**	**1,370**	**1,201**	**14.1**
Other vehicle expenses	**2,365**	**2,502**	**–5.5**	**1,901**	**2,041**	**–6.9**
Vehicle finance charges	323	360	–10.2	267	362	–26.2
Maintenance and repairs	652	684	–4.7	499	568	–12.2
Vehicle insurance	964	853	13.0	760	636	19.5
Vehicle rental, leases, licenses, other charges	426	604	–29.5	375	475	–21.0
Public transportation	**441**	**468**	**–5.8**	**274**	**340**	**–19.4**

	total consumer units			under age 30		
	2004	2000	percent change 2000–04	2004	2000	percent change 2000–04
HEALTH CARE	**$2,574**	**$2,266**	**13.6%**	**$982**	**$872**	**12.6%**
Health insurance	1,332	1,078	23.5	515	428	20.4
Medical services	648	623	4.0	266	261	1.9
Drugs	480	456	5.2	156	134	16.6
Medical supplies	114	109	5.0	46	48	−4.7
ENTERTAINMENT	**2,218**	**2,044**	**8.5**	**1,540**	**1,498**	**2.8**
Fees and admissions	528	565	−6.5	312	350	−10.8
Television, radio, sound equipment	788	682	15.5	657	607	8.3
Pets, toys, and playground equipment	381	366	4.0	288	260	10.8
Other entertainment supplies, services	522	431	21.1	283	283	0.0
PERSONAL CARE PRODUCTS AND SERVICES	**581**	**619**	**−6.1**	**433**	**489**	**−11.5**
READING	**130**	**160**	**−18.8**	**65**	**89**	**−26.8**
EDUCATION	**905**	**693**	**30.5**	**1,335**	**1,055**	**26.5**
TOBACCO PRODUCTS AND SMOKING SUPPLIES	**288**	**350**	**−17.7**	**265**	**298**	**−11.2**
MISCELLANEOUS	**690**	**851**	**−18.9**	**420**	**528**	**−20.4**
CASH CONTRIBUTIONS	**1,408**	**1,307**	**7.7**	**494**	**382**	**29.4**
PERSONAL INSURANCE AND PENSIONS	**4,823**	**3,691**	**30.7**	**2,921**	**2,347**	**24.4**
Life and other personal insurance	390	438	−10.9	103	124	−16.9
Pensions and Social Security	4,433	3,253	36.3	2,818	2,223	26.7
PERSONAL TAXES	**2,166**	**3,419**	**−36.6**	**877**	**1,889**	**−53.6**
Federal income taxes	1,519	2,642	−42.5	552	1,454	−62.0
State and local income taxes	472	616	−23.4	290	407	−28.7
Other taxes	175	160	9.3	35	27	27.6
GIFTS FOR NONHOUSEHOLD MEMBERS	**1,215**	**1,188**	**2.3**	**545**	**700**	**−22.1**

Note: The Bureau of Labor Statistics uses consumer unit rather than household as the sampling unit in the Consumer Expenditure Survey. For the definition of consumer unit, see the glossary. Spending on gifts is also included in the preceding product and service categories.
Source: Bureau of Labor Statistics, 2000 and 2004 Consumer Expenditure Surveys, Internet site http://www.bls.gov/cex/; calculations by New Strategist

Young Adults Spend Less than Average on Most Things

Householders under age 30 spend just 74 percent as much as the average household.

The incomes of householders under age 30 are well below average, and so is their spending. On some things, however, Millennials (aged 10 to 27 in 2004) spend more. They spend 11 percent more than the average household on alcoholic beverages. They spend 79 percent more on rent. Because many young householders are parents, they spend 89 percent more than the average household on clothes for children under age 2. They spend 15 percent more on used cars and trucks. Millennial householders spend 48 percent more than average on education. Many are students paying for college at least partly out of their own pocket.

On most items, Millennials spend far less than the average household. They spend 13 percent less than the average household on food away from home (with an index of 87). They spend 59 percent less than average on owned dwellings, because most are renters. They spend 62 percent less than average on health care since most are in good health and have few medical needs. Their spending on reading material is just half the average.

■ As Millennial householders age, their spending will rise with their income.

The youngest householders are big spenders on alcohol, rent, and education

(indexed spending by householders under age 30 on selected items, 2004)

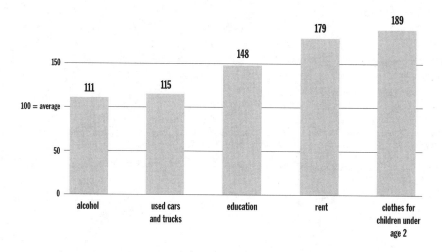

Table 8.2 Average, Indexed, and Market Share of Spending by Householders under Age 30, 2004

(average annual spending of total consumer units and average annual, indexed, and market share of spending by consumer units headed by people under age 30, 2004)

	total consumer units	consumer units headed by people under age 30		
		average spending	indexed spending	market share
Number of consumer units (in 000s)	116,282	18,107	–	15.6%
Average before-tax income	$54,453	$34,712	64	9.9
Average annual spending	43,395	32,018	74	11.5
FOOD	5,781	4,506	78	12.1
Food at home	3,347	2,395	72	11.1
Cereals and bakery products	461	328	71	11.1
Cereals and cereal products	154	125	81	12.6
Bakery products	307	203	66	10.3
Meats, poultry, fish, and eggs	880	640	73	11.3
Beef	265	195	74	11.5
Pork	181	129	71	11.1
Other meats	108	70	65	10.1
Poultry	156	134	86	13.4
Fish and seafood	128	79	62	9.6
Eggs	42	33	79	12.2
Dairy products	371	260	70	10.9
Fresh milk and cream	144	112	78	12.1
Other dairy products	226	149	66	10.3
Fruits and vegetables	561	380	68	10.5
Fresh fruits	187	120	64	10.0
Fresh vegetables	183	121	66	10.3
Processed fruits	110	81	74	11.5
Processed vegetables	82	58	71	11.0
Other food at home	1,075	788	73	11.4
Sugar and other sweets	128	81	63	9.9
Fats and oils	89	59	66	10.3
Miscellaneous foods	527	402	76	11.9
Nonalcoholic beverages	290	229	79	12.3
Food prepared by household on trips	41	16	39	6.1
Food away from home	2,434	2,111	87	13.5
ALCOHOLIC BEVERAGES	459	508	111	17.2
HOUSING	13,918	10,292	74	11.5
Shelter	7,998	6,341	79	12.3
Owned dwellings	5,324	2,183	41	6.4
Mortgage interest and charges	2,936	1,477	50	7.8
Property taxes	1,391	442	32	4.9
Maintenance, repairs, insurance, other expenses	997	264	26	4.1

	total consumer units	consumer units headed by people under age 30		
		average spending	indexed spending	market share
Rented dwellings	$2,201	$3,942	179	27.9%
Other lodging	473	216	46	7.1
Utilities, fuels, public services	**2,927**	**1,954**	**67**	**10.4**
Natural gas	424	221	52	8.1
Electricity	1,064	697	66	10.2
Fuel oil and other fuels	121	43	36	5.5
Telephone services	990	823	83	12.9
Water and other public services	327	170	52	8.1
Household services	**753**	**482**	**64**	**10.0**
Personal services	300	291	97	15.1
Other household services	453	191	42	6.6
Housekeeping supplies	**594**	**373**	**63**	**9.8**
Laundry and cleaning supplies	149	106	71	11.1
Other household products	290	155	53	8.3
Postage and stationery	155	112	72	11.3
Household furnishings and equipment	**1,646**	**1,142**	**69**	**10.8**
Household textiles	158	82	52	8.1
Furniture	417	347	83	13.0
Floor coverings	52	21	40	6.3
Major appliances	204	128	63	9.8
Small appliances, misc. housewares	105	80	76	11.9
Miscellaneous household equipment	711	485	68	10.6
APPAREL AND SERVICES	**1,816**	**1,714**	**94**	**14.7**
Men and boys	**406**	**353**	**87**	**13.5**
Men, aged 16 or older	317	291	92	14.3
Boys, aged 2 to 15	89	62	70	10.8
Women and girls	**739**	**614**	**83**	**12.9**
Women, aged 16 or older	631	555	88	13.7
Girls, aged 2 to 15	108	59	55	8.5
Children under age 2	**79**	**149**	**189**	**29.4**
Footwear	**329**	**329**	**100**	**15.6**
Other apparel products and services	**264**	**269**	**102**	**15.9**
TRANSPORTATION	**7,801**	**6,541**	**84**	**13.1**
Vehicle purchases	**3,397**	**2,996**	**88**	**13.7**
Cars and trucks, new	1,748	1,138	65	10.1
Cars and trucks, used	1,582	1,815	115	17.9
Gasoline and motor oil	**1,598**	**1,370**	**86**	**13.3**
Other vehicle expenses	**2,365**	**1,901**	**80**	**12.5**
Vehicle finance charges	323	267	83	12.9
Maintenance and repairs	652	499	77	11.9
Vehicle insurance	964	760	79	12.3
Vehicle rental, leases, licenses, other charges	426	375	88	13.7
Public transportation	**441**	**274**	**62**	**9.7**

	total consumer units	consumer units headed by people under age 30		
		average spending	indexed spending	market share
HEALTH CARE	**$2,574**	**$982**	**38**	**5.9%**
Health insurance	1,332	515	39	6.0
Medical services	648	266	41	6.4
Drugs	480	156	33	5.1
Medical supplies	114	46	40	6.3
ENTERTAINMENT	**2,218**	**1,540**	**69**	**10.8**
Fees and admissions	528	312	59	9.2
Television, radio, sound equipment	788	657	83	13.0
Pets, toys, and playground equipment	381	288	76	11.8
Other entertainment supplies, services	522	283	54	8.4
PERSONAL CARE PRODUCTS AND SERVICES	**581**	**433**	**75**	**11.6**
READING	**130**	**65**	**50**	**7.8**
EDUCATION	**905**	**1,335**	**148**	**23.0**
TOBACCO PRODUCTS AND SMOKING SUPPLIES	**288**	**265**	**92**	**14.3**
MISCELLANEOUS	**690**	**420**	**61**	**9.5**
CASH CONTRIBUTIONS	**1,408**	**494**	**35**	**5.5**
PERSONAL INSURANCE AND PENSIONS	**4,823**	**2,921**	**61**	**9.4**
Life and other personal insurance	390	103	26	4.1
Pensions and Social Security	4,433	2,818	64	9.9
PERSONAL TAXES	**2,166**	**877**	**40**	**6.3**
Federal income taxes	1,519	552	36	5.7
State and local income taxes	472	290	61	9.6
Other taxes	175	35	20	3.1
GIFTS FOR NONHOUSEHOLD MEMBERS	**1,215**	**545**	**45**	**7.0**

Note: The Bureau of Labor Statistics uses consumer unit rather than household as the sampling unit in the Consumer Expenditure Survey. For the definition of consumer unit, see the glossary. Spending on gifts is also included in the preceding product and service categories; "–" means not applicable.
Source: Bureau of Labor Statistics, 2004 Consumer Expenditure Survey, Internet site http://www.bls.gov/cex/; calculations by New Strategist

Parents of Preschoolers Spend Cautiously

The spending of married couples with preschoolers rose more slowly than their incomes between 2000 and 2004.

The incomes of married couples with preschoolers rose 9 percent between 2000 and 2004, after adjusting for inflation. Their spending increased by just 0.6 percent as they reined in their purchases.

Couples with preschoolers cut their spending on groceries (food at home) by 6 percent between 2000 and 2004. But they spent 7 percent more on food away from home. They spent 20 percent less on alcoholic beverages, but 27 percent more on television, radio, and sound equipment. As the homeownership rate rose, they spent more on owned dwellings and less on rent. They spent 5 percent more on women's clothes, but less on clothes for children. Their spending on new cars and trucks rose 2 percent, while spending on used vehicles fell 30 percent. Health insurance spending rose 13 percent.

■ The spending pattern of couples with preschoolers is a mixed bag, revealing the diversity of their economic status.

Married couples with preschoolers spent more on some things, less on others

(percent change in spending by married couples with children under age 6 at home, 2000 to 2004, in 2004 dollars)

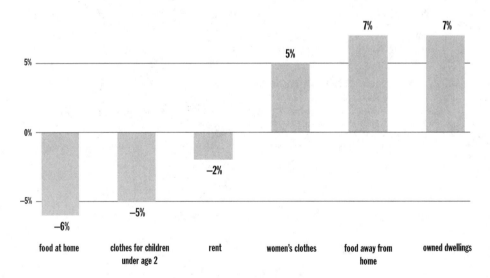

Table 8.3 Average Spending of Married Couples with Oldest Child under Age 6, 2000 and 2004

(average annual spending of married-couple consumer units with oldest child under age 6, 2000 and 2004; percent change, 2000–04; in 2004 dollars)

	2004	2000	percent change 2000–04
Number of consumer units (in 000s)	5,604	5,291	5.9%
Average before-tax income	$75,293	$69,025	9.1
Average annual spending	55,981	55,674	0.6
FOOD	6,300	6,381	–1.3
Food at home	3,765	4,014	–6.2
Cereals and bakery products	492	595	–17.2
Cereals and cereal products	160	204	–21.6
Bakery products	333	390	–14.7
Meats, poultry, fish, and eggs	875	898	–2.6
Beef	244	269	–9.2
Pork	175	166	5.7
Other meats	100	118	–15.6
Poultry	165	188	–12.0
Fish and seafood	147	120	22.9
Eggs	45	36	24.3
Dairy products	437	455	–4.0
Fresh milk and cream	190	193	–1.6
Other dairy products	246	262	–6.2
Fruits and vegetables	634	679	–6.6
Fresh fruits	211	206	2.3
Fresh vegetables	205	202	1.6
Processed fruits	136	167	–18.4
Processed vegetables	82	103	–20.5
Other food at home	1,327	1,388	–4.4
Sugar and other sweets	140	139	0.5
Fats and oils	88	81	8.4
Miscellaneous foods	772	804	–4.0
Nonalcoholic beverages	292	314	–6.9
Food prepared by household on trips	35	49	–29.1
Food away from home	2,535	2,367	7.1
ALCOHOLIC BEVERAGES	330	411	–19.8
HOUSING	21,045	20,514	2.6
Shelter	11,944	11,405	4.7
Owned dwellings	9,254	8,626	7.3
Mortgage interest and charges	6,243	6,016	3.8
Property taxes	1,907	1,650	15.6
Maintenance, repairs, insurance, other expenses	1,104	959	15.2

	2004	2000	percent change 2000–04
Rented dwellings	$2,334	$2,371	−1.6%
Other lodging	357	408	−12.5
Utilities, fuels, public services	**3,325**	**3,076**	**8.1**
Natural gas	546	395	38.3
Electricity	1,114	1,049	6.2
Fuel oil and other fuels	110	125	−12.0
Telephone services	1,166	1,146	1.7
Water and other public services	389	361	7.8
Household services	**2,699**	**2,611**	**3.4**
Personal services	2,146	2,183	−1.7
Other household services	554	428	29.5
Housekeeping supplies	**820**	**678**	**21.0**
Laundry and cleaning supplies	174	165	5.8
Other household products	450	331	35.8
Postage and stationery	196	182	7.6
Household furnishings and equipment	**2,257**	**2,744**	**−17.8**
Household textiles	168	196	−14.4
Furniture	626	792	−21.0
Floor coverings	47	50	−6.9
Major appliances	333	291	14.6
Small appliances, misc. housewares	180	137	31.3
Miscellaneous household equipment	903	1,278	−29.3
APPAREL AND SERVICES	**2,583**	**2,841**	**−9.1**
Men and boys	**575**	**590**	**−2.6**
Men, aged 16 or older	443	428	3.6
Boys, aged 2 to 15	132	162	−18.7
Women and girls	**873**	**852**	**2.4**
Women, aged 16 or older	719	683	5.2
Girls, aged 2 to 15	154	169	−8.8
Children under age 2	**518**	**546**	**−5.2**
Footwear	**323**	**493**	**−34.4**
Other apparel products and services	**294**	**360**	**−18.3**
TRANSPORTATION	**10,599**	**11,786**	**−10.1**
Vehicle purchases	**5,142**	**6,136**	**−16.2**
Cars and trucks, new	2,944	2,896	1.7
Cars and trucks, used	2,169	3,089	−29.8
Gasoline and motor oil	**1,991**	**1,748**	**13.9**
Other vehicle expenses	**3,015**	**3,455**	**−12.7**
Vehicle finance charges	484	604	−19.9
Maintenance and repairs	722	781	−7.6
Vehicle insurance	1,105	1,050	5.3
Vehicle rental, leases, licenses, other charges	703	1,019	−31.0
Public transportation	**451**	**446**	**1.0**

	2004	2000	percent change 2000–04
HEALTH CARE	**$2,369**	**$2,081**	**13.9%**
Health insurance	1,275	1,124	13.4
Medical services	690	601	14.8
Drugs	305	264	15.4
Medical supplies	99	92	7.4
ENTERTAINMENT	**2,442**	**2,403**	**1.6**
Fees and admissions	479	533	–10.1
Television, radio, sound equipment	1,001	786	27.3
Pets, toys, and playground equipment	520	528	–1.4
Other entertainment supplies, services	442	555	–20.4
PERSONAL CARE PRODUCTS AND SERVICES	**604**	**712**	**–15.2**
READING	**139**	**191**	**–27.2**
EDUCATION	**414**	**461**	**–10.1**
TOBACCO PRODUCTS, SMOKING SUPPLIES	**211**	**302**	**–30.1**
MISCELLANEOUS	**687**	**754**	**–8.8**
CASH CONTRIBUTIONS	**1,189**	**930**	**27.8**
PERSONAL INSURANCE AND PENSIONS	**7,069**	**5,910**	**19.6**
Life and other personal insurance	389	529	–26.4
Pensions and Social Security	6,680	5,381	24.1
PERSONAL TAXES	**2,891**	**4,567**	**–36.7**
Federal income taxes	1,947	3,576	–45.6
State and local income taxes	788	829	–5.0
Other taxes	156	161	–3.3
GIFTS FOR NONHOUSEHOLD MEMBERS	**1,078**	**1,007**	**7.1**

Note: The Bureau of Labor Statistics uses consumer unit rather than household as the sampling unit in the Consumer Expenditure Survey. For the definition of consumer unit, see the glossary. Spending on gifts is included in the preceding product and service categories.
Source: Bureau of Labor Statistics, 2000 and 2004 Consumer Expenditure Surveys, Internet site http://www.bls.gov/cex/; calculations by New Strategist

Couples with School-Aged Children Are Spending a Little More

They spent less on many categories between 2000 and 2004, however.

Married couples with school-aged children rank among the most-affluent households in the nation. But their incomes grew only 3 percent between 2000 and 2004, after adjusting for inflation. Average household spending, at $60,578, was only 2 percent greater than in 2000.

Spending trends among couples with school-aged children are a mixed bag reflecting compromises between budgeting for necessities and outfitting themselves with the accessories of a middle-class lifestyle. Couples with school-aged children cut their spending on food at home (groceries) by 0.1 percent between 2000 and 2004, after adjusting for inflation. But their spending on food away from home rose nearly 8 percent. They spent 14 percent more on alcoholic beverages, but 7 percent less on entertainment. Their spending on mortgage interest fell 6 percent as lower interest rates reduced costs, but spending on property taxes grew 11 percent. They spent 6 percent more on new cars and trucks, but 15 percent less on furniture.

Couples with school-aged children spent 34 percent more on out of pocket health insurance costs in 2004 than in 2000. They spent 27 percent more on education and 34 percent more on pensions and Social Security.

■ With income growing only slowly, parents with school-aged children have become cautious spenders.

Couples with school-aged children are spending much more for health insurance

(percent change in spending by married couples with children aged 6 to 17 on selected items, 2000 to 2004; in 2004 dollars)

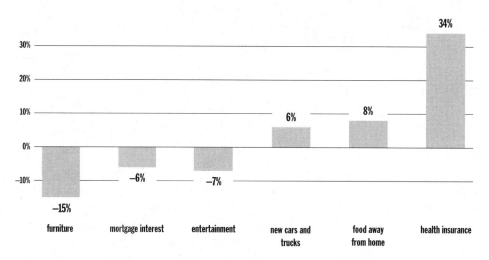

Table 8.4 Average Spending of Married Couples with Oldest Child Aged 6 to 17, 2000 and 2004

(average annual spending of married-couple consumer units with oldest child aged 6 to 17, 2000 and 2004; percent change, 2000–04; in 2004 dollars)

	2004	2000	percent change 2000–04
Number of consumer units (in 000s)	15,376	15,396	–0.1%
Average before-tax income	$78,508	$76,203	3.0
Average annual spending	60,578	59,419	2.0
FOOD	8,484	8,235	3.0
Food at home	4,887	4,890	–0.1
Cereals and bakery products	718	770	–6.8
Cereals and cereal products	246	281	–12.4
Bakery products	472	488	–3.3
Meats, poultry, fish, and eggs	1,216	1,267	–4.0
Beef	380	378	0.4
Pork	236	259	–8.8
Other meats	162	168	–3.5
Poultry	225	230	–2.3
Fish and seafood	159	184	–13.7
Eggs	54	48	11.9
Dairy products	580	545	6.4
Fresh milk and cream	233	229	1.6
Other dairy products	347	316	9.8
Fruits and vegetables	771	786	–2.0
Fresh fruits	255	236	8.1
Fresh vegetables	239	234	2.3
Processed fruits	160	185	–13.7
Processed vegetables	116	132	–11.9
Other food at home	1,602	1,522	5.2
Sugar and other sweets	187	193	–3.1
Fats and oils	125	129	–3.4
Miscellaneous foods	813	744	9.3
Nonalcoholic beverages	421	392	7.5
Food prepared by household on trips	55	65	–15.0
Food away from home	3,597	3,346	7.5
ALCOHOLIC BEVERAGES	455	400	13.6
HOUSING	18,900	19,122	–1.2
Shelter	10,838	11,007	–1.5
Owned dwellings	8,644	8,706	–0.7
Mortgage interest and charges	5,433	5,792	–6.2
Property taxes	1,961	1,759	11.5
Maintenance, repairs, insurance, other expenses	1,250	1,155	8.2

	2004	2000	percent change 2000–04
Rented dwellings	$1,545	$1,693	−8.7%
Other lodging	650	610	6.6
Utilities, fuels, public services	**3,809**	**3,502**	**8.8**
Natural gas	549	435	26.1
Electricity	1,419	1,283	10.6
Fuel oil and other fuels	149	129	15.1
Telephone services	1,249	1,202	3.9
Water and other public services	444	452	−1.8
Household services	**1,167**	**1,298**	**−10.1**
Personal services	608	725	−16.1
Other household services	558	574	−2.7
Housekeeping supplies	**824**	**794**	**3.8**
Laundry and cleaning supplies	217	248	−12.5
Other household products	415	378	9.7
Postage and stationery	192	168	14.4
Household furnishings and equipment	**2,262**	**2,520**	**−10.2**
Household textiles	164	172	−4.8
Furniture	590	697	−15.3
Floor coverings	64	66	−2.8
Major appliances	276	301	−8.2
Small appliances, misc. housewares	130	132	−1.2
Miscellaneous household equipment	1,038	1,154	−10.0
APPAREL AND SERVICES	**2,757**	**3,113**	**−11.4**
Men and boys	**739**	**786**	**−6.0**
Men, aged 16 or older	456	462	−1.3
Boys, aged 2 to 15	283	325	−12.8
Women and girls	**1,023**	**1,200**	**−14.7**
Women, aged 16 or older	671	762	−12.0
Girls, aged 2 to 15	352	439	−19.8
Children under age 2	100	112	−10.6
Footwear	**545**	**589**	**−7.5**
Other apparel products and services	**351**	**426**	**−17.5**
TRANSPORTATION	**11,377**	**11,675**	**−2.6**
Vehicle purchases	**5,370**	**5,596**	**−4.0**
Cars and trucks, new	2,769	2,610	6.1
Cars and trucks, used	2,526	2,916	−13.4
Gasoline and motor oil	**2,277**	**2,047**	**11.2**
Other vehicle expenses	**3,188**	**3,501**	**−8.9**
Vehicle finance charges	516	567	−9.0
Maintenance and repairs	881	907	−2.9
Vehicle insurance	1,199	1,077	11.3
Vehicle rental, leases, licenses, other charges	593	950	−37.6
Public transportation	**542**	**532**	**1.9**

	2004	2000	percent change 2000–04
HEALTH CARE	**$2,948**	**$2,469**	**19.4%**
Health insurance	1,579	1,182	33.5
Medical services	872	802	8.8
Drugs	372	359	3.7
Medical supplies	125	126	–0.9
ENTERTAINMENT	**3,320**	**3,565**	**–6.9**
Fees and admissions	991	1,151	–13.9
Television, radio, sound equipment	1,070	1,006	6.4
Pets, toys, and playground equipment	570	600	–5.0
Other entertainment supplies, services	690	807	–14.5
PERSONAL CARE PRODUCTS AND SERVICES	**732**	**849**	**–13.8**
READING	**158**	**191**	**–17.2**
EDUCATION	**1,439**	**1,132**	**27.1**
TOBACCO PRODUCTS, SMOKING SUPPLIES	**318**	**369**	**–13.7**
MISCELLANEOUS	**650**	**1,053**	**–38.3**
CASH CONTRIBUTIONS	**1,517**	**1,393**	**8.9**
PERSONAL INSURANCE AND PENSIONS	**7,524**	**5,851**	**28.6**
Life and other personal insurance	543	647	–16.1
Pensions and Social Security	6,981	5,204	34.2
PERSONAL TAXES	**2,738**	**5,193**	**–47.3**
Federal income taxes	1,836	3,999	–54.1
State and local income taxes	697	994	–29.9
Other taxes	205	200	2.7
GIFTS FOR NONHOUSEHOLD MEMBERS	**1,393**	**1,258**	**10.7**

Note: The Bureau of Labor Statistics uses consumer unit rather than household as the sampling unit in the Consumer Expenditure Survey. For the definition of consumer unit, see the glossary. Spending on gifts is also included in the preceding product and service categories.
Source: Bureau of Labor Statistics, 2000 and 2004 Consumer Expenditure Surveys, Internet site http://www.bls.gov/cex/; calculations by New Strategist

Couples with Adult Children at Home Are Spending More

Education and health insurance are two of the biggest gainers.

Married couples with grown children (aged 18 or older) at home are the most affluent household type. That's because these households have the most earners—2.5 versus 1.7 earners in the average household. Couples with adult children at home spent an average of $64,162 in 2004, 7 percent more than they spent in 2000, after adjusting for inflation.

Married couples with adult children at home are spending less on many items. They cut their grocery (food at home) spending by 1.5 percent between 2000 and 2004, and their spending on alcoholic beverages declined 3 percent. But they spent 4 percent more on food away from home (mostly restaurant meals). Spending on owned homes increased 3 percent, but spending on home furnishings and equipment fell 4 percent. Spending on entertainment rose 5 percent, but spending on apparel diminished 12 percent. This household type spent 27 percent more on out of pocket health insurance costs in 2004 than in 2000.

Many couples with adult children at home have at least one child in college. Their spending on education rose 18 percent between 2000 and 2004, after adjusting for inflation.

■ Many couples with adult children at home are trying to save for college expenses, tempering their discretionary purchases.

Couples with adult children at home are spending more on education

(percent change in spending by married couples with children aged 18 or older at home, 2000 and 2004; in 2004 dollars)

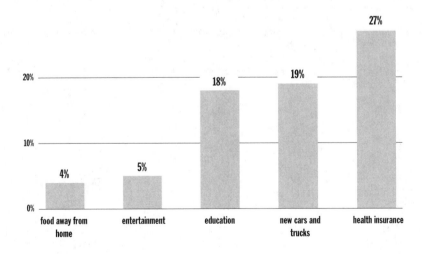

Table 8.5 Average Spending of Married Couples with Oldest Child Aged 18 or Older, 2000 and 2004

(average annual spending of married-couple consumer units with oldest child at home aged 18 or older, 2000 and 2004; percent change, 2000–04; in 2004 dollars)

	2004	2000	percent change 2000–04
Number of consumer units (in 000s)	8,300	8,090	2.6%
Average before-tax income	$85,109	$70,996	19.9
Average annual spending	64,162	59,835	7.2
FOOD	**8,682**	**8,619**	**0.7**
Food at home	**5,104**	**5,182**	**–1.5**
Cereals and bakery products	705	822	–14.2
Cereals and cereal products	242	275	–12.1
Bakery products	463	545	–15.1
Meats, poultry, fish, and eggs	1,465	1,394	5.1
Beef	480	429	11.9
Pork	300	294	2.1
Other meats	184	186	–1.3
Poultry	243	252	–3.7
Fish and seafood	191	171	11.6
Eggs	66	61	7.4
Dairy products	549	554	–0.9
Fresh milk and cream	219	226	–3.1
Other dairy products	330	328	0.6
Fruits and vegetables	823	846	–2.7
Fresh fruits	263	264	–0.5
Fresh vegetables	278	251	10.7
Processed fruits	155	179	–13.3
Processed vegetables	128	151	–15.4
Other food at home	1,561	1,566	–0.3
Sugar and other sweets	183	222	–17.4
Fats and oils	137	148	–7.5
Miscellaneous foods	750	689	8.9
Nonalcoholic beverages	439	453	–3.1
Food prepared by household on trips	51	55	–7.0
Food away from home	**3,578**	**3,438**	**4.1**
ALCOHOLIC BEVERAGES	**506**	**523**	**–3.3**
HOUSING	**17,503**	**17,042**	**2.7**
Shelter	**9,455**	**9,412**	**0.5**
Owned dwellings	7,628	7,396	3.1
Mortgage interest and charges	4,470	4,320	3.5
Property taxes	1,987	1,886	5.4
Maintenance, repairs, insurance, other expenses	1,171	1,191	–1.7

	2004	2000	percent change 2000–04
Rented dwellings	$1,058	$1,089	−2.9%
Other lodging	769	927	−17.0
Utilities, fuels, public services	**4,240**	**3,731**	**13.7**
Natural gas	594	458	29.6
Electricity	1,489	1,401	6.3
Fuel oil and other fuels	177	143	24.1
Telephone services	1,487	1,243	19.7
Water and other public services	492	486	1.3
Household services	**599**	**586**	**2.3**
Personal services	69	117	−41.2
Other household services	531	468	13.4
Housekeeping supplies	**794**	**801**	**−0.8**
Laundry and cleaning supplies	208	219	−5.2
Other household products	379	387	−2.1
Postage and stationery	207	194	6.6
Household furnishings and equipment	**2,415**	**2,513**	**−3.9**
Household textiles	299	179	67.2
Furniture	556	531	4.7
Floor coverings	66	118	−44.3
Major appliances	311	375	−17.1
Small appliances, misc. housewares	133	136	−2.2
Miscellaneous household equipment	1,049	1,175	−10.7
APPAREL AND SERVICES	**2,617**	**2,959**	**−11.6**
Men and boys	**618**	**797**	**−22.5**
Men, aged 16 or older	516	680	−24.1
Boys, aged 2 to 15	103	117	−12.2
Women and girls	**1,189**	**1,305**	**−8.9**
Women, aged 16 or older	1,061	1,184	−10.4
Girls, aged 2 to 15	128	122	5.1
Children under age 2	**35**	**69**	**−49.4**
Footwear	**490**	**424**	**15.4**
Other apparel products and services	**285**	**363**	**−21.5**
TRANSPORTATION	**13,694**	**13,336**	**2.7**
Vehicle purchases	**6,263**	**6,270**	**−0.1**
Cars and trucks, new	3,354	2,807	19.5
Cars and trucks, used	2,837	3,421	−17.1
Gasoline and motor oil	**2,770**	**2,295**	**20.7**
Other vehicle expenses	**3,986**	**4,161**	**−4.2**
Vehicle finance charges	548	610	−10.1
Maintenance and repairs	987	1,084	−8.9
Vehicle insurance	1,818	1,544	17.7
Vehicle rental, leases, licenses, other charges	634	922	−31.3
Public transportation	**674**	**612**	**10.1**

	2004	2000	percent change 2000–04
HEALTH CARE	**$3,554**	**$2,941**	**20.9%**
Health insurance	1,820	1,429	27.3
Medical services	947	803	17.9
Drugs	611	558	9.4
Medical supplies	176	151	16.3
ENTERTAINMENT	**2,975**	**2,837**	**4.9**
Fees and admissions	729	777	–6.1
Television, radio, sound equipment	1,081	905	19.5
Pets, toys, and playground equipment	495	464	6.7
Other entertainment supplies, services	670	690	–2.9
PERSONAL CARE PRODUCTS AND SERVICES	**891**	**927**	**–3.9**
READING	**154**	**199**	**–22.4**
EDUCATION	**2,294**	**1,940**	**18.2**
TOBACCO PRODUCTS, SMOKING SUPPLIES	**413**	**499**	**–17.2**
MISCELLANEOUS	**1,011**	**997**	**1.4**
CASH CONTRIBUTIONS	**1,610**	**1,503**	**7.1**
PERSONAL INSURANCE AND PENSIONS	**8,257**	**5,514**	**49.7**
Life and other personal insurance	742	770	–3.6
Pensions and Social Security	7,516	4,744	58.4
PERSONAL TAXES	**3,142**	**4,519**	**–30.5**
Federal income taxes	2,233	3,577	–37.6
State and local income taxes	690	744	–7.2
Other taxes	219	199	10.3
GIFTS FOR NONHOUSEHOLD MEMBERS	**1,722**	**1,895**	**–9.1**

Note: The Bureau of Labor Statistics uses consumer unit rather than household as the sampling unit in the Consumer Expenditure Survey. For the definition of consumer unit, see the glossary. Spending on gifts is also included in the preceding product and service categories.
Source: Bureau of Labor Statistics, 2000 and 2004 Consumer Expenditure Surveys, Internet site http://www.bls.gov/cex/; calculations by New Strategist

Single Parents Increased Their Spending

They are spending more on many items, but less on some.

Single parents with children under age 18 at home spent $32,824 in 2004—3 percent more than they spent in 2000, after adjusting for inflation. This household type spends more than it makes.

Spending trends for single-parent families have experienced both ups and downs in the past few years. Single parents spent 5 percent more on food away from home and 7 percent more on alcoholic beverages in 2004 than in 2000, after adjusting for inflation. They cut their spending on personal care products and services by 17 percent, however. Single parents boosted their spending on health care by 24 percent between 2000 and 2004, with an enormous 42 percent increase in their out of pocket spending on health insurance. Like most other household types, they spent more on owned dwellings as homeownership rates increased. As they outfitted those homes, their spending on furniture rose 20 percent. Single parents spent 39 percent more on new cars and trucks, but 26 percent less on used vehicles. Their spending on women's clothes rose 4 percent, while their spending on children's clothes fell.

■ With more and more money devoted to out of pocket health insurance costs, single parents may have less discretionary income in the years ahead.

The income of single parents is less than their spending

(average household income and average spending of single-parent families with children under age 18 at home, 2004)

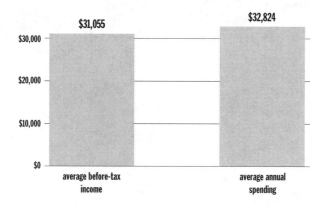

Table 8.6 Average Spending of Single Parents with Children under Age 18, 2000 and 2004

(average annual spending of single parents with children under age 18, 2000 and 2004; percent change, 2000–04; in 2004 dollars)

	2004	2000	percent change 2000–04
Number of consumer units (in 000s)	6,892	6,132	12.4%
Average before-tax income	$31,055	$27,526	12.8
Average annual spending	32,824	31,725	3.5
FOOD	4,873	4,667	4.4
Food at home	3,015	2,903	3.8
Cereals and bakery products	443	426	4.1
Cereals and cereal products	162	168	–3.5
Bakery products	281	257	9.5
Meats, poultry, fish, and eggs	835	827	1.0
Beef	258	245	5.5
Pork	188	174	7.8
Other meats	106	100	6.2
Poultry	135	168	–19.6
Fish and seafood	112	102	9.8
Eggs	37	36	2.2
Dairy products	317	306	3.6
Fresh milk and cream	140	128	9.1
Other dairy products	176	178	–1.0
Fruits and vegetables	456	448	1.9
Fresh fruits	149	125	19.2
Fresh vegetables	130	128	1.3
Processed fruits	102	115	–11.4
Processed vegetables	75	79	–5.0
Other food at home	964	897	7.4
Sugar and other sweets	123	117	4.8
Fats and oils	78	86	–8.8
Miscellaneous foods	474	394	20.4
Nonalcoholic beverages	269	264	1.8
Food prepared by household on trips	19	35	–45.9
Food away from home	1,858	1,764	5.3
ALCOHOLIC BEVERAGES	219	205	6.8
HOUSING	12,030	11,772	2.2
Shelter	7,043	6,944	1.4
Owned dwellings	3,314	3,068	8.0
Mortgage interest and charges	2,037	1,858	9.6
Property taxes	729	709	2.9
Maintenance, repairs, insurance, other expenses	548	501	9.3

	2004	2000	percent change 2000–04
Rented dwellings	$3,510	$3,636	−3.5%
Other lodging	219	240	−8.8
Utilities, fuels, public services	**2,755**	**2,561**	**7.6**
Natural gas	380	336	13.2
Electricity	1,065	947	12.5
Fuel oil and other fuels	67	47	42.1
Telephone services	979	980	−0.1
Water and other public services	263	252	4.2
Household services	**759**	**862**	**−12.0**
Personal services	483	643	−24.9
Other household services	276	219	25.8
Housekeeping supplies	**453**	**404**	**12.2**
Laundry and cleaning supplies	158	166	−4.6
Other household products	193	154	25.7
Postage and stationery	102	84	20.8
Household furnishings and equipment	**1,020**	**1,000**	**2.0**
Household textiles	85	66	29.2
Furniture	357	298	19.7
Floor coverings	42	24	74.0
Major appliances	101	114	−11.5
Small appliances, misc. housewares	70	39	77.3
Miscellaneous household equipment	365	457	−20.2
APPAREL AND SERVICES	**1,859**	**2,107**	**−11.8**
Men and boys	**304**	**445**	**−31.7**
Men, aged 16 or older	111	162	−31.6
Boys, aged 2 to 15	193	284	−32.1
Women and girls	**880**	**891**	**−1.2**
Women, aged 16 or older	608	584	4.2
Girls, aged 2 to 15	272	306	−11.1
Children under age 2	**89**	**122**	**−26.9**
Footwear	**424**	**451**	**−5.9**
Other apparel products and services	**164**	**197**	**−16.9**
TRANSPORTATION	**5,446**	**5,503**	**−1.0**
Vehicle purchases	**2,304**	**2,565**	**−10.2**
Cars and trucks, new	798	575	38.8
Cars and trucks, used	1,463	1,985	−26.3
Gasoline and motor oil	**1,216**	**981**	**24.0**
Other vehicle expenses	**1,716**	**1,665**	**3.1**
Vehicle finance charges	211	238	−11.4
Maintenance and repairs	477	516	−7.5
Vehicle insurance	725	608	19.3
Vehicle rental, leases, licenses, other charges	302	303	−0.2
Public transportation	**209**	**293**	**−28.6**

	2004	2000	percent change 2000–04
HEALTH CARE	**$1,384**	**$1,112**	**24.4%**
Health insurance	705	497	41.9
Medical services	415	398	4.2
Drugs	213	159	33.9
Medical supplies	51	59	–13.9
ENTERTAINMENT	**1,573**	**1,572**	**0.1**
Fees and admissions	391	443	–11.8
Television, radio, sound equipment	695	648	7.2
Pets, toys, and playground equipment	285	280	1.9
Other entertainment supplies, services	203	200	1.7
PERSONAL CARE PRODUCTS AND SERVICES	**517**	**624**	**–17.2**
READING	**68**	**83**	**–18.4**
EDUCATION	**700**	**433**	**61.6**
TOBACCO PRODUCTS, SMOKING SUPPLIES	**277**	**328**	**–15.5**
MISCELLANEOUS	**643**	**860**	**–25.2**
CASH CONTRIBUTIONS	**587**	**446**	**31.5**
PERSONAL INSURANCE AND PENSIONS	**2,648**	**2,012**	**31.6**
Life and other personal insurance	204	165	24.0
Pensions and Social Security	2,444	1,846	32.4
PERSONAL TAXES	**103**	**655**	**–84.3**
Federal income taxes	–	387	–
State and local income taxes	217	223	–2.5
Other taxes	82	45	82.3
GIFTS FOR NONHOUSEHOLD MEMBERS	**649**	**749**	**–13.4**

Note: The Bureau of Labor Statistics uses consumer unit rather than household as the sampling unit in the Consumer Expenditure Survey. For the definition of consumer unit, see the glossary. Spending on gifts is also included in the preceding product and service categories; "–" means sample is too small to make a reliable estimate.
Source: Bureau of Labor Statistics, 2000 and 2004 Consumer Expenditure Surveys, Internet site http://www.bls.gov/cex/; calculations by New Strategist

Married Couples with Children Spend More than Average

Single parents spend much less than average on most products and services.

Because married couples have higher-than-average incomes, their spending is also above average. Overall, couples with preschoolers spent 29 percent more than the average household in 2004. Couples with school-aged children spend 40 percent more, while those with grown children at home spend 48 percent more. In contrast, single-parent families spend 24 percent less than the average household. Married couples with children control 35 percent of total household spending, while single parents control just 4 percent.

Couples with preschoolers spend much more than average on items needed by young children. They spend more than seven times the average on household personal services (mostly day care) and more than six times the average on clothes for infants.

Couples with school-aged or older children at home spend much more than average on most products and services. Those with adult children at home spend substantially more on items needed by workers (since their households have more workers than the average household) and by college students (since many have children in college). They spend 63 percent more than average on "other" lodging (which includes college dorm room expenses) and more than twice the average on education.

Single parents spend less than average in all but a few categories. They are above-average spenders on rent, household personal services (mostly day care), and children's clothes.

■ Married couples with children spend more than the average household, but their spending is well within their means. Single parents are living closer to the edge.

Married couples with adult children at home spend the most

(indexed average annual spending of households with children, by type of household, 2004)

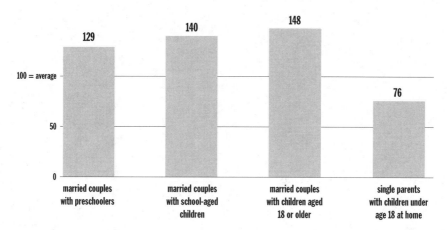

Table 8.7 Indexed Spending of Households with Children, 2004

(indexed spending of total consumer units and consumer units with children at home, by type of consumer unit, 2004)

	total consumer units	married couples with children				single parents with children under age 18
		total	oldest child under age 6	oldest child aged 6 to 17	oldest child 18 or older	
Number of consumer units (in 000s)	116,282	29,279	5,604	15,376	8,300	6,892
Indexed average before-tax income	100	146	138	144	156	57
Indexed average annual spending	100	140	129	140	148	76
FOOD	100	140	109	147	150	84
Food at home	100	141	112	146	152	90
Cereals and bakery products	100	145	107	156	153	96
Cereals and cereal products	100	147	104	160	157	105
Bakery products	100	144	108	154	151	92
Meats, poultry, fish, and eggs	100	138	99	138	166	95
Beef	100	142	92	143	181	97
Pork	100	133	97	130	166	104
Other meats	100	144	93	150	170	98
Poultry	100	139	106	144	156	87
Fish and seafood	100	129	115	124	149	88
Eggs	100	131	107	129	157	88
Dairy products	100	146	118	156	148	85
Fresh milk and cream	100	153	132	162	152	97
Other dairy products	100	142	109	154	146	78
Fruits and vegetables	100	135	113	137	147	81
Fresh fruits	100	133	113	136	141	80
Fresh vegetables	100	132	112	131	152	71
Processed fruits	100	140	124	145	141	93
Processed vegetables	100	137	100	141	156	91
Other food at home	100	143	123	149	145	90
Sugar and other sweets	100	138	109	146	143	96
Fats and oils	100	136	99	140	154	88
Miscellaneous foods	100	150	146	154	142	90
Nonalcoholic beverages	100	138	101	145	151	93
Food prepared by household on trips	100	122	85	134	124	46
Food away from home	100	139	104	148	147	76
ALCOHOLIC BEVERAGES	100	97	72	99	110	48
HOUSING	100	136	151	136	126	86
Shelter	100	133	149	136	118	88
Owned dwellings	100	159	174	162	143	62
Mortgage interest and charges	100	181	213	185	152	69
Property taxes	100	141	137	141	143	52
Maintenance, repairs, insurance, other expenses	100	120	111	125	117	55

	total consumer units	married couples with children				single parents with children under age 18
		total	oldest child under age 6	oldest child aged 6 to 17	oldest child 18 or older	
Rented dwellings	100	71	106	70	48	159
Other lodging	100	133	75	137	163	46
Utilities, fuels, public services	**100**	**131**	**114**	**130**	**145**	**94**
Natural gas	100	132	129	129	140	90
Electricity	100	130	105	133	140	100
Fuel oil and other fuels	100	123	91	123	146	55
Telephone services	100	131	118	126	150	99
Water and other public services	100	137	119	136	150	80
Household services	**100**	**173**	**358**	**155**	**80**	**101**
Personal services	100	250	715	203	23	161
Other household services	100	121	122	123	117	61
Housekeeping supplies	**100**	**137**	**138**	**139**	**134**	**76**
Laundry and cleaning supplies	100	138	117	146	140	106
Other household products	100	142	155	143	131	67
Postage and stationery	100	126	126	124	134	66
Household furnishings and equipment	**100**	**140**	**137**	**137**	**147**	**62**
Household textiles	100	126	106	104	189	54
Furniture	100	141	150	141	133	86
Floor coverings	100	117	90	123	127	81
Major appliances	100	146	163	135	152	50
Small appliances, misc. housewares	100	134	171	124	127	67
Miscellaneous household equipment	100	143	127	146	148	51
APPAREL AND SERVICES	**100**	**148**	**142**	**152**	**144**	**102**
Men and boys	**100**	**166**	**142**	**182**	**152**	**75**
Men, aged 16 or older	100	148	140	144	163	35
Boys, aged 2 to 15	100	229	148	318	116	217
Women and girls	**100**	**140**	**118**	**138**	**161**	**119**
Women, aged 16 or older	100	124	114	106	168	96
Girls, aged 2 to 15	100	232	143	326	119	252
Children under age 2	**100**	**213**	**656**	**127**	**44**	**113**
Footwear	**100**	**147**	**98**	**166**	**149**	**129**
Other apparel products and services	**100**	**122**	**111**	**133**	**108**	**62**
TRANSPORTATION	**100**	**152**	**136**	**146**	**176**	**70**
Vehicle purchases	**100**	**164**	**151**	**158**	**184**	**68**
Cars and trucks, new	100	170	168	158	192	46
Cars and trucks, used	100	161	137	160	179	92
Gasoline and motor oil	**100**	**148**	**125**	**142**	**173**	**76**
Other vehicle expenses	**100**	**143**	**127**	**135**	**169**	**73**
Vehicle finance charges	100	161	150	160	170	65
Maintenance and repairs	100	135	111	135	151	73
Vehicle insurance	100	141	115	124	189	75
Vehicle rental, leases, licenses, other charges	100	147	165	139	149	71
Public transportation	**100**	**127**	**102**	**123**	**153**	**47**

	total consumer units	married couples with children				single parents with children under age 18
		total	oldest child under age 6	oldest child aged 6 to 17	oldest child 18 or older	
HEALTH CARE	100	117	92	115	138	54
Health insurance	100	119	96	119	137	53
Medical services	100	133	106	135	146	64
Drugs	100	89	64	78	127	44
Medical supplies	100	118	87	110	154	45
ENTERTAINMENT	100	138	110	150	134	71
Fees and admissions	100	155	91	188	138	74
Television, radio, sound equipment	100	135	127	136	137	88
Pets, toys, and playground equipment	100	141	136	150	130	75
Other entertainment supplies, services	100	122	85	132	128	39
PERSONAL CARE PRODUCTS, SERVICES	100	129	104	126	153	89
READING	100	118	107	122	118	52
EDUCATION	100	164	46	159	253	77
TOBACCO PRODUCTS, SMOKING SUPPLIES	100	113	73	110	143	96
MISCELLANEOUS	100	110	100	94	147	93
CASH CONTRIBUTIONS	100	105	84	108	114	42
PERSONAL INSURANCE AND PENSIONS	100	159	147	156	171	55
Life and other personal insurance	100	146	100	139	190	52
Pensions and Social Security	100	160	151	157	170	55
PERSONAL TAXES	100	133	133	126	145	5
Federal income taxes	100	130	128	121	147	–
State and local income taxes	100	151	167	148	146	46
Other taxes	100	114	89	117	125	47
GIFTS FOR NONHOUSEHOLD MEMBERS	100	117	89	115	142	53

Note: The index compares the spending of consumer units with children with the spending of the average consumer unit. It is calculated by dividing the spending of consumer units with children by average spending in each category and multiplying by 100. An index of 100 means the spending equals average spending. An index of 130 means the spending is 30 percent above average, while an index of 70 means the spending is 30 percent below average. The Bureau of Labor Statistics uses consumer unit rather than household as the sampling unit in the Consumer Expenditure Survey. For the definition of consumer unit, see the glossary. "–" means sample is too small to make a reliable estimate.
Source: Bureau of Labor Statistics, 2004 Consumer Expenditure Survey, Internet site http://www.bls.gov/cex/; calculations by New Strategist

Table 8.8 Market Share of Spending Controlled by Households with Children, 2004

(percent of total household spending accounted for by consumer units with children at home, 2004)

| | total consumer units | married couples with children | | | | single parents with children under age 18 |
		total	oldest child under age 6	oldest child aged 6 to 17	oldest child 18 or older	
Number of consumer units (in 000s)	116,282	29,279	5,604	15,376	8,300	6,892
Share of consumer units	100.0%	25.2%	4.8%	13.2%	7.1%	5.9%
Share of before-tax income	100.0	36.9	6.7	19.1	11.2	3.4
Share of total spending	100.0	35.2	6.2	18.5	10.6	4.5
FOOD	100.0	35.2	5.3	19.4	10.7	5.0
Food at home	100.0	35.4	5.4	19.3	10.9	5.3
Cereals and bakery products	100.0	36.5	5.1	20.6	10.9	5.7
Cereals and cereal products	100.0	37.1	5.0	21.1	11.2	6.2
Bakery products	100.0	36.2	5.2	20.3	10.8	5.4
Meats, poultry, fish, and eggs	100.0	34.6	4.8	18.3	11.9	5.6
Beef	100.0	35.8	4.4	19.0	12.9	5.8
Pork	100.0	33.4	4.7	17.2	11.8	6.2
Other meats	100.0	36.1	4.5	19.8	12.2	5.8
Poultry	100.0	35.0	5.1	19.1	11.1	5.1
Fish and seafood	100.0	32.5	5.5	16.4	10.7	5.2
Eggs	100.0	33.0	5.2	17.0	11.2	5.2
Dairy products	100.0	36.8	5.7	20.7	10.6	5.1
Fresh milk and cream	100.0	38.5	6.4	21.4	10.9	5.8
Other dairy products	100.0	35.9	5.2	20.3	10.4	4.6
Fruits and vegetables	100.0	33.9	5.4	18.2	10.5	4.8
Fresh fruits	100.0	33.4	5.4	18.0	10.0	4.7
Fresh vegetables	100.0	33.3	5.4	17.3	10.8	4.2
Processed fruits	100.0	35.3	6.0	19.2	10.1	5.5
Processed vegetables	100.0	34.4	4.8	18.7	11.1	5.4
Other food at home	100.0	36.0	5.9	19.7	10.4	5.3
Sugar and other sweets	100.0	34.6	5.3	19.3	10.2	5.7
Fats and oils	100.0	34.2	4.8	18.6	11.0	5.2
Miscellaneous foods	100.0	37.6	7.1	20.4	10.2	5.3
Nonalcoholic beverages	100.0	34.6	4.9	19.2	10.8	5.5
Food prepared by household on trips	100.0	30.7	4.1	17.7	8.9	2.7
Food away from home	100.0	34.9	5.0	19.5	10.5	4.5
ALCOHOLIC BEVERAGES	100.0	24.3	3.5	13.1	7.9	2.8
HOUSING	100.0	34.2	7.3	18.0	9.0	5.1
Shelter	100.0	33.6	7.2	17.9	8.4	5.2
Owned dwellings	100.0	40.1	8.4	21.5	10.2	3.7
Mortgage interest and charges	100.0	45.6	10.2	24.5	10.9	4.1
Property taxes	100.0	35.4	6.6	18.6	10.2	3.1
Maintenance, repairs, insurance, other expenses	100.0	30.3	5.3	16.6	8.4	3.3

| | | married couples with children | | | single parents |
	total consumer units	total	oldest child under age 6	oldest child aged 6 to 17	oldest child 18 or older	with children under age 18
Rented dwellings	100.0%	17.8%	5.1%	9.3%	3.4%	9.5%
Other lodging	100.0	33.4	3.6	18.2	11.6	2.7
Utilities, fuels, public services	**100.0**	**33.0**	**5.5**	**17.2**	**10.3**	**5.6**
Natural gas	100.0	33.3	6.2	17.1	10.0	5.3
Electricity	100.0	32.7	5.0	17.6	10.0	5.9
Fuel oil and other fuels	100.0	31.0	4.4	16.3	10.4	3.3
Telephone services	100.0	33.1	5.7	16.7	10.7	5.9
Water and other public services	100.0	34.4	5.7	18.0	10.7	4.8
Household services	**100.0**	**43.4**	**17.3**	**20.5**	**5.7**	**6.0**
Personal services	100.0	62.9	34.5	26.8	1.6	9.5
Other household services	100.0	30.6	5.9	16.3	8.4	3.6
Housekeeping supplies	**100.0**	**34.5**	**6.7**	**18.3**	**9.5**	**4.5**
Laundry and cleaning supplies	100.0	34.8	5.6	19.3	10.0	6.3
Other household products	100.0	35.9	7.5	18.9	9.3	3.9
Postage and stationery	100.0	31.8	6.1	16.4	9.5	3.9
Household furnishings and equipment	**100.0**	**35.2**	**6.6**	**18.2**	**10.5**	**3.7**
Household textiles	100.0	31.7	5.1	13.7	13.5	3.2
Furniture	100.0	35.4	7.2	18.7	9.5	5.1
Floor coverings	100.0	29.5	4.4	16.3	9.1	4.8
Major appliances	100.0	36.7	7.9	17.9	10.9	2.9
Small appliances, misc. housewares	100.0	33.8	8.3	16.4	9.0	4.0
Miscellaneous household equipment	100.0	35.9	6.1	19.3	10.5	3.0
APPAREL AND SERVICES	**100.0**	**37.2**	**6.9**	**20.1**	**10.3**	**6.1**
Men and boys	**100.0**	**41.7**	**6.8**	**24.1**	**10.9**	**4.4**
Men, aged 16 or older	100.0	37.3	6.7	19.0	11.6	2.1
Boys, aged 2 to 15	100.0	57.7	7.1	42.0	8.3	12.9
Women and girls	**100.0**	**35.2**	**5.7**	**18.3**	**11.5**	**7.1**
Women, aged 16 or older	100.0	31.2	5.5	14.1	12.0	5.7
Girls, aged 2 to 15	100.0	58.5	6.9	43.1	8.5	14.9
Children under age 2	**100.0**	**53.5**	**31.6**	**16.7**	**3.2**	**6.7**
Footwear	**100.0**	**37.1**	**4.7**	**21.9**	**10.6**	**7.6**
Other apparel products and services	**100.0**	**30.6**	**5.4**	**17.6**	**7.7**	**3.7**
TRANSPORTATION	**100.0**	**38.4**	**6.5**	**19.3**	**12.5**	**4.1**
Vehicle purchases	**100.0**	**41.4**	**7.3**	**20.9**	**13.2**	**4.0**
Cars and trucks, new	100.0	42.8	8.1	20.9	13.7	2.7
Cars and trucks, used	100.0	40.5	6.6	21.1	12.8	5.5
Gasoline and motor oil	**100.0**	**37.2**	**6.0**	**18.8**	**12.4**	**4.5**
Other vehicle expenses	**100.0**	**36.0**	**6.1**	**17.8**	**12.0**	**4.3**
Vehicle finance charges	100.0	40.5	7.2	21.1	12.1	3.9
Maintenance and repairs	100.0	34.0	5.3	17.9	10.8	4.3
Vehicle insurance	100.0	35.4	5.5	16.4	13.5	4.5
Vehicle rental, leases, licenses, other charges	100.0	36.9	8.0	18.4	10.6	4.2
Public transportation	**100.0**	**32.0**	**4.9**	**16.3**	**10.9**	**2.8**

| | total consumer units | married couples with children | | | | single parents with children under age 18 |
		total	oldest child under age 6	oldest child aged 6 to 17	oldest child 18 or older	
HEALTH CARE	100.0%	29.4%	4.4%	15.1%	9.9%	3.2%
Health insurance	100.0	30.0	4.6	15.7	9.8	3.1
Medical services	100.0	33.4	5.1	17.8	10.4	3.8
Drugs	100.0	22.4	3.1	10.2	9.1	2.6
Medical supplies	100.0	29.6	4.2	14.5	11.0	2.7
ENTERTAINMENT	100.0	34.6	5.3	19.8	9.6	4.2
Fees and admissions	100.0	39.1	4.4	24.8	9.9	4.4
Television, radio, sound equipment	100.0	33.9	6.1	18.0	9.8	5.2
Pets, toys, and playground equipment	100.0	35.5	6.6	19.8	9.3	4.4
Other entertainment supplies, services	100.0	30.7	4.1	17.5	9.2	2.3
PERSONAL CARE PRODUCTS, SERVICES	100.0	32.4	5.0	16.7	10.9	5.3
READING	100.0	29.6	5.2	16.1	8.5	3.1
EDUCATION	100.0	41.3	2.2	21.0	18.1	4.6
TOBACCO PRODUCTS, SMOKING SUPPLIES	100.0	28.3	3.5	14.6	10.2	5.7
MISCELLANEOUS	100.0	27.6	4.8	12.5	10.5	5.5
CASH CONTRIBUTIONS	100.0	26.5	4.1	14.2	8.2	2.5
PERSONAL INSURANCE AND PENSIONS	100.0	39.9	7.1	20.6	12.2	3.3
Life and other personal insurance	100.0	36.8	4.8	18.4	13.6	3.1
Pensions and Social Security	100.0	40.2	7.3	20.8	12.1	3.3
PERSONAL TAXES	100.0	33.5	6.4	16.7	10.4	0.3
Federal income taxes	100.0	32.7	6.2	16.0	10.5	–
State and local income taxes	100.0	38.0	8.0	19.5	10.4	2.7
Other taxes	100.0	28.6	4.3	15.5	8.9	2.8
GIFTS FOR NONHOUSEHOLD MEMBERS	100.0	29.5	4.3	15.2	10.1	3.2

Note: Market shares are calculated by first multiplying average spending by the total number of households. Using those aggregate figures, the total spending of each segment is divided by the total for all households to determine each segment's share of the total. The Bureau of Labor Statistics uses consumer unit rather than household as the sampling unit in the Consumer Expenditure Survey. For the definition of consumer unit, see the glossary. "–" means sample is too small to make a reliable estimate.
Source: Bureau of Labor Statistics, 2004 Consumer Expenditure Survey, Internet site http://www.bls.gov/cex/; calculations by New Strategist

9

Time Use

■ Time use varies sharply by age. Teenagers get the most sleep, an average of 9.46 hours a night. Men aged 45 to 54 get the least amount of sleep—just 8.08 hours.

■ On an average day, women under age 35 spend at least three times as long as their male counterparts preparing meals.

■ Among teenagers, television is more popular than playing on a computer. Boys aged 15 to 19 spend 1.24 hours per day on their computer versus 2.45 hours per day watching TV.

■ The 62 percent majority of 18-to-29-year-olds uses instant messaging compared with a much smaller 26 to 36 percent of adults aged 30 or older.

■ The Millennial generation accounted for only 13 percent of voters in the 2004 presidential election, far behind the 40 percent share accounted for by Boomers.

■ Paying for college is a big worry for many college freshmen. When asked how concerned they are about their ability to finance their college education, only 34 percent have no concerns.

■ The great majority of college freshmen believe a national health care plan is needed to cover everyone's medical costs. They also support gun control and legal abortion.

Americans Spend More Time in Leisure than at Work

Driving around ranks fifth in time use, ahead of eating and drinking.

The average person spends 9.33 hours a day in personal care activities, primarily sleeping. Socializing, relaxing, and leisure activities take up 4.62 hours a day, and work accounts for another 3.37 hours, according to the Bureau of Labor Statistics' American Time Use Survey. Household activities (i.e., housework) rank fourth in importance in the time use statistics, followed by traveling—a category that includes driving to work, to stores, to leisure activities, and to children's events.

Time use varies sharply by age. Not surprisingly, people aged 25 to 54 spend the most time working (29 to 36 percent more than the average person) and consequently they have the least amount of leisure time (12 to 20 percent less than average). Older Americans have the most leisure time—even more than teenagers. People aged 65 or older have 6.87 hours of leisure per day compared with 4.82 hours per day for people aged 15 to 19.

Time use also varies greatly by sex. Among 15-to-19-year-olds, for example, boys spend more time than girls working, eating and drinking, socializing, and playing sports. Girls spend more time than boys doing most other activities including shopping, volunteering, and making phone calls.

■ Teenagers spend more time on educational activities than any other age group, an average of 2.98 hours per day.

Teens and young adults spend a lot of time driving around

(average number of hours per day spent traveling, by age, 2004)

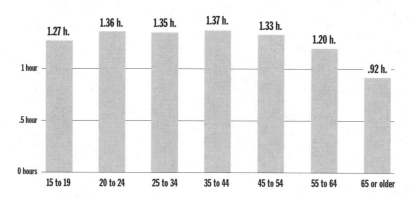

Table 9.1 Time Use by Primary Activity and Age, 2004

(average and indexed hours per day spent in primary activities, by age, 2004)

	total	15–19	20–24	25–34	35–44	45–54	55–64	65+
Total hours	**24.00**	**24.00**	**24.00**	**24.00**	**24.00**	**24.00**	**24.00**	**24.00**
Personal care activities	9.33	10.25	9.66	9.23	9.02	9.00	9.08	9.65
Household activities	1.82	0.69	1.02	1.53	1.89	2.07	2.18	2.62
Caring for and helping household members	0.48	0.10	0.44	1.01	0.88	0.32	0.14	0.09
Caring for and helping nonhousehold members	0.19	0.11	0.18	0.17	0.14	0.23	0.31	0.19
Work and related activities	3.37	1.14	3.49	4.35	4.60	4.50	3.49	0.65
Education	0.46	2.98	0.94	0.26	0.14	0.09	0.05	0.03
Consumer purchases	0.41	0.31	0.35	0.46	0.41	0.41	0.46	0.40
Professional and personal care services	0.09	0.05	0.03	0.07	0.08	0.11	0.09	0.16
Household services	0.02	–	–	0.01	0.01	0.02	0.02	0.03
Government services and civic obligations	0.01	–	0.01	0.01	0.01	–	0.01	–
Eating and drinking	1.11	0.86	0.97	1.05	1.06	1.12	1.23	1.38
Socializing, relaxing, and leisure	4.62	4.82	4.71	3.87	3.68	4.05	4.97	6.87
Sports, exercise, and recreation	0.33	0.71	0.44	0.30	0.28	0.25	0.26	0.25
Religious and spiritual activities	0.12	0.15	0.10	0.10	0.10	0.11	0.13	0.20
Volunteer activities	0.15	0.17	0.06	0.07	0.15	0.18	0.15	0.20
Telephone calls	0.12	0.26	0.14	0.08	0.08	0.11	0.10	0.14
Traveling	1.26	1.27	1.36	1.35	1.37	1.33	1.20	0.92
Unencodeable	0.12	0.14	0.09	0.07	0.09	0.10	0.13	0.22
Index of time use by age to total								
Personal care activities	100	110	104	99	97	96	97	103
Household activities	100	38	56	84	104	114	120	144
Caring for and helping household members	100	21	92	210	183	67	29	19
Caring for and helping nonhousehold members	100	58	95	89	74	121	163	100
Work and related activities	100	34	104	129	136	134	104	19
Education	100	648	204	57	30	20	11	7
Consumer purchases	100	76	85	112	100	100	112	98
Professional and personal care services	100	56	33	78	89	122	100	178
Household services	100	–	–	50	50	100	100	150
Government services and civic obligations	100	–	100	100	100	–	100	–
Eating and drinking	100	77	87	95	95	101	111	124
Socializing, relaxing, and leisure	100	104	102	84	80	88	108	149
Sports, exercise, and recreation	100	215	133	91	85	76	79	76
Religious and spiritual activities	100	125	83	83	83	92	108	167
Volunteer activities	100	113	40	47	100	120	100	133
Telephone calls	100	217	117	67	67	92	83	117
Traveling	100	101	108	107	109	106	95	73
Unencodeable	100	117	75	58	75	83	108	183

Note: "–" means number is less than .005 or sample is too small to make a reliable estimate.
Source: Bureau of Labor Statistics, unpublished tables from the American Time Use Survey, Internet site http://www.bls.gov/tus/ home.htm; calculations by New Strategist

Table 9.2 Time Use by Age and Sex, 2004: Aged 15 to 19

(hours per day spent in primary activities by people aged 15 or older and aged 15 to 19 by sex; index of age group time use to total time use by sex, and index of time use by people aged 15 to 19 by sex, 2004)

	total men	men aged 15 to 19		total women	women aged 15 to 19		aged 15 to 19 index of women's time to men's
		hours	index to total men		hours	index to total women	
Total hours	**24.00**	**24.00**	**100**	**24.00**	**24.00**	**100**	**100**
Personal care activities	9.14	10.05	110	9.50	10.47	110	104
Household activities	1.33	0.53	40	2.28	0.88	39	166
Caring for/helping household members	0.29	0.06	21	0.65	0.15	23	250
Caring for/helping nonhousehold members	0.16	0.08	50	0.22	0.14	64	175
Work and related activities	4.03	1.22	30	2.76	1.04	38	85
Education	0.46	2.90	630	0.46	3.06	665	106
Consumer purchases	0.30	0.25	83	0.50	0.37	74	148
Professional and personal care services	0.07	0.03	43	0.11	0.06	55	200
Household services	0.01	–	–	0.02	–	–	–
Government services, civic obligations	–	–	–	0.01	–	–	–
Eating and drinking	1.17	0.89	76	1.06	0.82	77	92
Socializing, relaxing, and leisure	4.89	5.25	107	4.38	4.33	99	82
Sports, exercise, and recreation	0.43	0.91	212	0.23	0.50	217	55
Religious and spiritual activities	0.12	0.14	117	0.13	0.16	123	114
Volunteer activities	0.12	0.15	125	0.17	0.21	124	140
Telephone calls	0.07	0.20	286	0.17	0.32	188	160
Traveling	1.29	1.22	95	1.22	1.32	108	108
Unencodeable	0.11	0.12	109	0.13	0.15	115	125

Note: "–" means number is less than .005 or sample is too small to make a reliable estimate.
Source: Bureau of Labor Statistics, unpublished tables from the American Time Use Survey, Internet site http://www.bls.gov/tus/home.htm; calculations by New Strategist

Table 9.3 Time Use by Age and Sex, 2004: Aged 20 to 24

(hours per day spent in primary activities by people aged 15 or older and aged 20 to 24 by sex; index of age group time use to total time use by sex, and index of time use by people aged 20 to 24 by sex, 2004)

		men aged 20 to 24			women aged 20 to 24		aged 20 to 24 index of
	total men	hours	index to total men	total women	hours	index to total women	women's time to men's
Total hours	**24.00**	**24.00**	**100**	**24.00**	**24.00**	**100**	**100**
Personal care activities	9.14	9.41	103	9.50	9.89	104	105
Household activities	1.33	0.68	51	2.28	1.33	58	196
Caring for/helping household members	0.29	0.11	38	0.65	0.74	114	673
Caring for/helping nonhousehold members	0.16	0.15	94	0.22	0.22	100	147
Work and related activities	4.03	4.07	101	2.76	2.97	108	73
Education	0.46	0.88	191	0.46	1.00	217	114
Consumer purchases	0.30	0.27	90	0.50	0.43	86	159
Professional and personal care services	0.07	0.01	14	0.11	0.05	45	500
Household services	0.01	–	–	0.02	–	–	–
Government services, civic obligations	–	–	–	0.01	0.01	100	–
Eating and drinking	1.17	0.91	78	1.06	1.02	96	112
Socializing, relaxing, and leisure	4.89	5.12	105	4.38	4.34	99	85
Sports, exercise, and recreation	0.43	0.63	147	0.23	0.26	113	41
Religious and spiritual activities	0.12	0.08	67	0.13	0.11	85	138
Volunteer activities	0.12	0.04	33	0.17	0.07	41	175
Telephone calls	0.07	0.10	143	0.17	0.19	112	190
Traveling	1.29	1.38	107	1.22	1.33	109	96
Unencodeable	0.11	0.14	127	0.13	0.05	38	36

Note: "–" means number is less than .005 or sample is too small to make a reliable estimate.
Source: Bureau of Labor Statistics, unpublished tables from the American Time Use Survey, Internet site http://www.bls.gov/tus/home.htm; calculations by New Strategist

Table 9.4 Time Use by Age and Sex, 2004: Aged 25 to 34

(hours per day spent in primary activities by people aged 15 or older and aged 25 to 34 by sex; index of age group time use to total time use by sex, and index of time use by people aged 25 to 34 by sex, 2004)

	total men	men aged 25 to 34		total women	women aged 25 to 34		aged 24 to 35 index of women's time to men's
		hours	index to total men		hours	index to total women	
Total hours	**24.00**	**24.00**	**100**	**24.00**	**24.00**	**100**	**100**
Personal care activities	9.14	9.07	99	9.50	9.40	99	104
Household activities	1.33	1.01	76	2.28	2.06	90	204
Caring for/helping household members	0.29	0.45	155	0.65	1.57	242	349
Caring for/helping nonhousehold members	0.16	0.17	106	0.22	0.17	77	100
Work and related activities	4.03	5.29	131	2.76	3.42	124	65
Education	0.46	0.24	52	0.46	0.27	59	113
Consumer purchases	0.30	0.35	117	0.50	0.56	112	160
Professional and personal care services	0.07	0.05	71	0.11	0.09	82	180
Household services	0.01	0.01	100	0.02	0.01	50	100
Government services, civic obligations	–	0.01	–	0.01	0.01	100	–
Eating and drinking	1.17	1.13	97	1.06	0.98	92	87
Socializing, relaxing, and leisure	4.89	4.13	84	4.38	3.62	83	88
Sports, exercise, and recreation	0.43	0.42	98	0.23	0.19	83	45
Religious and spiritual activities	0.12	0.09	75	0.13	0.10	77	111
Volunteer activities	0.12	0.07	58	0.17	0.07	41	100
Telephone calls	0.07	0.05	71	0.17	0.11	65	220
Traveling	1.29	1.41	109	1.22	1.29	106	91
Unencodeable	0.11	0.06	55	0.13	0.08	62	133

Note: "–" means number is less than .005 or sample is too small to make a reliable estimate.
Source: Bureau of Labor Statistics, unpublished tables from the American Time Use Survey, Internet site http://www.bls.gov/tus/home.htm; calculations by New Strategist

Most Americans Get More than Eight Hours of Sleep

Teenagers sleep the most.

On an average day, people aged 15 or older get 8.56 hours of sleep according to the American Time Use Survey. Not surprisingly, teenagers get the most sleep. People aged 15 to 19 sleep 9.46 hours a night (or day), or 11 percent more than the average person. Men aged 45 to 54 get the least amount of sleep—just 8.08 hours a day, or 6 percent less than average. Sleep time increases in the 55-to-64 age group but never matches the level achieved by teenagers.

The average person spends 0.67 hours (or 40 minutes) per day grooming—a category that includes bathing, hair care, dressing, and putting on make-up. Again, teens aged 15 to 19 spend the most time grooming, with teen girls devoting 39 percent more time than average to this task. In every age group, men spend less time than average grooming, with the oldest men spending 25 percent less time than average on grooming activities.

■ Women of all ages spend more than the average amount of time grooming.

The middle aged sleep the least

(average number of hours per day spent sleeping, by age, 2004)

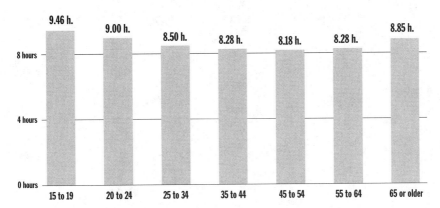

Table 9.5 Time Spent Sleeping by Age and Sex, 2004

(average hours per day spent sleeping as a primary activity and index of time to average, by age and sex, 2004)

	total	men	women
Aged 15 or older	**8.56**	**8.51**	**8.61**
Aged 15 to 19	9.46	9.44	9.49
Aged 20 to 24	9.00	8.83	9.16
Aged 25 to 34	8.50	8.47	8.54
Aged 35 to 44	8.28	8.26	8.29
Aged 45 to 54	8.18	8.08	8.27
Aged 55 to 64	8.28	8.29	8.27
Aged 65 or older	8.85	8.76	8.92
INDEX OF TIME TO AVERAGE			
Aged 15 or older	**100**	**99**	**101**
Aged 15 to 19	111	110	111
Aged 20 to 24	105	103	107
Aged 25 to 34	99	99	100
Aged 35 to 44	97	96	97
Aged 45 to 54	96	94	97
Aged 55 to 64	97	97	97
Aged 65 or older	103	102	104

Source: Bureau of Labor Statistics, unpublished tables from the American Time Use Survey, Internet site http://www.bls.gov/tus/home.htm; calculations by New Strategist

Table 9.6 Time Spent Grooming by Age and Sex, 2004

(average hours per day spent grooming as a primary activity and index of time to average, by age and sex, 2004)

	total	men	women
Aged 15 or older	**0.67**	**0.55**	**0.77**
Aged 15 to 19	0.74	0.56	0.93
Aged 20 to 24	0.66	0.58	0.73
Aged 25 to 34	0.65	0.57	0.73
Aged 35 to 44	0.66	0.55	0.76
Aged 45 to 54	0.69	0.57	0.80
Aged 55 to 64	0.68	0.54	0.80
Aged 65 or older	0.62	0.50	0.70
INDEX OF TIME TO AVERAGE			
Aged 15 or older	**100**	**82**	**115**
Aged 15 to 19	110	84	139
Aged 20 to 24	99	87	109
Aged 25 to 34	97	85	109
Aged 35 to 44	99	82	113
Aged 45 to 54	103	85	119
Aged 55 to 64	101	81	119
Aged 65 or older	93	75	104

Note: Time spent on this activity does not include travel time or professional grooming services.
Source: Bureau of Labor Statistics, unpublished tables from the American Time Use Survey, Internet site http://www.bls.gov/tus/ home.htm; calculations by New Strategist

People Aged 25 to 34 Spend the Most Time Caring for Household Children

Women spend much more time than men on this activity.

Women aged 15 or older spend 37 percent more time than the average person caring for household children as a primary activity, while men spend less time than average caring for household children. The time spent caring for household children as a primary activity peaks in the 25-to-44 age group, when most families have children under age 18 at home.

Few teenagers spend much time caring for household children, but the time devoted to this activity spikes among 20-to-24-year-olds. Women aged 20 to 24 spend an average of 0.62 hours (37 minutes) a day caring for household children compared with men's 0.08 hours (5 minutes) a day. These figures are low because they include those who cared for household children and those who did not. The many young adults who do not care for household children on an average day drive the numbers to these low levels. Women aged 25 to 34 spend the most time caring for household children as a primary activity, an average of 1.38 hours a day. Their male counterparts spend only 0.40 hours (24 minutes) doing so.

■ The time spent caring for household children drops below average in the 45-or-older age groups.

The time spent caring for household children rises above average for women in the 20-to-24 age group

*(index of time women spend caring for household children to the average, by age, 2004;
100 equals the average for all people aged 15 or older)*

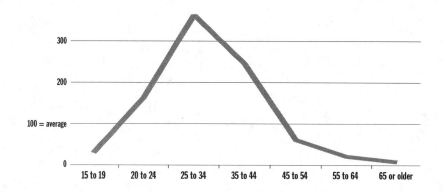

Table 9.7 Time Spent Caring for and Helping Household Children by Age and Sex, 2004

(average hours per day spent caring for and helping household children as a primary activity and index of time to average, by age and sex, 2004)

	total	men	women
Aged 15 or older	**0.38**	**0.23**	**0.52**
Aged 15 to 19	0.08	0.04	0.11
Aged 20 to 24	0.36	0.08	0.62
Aged 25 to 34	0.89	0.40	1.38
Aged 35 to 44	0.73	0.53	0.93
Aged 45 to 54	0.21	0.19	0.23
Aged 55 to 64	0.06	0.04	0.08
Aged 65 or older	0.02	–	0.03
INDEX OF TIME TO AVERAGE			
Aged 15 or older	**100**	**61**	**137**
Aged 15 to 19	21	11	29
Aged 20 to 24	95	21	163
Aged 25 to 34	234	105	363
Aged 35 to 44	192	139	245
Aged 45 to 54	55	50	61
Aged 55 to 64	16	11	21
Aged 65 or older	5	–	8

Note: Time spent on this activity does not include travel time. "–" means number is less than .005 or sample is too small to make a reliable estimate.
Source: Bureau of Labor Statistics, unpublished tables from the American Time Use Survey, Internet site http://www.bls.gov/tus/home.htm; calculations by New Strategist

Women Still Do the Housework

In the kitchen, younger generations are less egalitarian than older Americans.

Women spend 0.75 hours (45 minutes) a day preparing meals and 0.20 hours (12 minutes) cleaning up in the kitchen afterwards. Men spend much less time on these tasks—only 15 minutes cooking, on average, and 3 minutes cleaning up. The differential between the sexes in the time spent cooking is greater among the young than the old. Among 15-to-34-year-olds, women spend at least three times as long as men cooking on an average day. People aged 65 or older—both men and women—spend more time cooking than their younger counterparts, and older women spend only two times as long as older men in the kitchen.

The average woman spends 0.54 hours a day cleaning her house, or 32 minutes. Men spend only 9 minutes a day housecleaning. Women aged 65 or older spend the most time cleaning—nearly twice the average. Perhaps the biggest gap in men's and women's housework time can be found in the laundry room. Women spend 18 minutes a day doing the laundry while men spend less than 4 minutes a day on this task. Women aged 65 or older spend 89 percent more time than average doing the laundry although they are most likely to live alone.

■ As leisure time expands in retirement, people fill some of it with household tasks such as cleaning and laundry.

Young adults spend less than the average amount of time cleaning their house

(index of time spent housecleaning to the average, by age, 2004; 100 equals the average for all people aged 15 or older)

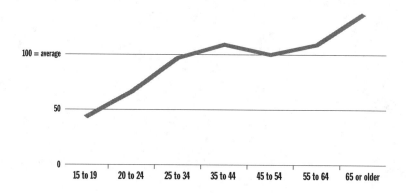

Table 9.8 Time Spent Preparing and Cleaning Up Meals by Age and Sex, 2004

(average hours per day spent on food and drink preparation and kitchen and food cleanup as primary activities, and index of time to average, by age and sex, 2004)

	food and drink preparation			kitchen and food cleanup		
	total	men	women	total	men	women
Aged 15 or older	**0.51**	**0.25**	**0.75**	**0.13**	**0.05**	**0.20**
Aged 15 to 19	0.10	0.05	0.15	0.03	0.01	0.05
Aged 20 to 24	0.23	0.11	0.34	0.05	0.02	0.08
Aged 25 to 34	0.37	0.16	0.58	0.11	0.04	0.18
Aged 35 to 44	0.42	0.24	0.59	0.15	0.05	0.24
Aged 45 to 54	0.43	0.23	0.61	0.15	0.06	0.22
Aged 55 to 64	0.43	0.22	0.63	0.15	0.06	0.23
Aged 65 or older	0.51	0.32	0.66	0.17	0.08	0.24
INDEX OF TIME TO AVERAGE						
Aged 15 or older	**100**	**49**	**147**	**100**	**38**	**154**
Aged 15 to 19	20	10	29	23	8	38
Aged 20 to 24	45	22	67	38	15	62
Aged 25 to 34	73	31	114	85	31	138
Aged 35 to 44	82	47	116	115	38	185
Aged 45 to 54	84	45	120	115	46	169
Aged 55 to 64	84	43	124	115	46	177
Aged 65 or older	100	63	129	131	62	185

Note: Time spent on these activities does not include travel time.
Source: Bureau of Labor Statistics, unpublished tables from the American Time Use Survey, Internet site http://www.bls.gov/tus/home.htm; calculations by New Strategist

Table 9.9 Time Spent Housecleaning and Doing Laundry by Age and Sex, 2004

(average hours per day spent on housecleaning and doing laundry as primary activities, and index of time to average, by age and sex, 2004)

	housecleaning			laundry		
	total	men	women	total	men	women
Aged 15 or older	**0.35**	**0.15**	**0.54**	**0.19**	**0.06**	**0.30**
Aged 15 to 19	0.15	0.08	0.24	0.05	0.03	0.07
Aged 20 to 24	0.23	0.08	0.38	0.09	0.05	0.11
Aged 25 to 34	0.34	0.15	0.54	0.18	0.06	0.29
Aged 35 to 44	0.38	0.15	0.60	0.23	0.07	0.38
Aged 45 to 54	0.35	0.16	0.53	0.23	0.08	0.37
Aged 55 to 64	0.38	0.16	0.58	0.20	0.05	0.33
Aged 65 or older	0.48	0.20	0.69	0.23	0.05	0.36
INDEX OF TIME TO AVERAGE						
Aged 15 or older	**100**	**43**	**154**	**100**	**32**	**158**
Aged 15 to 19	43	23	69	26	16	37
Aged 20 to 24	66	23	109	47	26	58
Aged 25 to 34	97	43	154	95	32	153
Aged 35 to 44	109	43	171	121	37	200
Aged 45 to 54	100	46	151	121	42	195
Aged 55 to 64	109	46	166	105	26	174
Aged 65 or older	137	57	197	121	26	189

Note: Time spent on these activities does not include travel time.
Source: Bureau of Labor Statistics, unpublished tables from the American Time Use Survey, Internet site http://www.bls.gov/tus/home.htm; calculations by New Strategist

Television Takes Up Time

Young adults spend more time watching TV than playing on their computers.

Watching television is by far the most popular leisure time activity—so popular, in fact, that the average person spends more time watching TV as a primary activity than eating and drinking or doing household chores. People aged 65 or older spend the most time watching TV—3.86 hours per day, or one-fourth of the waking hours of people in the age group. Women aged 35 to 44 spend the least amount of time watching TV (1.91 hours per day).

Even among teenagers, television is more popular than playing on a computer. Teen boys aged 15 to 19 spend 1.24 hours per day on their computer versus 2.45 hours per day watching TV. Teen boys spend the most time playing on a computer, more than three times the average.

People aged 65 or older spend the most time reading, an average of about one hour a day—more than twice the average. Teens and young adults spend much more time on a computer than reading. For men, reading is more popular than leisure computer use only among those aged 45 or older. Among women, reading becomes more popular than computer use in the 25-to-34 age group.

■ As younger generations age, they may spend more time reading and less time on the computer.

Television is popular in every age group

(average hours per day spent watching television as a primary activity, by age, 2004)

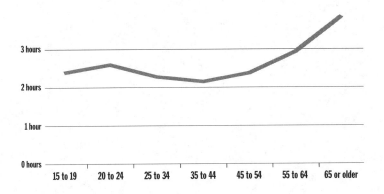

Table 9.10 Time Spent Watching TV, Reading, and Leisure Computer Use and Playing Games by Age and Sex, 2004

(average hours per day spent watching television, reading for personal interest, and leisure computer use and playing games as primary activities, and index of time to average, by age and sex, 2004)

	television			reading			computer use for leisure, games		
	total	men	women	total	men	women	total	men	women
Aged 15 or older	**2.64**	**2.85**	**2.43**	**0.38**	**0.32**	**0.44**	**0.34**	**0.44**	**0.26**
Aged 15 to 19	2.39	2.45	2.33	0.15	0.11	0.19	0.84	1.24	0.40
Aged 20 to 24	2.60	2.87	2.35	0.10	0.07	0.13	0.55	0.79	0.31
Aged 25 to 34	2.28	2.42	2.14	0.16	0.14	0.18	0.28	0.42	0.15
Aged 35 to 44	2.15	2.40	1.91	0.24	0.21	0.27	0.24	0.25	0.23
Aged 45 to 54	2.38	2.68	2.11	0.35	0.30	0.40	0.24	0.26	0.21
Aged 55 to 64	2.93	3.35	2.55	0.57	0.48	0.65	0.25	0.25	0.26
Aged 65 or older	3.86	4.16	3.64	0.99	0.94	1.03	0.35	0.35	0.36
INDEX OF TIME TO AVERAGE									
Aged 15 or older	**100**	**108**	**92**	**100**	**84**	**116**	**100**	**129**	**76**
Aged 15 to 19	91	93	88	39	29	50	247	365	118
Aged 20 to 24	98	109	89	26	18	34	162	232	91
Aged 25 to 34	86	92	81	42	37	47	82	124	44
Aged 35 to 44	81	91	72	63	55	71	71	74	68
Aged 45 to 54	90	102	80	92	79	105	71	76	62
Aged 55 to 64	111	127	97	150	126	171	74	74	76
Aged 65 or older	146	158	138	261	247	271	103	103	106

Note: Time spent on these activities does not include travel time.
Source: Bureau of Labor Statistics, unpublished tables from the American Time Use Survey, Internet site http://www.bls.gov/tus/home.htm; calculations by New Strategist

Many Parents and Adult Children Live Near One Another

Most adult children see their parents at least once a week.

Americans are known for their mobility, but despite the lure of distant places most parents and adult children live less than one hour's drive from each other, according to a survey by the Pew Research Center. Sixty-five percent of people aged 18 or older live less than an hour's drive from their parents. Conversely, 72 percent of parents live less than an hour away from an adult child.

The 54 percent majority of adults see a parent at least once a week. Adding telephone contact to the mix drives the proportion of Americans who see or talk on the telephone with a parent on a weekly basis up to a near-universal 86 percent. Women talk on the phone with their parents much more frequently than men, with 42 percent doing so daily compared with 23 percent of men. Women are also more likely than men to stay in touch with an adult child, 47 percent talking on the phone with a child every day compared with 24 percent of men.

Seventy-three percent of Americans aged 18 or older have children, with the proportion rising from 39 percent in the 18-to-29 age group to 78 percent among 30-to-49-year-olds. Sixty-eight percent of adults have a living parent, but only 29 percent have a grandparent still living.

■ Ninety percent of American adults have a brother or sister, making it the most common family relationship.

Few adult children live far from their parents

(percent distribution of people aged 18 or older by distance from parents' home, 2005)

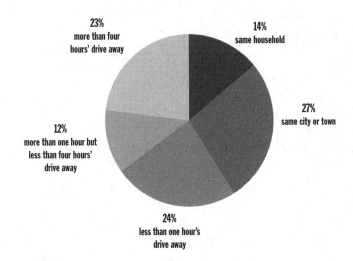

23%
more than four
hours' drive away

14%
same household

27%
same city or town

12%
more than one hour but
less than four hours'
drive away

24%
less than one hour's
drive away

Table 9.11 The Generations: Relationships and Contacts, 2005

(percent of people aged 18 or older with selected living relatives, by age; proximity of parents and adult children; frequency of contact with parents by type of contact; and telephone contact between parents and adult children by sex, 2005)

GENERATIONAL RELATIONSHIPS

	total	18 to 29	30 to 49	50 to 64	65 or older
Have grandchildren	32%	–	11%	56%	82%
Have children	73	39%	78	84	89
Have a brother or sister	90	92	94	91	78
Have at least one living parent	68	98	88	51	9
Have any living grandparents	29	79	31	2	–

PARENT/CHILD PROXIMITY

(among respondents with at least one living parent and among respondents with at least one financially independent adult child)

	parent(s)	adult child
Live in same household	14%	14%
Live in same city or town	27	30
Live less than an hour away	24	28
Live less than four hour's drive away	12	11
Live more than 4 hour's drive away	23	17

FREQUENCY OF CONTACT WITH PARENT(S)

(among respondents with at least one living parent)

	email	see	phone	see or phone
Every day	3%	24%	32%	42%
Once a week or more	10	30	47	44
Once a month or more	8	15	11	10
Several times a year	3	17	2	2
Once a year	–	7	1	1
Less often than once a year	–	7	5	1
Never	76	–	–	–
Don't know	–	–	2	–

TELEPHONE CONTACT WITH PARENT(S)

(among respondents with at least one living parent)

	total	men	women
Daily	32%	23%	42%
Weekly	47	52	41
Less often	19	23	15
Don't know	2	2	2

TELEPHONE CONTACT WITH ADULT CHILD

(among respondents with a financially independent adult child aged 18 or older)

	total	men	women
Daily	37%	24%	47%
Weekly	48	55	43
Less often	13	19	9
Don't know	2	2	1

Note: "–" means zero or sample too small to make a reliable estimate.
Source: Pew Research Center, Families Drawn Together by Communications Revolution, February 21, 2006; Internet site http://pewresearch.org/reports/?ReportID=9

More than Two-Thirds of Americans Are Online

Young adults are most likely to go online.

Sixty-eight percent of Americans aged 18 or older were Internet users in 2005, up substantially from the 46 percent of 2000, according to surveys by the Pew Internet & American Life Project. Fully 84 percent of young adults—those aged 18 to 29—use the Internet, but those aged 30 to 49 are not far behind at 80 percent. The 30-to-49 age group is most likely to have been online yesterday (64 percent).

Emailing is the most popular online activity, engaged in by 91 percent of Internet users. The oldest Internet users are just as likely to email as young adults. But young adults are far more likely to do instant messaging. The 62 percent majority of 18-to-29-year-olds uses instant messaging versus only 26 to 36 percent of older adults. Downloading music shows the biggest gap in Internet use by age, with 46 percent of young adults doing downloads compared with only 6 percent of people aged 65 or older.

■ The Internet is changing the way young and middle-aged adults interact with the world, affecting both government and business.

The oldest Americans are least likely to use the Internet

(percent of people using the Internet, by age, 2005)

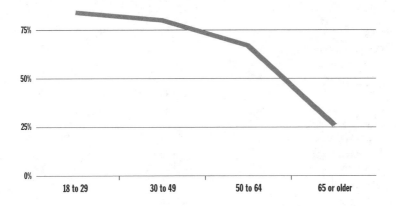

Table 9.12 Computer and Internet Use by Age, 2005

(percent of people aged 18 or older who use a computer, go online, and went online yesterday, by age, 2005)

	use a computer	go online	went online yesterday
Total people	**72%**	**68%**	**60%**
Aged 18 to 29	87	84	58
Aged 30 to 49	84	80	64
Aged 50 to 64	71	67	58
Aged 65 or older	29	26	49

Source: Pew Internet & American Life Project, Internet site http://www.pewinternet.org/trends.asp#demographics; calculations by New Strategist

Table 9.13 Online Activities Ever Done by Age, 2005

(percent of Internet users who have ever used the Internet for selected activities, by age, 2005)

	total	18 to 29	30 to 49	50 to 64	65 or older
Send or read email	91%	91%	91%	92%	91%
Research a product or service	78	79	82	78	65
Get news	72	75	75	71	56
Buy a product	67	68	69	66	48
Do research for job	51	44	59	51	17
Bank online	41	40	48	35	27
Instant messaging	40	62	36	31	26
Download computer programs	39	46	40	32	26
Play a game	36	54	33	26	30
Use online classified ads to sell/buy/ find job, meet people	36	44	40	26	15
Read someone else's blog	27	32	27	24	17
Share files with others	27	39	24	22	14
Search for information about someone you know or might meet	27	32	27	23	29
Download music	25	46	22	12	6
Participate in an auction	24	27	27	19	12
Download screensavers	23	28	22	24	20
Download computer games	21	29	19	15	14
Download video files	18	28	18	8	3
Take part in chat rooms or discussions	17	34	15	7	5
View live remote images via a webcam	16	18	17	16	6
Visit an adult web site	13	18	13	9	2
Make a donation to charity	11	10	13	11	4
Create a blog	7	13	6	4	3

Source: Pew Internet & American Life Project, Internet site http://www.pewinternet.org/trends.asp#demographics

Voting Has Decreased among All but the Oldest Americans

Older Americans have considerable influence because so many vote.

The older people are, the more likely they are to vote. This has long been true, but the gap between young and old has widened over the years. In the 1972 presidential election (the first in which 18-to-20-year-olds could vote), 64 percent of people aged 65 or older voted compared with 50 percent of those aged 18 to 24—a gap of 14 percentage points. In the 2004 election, 69 percent of people aged 65 or older voted versus only 42 percent of people aged 18 to 24—a 27 percentage point difference.

A look at voting patterns in 2004 by generation reveals that voting rates rose from a low of 42 percent among Millennials to just over 50 percent among Gen Xers. Sixty-four percent of Boomers voted in 2004, as did 69 percent of Americans aged 59 or older. Because of their numbers, Boomers accounted for the largest share (40 percent) of voters in 2004. Older Americans were 28 percent of voters, while Gen Xers and Millennials were far behind at 19 and 13 percent, respectively.

■ The political power of Millennials will grow as their voting rate increases.

Millennials account for the smallest share of voters

(percent distribution of people voting in the 2004 presidential election, by generation)

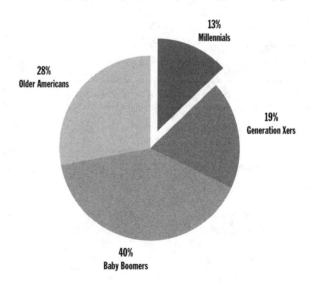

Table 9.14 Voting Rate by Age, 1964 to 2004

(percent of people who reported voting in presidential elections by age, and percentage point change, 1964 to 2004)

		presidential election years			
	total	18–24	25–44	45–64	65+
2004	58.3%	41.9%	52.2%	66.6%	68.9%
2000	54.7	32.3	49.8	64.1	67.6
1996	54.2	32.4	49.2	64.4	67.0
1992	61.3	42.8	58.3	70.0	70.1
1988	57.4	36.2	54.0	67.9	68.8
1984	59.9	40.8	58.4	69.8	67.7
1980	59.3	39.9	58.7	69.3	65.1
1976	59.2	42.2	58.7	68.7	62.2
1972	63.0	49.6	62.7	70.8	63.5
1968	67.8	50.4	66.6	74.9	65.8
1964	69.3	50.9	69.0	75.9	66.3
Percentage point change					
1964 to 2004	−11.0	−9.0	−16.8	−9.3	2.6

Note: Before 1972, data for 18-to-24-year-olds include only 21-to-24-year-olds.
Source: Bureau of the Census, Voting and Registration in the Election of November 2004, detailed tables, Internet site http://www.census.gov/population/www/socdemo/voting/cps2004.html; calculations by New Strategist

Table 9.15 Voting by Generation, 2004

(total number of people aged 18 or older, and number and percent who reported voting in the presidential election, and percent distribution of voters, by generation, 2004; numbers in thousands)

		voted		
	total	number	percent	percent distribution
Total people aged 18 or older	**215,694**	**125,736**	**58.3%**	**100.0%**
Millennials (aged 18 to 27)	39,335	16,636	42.3	13.2
Generation X (aged 28 to 39)	47,972	24,352	50.8	19.4
Baby Boom (aged 40 to 58)	78,253	50,060	64.0	39.8
Older Americans (aged 59 or older)	50,132	34,689	69.2	27.6

Source: Bureau of the Census, Voting and Registration in the Election of November 2004, detailed tables, Internet site http://www.census.gov/population/www/socdemo/voting/cps2004.html; calculations by New Strategist

Young Adults Dominate Some Religious Groups

Presbyterians and Methodists are much older than Catholics or Baptists.

The religious affiliations of Americans are changing, in large part because younger adults adhere to different religious groups than older adults. The American Religious Identification Survey, taken in 2001 through the efforts of Egon Mayer, Barry A. Kosmin, and Ariela Keysar and sponsored by the Graduate Center of the City University of New York, reveals the differing age distributions of religious groups. In the nationally representative survey, respondents were asked to identify the religious group to which they belonged.

Catholics are by far the most numerous, with an estimated 51 million American adults identifying themselves as belonging to the Catholic Church.

Twenty-four percent of Catholics are aged 18 to 29, 62 percent are aged 30 to 64, and only 14 percent are aged 65 or older. Many religious groups are much older. Fully 35 percent of people who identify themselves as Congregational/UCC are aged 65 or older, as are 30 percent of self-identified Protestants, 29 percent of Presbyterians, and 27 percent of Methodists. At the other extreme, more than half of Muslims and Buddhists are aged 18 to 29. Typically, younger denominations have a greater potential for growth.

■ Twenty-nine million Americans do not identify with any religious group. Among those with no religion, only 8 percent are aged 65 or older.

Mormons are much younger than Methodists

(percent distribution of self-identified Methodists and Mormons, by age, 2001)

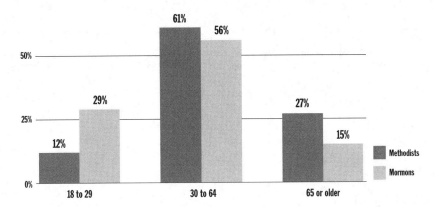

Table 9.16 Age Distribution of Religious Groups, 2001

(total number of adult members of selected religious groups and percent distribution by age, 2001; numbers in thousands)

	number	percent distribution			
		total	18–29	30–64	65 or older
Total U.S. adults	**208,000**	**100%**	**23%**	**61%**	**16%**
Catholic	50,873	100	24	62	14
Baptist	33,830	100	21	63	16
No religion	29,481	100	35	57	8
Christian	14,190	100	35	58	7
Methodist	14,140	100	12	61	27
Lutheran	9,580	100	15	63	22
Presbyterian	5,596	100	10	61	29
Protestant	4,647	100	13	57	30
Pentecostal	4,407	100	24	67	9
Episcopalian/Anglican	3,451	100	10	62	28
Jewish	2,831	100	14	58	28
Mormon	2,787	100	29	56	15
Churches of Christ	2,503	100	17	58	25
Non-denominational	2,489	100	23	65	12
Congregational/UCC	1,378	100	11	54	35
Jehovah's Witnesses	1,331	100	24	66	10
Assemblies of God	1,105	100	21	69	10
Muslim/Islamic	1,104	100	58	42	–
Buddhist	1,082	100	56	41	3
Evangelical/born again	1,032	100	19	72	9
Church of God	944	100	16	65	19
Seventh Day Adventist	724	100	10	64	26

Note: Religious group is self-identified; numbers will not add to total because not all groups are shown. "–" means sample is too small to make a reliable estimate.
Source: American Religious Indentification Survey 2001, Barry A. Kosmin, Egon Mayer, and Ariela Keysar. For further details see: Barry A. Kosmin and Ariela Keysar, Religion in a Free Market, Paramount Market Publishing, Inc. Ithaca, NY, 2006.

More than One in Four Volunteer

Young adults are least likely to volunteer.

Among people aged 16 or older, 29 percent volunteered their time between September 2004 and September 2005, according to the Bureau of Labor Statistics, which defines volunteers as those who performed unpaid activities for an organization at least once during the time period. Volunteering peaks in middle age at 29 percent among men aged 35 to 54 and 40 percent among women aged 35 to 44. Many teenagers also volunteer, perhaps through school clubs and activities. Thirty percent of 16-to-19-year-olds volunteered during the past year. Among 20-to-24-year-olds, volunteering drops to just 19 percent—the lowest level among age groups.

Volunteers donate a median of 50 hours a year to the task, or an average of one hour a week. Among volunteers under age 45, the largest share donates time to educational and youth service organizations. Among volunteers aged 45 or older, the largest share works for a religious organization.

■ The most important reason people say they volunteer is because someone asked them to, cited by 43 percent. A slightly smaller share (40 percent) say they volunteered to volunteer.

Volunteering is lowest among 20-to-24-year-olds

(percent of people volunteering, by age, 2005)

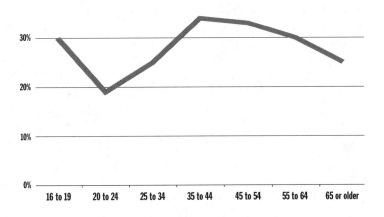

Table 9.17 Volunteering by Sex and Age, 2005

(number of people aged 16 or older, and number and percent who performed unpaid volunteer activities for an organization at any point during the past year, by sex and age, September 2005; numbers in thousands)

	total	volunteers	
		number	percent of total
Total people	**226,693**	**65,357**	**28.8%**
Aged 16 to 19	16,443	5,000	30.4
Aged 20 to 24	20,291	3,956	19.5
Aged 25 to 34	39,118	9,881	25.3
Aged 35 to 44	42,968	14,809	34.5
Aged 45 to 54	42,316	13,826	32.7
Aged 55 to 64	30,410	9,173	30.2
Aged 65 or older	35,146	8,712	24.8
Total men	**109,475**	**27,370**	**25.0**
Aged 16 to 19	8,339	2,282	27.4
Aged 20 to 24	10,193	1,576	15.5
Aged 25 to 34	19,479	3,949	20.3
Aged 35 to 44	21,165	6,105	28.8
Aged 45 to 54	20,701	5,999	29.0
Aged 55 to 64	14,622	3,999	27.3
Aged 65 or older	14,975	3,460	23.1
Total women	**117,218**	**37,987**	**32.4**
Aged 16 to 19	8,104	2,718	33.5
Aged 20 to 24	10,098	2,380	23.6
Aged 25 to 34	19,639	5,931	30.2
Aged 35 to 44	21,803	8,704	39.9
Aged 45 to 54	21,615	7,828	36.2
Aged 55 to 64	15,788	5,174	32.8
Aged 65 or older	20,170	5,252	26.0

Source: Bureau of Labor Statistics, Volunteering in the United States, 2005, Internet site http://www.bls.gov/news.release/volun .toc.htm

Table 9.18 Volunteering by Age and Type of Organization, 2005

(number of people aged 16 or older who performed unpaid volunteer activities for an organization at any point in the past year, median annual hours of volunteer work performed, and percent distribution by type of organization for which the volunteer worked the most hours, by age, September 2005)

	total	16 to 19	20 to 24	25 to 34	35 to 44	45 to 54	55 to 64	65 or older
Total volunteers (in 000s)	**65,357**	**5,000**	**3,956**	**9,881**	**14,809**	**13,826**	**9,173**	**8,712**
Median annual hours	50	36	40	36	48	50	56	96
TYPE OF ORGANIZATION								
Total volunteers	**100.0%**	**100.0%**	**100.0%**	**100.0%**	**100.0%**	**100.0%**	**100.0%**	**100.0%**
Civic, political, professional, or international	6.4	3.4	5.3	6.8	4.8	6.8	8.0	8.2
Educational or youth service	26.2	36.5	27.3	33.6	37.9	25.6	13.5	6.2
Environmental or animal care	1.8	2.1	2.9	2.1	1.3	2.1	2.1	0.9
Hospital or other health	7.7	7.6	9.0	6.6	5.8	7.7	8.9	10.1
Public safety	1.3	1.0	2.3	1.7	1.1	1.3	1.4	0.8
Religious	34.8	27.7	27.3	29.1	31.2	36.8	41.2	45.0
Social or community service	13.4	13.6	16.6	13.1	10.5	11.4	15.5	18.0
Sport, hobby, cultural, or arts	3.3	2.8	2.7	3.0	3.0	3.6	3.8	3.7
Other	3.5	2.9	4.5	3.1	3.1	3.1	4.0	4.7
Not determined	1.7	2.5	2.1	1.0	1.3	1.7	1.7	2.3

Source: Bureau of Labor Statistics, Volunteering in the United States, 2005, Internet site http://www.bls.gov/news.release/volun .toc.htm

Table 9.19 Volunteering by Age and Type of Work Performed, 2005

(number of people aged 16 or older who performed unpaid volunteer activities for an organization at any point in the past year, and percent distribution by type of work performed for the organization for which the volunteer worked the most hours, by age, September 2005)

	total	16 to 19	20 to 24	25 to 34	35 to 44	45 to 54	55 to 64	65 or older
Total volunteers (in 000s)	65,357	5,000	3,956	9,881	14,809	13,826	9,173	8,712

TYPE OF WORK PERFORMED FOR MAIN ORGANIZATION

	total	16 to 19	20 to 24	25 to 34	35 to 44	45 to 54	55 to 64	65 or older
Total volunteers	100.0%	100.0%	100.0%	100.0%	100.0%	100.0%	100.0%	100.0%
Coach, referee, or surpervise sports teams	8.9	12.0	11.1	11.6	13.0	9.1	3.4	1.5
Tutor or teach	21.3	21.4	22.8	24.0	24.6	21.4	19.4	13.6
Mentor youth	17.6	20.2	24.6	20.5	20.9	18.0	13.9	7.3
Be an usher, greeter, or minister	13.1	10.0	8.7	9.5	11.0	15.0	17.1	17.7
Collect, prepare, distribute, or serve food	26.3	25.2	21.4	23.4	25.5	27.3	28.5	29.9
Collect, make, distribute goods other than food	16.2	14.5	14.5	15.7	16.4	15.7	16.7	18.6
Fundraise or sell items to raise money	29.7	29.3	23.3	29.7	32.9	32.6	30.1	22.9
Provide counseling, medical care, fire/ EMS or protective services	7.4	3.9	9.1	7.9	6.6	8.3	8.7	6.8
Provide general office services	12.8	9.5	8.8	10.8	13.2	13.0	14.4	15.9
Provide professional or management assistance, including serving on a board or committee	17.7	4.4	8.1	12.8	18.9	21.6	23.8	20.6
Engage in music performance or other artistic activity	11.5	16.3	14.9	12.5	11.3	10.3	10.7	8.7
Engage in general labor, supply transportation	22.5	23.2	19.7	22.2	23.1	24.4	22.9	19.6
Other or not reported	15.3	14.9	15.8	15.4	14.0	14.5	14.3	19.9

Note: Percentages will sum to more than 100 because more than one type of activity may have been performed.
Source: Bureau of Labor Statistics, Volunteering in the United States, 2005, Internet site http://www.bls.gov/news.release/volun .toc.htm

Table 9.20 Volunteering by Method of Involvement and Age, 2005

(number of people aged 16 or older who performed unpaid volunteer activities for an organization at any point in the past year, and percent distribution by how they became involved with main organization for which they volunteered, by age, September 2005)

	total	16 to 19	20 to 24	25 to 34	35 to 44	45 to 54	55 to 64	65 or older
Total volunteers (in 000s)	65,357	5,000	3,956	9,881	14,809	13,826	9,173	8,712

HOW VOLUNTEERS BECAME INVOLVED WITH MAIN ORGANIZATION

	total	16 to 19	20 to 24	25 to 34	35 to 44	45 to 54	55 to 64	65 or older
Total volunteers	100.0%	100.0%	100.0%	100.0%	100.0%	100.0%	100.0%	100.0%
Approached the organization	40.3	40.0	39.0	39.4	40.2	40.2	40.6	42.1
Were asked to volunteer	42.8	40.0	41.5	44.9	43.3	43.7	42.4	41.0
Asked by boss or employer	1.5	0.5	2.3	2.6	1.5	1.6	1.2	0.4
Asked by relative, friend, or co-worker	14.1	14.8	18.7	15.3	13.3	12.8	14.1	13.7
Asked by someone in organization/school	25.9	23.1	18.4	25.5	27.5	28.0	25.8	25.2
Asked by someone else	1.2	1.4	1.8	1.4	0.9	1.0	1.1	1.6
Other or not reported	16.9	20.0	19.6	15.7	16.5	16.0	17.1	16.9

Source: Bureau of Labor Statistics, Volunteering in the United States, 2005, Internet site http://www.bls.gov/news.release/volun .toc.htm

Vietnam Veterans Outnumber Others

One-third of veterans served in Vietnam.

Twenty-five million Americans are veterans, and 38 percent of them are aged 65 or older. Despite the older age of the nation's veterans, the largest share of vets served not in World War II, but in Vietnam. Seventeen percent served in the Gulf war, which includes anyone serving in the military from August 2, 1990, to the present.

World War II veterans, once most numerous, now number only 3.9 million and account for just 16 percent of the veteran population. The 8.1 million Vietnam vets account for a much larger 33 percent of the veteran population. Only 3.4 million veterans served during the Korean conflict, accounting for 14 percent of the total.

■ Women account for 7 percent of all veterans, but for 16 percent of Gulf war veterans.

Few living veterans served during World War II

(percent distribution of veterans by time of service, 2004)

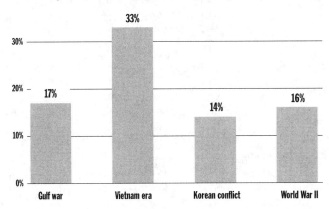

Table 9.21 Veterans by Age and Service, 2004

(number and percent distribution of living veterans by age and service, 2004; numbers in thousands)

	total veterans	wartime veterans total	Gulf war	Vietnam era	Korean conflict	World War II	peacetime veterans
Total veterans	24,793	18,477	4,105	8,147	3,423	3,916	6,316
Under age 35	2,007	1,946	1,946	0	0	0	61
Aged 35 to 39	1,332	768	768	0	0	0	564
Aged 40 to 44	1,732	520	520	0	0	0	1,212
Aged 45 to 49	1,906	738	383	393	0	0	1,168
Aged 50 to 54	2,172	1,858	267	1,731	0	0	314
Aged 55 to 59	3,572	3,448	151	3,409	0	0	124
Aged 60 to 64	2,553	1,762	48	1,755	0	0	791
Aged 65 or older	9,520	7,437	22	859	3,423	3,916	2,083
Female	1,692	1,130	647	262	80	178	562

PERCENT DISTRIBUTION BY AGE

	total veterans	total	Gulf war	Vietnam era	Korean conflict	World War II	peacetime veterans
Total veterans	100.0%	100.0%	100.0%	100.0%	100.0%	100.0%	100.0%
Under age 35	8.1	10.5	47.4	0.0	0.0	0.0	1.0
Aged 35 to 39	5.4	4.2	18.7	0.0	0.0	0.0	8.9
Aged 40 to 44	7.0	2.8	12.7	0.0	0.0	0.0	19.2
Aged 45 to 49	7.7	4.0	9.3	4.8	0.0	0.0	18.5
Aged 50 to 54	8.8	10.1	6.5	21.2	0.0	0.0	5.0
Aged 55 to 59	14.4	18.7	3.7	41.8	0.0	0.0	2.0
Aged 60 to 64	10.3	9.5	1.2	21.5	0.0	0.0	12.5
Aged 65 or older	38.4	40.3	0.5	10.5	100.0	100.0	33.0
Percent female	6.8	6.1	15.8	3.2	2.3	4.5	8.9

PERCENT DISTRIBUTION BY SERVICE

	total veterans	total	Gulf war	Vietnam era	Korean conflict	World War II	peacetime veterans
Total veterans	100.0%	74.5%	16.6%	32.9%	13.8%	15.8%	25.5%
Under age 35	100.0	97.0	97.0	0.0	0.0	0.0	3.0
Aged 35 to 39	100.0	57.7	57.7	0.0	0.0	0.0	42.3
Aged 40 to 44	100.0	30.0	30.0	0.0	0.0	0.0	70.0
Aged 45 to 49	100.0	38.7	20.1	20.6	0.0	0.0	61.3
Aged 50 to 54	100.0	85.5	12.3	79.7	0.0	0.0	14.5
Aged 55 to 59	100.0	96.5	4.2	95.4	0.0	0.0	3.5
Aged 60 to 64	100.0	69.0	1.9	68.7	0.0	0.0	31.0
Aged 65 or older	100.0	78.1	0.2	9.0	36.0	41.1	21.9
Female	100.0	66.8	38.2	15.5	4.7	10.5	33.2

Note: Veterans who served in more than one wartime period are counted only once in the wartime veterans total. Gulf war veterans are those serving from August 2, 1990, to present.
Source: Bureau of the Census, Statistical Abstract of the United States: 2006, Internet site http://www.census.gov/statab/www/; calculations by New Strategist

The Young Are Most Likely to Be Crime Victims

Victimization rate drops sharply with age.

Although older Americans are most fearful of crime, young people are more likely to become victims of crime. Among people aged 12 to 24, the violent-crime victimization rate stands at 43 to 50 crimes per 1,000 people in the age group. This is more than twice the rate for all Americans aged 12 or older. Among people aged 65 or older, the violent-crime victimization rate is just 2 per 1,000.

A variety of factors contribute to the higher victimization rate of young people, who are also more likely than their elders to commit crimes. Because older Americans are more fearful of crime, they take steps to protect themselves—such as avoiding going out at night or venturing into certain areas. Young people, on the other hand, are notorious for living on the edge, believing they are invulnerable to danger. As people enter middle age, they become increasingly aware of their vulnerability, which in turn reduces their chances of becoming a crime victim. People aged 35 or older are less likely than average to be victims of violent crime.

■ The crime rate has dropped over the past few years, but young adults are still most likely to be victims of crime.

The oldest Americans are least likely to be victims of crime

(number of crimes per 1,000 people in age group, by age of victim, 2004)

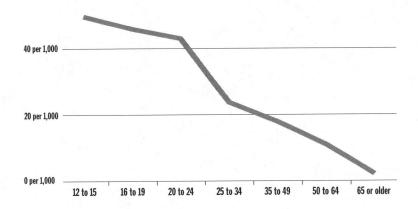

Table 9.22 Violent Crime and Personal Theft Victimization by Age, 2004

(population aged 12 or older, and number of victimizations per 1,000 people aged 12 or older, by age and type of crime, 2004)

	number (in 000s)	victimizations per 1,000 persons aged 12 or older						personal theft
		violent crime						
			rape, sexual		assault			
		total	assault	robbery	total	aggravated	simple	
Total people	**241,704**	**21.4**	**0.9**	**2.1**	**18.5**	**4.3**	**14.2**	**0.9**
Aged 12 to 15	17,083	49.7	2.2	3.8	43.6	6.2	37.5	2.1
Aged 16 to 19	16,256	45.9	2.5	4.8	38.6	11.3	27.2	3.3
Aged 20 to 24	20,273	43.0	2.5	3.1	37.4	9.4	28.0	0.7
Aged 25 to 34	39,510	23.7	0.7	2.4	20.6	4.8	15.8	0.6
Aged 35 to 49	65,580	17.9	0.5	2.1	15.2	3.9	11.4	0.7
Aged 50 to 64	48,412	11.0	0.3	1.1	9.6	1.9	7.8	0.5
Aged 65 or older	34,590	2.1	0.1	0.3	1.8	0.5	1.3	0.8

Note: Violent crime as defined in the National Crime Victimization Survey includes rape/sexual assault, robbery, and assault. It does not include murder or manslaughter because it is based on interviews with victims. Personal theft includes pocket picking, purse snatching, and attempted purse snatching.
Source: Bureau of Justice Statistics, Criminal Victimization 2004, Internet site http://www.ojp.usdoj.gov/bjs/abstract/cv04.htm

Table 9.24   Risk Behavior of 10th Graders by Sex, 2003

(percent of 10th graders engaging in selected risk behaviors, by sex, 2003)

	10th graders		
	total	female	male
Was in a physical fight in the past 12 months	33.5%	25.0%	41.8%
Property stolen or deliberately damaged on school property	30.5	26.6	34.3
Felt so sad/hopeless almost every day for two+ weeks that stopped usual activities	29.7	36.9	22.7
In past 30 days rode with a driver who had been drinking alcohol	29.3	31.0	27.6
Seriously considered attempting suicide in past 12 months	18.3	23.8	13.2
Rarely or never wore seatbelts when riding in a car driven by someone else	16.9	13.3	20.4
Carried a weapon on at least one day during the past 30 days	15.9	5.2	26.5
Engaged in a physical fight on school property during past 12 months	12.8	7.3	18.1
Was forced to have sexual intercourse	9.4	11.0	7.7
Was threatened or injured with a weapon on school property during past 12 months	9.2	7.0	11.3
Drove after drinking alcohol in past 30 days	9.2	6.9	11.3
Attempted suicide in past 12 months	9.1	12.7	5.5
Was physically hurt by boyfriend/girlfriend on purpose in the past 12 months	8.8	8.2	9.3
Carried a weapon on school property in past 30 days	6.0	3.0	8.9
Carried a gun on at least one day during the past 30 days	5.9	1.4	10.4
Felt too unsafe to go to school at least once in the past 30 days	5.2	5.1	5.3
Suicide attempt required medical attention in past 12 months	2.6	3.2	2.1

Source: Grunbaum, Jo Anne, et. al., "Youth Risk Behavior Surveillance–United States, 2003," Mortality and Morbidity Weekly Report, Vol. 53/SS-2, Centers for Disease Control and Prevention, May 21, 2004, Internet site http://www.cdc.gov/mmwr/preview/mmwrhtml/ss5302a1.htm

Table 9.25 Risk Behavior of 11th Graders by Sex, 2003

(percent of 11th graders engaging in selected risk behaviors, by sex, 2003)

	11th graders		
	total	female	male
Was in a physical fight in the past 12 months	30.9%	23.0%	38.5%
In past 30 days, rode with a driver who had been drinking alcohol	30.5	30.7	30.3
Felt so sad/hopeless almost every day for two+ weeks that stopped usual activities	28.9	35.9	22.1
Property stolen or deliberately damaged on school property	27.2	23.9	30.5
Rarely or never wore seatbelts when riding in a car driven by someone else	18.5	15.5	21.4
Carried a weapon on at least one day during the past 30 days	18.2	6.8	29.2
Seriously considered attempting suicide in past 12 months	16.4	20.0	12.9
Drove after drinking alcohol in past 30 days	15.3	11.1	19.5
Engaged in a physical fight on school property during past 12 months	10.4	6.4	14.2
Was forced to have sexual intercourse	9.2	13.5	4.8
Was physically hurt by boyfriend/girlfriend on purpose in the past 12 months	8.1	8.2	7.9
Was threatened or injured with a weapon on school property during past 12 months	7.3	5.4	9.2
Attempted suicide in past 12 months	7.3	10.0	4.6
Carried a weapon on school property in past 30 days	6.6	2.7	10.3
Carried a gun on at least one day during the past 30 days	6.3	1.6	10.8
Felt too unsafe to go to school at least once in the past 30 days	4.5	4.6	4.3
Suicide attempt required medical attention in past 12 months	2.4	2.9	2.0

Source: Grunbaum, Jo Anne, et. al., "Youth Risk Behavior Surveillance–United States, 2003," Mortality and Morbidity Weekly Report, Vol. 53/SS-2, Centers for Disease Control and Prevention, May 21, 2004, Internet site http://www.cdc.gov/mmwr/preview/mmwrhtml/ss5302a1.htm

Table 9.26 Risk Behavior of 12th Graders by Sex, 2003

(percent of 12th graders engaging in selected risk behaviors, by sex, 2003)

	12th graders		
	total	female	male
In past 30 days, rode with a driver who had been drinking alcohol	33.3%	32.6%	34.0%
Felt so sad/hopeless almost every day for two+ weeks that stopped usual activities	27.4	32.6	22.0
Was in a physical fight in the past 12 months	26.5	17.7	35.0
Property stolen or deliberately damaged on school property	24.2	20.2	27.9
Drove after drinking alcohol in past 30 days	19.8	13.6	25.6
Rarely or never wore seatbelts when riding in a car driven by someone else	16.2	10.9	21.1
Carried a weapon on at least one day during the past 30 days	15.5	5.2	25.2
Seriously considered attempting suicide in past 12 months	15.5	18.0	13.2
Was physically hurt by boyfriend/girlfriend on purpose in the past 12 months	10.1	10.2	10.1
Was forced to have sexual intercourse	9.1	11.6	6.6
Engaged in a physical fight on school property during past 12 months	7.3	4.7	9.6
Carried a weapon on school property in past 30 days	6.4	2.5	10.2
Was threatened or injured with a weapon on school property during past 12 months	6.3	3.9	8.5
Attempted suicide in past 12 months	6.1	6.9	5.2
Carried a gun on at least one day during the past 30 days	5.7	1.0	10.0
Felt too unsafe to go to school at least once in the past 30 days	3.8	3.9	3.8
Suicide attempt required medical attention in past 12 months	2.1	2.2	1.8

Source: Grunbaum, Jo Anne, et. al., "Youth Risk Behavior Surveillance–United States, 2003," Mortality and Morbidity Weekly Report, Vol. 53/SS-2, Centers for Disease Control and Prevention, May 21, 2004, Internet site http://www.cdc.gov/mmwr/preview/ mmwrhtml/ss5302a1.htm

Delinquent Behavior Is Not the Norm

Most 12th graders do not engage in delinquent behavior, but a substantial minority cross the line.

Most teenagers follow the rules, but not all of them. When asked which delinquent behaviors they have participated in during the past year, 28 percent admit taking something worth less than $50 that did not belong to them. Twenty-seven percent have taken something from a store without paying for it. Fourteen percent have gotten into a serious fight at school or work.

Boys are more likely than girls to engage in almost all types of problem behavior. While 19 percent of boys have hurt someone badly enough in the past year that the victim needed bandages or a doctor, only 5 percent of girls have done so. Twelve percent of boys say they have been arrested and taken to a police station in the past year versus 4 percent of girls. The only problem behavior girls are more likely to engage in than boys is fighting with parents—92 percent of girls have done so in the past 12 months versus 88 percent of boys.

■ While delinquent behavior is not the norm among teens, it is widespread enough to raise alarm among parents, teachers, and community leaders.

Many boys cross the line

(percent of 12th grade boys engaging in delinquent behavior in the past 12 months, 2003)

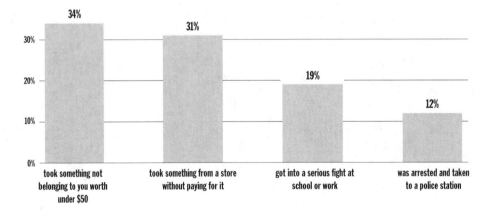

Table 9.27 Delinquent Behavior of 12th Graders, 2003

(percent of 12th graders reporting delinquent behavior in the past 12 months, by type of behavior and sex, 2003)

	total	females	males
Argued or had a fight with either of your parents	89.7%	92.4%	87.6%
Took something not belonging to you worth under $50	27.7	21.1	34.2
Took something from a store without paying for it	26.8	22.8	30.9
Went into a house or building when you weren't supposed to be there	23.0	17.3	29.0
Took part in a fight with a group of friends against another group	19.8	14.9	24.6
Got into a serious fight at school or work	14.3	8.8	19.4
Damaged school property on purpose	13.2	6.4	19.9
Hurt someone badly enough to need bandages or a doctor	12.0	5.1	18.9
Took something not belonging to you worth over $50	9.6	5.1	13.7
Been arrested and taken to a police station	8.0	4.1	11.6
Damaged property at work on purpose	6.8	2.6	11.1
Took part of a car without permission	5.5	2.1	9.0
Took a car that didn't belong to someone in your family without permission	5.3	2.4	8.0
Used a knife, gun, or other weapon to get something from someone	3.9	0.9	6.5
Set fire to someone's property on purpose	3.8	0.9	6.7
Hit an instructor or supervisor	3.2	0.9	5.2

Source: Monitoring the Future Survey, Institute for Social Research, University of Michigan, published in Sourcebook of Criminal Justice Statistics Online, Internet site http://www.albany.edu/sourcebook

Movies Lure Most People out of Their Home

Young adults are most likely to go to the movies.

Among the arts, movies attract the largest audience according to a study by the National Endowment for the Arts. Eighty-three percent of 18-to-24-year-olds attended at least one movie in the past year. Movie attendance falls slowly with age, dropping below 50 percent in the 55-to-64 age group. But even among people aged 75 or older, about one in five went to a movie in the past year.

Literature also has a large audience. Forty-seven percent of people aged 18 or older read literature during the past year, with the figure peaking at 52 percent among people aged 45 to 54. Arts and crafts fairs or festivals attract about one-third of Americans each year, with attendance ranging from a low of 16 percent among people aged 75 or older to a high of 39 percent among those aged 45 to 54.

The most popular personal arts activity is purchasing original pieces of art—30 percent have done so in the past year and among young adults the figure is 41 percent. Sewing and needlework is especially popular among older Americans, with more than one in five 65-to-74-year-olds participating. Among 18-to-24-year-olds, however, only 10 percent participate in sewing crafts.

■ The arts audience is huge and diverse, spanning the age groups.

Movie attendance falls slowly with age

(percent of people aged 18 or older who went to the movies in the past year, by age, 2002)

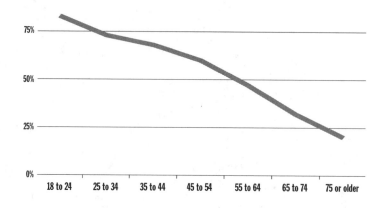

Table 9.28 Attendance at Arts Events by Age, 2002

(percent of people aged 18 or older who attended/visited/read selected arts during the past year, by age, 2002)

	total	18–24	25–34	35–44	45–54	55–64	65–74	75+
Read literature (novels, poetry, or plays)	46.7%	42.8%	47.7%	46.6%	51.6%	48.9%	45.3%	36.7%
Attended art fair/festival or craft fair/festival	33.4	29.2	33.5	37.2	38.8	35.1	31.1	15.7
Visited historic site	31.6	28.3	33.3	35.8	38.0	31.6	24.2	12.8
Visited art museum or gallery	26.5	23.7	26.7	27.4	32.9	27.8	23.4	13.4
Attended musical	17.1	14.8	15.4	19.1	19.3	19.7	16.6	10.1
Attended nonmusical play	12.3	11.4	10.7	13.0	15.2	13.8	13.0	5.4
Attended classical music performance	11.6	7.8	9.0	10.7	15.2	15.6	12.5	9.5
Attended jazz performance	10.8	10.5	10.8	13.0	13.9	8.8	7.6	3.9
Attended dance performance (except ballet)	6.3	6.2	5.9	7.0	8.0	6.0	5.4	3.0
Attended ballet	3.9	2.6	3.5	4.9	5.1	3.3	3.3	2.2
Attended opera	3.2	2.0	3.0	2.8	4.0	4.2	4.0	1.8

Source: National Endowment for the Arts, 2002 Survey of Public Participation in the Arts: Summary Report, Research Division Report No. 45, Internet site http://www.nea.gov/pub/ResearchReports_chrono.html

Table 9.29 Participation in the Arts through Media, 2002

(percent of people aged 18 or older who participated in the arts through media during the past year, by age, 2002)

	total	18–24	25–34	35–44	45–54	55–64	65–74	75+
Jazz								
TV	16.4%	10.7%	13.8%	17.7%	20.7%	17.0%	18.5%	15.1%
Radio	23.5	16.1	23.8	28.1	29.6	24.1	18.4	11.9
Recordings	17.2	13.1	17.5	21.1	21.8	16.8	11.8	7.7
Classical music								
TV	18.1	8.9	12.4	15.9	20.9	23.8	28.3	25.8
Radio	23.9	13.8	21.1	23.9	29.9	29.5	26.5	20.8
Recordings	19.3	14.1	18.1	19.3	23.1	22.9	20.8	14.2
Opera								
TV	5.8	3.0	3.7	4.5	5.7	8.1	10.5	9.7
Radio	5.7	2.0	4.5	4.3	6.4	8.7	9.4	7.7
Recordings	5.5	2.7	4.4	4.7	6.8	8.1	7.9	5.4
Musical play								
TV	11.7	7.2	9.8	11.8	13.3	12.3	16.2	14.1
Radio	2.4	1.9	1.7	2.5	2.6	2.8	3.2	2.6
Recordings	4.3	3.1	3.2	4.4	5.9	5.1	4.4	2.9
Non-musical play								
TV	9.4	7.0	7.3	8.5	9.7	12.3	13.6	11.1
Radio	2.1	1.3	2.1	2.3	2.8	1.6	2.4	1.4
Dance (on TV)	**12.6**	**8.7**	**10.0**	**13.0**	**13.8**	**15.0**	**15.1**	**14.4**
Artists, art work, or art museums (on TV)	**25.0**	**21.1**	**25.3**	**24.8**	**28.5**	**27.2**	**24.5**	**19.1**

Source: National Endowment for the Arts, 2002 Survey of Public Participation in the Arts: Summary Report, Research Division Report No. 45, Internet site http://www.nea.gov/pub/ResearchReports_chrono.html

Table 9.30 Personal Participation in the Arts, 2002

(percent of people aged 18 or older who personally participated in the arts during the past year, by age, 2002)

	total	18–24	25–34	35–44	45–54	55–64	65–74	75+
Purchased art in past year	29.5%	41.0%	39.1%	31.2%	27.9%	26.1%	23.7%	11.4%
Own original pieces of art	19.3	9.4	15.3	20.9	25.8	24.5	20.1	14.8
Sewing, weaving, crocheting, quilting, or needlepoint	16.0	10.4	13.0	15.3	18.6	19.1	20.5	18.0
Photography	11.5	12.9	12.3	14.1	12.1	10.5	8.1	3.8
Painting, drawing, sculpture, or printmaking	8.6	15.4	10.2	8.1	8.2	6.7	4.8	3.1
Writing	7.0	12.7	7.9	6.7	6.8	5.0	4.1	3.7
Pottery, jewelry, leatherwork, or metalwork	6.9	9.3	7.8	7.4	7.5	5.6	4.6	2.4
Choir/chorale	4.8	4.9	3.9	4.8	5.1	5.6	5.3	3.7
Dance (except ballet)	4.2	6.0	4.5	3.9	4.2	3.4	3.7	2.5
Musical play	2.4	2.5	2.1	2.1	2.7	2.6	2.1	2.2
Music composition	2.3	5.7	3.3	2.3	1.8	0.9	0.4	0.1
Classical music performance	1.8	2.5	1.4	1.8	2.5	1.5	1.4	0.7
Act in play	1.4	3.0	1.4	1.7	1.1	0.9	0.6	0.2
Jazz performance	1.3	1.9	1.2	1.5	2.0	0.8	0.5	0.4
Opera	0.7	0.7	0.6	0.6	0.9	0.9	0.8	0.7
Ballet	0.3	1.1	0.2	0.4	0.2	0.2	0.0	0.2

Source: National Endowment for the Arts, 2002 Survey of Public Participation in the Arts: Summary Report, Research Division Report No. 45, Internet site http://www.nea.gov/pub/ResearchReports_chrono.html

Table 9.31 Participation in Selected Leisure Activities, 2002

(percent of people aged 18 or older who participated in selected leisure activities during the past year, by age, 2002)

	total	18–24	25–34	35–44	45–54	55–64	65–74	75+
Go to the movies	60.0%	82.8%	73.3%	68.0%	60.4%	46.6%	32.2%	19.5%
Jog, lift weights, walk, or participate in any other exercise routine	55.1	61.3	60.2	59.5	58.6	48.4	47.0	31.3
Garden indoor or outdoor	47.3	20.7	41.4	51.0	55.4	56.6	57.2	47.9
Participate in home improvement or repair to own home	42.4	21.1	41.1	53.0	54.9	44.8	38.4	22.1
Go to an amusement park or carnival	41.7	57.6	56.2	53.3	37.1	27.1	18.4	9.6
Attend sports events (except youth sports)	35.0	46.0	41.8	42.2	35.8	25.5	19.7	11.1
Participate in outdoor activities such as camping, hiking, or canoeing	30.9	37.7	38.8	39.0	33.0	21.7	14.9	5.8
Participate in sports, such as golf, bowling, skiing, or basketball	30.4	49.4	39.6	36.6	28.6	16.0	13.7	6.0
Perform volunteer or charity work	29.0	25.3	26.0	33.2	33.4	28.1	28.8	21.3

Source: National Endowment for the Arts, 2002 Survey of Public Participation in the Arts: Summary Report, Research Division Report No. 45, Internet site http://www.nea.gov/pub/ResearchReports_chrono.html

Most Students Go to College Close to Home

The majority have college-educated parents.

The 56 percent majority of college freshmen attend a college that is no more than 100 miles from their home, according to the 2005 American Freshman Survey of UCLA's Higher Education Research Institute. Only 13 percent attend a college that is more than 500 miles from their home.

Because college costs are high and rising, college students are more likely to come from high-income than from low-income families. Only 9 percent of college freshmen are from families with incomes of less than $20,000, while more than one-third are from families with incomes of $100,000 or more. Parental education also plays a role in college attendance. More than half of today's college freshmen have mothers and fathers who are college graduates.

■ As college costs continue to soar, the children who can afford to go to college are increasingly from high-income, highly educated families.

More than one-third of college freshmen are from families with incomes of $100,000 or more

(percent distribution of college freshmen by parents' total income, 2005)

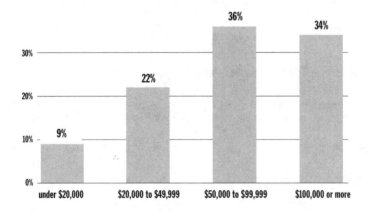

Table 9.32 Family Characteristics of College Freshmen, 2005

(percent distribution of college freshmen in institutions offering baccalaureate degrees by family characteristics, 2005)

	percent distribution
How many miles from college is your permanent home?	
Ten or less	10.9%
11 to 50	26.9
51 to 100	18.1
101 to 500	31.5
More than 500	12.6
Estimate of parents' total income	
Under $20,000	8.9
$20,000 to $29,999	7.0
$30,000 to $39,999	6.8
$40,000 to $49,999	7.8
$50,000 to $59,999	9.0
$60,000 to $74,999	12.0
$75,000 to $99,999	15.0
$100,000 to $150,000	16.9
$150,000 or more	16.9
Father's educational attainment	
Less than high school graduate	7.4
High school graduate	21.3
Some college or vocational school	18.4
College graduate	27.9
Some graduate school or graduate degree	25.0
Mother's educational attainment	
Less than high school graduate	5.8
High school graduate	20.7
Some college or vocational school	21.2
College graduate	31.8
Some graduate school or graduate degree	20.4

Source: The American Freshman: National Norms for Fall 2005, John H. Pryor, Sylvia Hurtado, Victor B. Saenz, Jennifer A. Lindholm, William S. Korn, and Kathryn M. Mahoney, Higher Education Research Institute, UCLA, 2005

Most Students Depend on Family to Pay the Bills

Many are worried about college costs.

Seventy-nine percent of college freshmen are paying for tuition, room, and board using money from their parents or other relatives, according UCLA's Higher Education Research Institute's American Freshman Survey. The majority of students say they will receive at least $3,000 from parents or relatives to pay for their first-year expenses, and 31 percent say they will receive $10,000 or more.

Grants, scholarships, and military funding—aid that does not have to be repaid—ranks second as a source of funding for tuition, room, and board. Sixty-five percent of students will receive at least some funding from this source, and 18 percent will receive $10,000 or more. A student's personal resources from work or work-study rank third in importance, with 57 percent using money from this source. Forty-nine percent of students say they will use student loans to pay for first-year expenses. Eleven percent are depending on loans of $10,000 or more.

Paying for college is a big worry for many students. When asked how concerned they are about their ability to finance their college education, only 34 percent of college freshmen say they have no concerns. The 53 percent majority has "some" concerns. Thirteen percent have major concerns, not knowing whether they will have enough to pay for school.

■ As college tuitions soar, many colleges are offering grants to lure the best students.

Many freshmen worry about paying for college

(percent distribution of college freshmen by level of concern about paying for college, 2005)

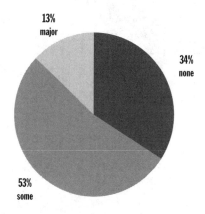

13%
major

34%
none

53%
some

Table 9.33 How Students Will Pay for College, 2005

(percent distribution of college freshmen in institutions offering baccalaureate degrees by amount paid for tuition, fees, room, and board by selected sources, and concern about ability to pay for college, 2005)

How much of your first year's educational expenses do you expect to cover from...

• Family resources (parents, relatives, spouses, etc.):

None	21.2%
Some	78.8
Less than $1,000	11.0
$1,000 to $2,999	13.1
$3,000 to $5,999	12.7
$6,000 to $9,999	11.1
$10,000 or more	30.9

• Aid that need not be repaid (grants, scholarships, military funding, etc.):

None	35.5
Some	64.5
Less than $1,000	7.6
$1,000 to $2,999	15.4
$3,000 to $5,999	13.5
$6,000 to $9,999	10.4
$10,000 or more	17.6

• My own resources (savings from work, work-study, other):

None	43.2
Some	56.8
Less than $1,000	26.4
$1,000 to $2,999	20.3
$3,000 to $5,999	6.4
$6,000 to $9,999	1.9
$10,000 or more	1.8

• Aid that must be repaid (loans, etc.):

None	51.4
Some	48.6
Less than $1,000	4.2
$1,000 to $2,999	14.2
$3,000 to $5,999	11.6
$6,000 to $9,999	8.2
$10,000 or more	10.5

Do you have any concern about your ability to finance your college education?

None (I am confident that I will have sufficient funds)	34.0
Some (but I probably will have enough funds)	52.7
Major (not sure I will have enough funds to complete college)	13.2

Source: The American Freshman: National Norms for Fall 2005, John H. Pryor, Sylvia Hurtado, Victor B. Saenz, Jennifer A. Lindholm, William S. Korn, and Kathryn M. Mahoney, Higher Education Research Institute, UCLA, 2005

Fewer than Half of College Freshmen Say They Drank Beer during Senior Year

More than three out of four performed volunteer work.

Every year for more than 35 years, the Higher Education Research Institute of UCLA has asked the nation's college freshmen a battery of questions about their attitudes, experiences, college plans, and life objectives. Over the decades, those answers reveal the character of generations of Americans. Based on the answers supplied by college freshmen in 2005, it is apparent that the Millennial generation is involved with their community. Seventy-nine percent of men and 87 percent of women performed volunteer work during their senior year in high school. Forty-seven percent of men and 52 percent of women participated in an organized demonstration during their senior year—an all-time high for the survey.

Surprisingly, fewer than half of freshmen drank beer during the past year—49 percent of men and 39 percent of women. About half say they drank wine or liquor. More than three out of four attended a religious service in the past year, and 68 to 72 percent socialized with someone from another racial or ethnic group.

Women freshmen are more likely than their male counterparts to feel overwhelmed by all they had to do (36 versus 16 percent). Men are more likely than women to do such things as drink beer, play a musical instrument, and frequently discuss politics.

■ The war in Iraq, Hurricane Katrina, and the Indian Ocean tsunami appear to have raised the civic involvement of young adults.

Many students are talking about religion and politics

(percent of students who frequently discussed religion or politics during the past year, by sex, 2005)

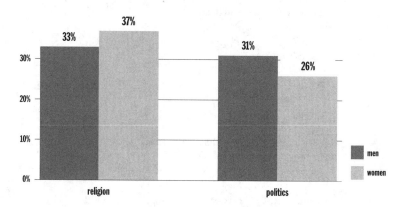

Table 9.34 Experiences of College Freshmen by Sex, 2005

(percent of college freshmen in institutions offering baccalaureate degrees who have participated in selected activities in the past year, by sex, 2005)

	men	women	percentage point difference between men and women
Used a personal computer frequently	85.4%	85.8%	−0.4
Performed volunteer work	78.5	87.0	−8.5
Attended a religious service	76.8	81.9	−5.1
Used the Internet for research or homework frequently	75.2	83.3	−8.1
Socialized with someone of another racial/ethnic group	68.4	71.7	−3.3
Drank wine or liquor	50.9	50.2	0.7
Drank beer	49.1	38.8	10.3
Played a musical instrument	46.8	41.2	5.6
Participated in organized demonstrations	46.7	52.1	−5.4
Discussed religion frequently	32.7	36.8	−4.1
Discussed politics with friends frequently	30.6	25.5	5.1
Voted in student election	20.8	25.3	−4.5
Frequently felt overwhelmed by all I had to do	15.9	35.6	−19.7
Smoked cigarettes frequently	5.8	5.7	0.1
Frequently felt depressed	5.2	8.4	−3.2

Source: The American Freshman: National Norms for Fall 2005, John H. Pryor, Sylvia Hurtado, Victor B. Saenz, Jennifer A. Lindholm, William S. Korn, and Kathryn M. Mahoney, Higher Education Research Institute, UCLA, 2005; calculations by New Strategist

College Freshmen Support National Health Insurance

Their top objectives are to make a lot of money and raise a family.

The great majority of college freshmen believe a national health care plan is needed to cover everyone's medical costs. They think the federal government is not doing enough to curb environmental pollution, and they want more control over the sale of handguns, according to the Higher Education Research Institute's American Freshman Survey. Sixty percent of women and 67 percent of men agree that dissent is a critical component of the political process. More than 60 percent say only volunteers should serve in the armed forces, and most want abortion to be legal.

Women are more likely than men to support legal marital status for same-sex couples, 64 versus 50 percent. Conversely, a larger proportion of men than women want to see laws prohibiting homosexual relations (35 versus 21 percent). Just 16 percent of women believe the activities of married women are best confined to the home and family versus 26 percent of men.

Both men and women want to make a lot of money. Fully 76 percent of men and 73 percent of women say that being very well off financially is essential or very important to them. Seventy-five percent of men and 76 percent of women say raising a family is essential or very important. Women are more likely than men to want to help others in difficulty, while men are more likely than women to want to be successful in their own business.

■ Most college students are liberal in their attitudes toward health care, gun control, taxes, homosexuality, and abortion.

College freshmen are decidedly liberal in their attitudes toward social issues

(percent of college freshmen agreeing somewhat or strongly with selected statements, by sex, 2005)

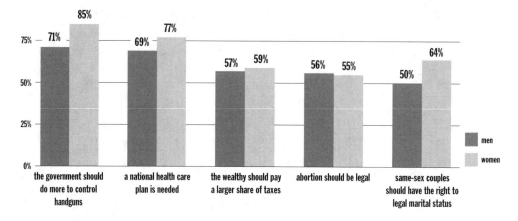

Table 9.35 Attitudes of College Freshmen by Sex, 2005

(percent of college freshmen in institutions offering baccalaureate degrees who somewhat or strongly agree with selected statements, by sex, 2005)

	men	women	percentage point difference between men and women
The federal government is not doing enough to control environmental pollution	73.9%	79.8%	−5.9
Federal government should do more to control the sale of handguns	71.0	84.9	−13.9
A national health care plan is needed to cover everyone's medical costs	69.3	77.1	−7.8
Dissent is a critical component of the political process	66.8	59.8	7.0
Only volunteers should serve in the armed forces	64.2	62.2	2.0
There is too much concern in the courts for the rights of criminals	60.7	55.5	5.2
Wealthy people should pay a larger share of taxes than they do now	57.3	58.9	−1.6
Abortion should be legal	55.8	54.8	1.0
Colleges should prohibit racist/sexist speech on campus	55.7	62.0	−6.3
Affirmative action in college admissions should be abolished	54.0	44.0	10.0
Same-sex couples should have the right to legal marital status	50.1	64.3	−14.2
Undocumented immigrants should be denied access to public education	49.6	36.1	13.5
Marijuana should be legalized	42.8	33.6	9.2
Federal military spending should be increased	37.6	31.4	6.2
It is important to have laws prohibiting homosexual relations	35.2	21.0	14.2
Realistically, an individual can do little to bring about changes in our society	31.4	23.9	7.5
The death penalty should be abolished	29.7	36.3	−6.6
The activities of married women are best confined to the home and family	26.2	15.5	10.7
Racial discrimination is no longer a major problem in America	25.9	17.1	8.8

Source: The American Freshman: National Norms for Fall 2005, John H. Pryor, Sylvia Hurtado, Victor B. Saenz, Jennifer A. Lindholm, William S. Korn, and Kathryn M. Mahoney, Higher Education Research Institute, UCLA, 2005; calculations by New Strategist

Table 9.36 Objectives of College Freshmen by Sex, 2005

(percent of college freshmen in institutions offering baccalaureate degrees who say the objective is essential or very important, by sex, 2005)

	men	women	percentage point difference between men and women
Being very well off financially	75.9%	73.4%	2.5
Raising a family	75.2	76.4	−1.2
Becoming an authority in my field	60.5	58.0	2.5
Helping others who are in difficulty	58.4	72.7	−14.3
Obtaining recognition from my colleagues for contributions to my special field	54.6	53.9	0.7
Becoming successful in a business of my own	47.3	38.7	8.6
Developing a meaningful philosophy of life	45.1	44.9	0.2
Improving my understanding of other countries and cultures	43.5	53.2	−9.7
Keeping up to date with political affairs	39.3	34.0	5.3
Influencing social values	37.4	44.4	−7.0
Integrating spirituality into my life	36.8	43.5	−6.7
Becoming a community leader	34.3	33.7	0.6
Helping to promote racial understanding	30.5	35.6	−5.1
Influencing the political structure	24.1	19.9	4.2
Making a theoretical contribution to science	21.5	16.8	4.7
Participating in a community action program	21.0	29.3	−8.3
Becoming involved in programs to clean up the environment	19.6	20.9	−1.9
Writing original works	16.3	15.7	3.9
Becoming accomplished in one of the performing arts	15.3	16.9	−1.6
Creating artistic work	15.2	17.6	−2.4

Source: The American Freshman: National Norms for Fall 2005, John H. Pryor, Sylvia Hurtado, Victor B. Saenz, Jennifer A. Lindholm, William S. Korn, and Kathryn M. Mahoney, Higher Education Research Institute, UCLA, 2005; calculations by New Strategist

10

Wealth

■ Householders under age 35 (the oldest Millennials turned 27 in 2004) saw their median net worth increase 15 percent between 2001 and 2004, to $14,200 after adjusting for inflation.

■ Only 39 percent of householders under age 35 owned stock in 2004, down from 49 percent in 2001. Householders under age 35 saw the value of their stock drop 31 percent during those years.

■ The value of the nonfinancial assets owned by householders under age 35 rose by only 2 percent between 2001 and 2004. Because housing equity accounts for the largest share of nonfinancial assets, the relatively low homeownership rate of the age group has dampened gains in the category.

■ The percentage of householders under age 35 with debt declined between 2001 and 2004—the only drop among the age groups. In 2004, 80 percent of the youngest householders were in debt, down from 83 percent in 2004.

■ Only 42 percent of American workers were included in an employer's retirement plan in 2004. Among workers under age 35, the figure ranged from just 4 to 40 percent.

The Youngest Householders Made Gains in Net Worth

But their net worth was lower in 2004 than in 1995, after adjusting for inflation.

Net worth is one of the most important measures of wealth. It is the amount remaining after a household's debts are subtracted from its assets. Householders under age 35 (the oldest Millennials turned 27 in 2004) saw their median net worth increase by 15 percent between 2001 and 2004, to $14,200, after adjusting for inflation. Despite this increase, the net worth of householders under age 35 was 4 percent lower in 2004 than in 1995, after adjusting for inflation.

The net worth of the youngest householders grew, although the median value of their financial assets fell by 21 percent between 2001 and 2004, after adjusting for inflation. The median value of their nonfinancial assets rose by just 2 percent during those years. Fewer householders in the age group were in debt, however, the percentage dropping from 83 to 80 percent between 2001 and 2004. Among householders under age 35 with debt, the median amount owed rose by a substantial 27 percent.

■ The net worth of householders under age 35 should get a boost from their rising homeownership rate, if they can pay down their mortgages.

Householders under age 35 saw their net worth grow by 15 percent

(percent change in net worth of households by age of householder, 2001 to 2004; in 2004 dollars)

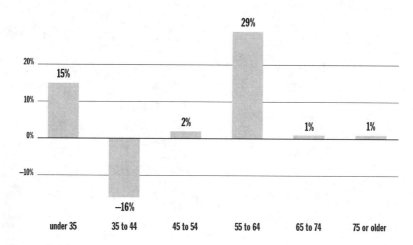

Table 10.1 Net Worth of Households by Age of Householder, 1995 to 2004

(median net worth of households by age of householder, 1995 to 2004; percent change, 1995–2004 and 2001–04; in 2004 dollars)

	2004	2001	1998	1995	percent change 2001–04	percent change 1995–2004
Total households	**$93,100**	**$91,700**	**$83,100**	**$70,800**	**1.5%**	**31.5%**
Under age 35	14,200	12,300	10,600	14,800	15.4	–4.1
Aged 35 to 44	69,400	82,600	73,500	64,200	–16.0	8.1
Aged 45 to 54	144,700	141,600	122,300	116,800	2.2	23.9
Aged 55 to 64	248,700	193,300	148,200	141,900	28.7	75.3
Aged 65 to 74	190,100	187,800	169,800	136,600	1.2	39.2
Aged 75 or older	163,100	161,200	145,600	114,500	1.2	42.4

Source: Federal Reserve Board, "Recent Changes in U.S. Family Finances: Evidence from the 2001 and 2004 Survey of Consumer Finances," Federal Reserve Bulletin, February 23, 2006, Internet site http://www.federalreserve.gov/pubs/bulletin/default.htm; calculations by New Strategist

Most Millennials Do Not Own Stock

The value of their financial assets has fallen.

Between 2001 and 2004, the financial assets of the average American household fell 23 percent after adjusting for inflation—to a median of $23,000, according to the Federal Reserve Board's Survey of Consumer Finances. The median value of the financial assets owned by householders under age 35 fell by 21 percent during those years to $5,200.

Only 39 percent of householders under age 35 owned stock in 2004, down from 49 percent in 2001. Householders under age 35 saw the value of their stock drop 31 percent during those years.

Slightly fewer than half (49.7 percent) of households owned a retirement account in 2004. Not surprisingly, among householders under age 35 the figure is a lower 40 percent. Among those with retirement accounts, median value is just $11,000.

■ Nonfinancial assets have become increasingly important to household wealth because of declining stock values and rising housing prices.

Millennials have few financial assets

(median value of financial assets of households by age of householder, 2004)

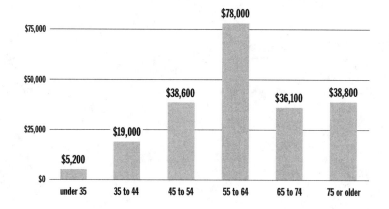

Table 10.2 Financial Assets of Households by Age of Householder, 2001 and 2004

(percentage of households owning financial assets and median value of assets for owners, by age of householder, 2001 and 2004; percentage point change in ownership and percent change in value of asset, 2001–04; in 2004 dollars)

	2004	2001	percentage point change
PERCENT OWNING ANY FINANCIAL ASSET			
Total households	**93.8%**	**93.4%**	**0.4**
Under age 35	90.1	89.7	0.4
Aged 35 to 44	93.6	93.5	0.1
Aged 45 to 54	93.6	94.7	−1.1
Aged 55 to 64	95.2	95.0	0.2
Aged 65 to 74	96.5	94.6	1.9
Aged 75 or older	97.6	95.1	2.5

	2004	2001	percent change
MEDIAN VALUE OF FINANCIAL ASSETS			
Total households	**$23,000**	**$29,800**	**−22.8%**
Under age 35	5,200	6,600	−21.2
Aged 35 to 44	19,000	28,600	−33.6
Aged 45 to 54	38,600	48,000	−19.6
Aged 55 to 64	78,000	59,800	30.4
Aged 65 to 74	36,100	54,700	−34.0
Aged 75 or older	38,800	42,600	−8.9

Source: Federal Reserve Board, "Recent Changes in U.S. Family Finances: Evidence from the 2001 and 2004 Survey of Consumer Finances," Federal Reserve Bulletin, February 23, 2006, Internet site http://www.federalreserve.gov/pubs/bulletin/default.htm; calculations by New Strategist

Table 10.3 Financial Assets of Households by Type of Asset and Age of Householder, 2004

(percentage of households owning financial assets, and median value of asset for owners, by type of asset and age of householder, 2004)

	total	under 35	35 to 44	45 to 54	55 to 64	65 to 74	75 or older
PERCENT OWNING ASSET							
Any financial asset	**93.8%**	**90.1%**	**93.6%**	**93.6%**	**95.2%**	**96.5%**	**97.6%**
Transaction accounts	91.3	86.4	90.8	91.8	93.2	93.9	96.4
Certificates of deposit	12.7	5.6	6.7	11.9	18.1	19.9	25.7
Savings bonds	17.6	15.3	23.3	21.0	15.2	14.9	11.0
Bonds	1.8	–	0.6	1.8	3.3	4.3	3.0
Stocks	20.7	13.3	18.5	23.2	29.1	25.4	18.4
Pooled investment funds	15.0	8.3	12.3	18.2	20.6	18.6	16.6
Retirement accounts	49.7	40.2	55.9	57.7	62.9	43.2	29.2
Cash value life insurance	24.2	11.0	20.1	26.0	32.1	34.8	34.0
Other managed assets	7.3	2.9	3.7	6.2	9.4	12.8	16.7
Other financial assets	10.0	11.6	10.0	12.1	7.2	8.1	8.1
MEDIAN VALUE OF ASSET							
Any financial asset	**$23,000**	**$5,200**	**$19,000**	**$38,600**	**$78,000**	**$36,100**	**$38,800**
Transaction accounts	3,800	1,800	3,000	4,800	6,700	5,500	6,500
Certificates of deposit	15,000	4,000	10,000	11,000	29,000	20,000	22,000
Savings bonds	1,000	500	500	1,000	2,500	3,000	5,000
Bonds	65,000	–	10,000	30,000	80,000	40,000	295,000
Stocks	15,000	4,400	10,000	14,500	25,000	42,000	50,000
Pooled investment funds	40,400	8,000	15,900	50,000	75,000	60,000	60,000
Retirement accounts	35,200	11,000	27,900	55,500	83,000	80,000	30,000
Cash value life insurance	6,000	3,000	5,000	8,000	10,000	8,000	5,000
Other managed assets	45,000	5,000	18,300	43,000	65,000	60,000	50,000
Other financial assets	4,000	1,000	3,500	5,000	7,000	10,000	22,000

Note: "–" means sample is too small to make a reliable estimate.
Source: Federal Reserve Board, "Recent Changes in U.S. Family Finances: Evidence from the 2001 and 2004 Survey of Consumer Finances," Federal Reserve Bulletin, February 23, 2006, Internet site http://www.federalreserve.gov/pubs/bulletin/default.htm; calculations by New Strategist

Table 10.4 Stock Ownership of Households by Age of Householder, 2001 and 2004

(percentage of householders owning stocks directly or indirectly, median value of stock for owners, and share of total household financial assets accounted for by stock holdings, by age of householder, 2001 and 2004; percent and percentage point change, 2001–04; in 2004 dollars)

	2004	2001	percentage point change
PERCENT OWNING STOCK			
Total households	**48.6%**	**51.9%**	**–3.3**
Under age 35	38.8	48.9	–10.1
Aged 35 to 44	52.3	59.5	–7.2
Aged 45 to 54	54.4	59.2	–4.8
Aged 55 to 64	61.6	57.1	4.5
Aged 65 to 74	45.8	39.2	6.6
Aged 75 or older	34.8	34.2	0.6

	2004	2001	percent change
MEDIAN VALUE OF STOCK			
Total households	**$24,300**	**$36,700**	**–33.8%**
Under age 35	5,200	7,500	–30.7
Aged 35 to 44	12,700	29,300	–56.7
Aged 45 to 54	30,600	53,300	–42.6
Aged 55 to 64	59,500	86,500	–31.2
Aged 65 to 74	75,000	159,800	–53.1
Aged 75 or older	85,900	127,800	–32.8

	2004	2001	percentage point change
STOCK AS SHARE OF FINANCIAL ASSETS			
Total households	**47.4%**	**56.0%**	**–8.6**
Under age 35	30.0	52.5	–22.5
Aged 35 to 44	47.7	57.3	–9.6
Aged 45 to 54	46.8	59.1	–12.3
Aged 55 to 64	51.1	56.2	–5.1
Aged 65 to 74	51.1	55.2	–4.1
Aged 75 or older	39.1	51.4	–12.3

Source: Federal Reserve Board, "Recent Changes in U.S. Family Finances: Evidence from the 2001 and 2004 Survey of Consumer Finances," Federal Reserve Bulletin, February 23, 2006, Internet site http://www.federalreserve.gov/pubs/bulletin/default.htm; calculations by New Strategist

The Nonfinancial Assets of Millennials Barely Grew

A rising homeownership rate hasn't boosted assets by much.

The median value of the nonfinancial assets owned by the average American household stood at $147,800 in 2004, a gain of 22 percent since 2001, after adjusting for inflation. The value of the nonfinancial assets owned by householders under age 35 rose by only 2 percent during those years. In 2004, the median value of the nonfinancial assets owned by house-holders in the age group stood at a modest $32,300.

Because housing equity accounts for the largest share of nonfinancial assets, the relatively low homeownership rate of the age group has dampened gains in the category. Only 42 percent of householders under age 35 owned a home in 2004. While this rate is higher than in 2001, it is still low compared to other age groups. Among homeowners under age 35, median home value rose 33 percent between 2001 and 2004, after adjusting for inflation. The homes of householders under age 35 had a median value of $135,000 in 2004.

■ Nonfinancial assets grew as a share of the average household's total assets between 2001 and 2004, rising from 58 to 64 percent.

The nonfinancial assets of Millennials are well below average

(median value of nonfinancial assets of households by age of householder, 2004)

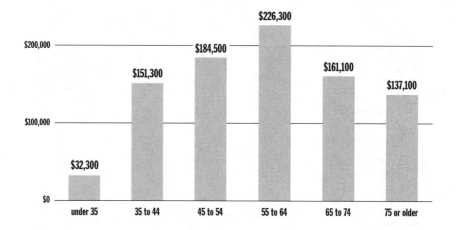

Table 10.5 Nonfinancial Assets of Households by Age of Householder, 2001 and 2004

(percentage of households owning nonfinancial assets and median value of assets for owners, by age of house-holder, 2001 and 2004; percentage point change in ownership and percent change in value of asset, 2001–04; in 2004 dollars)

	2004	2001	percentage point change
PERCENT OWNING ANY NONFINANCIAL ASSET			
Total households	**92.5%**	**90.7%**	**1.8**
Under age 35	88.6	83.0	5.6
Aged 35 to 44	93.0	93.2	–0.2
Aged 45 to 54	94.7	95.2	–0.5
Aged 55 to 64	92.6	95.4	–2.8
Aged 65 to 74	95.6	91.6	4.0
Aged 75 or older	92.5	86.4	6.1

	2004	2001	percent change
MEDIAN VALUE OF NONFINANCIAL ASSETS			
Total households	**$147,800**	**$120,900**	**22.2%**
Under age 35	32,300	31,700	1.9
Aged 35 to 44	151,300	125,500	20.6
Aged 45 to 54	184,500	150,800	22.3
Aged 55 to 64	226,300	157,500	43.7
Aged 65 to 74	161,100	158,900	1.4
Aged 75 or older	137,100	130,600	5.0

Source: Federal Reserve Board, "Recent Changes in U.S. Family Finances: Evidence from the 2001 and 2004 Survey of Consumer Finances," Federal Reserve Bulletin, February 23, 2006, Internet site http://www.federalreserve.gov/pubs/bulletin/default.htm; calculations by New Strategist

Table 10.6 Nonfinancial Assets of Households by Type of Asset and Age of Householder, 2004

(percentage of households owning nonfinancial assets, and median value of asset for owners, by type of asset and age of householder, 2004)

	total	under 35	35 to 44	45 to 54	55 to 64	65 to 74	75 or older
PERCENT OWNING ASSET							
Any nonfinancial asset	**92.5%**	**88.6%**	**93.0%**	**94.7%**	**92.6%**	**95.6%**	**92.5%**
Vehicles	86.3	82.9	89.4	88.8	88.6	89.1	76.9
Primary residence	69.1	41.6	68.3	77.3	79.1	81.3	85.2
Other residential property	12.5	5.1	9.4	16.3	19.5	19.9	9.7
Equity in nonresidential property	8.3	3.3	6.4	11.4	12.8	10.6	7.7
Business equity	11.5	6.9	13.9	15.7	15.8	8.0	5.3
Other nonfinancial assets	7.8	5.5	6.0	9.7	9.2	9.0	8.5
MEDIAN VALUE OF ASSET							
Total nonfinancial assets	**$147,800**	**$32,300**	**$151,300**	**$184,500**	**$226,300**	**$161,100**	**$137,100**
Vehicles	14,200	11,300	15,600	18,800	18,600	12,400	8,400
Primary residence	160,000	135,000	160,000	170,000	200,000	150,000	125,000
Other residential property	100,000	82,500	80,000	90,000	135,000	80,000	150,000
Equity in nonresidential property	60,000	55,000	42,200	43,000	75,000	78,000	85,800
Business equity	100,000	50,000	100,000	144,000	190,900	100,000	80,300
Other nonfinancial assets	15,000	5,000	10,000	20,000	25,000	30,000	11,000

Source: Federal Reserve Board, "Recent Changes in U.S. Family Finances: Evidence from the 2001 and 2004 Survey of Consumer Finances," Federal Reserve Bulletin, February 23, 2006, Internet site http://www.federalreserve.gov/pubs/bulletin/default.htm; calculations by New Strategist

Table 10.7 Household Ownership of Primary Residence by Age of Householder, 2001 and 2004

(percentage of households owning their primary residence, median value of asset for owners, and median value of home-secured debt for owners, by age of householder, 2001 and 2004; percentage point change in ownership and percent change in value of asset, 2001–04; in 2004 dollars)

	2004	2001	percentage point change
PERCENT OWNING PRIMARY RESIDENCE			
Total households	**69.1%**	**67.7%**	**1.4**
Under age 35	41.6	39.9	1.7
Aged 35 to 44	68.3	67.8	0.5
Aged 45 to 54	77.3	76.2	1.1
Aged 55 to 64	79.1	83.2	–4.1
Aged 65 to 74	81.3	82.5	–1.2
Aged 75 or older	85.2	76.2	9.0

	2004	2001	percent change
MEDIAN VALUE OF PRIMARY RESIDENCE			
Total households	**$160,000**	**$131,000**	**22.1%**
Under age 35	135,000	101,200	33.4
Aged 35 to 44	160,000	133,100	20.2
Aged 45 to 54	170,000	143,800	18.2
Aged 55 to 64	200,000	138,500	44.4
Aged 65 to 74	150,000	137,400	9.2
Aged 75 or older	125,000	118,200	5.8

	2004	2001	percent change
MEDIAN VALUE OF HOME-SECURED DEBT			
Total households	**$95,000**	**$74,600**	**27.3%**
Under age 35	107,000	82,000	30.5
Aged 35 to 44	110,000	85,200	29.1
Aged 45 to 54	97,000	79,900	21.4
Aged 55 to 64	83,000	58,600	41.6
Aged 65 to 74	51,000	41,500	22.9
Aged 75 or older	31,000	47,700	–35.0

Source: Federal Reserve Board, "Recent Changes in U.S. Family Finances: Evidence from the 2001 and 2004 Survey of Consumer Finances," Federal Reserve Bulletin, February 23, 2006, Internet site http://www.federalreserve.gov/pubs/bulletin/default.htm; calculations by New Strategist

Debt Increased for Millennials

The biggest debtors are householders aged 35 to 44, however.

The debt of the average American household grew by a substantial 34 percent between 2001 and 2004, to $55,300, after adjusting for inflation. Among householders under age 35, debt rose by a slightly smaller 27 percent during those years, to $33,600. The percentage of householders under age 35 with debt declined between 2001 and 2004—the only drop among the age groups. In 2004, 80 percent of the youngest householders were in debt, down from 83 percent in 2004.

Home-secured debt accounts for the largest share of debt by far. Forty-eight percent of households have home-secured debt, owing a median of $95,000. Householders under age 35 owe $107,000 for their homes, behind only householders aged 35 to 44. But only 38 percent of householders under age 35 have home-secured debt. The 48 percent minority of householders under age 35 carry a credit card balance, owing a median of $1,500 on their credit cards in 2004. Fifty-nine percent of householders under age 35 have an installment loan (primarily car loans), owing a median of $11,900.

■ As more Millennials buy homes, their debts will increase.

Millennials owe relatively little—yet

(median amount of debt owed by households by age of householder, 2004)

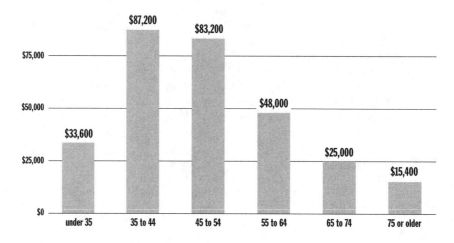

Table 10.8 Debt of Households by Age of Householder, 2001 and 2004

(percentage of households with debt and median amount of debt for debtors, by age of householder, 2001 and 2004; percentage point change in households with debt and percent change in amount of debt, 2001–04; in 2004 dollars)

	2004	2001	percentage point change
PERCENT WITH DEBT			
Total households	**76.4%**	**75.1%**	**1.3**
Under age 35	79.8	82.7	–2.9
Aged 35 to 44	88.6	88.6	0.0
Aged 45 to 54	88.4	84.6	3.8
Aged 55 to 64	76.3	75.4	0.9
Aged 65 to 74	58.8	56.8	2.0
Aged 75 or older	40.3	29.2	11.1

	2004	2001	percent change
MEDIAN AMOUNT OF DEBT			
Total households	**$55,300**	**$41,300**	**33.9%**
Under age 35	33,600	26,500	26.8
Aged 35 to 44	87,200	65,500	33.1
Aged 45 to 54	83,200	57,800	43.9
Aged 55 to 64	48,000	36,900	30.1
Aged 65 to 74	25,000	14,000	78.6
Aged 75 or older	15,400	5,300	190.6

Source: Federal Reserve Board, "Recent Changes in U.S. Family Finances: Evidence from the 2001 and 2004 Survey of Consumer Finances," Federal Reserve Bulletin, February 23, 2006, Internet site http://www.federalreserve.gov/pubs/bulletin/default.htm; calculations by New Strategist

Table 10.9 Debt of Households by Type of Debt and Age of Householder, 2004

(percentage of householders with debt, and median value of debt for those with debt, by type of debt and age of householder, 2004)

	total	under 35	35 to 44	45 to 54	55 to 64	65 to 74	75 or older
PERCENT WITH DEBT							
Any debt	**76.4%**	**79.8%**	**88.6%**	**88.4%**	**76.3%**	**58.8%**	**40.3%**
Secured by residential property							
Primary residence	47.9	37.7	62.8	64.6	51.0	32.1	18.7
Other	4.0	2.1	4.0	6.3	5.9	3.2	1.5
Lines of credit not secured by residential property	1.6	2.2	1.5	2.9	0.7	0.4	–
Installment loans	46.0	59.4	55.7	50.2	42.8	27.5	13.9
Credit card balances	46.2	47.5	58.8	54.0	42.1	31.9	23.6
Other debt	7.6	6.2	11.3	9.4	8.4	4.0	2.5
MEDIAN AMOUNT OF DEBT							
Any debt	**$55,300**	**$33,600**	**$87,200**	**$83,200**	**$48,000**	**$25,000**	**$15,400**
Secured by residential property							
Primary residence	95,000	107,000	110,000	97,000	83,000	51,000	31,000
Other	87,000	62,500	75,000	87,000	108,800	100,000	39,000
Lines of credit not secured by residential property	3,000	1,000	1,900	7,000	14,000	4,000	–
Installment loans	11,500	11,900	12,000	12,000	12,900	8,300	6,700
Credit card balances	2,200	1,500	2,500	2,900	2,200	2,200	1,000
Other debt	4,000	3,000	4,000	4,000	5,500	5,000	2,000

Note: "–" means sample is too small to make a reliable estimate.
Source: Federal Reserve Board, "Recent Changes in U.S. Family Finances: Evidence from the 2001 and 2004 Survey of Consumer Finances," Federal Reserve Bulletin, February 23, 2006, Internet site http://www.federalreserve.gov/pubs/bulletin/default.htm; calculations by New Strategist

Few Millennials Participate in a Workplace Retirement Plan

Many think they will have to work in retirement.

Only 42 percent of American workers were included in an employer's retirement plan in 2004, according to an analysis of government statistics by the Employee Benefit Research Institute (EBRI). Retirement plan participation peaks among older workers at just over 50 percent. Among workers aged 21 to 25, only 19 percent participate in an employer's retirement plan. Among those aged 25 to 34, participation is a higher 40 percent.

Another EBRI study shows only 11 percent of workers aged 21 to 25 own an IRA or participate in a 401(k)-type (defined-contribution) retirement plan. In the 25 to 34 age group, the figure rises to 34 percent. Among those aged 25 to 44 participating in 401(k)-type plans, the median balance was just $6,000.

Even at their youthful age, many young adults worry about retirement. Only 26 percent of workers aged 25 to 34 are "very confident" they will have enough money to live comfortably throughout retirement, according to EBRI's Retirement Confidence Survey. Nevertheless, one in four thinks he or she will be able to retire before age 60. Of course, the meaning of retirement is questionable here, since 26 percent say their main source of income in retirement will be employment.

■ The substitution of defined-contribution for defined-benefit pension plans puts the burden of retirement savings on workers rather than employers.

Among workers under age 35, fewer than half participate in an employer-sponsored retirement plan

(percent of workers participating in an employer-sponsored retirement plan, by age, 2004)

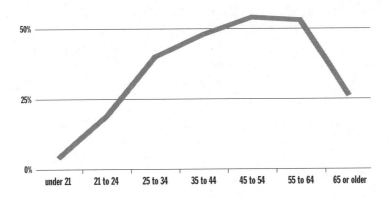

Table 10.10 Retirement-Plan Coverage by Age, 2004

(total number of workers, percent whose employer offers a retirement plan, and percent participating in plan, by type of employment and age of worker, 2004; numbers in thousands)

	number of workers	percent with an employer who sponsors a retirement plan	percent participating in employer's retirement plan
Total workers	**152,708**	**53.2%**	**41.9%**
Under age 21	10,824	24.9	4.1
Aged 21 to 24	12,602	41.0	19.4
Aged 25 to 34	32,468	52.8	39.7
Aged 35 to 44	36,214	57.3	48.3
Aged 45 to 54	34,585	61.2	53.9
Aged 55 to 64	19,654	60.3	53.0
Aged 65 or older	6,361	38.4	25.8
Private wage and salary workers aged 21 to 64			
Total workers	**105,703**	**54.5**	**43.0**
Aged 21 to 24	11,163	39.4	18.2
Aged 25 to 34	26,949	51.0	37.1
Aged 35 to 44	28,344	56.7	46.8
Aged 45 to 54	25,497	59.8	51.5
Aged 55 to 64	13,750	59.3	51.1
Public wage and salary workers aged 21 to 64			
Total workers	**20,529**	**85.1**	**75.8**
Aged 21 to 24	1,156	64.4	35.6
Aged 25 to 34	3,985	82.5	69.8
Aged 35 to 44	5,216	85.1	77.0
Aged 45 to 54	6,319	88.4	82.5
Aged 55 to 64	3,853	88.8	81.7

Source: Employee Benefit Research Institute, "Employment-Based Retirement Plan Participation: Geographic Differences and Trends, 2004," Issue Brief, No. 286, October 2005, Internet site http://www.ebri.org/publications/ib/index.cfm?fa=ibDisp&content_id=3590

Table 10.11 Ownership of IRAs and Participation in 401(k)s by Age, 2002

(percentage of workers aged 21 to 64 owning IRAs and/or participating in a 401(k)-type plan, by age, 2002)

	IRA and/or 401(k)-type plan	IRA only	401(k)-type plan only	both IRA and 401(k)-type plan	neither IRA nor 401(k)-type plan
Total workers	**40.4%**	**9.6%**	**21.7%**	**9.2%**	**59.6%**
Aged 21 to 24	10.6	1.5	8.4	0.7	89.4
Aged 25 to 34	34.3	5.7	22.9	5.7	65.7
Aged 35 to 44	43.0	9.1	24.4	9.6	57.0
Aged 45 to 54	48.3	12.0	23.9	12.4	51.7
Aged 55 to 64	50.6	18.3	18.5	13.8	49.4

Source: Employee Benefit Research Institute, "401(k)-Type Plan and IRA Ownership," by Craig Copeland, Notes, Vol. 26, No. 1, January 2005, Internet site http://www.ebri.org/

Table 10.12 Amount Saved in IRAs and 401(k)s by Age, 2002

(percentage of workers aged 21 to 64 owning an IRA or participating in a 401(k)-type plan, and average and median balance of IRA and 401(k), by age, 2002)

	percent owning IRA	IRA balance		percent participating in 401(k)	401(k) balance	
		average	median		average	median
Total workers	**18.7%**	**$26,951**	**$10,000**	**30.9%**	**$33,647**	**$14,000**
Aged 21 to 24	2.3	3,841	2,000	9.1	4,641	2,500
Aged 25 to 34	11.4	10,146	5,000	28.6	12,067	6,000
Aged 35 to 44	18.7	21,235	9,000	33.9	32,026	15,000
Aged 45 to 54	24.5	29,600	13,000	36.3	44,829	20,000
Aged 55 to 64	32.1	42,003	19,000	32.3	53,184	25,000

Source: Employee Benefit Research Institute, "401(k)-Type Plan and IRA Ownership," by Craig Copeland, Notes, Vol. 26, No. 1, January 2005, Internet site http://www.ebri.org/

Table 10.13 Retirement Planning by Age, 2005

(percentage of workers aged 25 or older responding by age, 2005)

	total	25 to 34	35 to 44	45 to 54	55 or older
Very confident in having enough money to live comfortably throughout retirement	25%	26%	25%	26%	20%
Very confident in having enough money to take care of medical expenses in retirement	20	21	19	20	19
Worker and/or spouse have saved for retirement	69	60	71	73	71
Worker and/or spouse are currently saving for retirement	62	53	67	65	66
Contribute to a workplace retirement savings plan	42	40	44	45	36
Have an IRA opened with money saved outside of an employer's retirement plan	31	25	27	38	38
Expected retirement age					
Less than 60	16	24	15	14	6
Aged 60 to 64	19	15	14	20	31
Aged 65	26	28	30	25	19
Aged 66 or older	24	19	28	26	24
Never retire	6	6	4	8	8
Don't know/refused	9	9	8	7	11
Expected sources of income in retirement					
Money from a workplace retirement savings plan	69	79	73	66	51
Money from a defined-benefit plan	33	34	37	29	33
Largest expected source of income in retirement					
A workplace retirement savings plan, such as a 401(k)	21	26	27	15	12
Other personal savings such as an IRA	18	22	17	19	15
Social Security	18	7	16	22	33
Employer-provided pension that pays a set amount each month for life	16	12	15	18	20
Employment	14	26	14	10	5
Sale or refinancing of your home	3	1	3	3	6
An inheritance	3	2	5	2	2
Other/don't know	6	4	4	11	7
Total savings and investments (not including value of primary residence)					
Less than $25,000	52	70	50	41	39
$25,000 to $49,999	13	12	15	14	12
$50,000 to $99,999	11	9	14	13	7
$100,000 to $249,999	12	5	10	17	23
$250,000 or more	11	4	10	16	19

Source: 2005 Retirement Confidence Survey, Employee Benefit Research Institute, American Savings Education Council, and Mathew Greenwald & Associates; Internet site http://www.ebri.org/surveys/rcs/

Glossary

adjusted for inflation Income or a change in income that has been adjusted for the rise in the cost of living, or the consumer price index (CPI-U-RS).

age Classification by age is based on the age of the person at his/her last birthday.

American Freshman Survey This is an annual survey taken each fall of students entering American colleges and universities as first-time, full-time freshmen. Initiated in Fall 1966, the survey is a project of the Cooperative Institutional Research Program sponsored by the American Council on Education and the Graduate School of Education & Information Studies at the University of California, Los Angeles. Survey results are based on the answers to the Student Information Form filled out by nearly 300,000 freshmen at more than 400 baccalaureate institutions during registration, freshman orientation, or the first few weeks of classes. Results are weighted to provide a normative picture of the American college freshman population.

American Housing Survey The AHS collects national and metropolitan-level data on the nation's housing, including apartments, single-family homes, and mobile homes. The nationally representative survey, with a sample of 55,000 homes, is conducted by the Census Bureau for the Department of Housing and Urban Development every other year.

American Indians In this book, American Indians include Alaska Natives (Eskimos and Aleuts) unless those groups are shown separately.

American Religious Identification Survey The 2001 ARIS, sponsored by the Graduate Center of the City University of New York, was based on a random telephone survey of 50,281 households in the continental U.S. Interviewers asked respondents aged 18 or older for their demographic characteristics and their religion. The 2001 ARIS updates the 1990 National Survey of Religious Identification.

American Time Use Survey Under contract with the Bureau of Labor Statistics, the Census Bureau collects ATUS information, revealing how people spend their time. The ATUS sample is drawn from U.S. households that have completed their final month of interviews for the Current Population Survey. One individual from each selected household is chosen to participate in the ATUS. Respondents are interviewed by telephone only once about their time use on the previous day. In 2003, the sample consisted of approximately 3,000 cases each month, which yielded about 1,700 completed interviews.

Asian The term "Asian" includes Native Hawaiians and other Pacific Islanders unless those groups are shown separately.

Baby Boom Americans born between 1946 and 1964.

Baby Bust Americans born between 1965 and 1976, also known as Generation X.

Behavioral Risk Factor Surveillance System The BRFSS is a collaborative project of the Centers for Disease Control and Prevention and U.S. states and territories. It is an ongoing data collection program designed to measure behavioral risk factors in the adult population aged 18 or older. All 50 states, three territories, and the District of Columbia take part in the survey, making the BRFSS the primary source of information on the health-related behaviors of Americans.

black The black racial category includes those who identified themselves as "black" or "African American."

central cities The largest city in a metropolitan area is called the central city. The balance of the metropolitan area outside the central city is regarded as the "suburbs."

Consumer Expenditure Survey The Consumer Expenditure Survey (CEX) is an ongoing study of the day-to-day spending of American households administered by the Bureau of Labor Statistics. The CEX includes an interview survey and a diary survey. The average spending figures shown in this book are the integrated data from both the diary and interview components of the survey. Two separate, nationally representative samples are used for the interview and diary surveys. For the interview survey, about 7,500 consumer units are interviewed on a rotating panel basis each quarter for five consecutive quarters. For the diary survey, 7,500 consumer units keep weekly diaries of spending for two consecutive weeks.

consumer unit *(on spending tables only)* For convenience, the term consumer unit and households are used interchangeably in the spending section of this book, although consumer units are somewhat different from the Census Bureau's households. Consumer units are all related members of a household, or financially independent members of a household. A household may include more than one consumer unit.

Current Population Survey The CPS is a nationally representative survey of the civilian noninstitutional population aged 15 or older. It is taken monthly by the Census Bureau for the Bureau of Labor Statistics, collecting information from more than 50,000 households on employment and unemployment. In March of each year, the survey includes the Annual Social and Economic Supplement (formerly called the Annual Demographic Survey), which is the source of most national data on the characteristics of Americans, such as educational attainment, living arrangements, and incomes.

disability As defined by the American Community Survey, respondents are asked whether they have a sensory, physical, mental, or self-care disability. Those who answer "yes" are classified as disabled.

disability As defined by the National Health Interview Survey, respondents aged 18 or older are asked whether they have difficulty in physical functioning, probing whether they can perform nine activities by themselves without using special equipment. The categories are walking a quarter mile; standing for two hours; sitting for two hours; walking up 10 steps without resting; stooping, bending, kneeling; reaching over one's head; grasping or handling small objects; carrying a 10-pound object; and pushing/pulling a large object. Adults who report that any of these activities is very difficult or they cannot do it at all are defined as having physical difficulties.

disability, work The Current Population Survey defines a work disability as a specific physical or mental condition that prevents an individual from working. The disability must be so severe that it completely incapacitates the individual and prevents him/her from doing any kind of work for at least the next six months.

dual-earner couple A married couple in which both the householder and the householder's spouse are in the labor force.

earnings A type of income, earnings is the amount of money a person receives from his or her job. *See also* Income.

employed All civilians who did any work as a paid employee or farmer/self-employed worker, or who worked 15 hours or more as an unpaid farm worker or in a family-owned business, during the reference period. All those who have jobs but who are temporarily absent from their jobs due to illness, bad weather, vacation, labor management dispute, or personal reasons are considered employed.

expenditure The transaction cost including excise and sales taxes of goods and services acquired during the survey period. The full cost of each purchase is recorded even though full payment may not have been made at the date of purchase. Average expenditure figures may be artificially low for infrequently purchased items such as cars because figures are calculated using all consumer units within a demographic segment rather than just purchasers. Expenditure estimates include money spent on gifts for others.

family A group of two or more people (one of whom is the householder) related by birth, marriage, or adoption and living in the same household.

family household A household maintained by a householder who lives with one or more people related to him or her by blood, marriage, or adoption.

female/male householder A woman or man who maintains a household without a spouse present. May head family or nonfamily households.

foreign-born population People who are not United States citizens at birth.

full-time employment Full-time is 35 or more hours of work per week during a majority of the weeks worked.

full-time, year-round Indicates 50 or more weeks of full-time employment during the previous calendar year.

Generation X Americans born between 1965 and 1976, also known as the baby-bust generation.

Hispanic Because Hispanic is an ethnic origin rather than a race, Hispanics may be of any race. While most Hispanics are white, there are black, Asian, and American Indian Hispanics.

household All the persons who occupy a housing unit. A household includes the related family members and all the unrelated persons, if any, such as lodgers, foster children, wards, or employees who share the housing unit. A person living alone is counted as a household. A group of unrelated people who share a housing unit as roommates or unmarried partners is also counted as a household. Households do not include group quarters such as college dormitories, prisons, or nursing homes.

household, race/ethnicity of Households are categorized according to the race or ethnicity of the householder only.

householder The householder is the person (or one of the persons) in whose name the housing unit is owned or rented or, if there is no such person, any adult member. With married couples, the householder may be either the husband or wife. The householder is the reference person for the household.

householder, age of The age of the householder is used to categorize households into age groups such as those used in this book. Married couples, for example, are classified according to the age of either the husband or wife, depending on which one identified him or herself as the householder.

housing unit A housing unit is a house, an apartment, a group of rooms, or a single room occupied or intended for occupancy as separate living quarters. Separate living quarters are those in which the occupants do not live and eat with any other persons in the structure and that have direct access from the outside of the building or through a common hall that is used or intended for use by the occupants of another unit or by the general public. The occupants may be a single family, one person living alone, two or more families living together, or any other group of related or unrelated persons who share living arrangements.

Housing Vacancy Survey The HVS is a supplement to the Current Population Survey, providing quarterly and annual data on rental and homeowner vacancy rates, characteristics of units available for occupancy, and homeownership rates by age, household type, region, state, and metropolitan area. The Current Population Survey sample includes 51,000 occupied housing units and 9,000 vacant units.

housing value The respondent's estimate of how much his or her house and lot would sell for if it were for sale.

immigration The relatively permanent movement (change of residence) of people into the country of reference.

income Money received in the preceding calendar year by each person aged 15 or older from each of the following sources: (1) earnings from longest job (or self-employment); (2) earnings from jobs other than longest job; (3) unemployment compensation; (4) workers' compensation; (5) Social Security; (6) Supplemental Security income; (7) public assistance; (8) veterans' payments; (9) survivor benefits; (10) disability benefits; (11) retirement pensions; (12) interest; (13) dividends; (14) rents and royalties or estates and trusts; (15) educational assistance; (16) alimony; (17) child support; (18) financial assistance from outside the household, and other periodic income. Income is reported in several ways in this book. Household income is the combined income of all household members. Income of persons is all income accruing to a person from all sources. Earnings are the money a person receives from his or her job.

industry Refers to the industry in which a person worked longest in the preceding calendar year.

job tenure The length of time a person has been employed continuously by the same employer.

labor force The labor force tables in this book show the civilian labor force only. The labor force includes both the employed and the unemployed (people who are looking for work). People are counted as in the labor force if they were working or looking for work during the reference week in which the Census Bureau fields the Current Population Survey.

labor force participation rate The percent of the civilian noninstitutional population that is in the civilian labor force, which includes both the employed and the unemployed.

married couples with or without children under age 18 Refers to married couples with or without own children under age 18 living in the same household. Couples without children under age 18 may be parents of grown children who live elsewhere, or they could be childless couples.

median The median is the amount that divides the population or households into two equal portions: one below and one above the median. Medians can be calculated for income, age, and many other characteristics.

median income The amount that divides the income distribution into two equal groups, half having incomes above the median, half having incomes below the median. The medians for households or families are based on all households or families. The median for persons are based on all persons aged 15 or older with income.

Medical Expenditure Panel Survey MEPS is a nationally representative survey that collects detailed information on the health status, access to care, health care use and expenses and health insurance coverage of the civilian noninstitutionalized population of the U.S. and nursing home residents. MEPS comprises four component surveys: the Household Component, the Medical Provider Component, the Insurance Component, and the Nursing Home Component. The Household Component, which is the core survey, is conducted each year and includes 15,000 households and 37,000 people.

metropolitan statistical area To be defined as a metropolitan statistical area (or MSA), an area must include a city with 50,000 or more inhabitants, or a Census Bureau-defined urbanized area of at least 50,000 inhabitants and a total metropolitan population of at least 100,000 (75,000 in New England). The county (or counties) that contains the largest city becomes the "central county" (counties), along with any adjacent counties that have at least 50 percent of their population in the urbanized area surrounding the largest city. Additional "outlying counties" are included in the MSA if they meet specified requirements of commuting to the central counties and other selected requirements of metropolitan character (such as population density and percent urban). In New England, MSAs are defined in terms of cities and towns rather than counties. For this reason, the concept of NECMA is used to define metropolitan areas in the New England division.

Millennial generation Americans born between 1977 and 1994.

mobility status People are classified according to their mobility status on the basis of a comparison between their place of residence at the time of the March Current Population Survey and their place of residence in March of the previous year. Nonmovers are people living in the same house at the end of the period as at the beginning of the period. Movers are people living in a different house at the end of the period than at the beginning of the period. Movers from abroad are either citizens or aliens whose place of residence is outside the United States at the beginning of the period, that is, in an outlying area under the jurisdiction of the United States or in a foreign country. The mobility status for children is fully allocated from the mother if she is in the household; otherwise it is allocated from the householder.

Monitoring the Future Project The MTF survey is conducted by the University of Michigan Survey Research Center. The survey is administered to approximately 50,000 students in 420 public and private secondary schools every year. High school seniors have been surveyed annually since 1975. Students in 8th and 10th grade have been surveyed annually since 1991.

National Ambulatory Medical Care Survey The NAMCS is an annual survey of visits to nonfederally employed office-based physicians who are primarily engaged in direct patient care. Data are collected from physicians rather than patients, with each physician assigned a one-week reporting period. During that week, a systematic random sample of visit characteristics are recorded by the physician or office staff.

National Crime Victimization Survey The NCVS collects data each year on nonfatal crimes against people age 12 or older, reported and not reported to the police, from a nationally representative sample of 42,000 households and 76,000 persons in the United States. The NCVS provides information about victims, offenders, and criminal offenses.

National Health and Nutrition Examination Survey The NHANES is a continuous survey of a representative sample of the U.S. civilian noninstitutionalized population. Respondents are interviewed at home about their health and nutrition, and the interview is followed up by a physical examination that measures such things as height and weight in mobile examination centers.

National Health Interview Survey The NHIS is a continuing nationwide sample survey of the civilian noninstitutional population of the U.S. conducted by the Census Bureau for the National Center for

Health Statistics. Each year, data are collected from more than 100,000 people about their illnesses, injuries, impairments, chronic and acute conditions, activity limitations, and the use of health services.

National Home and Hospice Care Survey These are a series of surveys of a nationally representative sample of home and hospice care agencies in the U.S., sponsored by the National Center for Health Statistics. Data on the characteristics of patients and services provided are collected through personal interviews with administrators and staff.

National Hospital Ambulatory Medical Care Survey The NHAMCS, sponsored by the National Center for Health Statistics, is an annual national probability sample survey of visits to emergency departments and outpatient departments at non-Federal, short stay and general hospitals. Data are collected by hospital staff from patient records.

National Hospital Discharge Survey This survey has been conducted annually since 1965, sponsored by the National Center for Health Statistics, to collect nationally representative information on the characteristics of inpatients discharged from nonfederal, short-stay hospitals in the U.S. The survey collects data from a sample of approximately 270,000 inpatient records acquired from a national sample of about 500 hospitals.

National Household Education Survey The NHES, sponsored by the National Center for Education Statistics, provides descriptive data on the educational activities of the U.S. population, including after-school care and adult education. The NHES is a system of telephone surveys of a representative sample of 45,000 to 60,000 households in the U.S. It has been conducted in 1991, 1993, 1995, 1996, 1999, 2001, and 2003.

National Nursing Home Survey This is a series of national sample surveys of nursing homes, their residents, and staff conducted at various intervals since 1973-74 and sponsored by the National Center for Health Statistics. The latest survey was taken in 1999. data for the survey are obtained through personal interviews with administrators and staff, and occasionally with self-administered questionnaires, in a sample of about 1,500 facilities.

National Survey of Family Growth The 2002 NSFG, sponsored by the National Center for Health Statistics, is a nationally representative survey of the civilian noninstitutional population aged 15 to 44. In-person interviews were completed with 12,571 men and women, collecting data on marriage, divorce, contraception, and infertility. The 2002 survey updates previous NSFG surveys taken in 1973, 1976, 1988, and 1995.

National Survey on Drug Use and Health *(formerly called the National Household Survey on Drug Abuse)* This survey, sponsored by the Substance Abuse and Mental Health Services Administration, has been conducted since 1971. It is the primary source of information on the use of illegal drugs by the U.S. population. Each year, a nationally representative sample of about 70,000 individuals aged 12 or older are surveyed in the 50 states and the District of Columbia.

net worth The amount of money left over after a household's debts are subtracted from its assets.

nonfamily household A household maintained by a householder who lives alone or who lives with people to whom he or she is not related.

nonfamily householder A householder who lives alone or with nonrelatives.

non-Hispanic People who do not identify themselves as Hispanic are classified as non-Hispanic. Non-Hispanics may be of any race.

non-Hispanic white People who identify their race as white and who do not indicate a Hispanic origin.

nonmetropolitan area Counties that are not classified as metropolitan areas.

occupation Occupational classification is based on the kind of work a person did at his or her job during the previous calendar year. If a person changed jobs during the year, the data refer to the occupation of the job held the longest during that year.

occupied housing units A housing unit is classified as occupied if a person or group of people is living in it or if the occupants are only temporarily absent—on vacation, example. By definition, the count of occupied housing units is the same as the count of households.

outside central city The portion of a metropolitan county or counties that falls outside of the central city or cities; generally regarded as the suburbs.

own children Own children are sons and daughters, including stepchildren and adopted children, of the householder. The totals include never-married children living away from home in college dormitories.

owner occupied A housing unit is "owner occupied" if the owner lives in the unit, even if it is mortgaged or not fully paid for. A cooperative or condominium unit is "owner occupied" only if the owner lives in it. All other occupied units are classified as "renter occupied."

part-time employment Part-time is less than 35 hours of work per week in a majority of the weeks worked during the year.

percent change The change (either positive or negative) in a measure that is expressed as a proportion of the starting measure. When median income changes from $20,000 to $25,000, for example, this is a 25 percent increase.

percentage point change The change (either positive or negative) in a value which is already expressed as a percentage. When a labor force participation rate changes from 70 percent of 75 percent, for example, this is a 5 percentage point increase.

poverty level The official income threshold below which families and people are classified as living in poverty. The threshold rises each year with inflation and varies depending on family size and age of householder.

primary activity In the time use tables, primary activities are those that respondents identify as their main activity. Other activities done simultaneously are not included.

proportion or share The value of a part expressed as a percentage of the whole. If there are 4 million people aged 25 and 3 million of them are white, then the white proportion is 75 percent.

race Race is self-reported and can be defined in three ways. The "race alone" population comprises people who identify themselves as only one race. The "race in combination" population comprises people who identify themselves as more than one race, such as white and black. The "race, alone or in combination" population includes both those who identify themselves as one race and those who identify themselves as more than one race.

regions The four major regions and nine census divisions of the United States are the state groupings as shown below:

Northeast:
—New England: Connecticut, Maine, Massachusetts, New Hampshire, Rhode Island, and Vermont
—Middle Atlantic: New Jersey, New York, and Pennsylvania

Midwest:
—East North Central: Illinois, Indiana, Michigan, Ohio, and Wisconsin
—West North Central: Iowa, Kansas, Minnesota, Missouri, Nebraska, North Dakota, and South Dakota

South:
—South Atlantic: Delaware, District of Columbia, Florida, Georgia, Maryland, North Carolina, South Carolina, Virginia, and West Virginia
—East South Central: Alabama, Kentucky, Mississippi, and Tennessee
—West South Central: Arkansas, Louisiana, Oklahoma, and Texas

West:
—Mountain: Arizona, Colorado, Idaho, Montana, Nevada, New Mexico, Utah, and Wyoming
—Pacific: Alaska, California, Hawaii, Oregon, and Washington

renter occupied *See* Owner occupied.

Retirement Confidence Survey The RCS, sponsored by the Employee Benefit Research Institute (EBRI), the American Savings Education Council (ASEC), and Mathew Greenwald & Associates (Greenwald), is an annual survey of a nationally representative sample of 1,000 people aged 25 or older. Respondents are asked a core set of questions that have been asked since 1996, measuring attitudes and behavior towards retirement. Additional questions are also asked about current retirement issues such as 401(k) participation.

rounding Percentages are rounded to the nearest tenth of a percent; therefore, the percentages in a distribution do not always add exactly to 100.0 percent. The totals, however, are always shown as 100.0. Moreover, individual figures are rounded to the nearest thousand without being adjusted to group totals, which are independently rounded; percentages are based on the unrounded numbers.

self-employment A person is categorized as self-employed if he or she was self-employed in the job held longest during the reference period. Persons who report self-employment from a second job are excluded, but those who report wage-and-salary income from a second job are included. Unpaid workers in family businesses are excluded. Self-employment statistics include only nonagricultural workers and exclude people who work for themselves in incorporated business.

sex ratio The number of men per 100 women.

suburbs See Outside central city.

Survey of Consumer Finances The Survey of Consumer Finances is a triennial survey taken by the Federal Reserve Board. It collects data on the assets, debts, and net worth of American households. For the 2004 survey, the Federal Reserve Board interviewed more than 4,000 households.

Survey of Public Participation in the Arts Initiated in 1982 by the National Endowment for the Arts, this survey examines the public's participation in the performing arts, visual arts, historic site visits, music, and literature. The 2002 survey is the fifth (earlier surveys were in 1982, 1985, 1992, and 1997) and was conducted as a supplement to the Current Population Survey. More than 17,000 respondents to the August 2002 Current Population Survey were asked about their arts participation and involvement.

unemployed Unemployed people are those who, during the survey period, had no employment but were available and looking for work. Those who were laid off from their jobs and were waiting to be recalled are also classified as unemployed.

white The "white" racial category includes many Hispanics (who may be of any race) unless the term "non-Hispanic white" is used.

Youth Risk Behavior Surveillance System The YRBSS was created by the Centers for Disease Control to monitor health risks being taken by young people at the national, state, and local level. The national survey is taken every two years based on a nationally representative sample of 16,000 students in 9th through 12th grade in public and private schools.

Bibliography

Agency for Healthcare Research and Quality
　　Internet site http://www.ahrq.gov/
　　—Medical Expenditure Panel Survey, Internet site http://www.meps.ahrq.gov/
　　CompendiumTables/TC_TOC.htm

Bureau of Justice Statistics
　　Internet site http://www.ojp.usdoj.gov/bjs/welcome.html
　　—*Criminal Victimization 2004*, Internet site http://www.ojp.usdoj.gov/bjs/abstract/cv04.htm
　　—Sourcebook of Criminal Justice Statistics Online, Internet site http://www.albany.edu/
　　sourcebook

Bureau of Labor Statistics
　　Internet site http://www.bls.gov
　　—American Time Use Survey, Internet site http://www.bls.gov/tus/home.htm and unpub-
　　lished data
　　—Characteristics of Minimum Wage Workers, Internet site http://www.bls.gov/cps/
　　minwage2004.htm
　　—Consumer Expenditure Survey, Internet site http://www.bls.gov/cex/
　　—Contingent and Alternative Employment Arrangements, Internet site http://www.bls
　　.gov/news.release/conemp.toc.htm
　　—Current Population Survey, Internet site http://www.bls.gov/cps/home.htm and unpub-
　　lished data
　　—Employee Tenure, Internet site http://www.bls.gov/news.release/tenure.toc.htm
　　—Employment Characteristics of Families, Internet site http://www.bls.gov/news.release/
　　famee.toc.htm
　　—Labor force participation rates, historical, Public Query Data Tool, Internet site http://
　　www.bls.gov/data
　　—Labor force projections, 2004–2014, Internet site http://www.bls.gov/emp/emplab1.htm
　　—Statistical Abstract of the United States: 2006, Internet site, http://www.census.gov/
　　statab/www/
　　—Volunteering in the United States, Internet site http://www.bls.gov/news.release/volun
　　.toc.htm
　　—Workers on Flexible and Shift Schedules, Internet site http://www.bls.gov/news.release/
　　flex.toc.htm

Bureau of the Census
　　Internet site http://www.census.gov
　　—*Adopted Children and Stepchildren: 2000*, Census 2000 Special Reports, CENSR-GRV, 2003,
　　Internet site http://www.census.gov/population/www/cen2000/phc-t21.html
　　—American Community Survey, 2004 custom tables, Internet site http://factfinder.census
　　.gov/servlet/DatasetMainPageServlet?_program=ACS&_lang=en
　　—American Housing Survey National Tables: 2003, Internet site http://www.census.gov/
　　hhes/www/housing/ahs/ahs03/ahs03.html
　　—America's Families and Living Arrangements: 2004, Internet site http://www.census.gov/
　　population/www/socdemo/hh-fam/cps2004.html

—Current Population Survey, Detailed Income Tabulations, 2005 Annual Social and Economic Supplement, Internet site http://www.census.gov/hhes/www/income/dinctabs.html

—Current Population Survey, Historical Income Tables, Internet site http://www.census.gov/hhes/income/histinc/histinctb.html

—Disability, 2003, Internet site http://www.census.gov/hhes/www/disability/data_title.html#2003

—Educational Attainment, Historical Tables, Internet site http://www.census.gov/population/www/socdemo/educ-attn.html

—Educational Attainment in the United States: 2004, Detailed Tables, Internet site http://www.census.gov/population/www/socdemo/education/cps2004.html

—Fertility of American Women, Current Population Survey—June 2004, Detailed Tables, Internet site http://www.census.gov/population/www/socdemo/fertility/cps2004.html

—Foreign Born Population of the United States, Current Population Survey—March 2004, Detailed Tables, (PPL-176), Internet site http://www.census.gov/population/www/socdemo/foreign/ppl-176.html

—Geographic Mobility: 2004, Detailed Tables, Internet site http://www.census.gov/population/www/socdemo/migrate/cps2004.html

—Health Insurance Coverage: 2004, Internet site http://pubdb3.census.gov/macro/032005/health/toc.htm

—Housing Vacancy Survey, Annual Statistics: 2005, Internet site http://www.census.gov/hhes/www/housing/hvs/annual05/ann05ind.html

—National and State Population Estimates, Internet site http://www.census.gov/popest/states/NST-ann-est.html

—Population Estimates by State, Internet site http://www.census.gov/popest/states/asrh/SC-est2004-02.html

—Poverty, Detailed Tables, Internet site http://pubdb3.census.gov/macro/032005/pov/toc.htm

—School Enrollment, Historical Tables, Internet site http://www.census.gov/population/www/socdemo/school.html

—School Enrollment—Social and Economic Characteristics of Students: October 2004, Internet site http://www.census.gov/population/www/socdemo/school/cps2004.html

—State Interim Population Projections by Age and Sex, Internet site http://www.census.gov/population/www/projections/projectionsagesex.html

—U.S. Interim Projections by Age, Sex, Race, and Hispanic Origin; Internet site http://www.census.gov/ipc/www/usinterimproj/

—Voting and Registration, Historical Time Series Tables, Internet site http://www.census.gov/population/www/socdemo/voting.html

—Voting and Registration in the Election of November 2004, Detailed Tables, Internet site http://www.census.gov/population/www/socdemo/voting/cps2004.html

Centers for Disease Control and Prevention

Internet site http://www.cdc.gov

—Behavioral Risk Factor Surveillance System Prevalence Data, Internet site http://apps.nccd.cdc.gov/brfss/index.asp

—"Youth Risk Behavior Surveillance–United States, 2003," *Mortality and Morbidity Weekly Report*, Vol. 53/SS-2, May 21, 2004; Internet site http://www.cdc.gov/mmwr/indss_2004.html

Employee Benefit Research Institute
  Internet site http://www.ebri.org/
  —"401(k)-Type Plan and IRA Ownership," Craig Copeland, *Notes*, Vol. 26, No. 1, January 2005
  —"Employment-Based Retirement Plan Participation: Geographic Differences and Trends, 2004," *Issue Brief*, No. 286, October 2005
  —"Income and the Elderly Population, Age 65 and Over, 2004," by Ken McDonnell, *Notes*, Vol. 27, No. 1, January 2006

Employee Benefit Research Institute, American Savings Education Council, and Mathew Greenwald & Associates
  Internet site http://www.ebri.org/
  —2005 Retirement Confidence Survey, Internet site http://www.ebri.org/surveys/rcs/2005/

Federal Interagency Forum on Child and Family Statistics
  Internet site http://www.childstats.gov/index.asp
  —America's Children: Key National Indicators of Well-Being, Internet site http://www.childstats.gov/americaschildren/index.asp

Federal Reserve Board
  Internet site http://www.federalreserve.gov/
  —"Recent Changes in U.S. Family Finances: Evidence from the 2001 and 2004 Survey of Consumer Finances," Federal Reserve Board, Internet site http://www.federalreserve.gov/pubs/oss/oss2/2004/scf2004home.html

Graduate Center of the City University of New York
  Internet site http://www.gc.cuny.edu/index.htm
  —American Religious Identification Survey 2001, Egon Mayer, Barry A. Kosmin, and Ariela Keysar, Internet site http://www.gc.cuny.edu/faculty/research_briefs/aris/aris_index.htm

Higher Education Research Institute
  Internet site http://www.gseis.ucla.edu/heri/whatis.html
  —*The American Freshman: National Norms for Fall 2005*, John H. Pryor, Sylvia Hurtado, Victor B. Saenz, Jennifer A. Lindholm, William S. Korn, and Kathryn M. Mahoney, Higher Education Research Institute, UCLA, 2005, Internet site http://www.gseis.ucla.edu/heri/american_freshman.html

Institute for Social Research, University of Michigan
  Internet site http://www.isr.umich.edu/
  —Monitoring the Future Survey, Internet site http://monitoringthefuture.org/index.html

National Center for Education Statistics
  Internet site http://nces.ed.gov
  —Digest of Education Statistics, 2004, Internet site http://nces.ed.gov/programs/digest/d04_tf.asp

National Center for Health Statistics
  Internet site http://www.cdc.gov/nchs
  —*2003 National Hospital Discharge Survey*, Advance Data, No. 359, 2005, Internet site http://www.cdc.gov/nchs/about/major/hdasd/listpubs.htm

—1999 National Nursing Home Survey, Internet site http://www.cdc.gov/nchs/nnhs.htm

—*Births: Final Data for 2003*, National Vital Statistics Reports, Vol. 54, No. 2, 2005, Internet site http://www.cdc.gov/nchs/products/pubs/pubd/nvsr/54/54-pre.htm

—*Births: Preliminary Data for 2004*, National Vital Statistics Reports, Vol. 54, No. 8, 2005, Internet site http://www.cdc.gov/nchs/products/pubs/pubd/nvsr/54/54-pre.htm

—*Characteristics of Hospice Care Discharges and Their Length of Service: United States, 2000*, Vital and Health Statistics, Series 13, No. 154, 2003; Internet site http://www.cdc.gov/nchs/pressroom/03facts/hospicecare.htm

—*Deaths: Final Data for 2002*, National Vital Statistics Reports, Vol. 53, No. 5, 2004, Internet site http://www.cdc.gov/nchs/about/major/dvs/mortdata.htm

—*Deaths: Preliminary Data for 2003*, National Vital Statistics Reports, Vol. 53, No. 15, 2005, Internet site http://www.cdc.gov/nchs/products/pubs/pubd/nvsr/53/53-21.htm

—*Fertility, Family Planning, and Reproductive Health of U.S. Women: Data from the 2002 National Survey of Family Growth*, Vital and Health Statistics, Series 23, No. 25, 2005; Internet site http://www.cdc.gov/nchs/nsfg.htm

—*Health, United States, 2005*, Internet site http://www.cdc.gov/nchs/hus.htm

—*Mean Body Weight, Height, and Body Mass Index, United States 1960–2002*, Advance Data, No. 347, 2004, Internet site http://www.cdc.gov/nchs/pressroom/04news/americans.htm

—*National Ambulatory Medical Care Survey: 2003 Summary*, Advance Data No. 365, 2005, Internet site http://www.cdc.gov/nchs/about/major/ahcd/adata.htm

—*National Hospital Ambulatory Medical Care Survey: 2003 Emergency Department Summary*, Advance Data No. 358, 2005, Internet site http://www.cdc.gov/nchs/about/major/ahcd/adata.htm

—*National Hospital Ambulatory Medical Care Survey: 2003 Outpatient Department Summary*, Advance Data, No. 366, 2005, Internet site http://www.cdc.gov/nchs/about/major/ahcd/adata.htm

—*Revised Birth and Fertility Rates for the 1990s and New Rates for the Hispanic Populations 2000 and 2001: United States*, National Vital Statistics Reports, Vol. 51, No. 12, 2003

—*Sexual Behavior and Selected Health Measures: Men and Women 15-44 Years of Age, United States, 2002*, Advance Data, No. 362, 2005; Internet site http://www.cdc.gov/nchs/nsfg.htm

—*Summary Health Statistics for U.S. Adults: National Health Interview Survey, 2003*, Vital and Health Statistics, Series 10, No. 225, 2005; Internet site http://www.cdc.gov/nchs/nhis.htm

—*Summary Health Statistics for U.S. Children: National Health Interview Survey, 2004*, Vital and Health Statistics, Series 10, No. 227, 2003; Internet site http://www.cdc.gov/nchs/nhis.htm

—*Teenagers in the United States: Sexual Activity, Contraceptive Use, and Childbearing, 2002*; Vital and Health Statistics, Series 23, No. 24, 2004; Internet site http://www.cdc.gov/nchs/nsfg.htm

National Endowment for the Arts

Internet site http://www.arts.endow.gov/

—*2002 Survey of Public Participation in the Arts: Summary Report*, Research Division Report No. 45, Internet site http://www.nea.gov/pub/ResearchReports_chrono.html

National Sporting Goods Association

Internet site http://www.nsga.org

—Sports Participation, Internet site http://www.nsga.org/public/pages/index.cfm?pageid=158

Office of Immigration Statistics

—2004 Yearbook of Immigration Statistics, Internet site http://uscis.gov/graphics/shared/statistics/index.htm

Pew Internet & American Life Project

Internet site http://www.pewinternet.org

—Latest Trends, Internet site http://www.pewinternet.org/trends.asp#usage

Pew Research Center

Internet site http://people-press.org/

—"Families Drawn Together by Communications Revolution," February 21, 2006

Substance Abuse and Mental Health Services Administration

Internet site http://www.samhsa.gov/

—National Survey on Drug Use and Health, Internet site http://oas.samhsa.gov/nsduh.htm

Index